GEORGE BAILEY was born in Chicago in 1919. A graduate of Columbia University and Magdalen College, Oxford, he has spent over 30 years in Europe, mostly in Germany and Austria, and has been a Fellow in Russian of the American Council of Learned Societies. During World War II Bailey served as an American Army intelligence liaison officer with the Red Army. He was interpreter/translator in Russian and German at the surrender negotiations, and from 1950–51 he was a resettlement officer for Soviet Army defectors. Since then Bailey has worked as a liaison officer with the German police, as a literary agent, and as an Eastern European correspondent. In 1959 he won the Overseas Press Club's award for best magazine reporting of foreign affairs. Since 1974 Bailey has been the coordinating editor for *Kontinent* magazine. He co-authored THE EXPERTS, MUNICH, and C.S. LEWIS SPEAKS, and is also the author of KÜNSTLER IM EXILE and of GERMANS, which is available in an Avon Discus edition. He now lives in France.

Other Avon Books by
George Bailey

GERMANS

Avon Books are available at special quantity discounts for bulk purchases for sales promotions, premiums, fund raising or educational use. Special books, or book excerpts, can also be created to fit specific needs.

For details write or telephone the office of the Director of Special Markets, Avon Books, 959 8th Avenue, New York, New York 10019, 212-262-3361.

KONTINENT 4
CONTEMPORARY RUSSIAN WRITERS

Edited by
GEORGE BAILEY

 A BARD BOOK/PUBLISHED BY AVON BOOKS

PG
3213
K6
1982

KONTINENT 4: CONTEMPORARY RUSSIAN WRITERS
is an original publication of Avon Books. This work has never
before appeared in book form.

AVON BOOKS
A division of
The Hearst Corporation
959 Eighth Avenue
New York, New York 10019

Copyright © 1982 by Kontinent Verlag GmbH.
English translation Copyright © 1982 by Avon Books
Published by arrangement with Kontinent Verlag GmbH.
Library of Congress Catalog Card Number: 82-90467
ISBN: 0-380-81182-0

All rights reserved, which includes the right to
reproduce this book or portions thereof in any form
whatsoever except as provided by the U. S. Copyright Law.
For information address Avon Books

First Bard Printing, November, 1982

BARD TRADEMARK REG. U. S. PAT. OFF. AND IN
OTHER COUNTRIES, MARCA REGISTRADA, HECHO EN
U. S. A.

Printed in the U. S. A.

OP   10   9   8   7   6   5   4   3   2   1

105245

Contents

PART ONE: In the "Big Zone" —Life in the U.S.S.R. Today

PART TWO: Justice?—Notes from the Prisons and Labor Camps

PART THREE: Out of the Frying Pan —The Emigrant Experience in the West

PART FOUR: Clues from the Past— History as Investigation and Reminiscence

Foreword

This book is made up of selected articles, stories, and other pieces from some sixteen issues of the quarterly dissident magazine *Kontinent*. It contains no poetry. As editor of this collection I could not bring myself to include any. I regret this decision, especially because it deprives the reader of this book of the opportunity of acquainting himself with examples of the work of Joseph Brodsky, among others. But there are simply too many difficulties involved in the translation of poetry. Unless the translator is a poet himself and virtually bilingual in Russian and the language into which he is translating, the result is almost certain to be at best a poor, pale reflection, and at worst a disastrous distortion of the original.

Nobody is happy with the term "dissident." For many people "dissident" connotes a kind of political professional, an activist with a definite, alternative political program. This is way off. Far closer to the truth is Ernst Neizvestny's definition: "In Russia everything that is not official is dissidence." Or Alexander Piatigorsky's statement: "I considered myself an absolutely model, first-class Soviet citizen . . . and all of a sudden—wham! I was kicked out!" The point, of course, is that regardless of what Piatigorsky considered himself, the Communist Party and government of the Soviet Union considered him a dissident. And rightly so. Anyone who chooses, however unwittingly, to assert his individuality in a totalitarian society can only do so by becoming a political activist against the state. This does not require a political program. The only requirement is "doing what comes naturally."

For this reason dissident literature is the literature of penal servitude, the work—for the most part—of men and women who have done time, and usually a long time, for "political crimes" against the Soviet Union or its satellites. It is the literature of suffering, the bearing of witness against injustice—testimonials in one form or another

1

from prisons, labor camps, and exile, in that order. This is a fact that poses several problems. In the first place it makes the authors a kind of an elite of sufferers. This in turn makes for invidious comparisons: say, of the Russian writer, like Solzhenitsyn, who is more than likely to have gone through various versions of hell and high water, with —well, with the British gentleman author (Laurie Lee comes to mind) who writes whimsical accounts of roughing it in high summer in the Toscana. Or to compare, as one must if one has read both books, Lillian Hellman's *Scoundrel Time* with Nadezhda Mandelstam's first book of memoirs.

In the second place it poses problems for the Western reviewer, commentator, or critic coming to grips with dissident literature. I am reminded of the young British author who reviewed Vladimir Bukovsky's *To Build a Castle*. So overwhelmed was he with the catalogue of calamities visited upon Bukovsky by the Soviet state that he felt obliged to confess to his readers the magnitude of his own worst ordeal: an appendectomy.

There is, and it is better to come right out with it, an arrogance that comes with suffering—even if it is only the determination not to suffer fools, particularly fools without power (after having been forced to suffer fools *with* power for years and years on end). No, the dissidents of the Soviet Union and its satellites (the exceptions prove the rule) will never harbor anything but contempt for the Left. The setting of their ordeal is socialism. The Soviet Union has preempted the position of bulwark of the international Left. This may be fortunate or unfortunate, depending on one's point of view. But nothing can be done about it. The dissidents have been there. They have seen the "future" and they know it doesn't work. As a result they are filled with horror, loathing, inspired defiance, and—strangest of all—laughter.

For me the most striking characteristic of dissident writing is its humor. Albert Camus pointed out that totalitarian regimes were forced to resort to terror in order to be taken seriously. The Third Reich was billed as "the fiercest political order since Genghis Khan." Necessarily so: With its absurd program, the Nazi party pullulated with perfectly ludicrous figures. One only need remember (I admit the difficulty) that Hermann Goering was the Prime Minister and Minister of the Interior of Prussia (and de facto Minister of State Theatres). If one could take away the apparatus of oppression the Soviet Union would be the most comical form of government on the face of the earth. But, unable to be dignified, the Soviet system needs must be fierce. It is this consideration that prompted Vladimir Maximov, the editor-in-chief of *Kontinent*, to call his series of novels about life in the Soviet Union "The Inhuman Comedy." Thanks to the courage of the dissidents, life in the Soviet Union is less inhuman than it was. It is certainly no less comical.

GEORGE BAILEY

About the Magazine *Kontinent*

An Address by Vladimir Bukovsky
at the *Kontinent* Conference of
Editors and Writers
in Berlin, 1978

Translated by Albert C. and Tanya Schmidt

I was an inmate of Zone 35, at the Perm penal complex for political prisoners, when I learned that the magazine *Kontinent* had come into existence. I found out about it from the Soviet press. As usual, the Soviet press camouflaged its own attacks on the magazine by using quotes from the foreign press—Yugoslav and West German, for instance—without indicating, moreover, that the references came from Communist publications. "Well, thank heaven," I said to myself with a sigh of relief, "our idea has been realized." The realization was not exactly as I had originally imagined it would be. For who would have thought that they would start throwing writers out of the country one after another?

Shortly before my arrest I suggested to Vladimir Maximov that a magazine be published, proposing that it be put together and distributed entirely inside the country. Maximov has revived that original idea and brought it to fulfillment.

Kontinent does not, of course, correspond altogether to the conception we had of it at that time. This is not simply one more Russian journal; it is, rather, a Western European journal: We would not have been able to carry out such a project inside the country. And furthermore, it does not draw exclusively on *samizdat* material for its contents. Yet we should bear in mind that, in the years that have passed since then, a huge new wave of emigration has taken place, and this third emigration, as it is called, has very close ties to Russia. The same people who only yesterday were demanding civil rights for themselves and for their fellow citizens inside the Soviet Union are at last able to exercise those rights within the framework of a magazine published under free conditions.

To be sure, a certain balance must be maintained. There is a taciturnity about manuscripts emanating from Russia: The authors cannot call on the telephone; they cannot bombard the editorial office with letters; and they cannot annoy the editor-in-chief by threatening to break off relations or to make embarrassing disclosures in the press. The opportunities available to émigrés in this regard are much greater. And I ask myself uneasily whether the editors might not in some instances succumb to psychological pressure exerted by certain authors.

We should remember, furthermore, that there are many persons in the new emigration who at one time preferred to take no risks, except perhaps by "signing up as dissidents" while waiting for permission to leave the country, and who now pose as fighters and as martyrs for the oppressed homeland. In the words of one former political prisoner: "After the Soviet border has been crossed, the number of dissidents doubles, and it triples when the border is left far behind." So the editors must be more cautious. I do not wish to say that I have encountered material of this kind in *Kontinent*, but the danger does exist.

Let me return to the subject of the writers who are living in the Soviet Union. For my part, I am not about to claim that those who have not crossed the frontier possess a monopoly on wisdom and talent, but I do think that, all else being equal, the advantage must always be conceded to them. People run a definite risk when they send their manuscripts abroad, and by the force of their example they demonstrate that liberty is worth taking risks for. Here the example in question is not simply a matter of smuggling manuscripts out of the country, not at all. It is far more than that. The example is set by persons who, irrespective of illegal and artificial barriers, are exercising their civil rights in the broadest sense of the term. In this way the conscience of society becomes actively imbued with the notion that each individual bears responsibility for actualizing those rights with which he is endowed.

At the editorial office I was told of the complications that arise in connection with publishing *samizdat* manuscripts. All of these problems have to do with the question of copyright. In the first place, they tell me, there are no controls over the distribution of *samizdat*, and it happens that material chosen to be printed in *Kontinent* may turn out to have been published elsewhere previously. Well, in my opinion, this is the editors' job. They should establish contacts so close as to insure that *Kontinent* does receive each manuscript which a writer or his trusted representative would like to have published in the magazine. This question is almost solely one of administrative procedure. A great deal depends, of course, on what channels are used—that is, on the persons in the West who do (or who do not) agree to help Soviet citizens. Everyone tells me in this context that the situation is considerably worse than it was in my day. Foreign journalists, diplomats, and tourists are becoming increasingly better acquainted with the ways in which Soviet authorities disregard legality in dealing with transmittal of manuscripts abroad, and as a consequence they are either afraid to lend a hand at all or else they do it haphazardly. During the months that have passed since I came to the West, I have heard dozens of complaints from all kinds of people who say that the transmitted documents either have not arrived at all, or have arrived very late, or in many instances have reached the wrong destination.

The second problem mentioned to me in connection with *samizdat* manuscripts is a more complicated one. The Russian editors of *Kontinent* will hardly be able to solve it without assistance from the Western publishers. As you know, the copyright arrangement is such that no piece of writing printed in *Kontinent* is authorized to appear in Western languages except in the respective non-Russian editions of the magazine. What does this mean? The Western editions appear much later than the Russian edition, and consequently the material of current interest to the Western reader either does not reach him at all or else is

stale by the time it does. Here is an example. In *Kontinent*
Number 9, a whole year ago, there appeared an article by
Marchenko entitled *"Tret'ye dano."* The author, a veteran
political prisoner, wrote from his exile in Siberia, presenting his thoughts on the subject of détente with interest-
ingly reasoned arguments. To this day, however, not one
of the Western editions of *Kontinent* has gotten around to
publishing a translation of this article.

I am not a legal consultant, and I am not about to give
concrete advice, but I do believe that the Western editors
who enjoy a copyright on all *Kontinent* material should remain fully aware of its special character and should take
certain definite obligations upon themselves. For us and
for our compatriots, *Kontinent* is not a purely literary enterprise and even less a commercial one. Those persons here
in the free world, those free citizens who have undertaken
to let the West hear the voice of free Russia and the voice of
free Eastern Europe, must find it within themselves to assume at least a share of the risks, and to display at least
some of the spirit of active self-sacrifice that has become a
matter of course for so many people who live under the
most suffocating of all totalitarian regimes.

I have been dwelling on what may appear to be details
because actually they have to do with fundamentals,
namely, with what people inside our huge "socialist camp"
expect from *Kontinent*. The journal should provide as complete a reflection as possible of the literary, political, and
social thinking of our peoples. It should be a platform for
the discussion of basic and essential issues having to do
with our past, our present, and our future. It should be a
forum for democracy, for tolerance, and for pluralism. Yet
concomitantly its task is to become our "window to Europe"—our window to the West—and it ought to be a place
where East and West meet and achieve a common understanding. And a place where the peoples of Eastern Europe
themselves can foregather and attain mutual comprehension.

I believe that *Kontinent* is coping, to a certain extent successfully, with these problems, and that it is improving
with each issue. But none of us can be entirely satisfied
with the level thus far attained. The opportunity is always
there to do the thing better, to do it in a more serious and a
more responsible way.

Now I should like to read you a letter from Milovan Djilas, a member of our editorial board, which he sent to Vladimir Maximov and to the *Kontinent* editorial office. Some
time ago I received my initiation into the prison world
thanks to his book *The New Class*: For having it in my possession I was arrested in 1963.

Dear friends!

It is through no fault of my own, and it is not to my
discredit, that I am unable to attend the *Kontinent* symposium in Berlin. I would have come, notwithstanding
the poor state of my health, but for the fact that for
several years now the authorities have been refusing
to issue me a passport for travel abroad—while at the
same time the functionaries are deafening themselves
with shouts about adherence to civil rights in their
democratic and participatory system.

Eastern Europe no longer fits the depiction pur-
veyed by its self-appointed rulers. Nowhere in the
world, and certainly not in Europe, is it possible any
longer for an all-engulfing censorship system or for
prison walls to hide the truth and to frighten those
who think freely, those who are fighting for human
dignity and national selfhood. Hence the futility of all
the obstacles erected by bureaucrats and others in the
way of solidarity and cooperation among all those who
are giving unstintingly of themselves in the struggle
for personal liberty in an undivided Europe and in a
world unclouded by fear.

And so I am with you. I might add that our bond of
friendship is all the stronger in that I am condemned
to absence and solitude. Were there now to arise a center of resistance to the obscurantism of Soviet totalitarian ideology, institutionalization and functionaliza-
tion of such a center would not be necessary. Respect
for the human being and love for humanity are shaped
and bred in fidelity to one's idea, to one's form, to
one's nation. That is why I see cooperation and solidarity as being so essential. Particularities and divergences are the foundation and the soul of the indomi-
table movement toward freedom of the person in an
open democratic society, toward equal rights for all

peoples in the union of mankind. The human spirit, generative of emancipatory ideas, has formed the central core of all activity throughout the ages. And that is how it should be in the future. That spirit will rally and guide its champions with a reliability equal to their readiness to serve, to be loyal to the spirit and to themselves. I need not name the States and the ideologies, or the ideologists; you already know at whom the critical words in my letter are aimed. Is this not further proof of mutual understanding, of tolerance and cooperation on our rocky road to freedom—a road where no one has ever been left to wander astray in loneliness? With all my heart I wish you success in adding to your store of knowledge and in opening up new opportunities. Especially in these days, at a moment when the "saviors of mankind"—ideologically divided though they be—are assembling to commemorate an event that proclaimed the downfall of the human spirit in a welter of tragic illusions, and the descent of a great people into an abyss of suffering which rendered its fate inseparable from the fate of all mankind.

MILOVAN DJILAS
Belgrade, October 31, 1977

PART ONE

In the "Big Zone"*

Life in the U.S.S.R. Today

*An expression used to refer to the entire Soviet Union as a labor camp.

Unwritten Reportage

BY ALEXEI LOSEV

Translated by Albert C. and Tanya Schmidt

From Kontinent No. IX, 1976

Eats

"Are you going to be at Smolny today?"

"Yes."

"Buy me a carton of Bulgarian cigarettes;

—some fresh cucumbers if they have any;

—half a kilo of frankfurters;

—some nice candy to hang on the Christmas tree;

—a pack of Marias;[1]

—some sausage;

—a couple of bottles of Borzhom water."

"They don't have Borzhom to take out. You have to drink it on the premises."

"Couldn't you ask them, at least? The doctor told my wife to gargle with hot Borzhom, but you know the way things are around here: When you need something, you can't get it anywhere. That's for sure."

"I'll see what I can do."

ALEXEI LOSEV *was born in 1937 in Leningrad. Having taken his degree in philology at the University of Leningrad, he worked on newspapers and became a member of the editorial staff of the children's magazine* Bonfire. *He is the author of five books and ten plays for children, all of which were published and performed in the Soviet Union. Losev emigrated to the West in 1976 and now lives in the United States.*

[1]Expensive cigarettes.

In the 1920s, Architect Shchusev built a modest yet tasteful propylaeum, lending bureaucratic solemnity to the front of the Smolny Palace. A statue of Lenin, discreetly waving his hand, was mounted neatly onto what looks like a glass-coaster. And they stuck a flag atop the pediment. It is as if they had taken a ruler and drawn a line with a red military pencil straight down the middle of the symmetrical composition, so that now, in order to see Smolny as Quarenghi built it, you need the Soviet knack of censoring what the eye perceives: An effort of the will is required to remove from your retina the image of propylaeum, statue, and flag. That is not always easy to do.

A flock of tourists are climbing the steps. They will be shown Lenin's cot and Krupskaya's stool. The foreigners emerge looking somewhat stunned by what they have seen; our own people are accustomed to that sort of thing.

To the left of the entrance is a hall, sterile and empty. This is the pass office. Through an arched window you can see the beard of the sergeant on duty. Another sergeant walks back and forth in the hall, maintaining order. There is almost always some mad truth-seeker, an old lady or a student, a Jew or a worker, waiting on the bench in the hope of being admitted. Though they try to look a little dressed up, on the wild chance of getting into Smolny, these people actually look like piles of rags against the sleek marble background. Visibly nervous, some of them tell their troubles to the guard, in a vain attempt to move their pawn one square forward by striking up a personal relationship with the authorities. Their voices are indecently loud, causing an echo that sounds incongruous under those high ceilings. Great patience and fortitude are needed to refrain from interrupting, from telling them to shut up, from chasing them off without further ado. The sergeant on duty displays these virtues: Over and over he tells them which organizations they should turn to with their problems—although they are welcome to wait if they wish, of course, and the comrade will receive them today if he is free. The guard explains all this in a clear and reasonable manner. And without an echo.

But few of the visitors to Smolny enter via the pass office. Comrades summoned by Comrade So-and-so for such-and-such a time stride in briskly with their briefcases and head straight for the first guard facing the entrance. A right hand dives into a left-hand jacket pocket; the sergeant glances at the Party card and at the comrade's face, and allows him to proceed.

From the expressions on the faces it is plain to see that for most of the people here an expedition to Smolny is a festive occasion (except for those who are being called on the carpet). The reasons for this holiday atmosphere may be simply that everything is so clean, so quiet, so solemn—the marble, the red runner under foot, the courtesy and efficiency of the guards. No fidgeting around like your uncle Vasya at the factory gate, no, here they make it snappy and in you go. The shining parquet has been polished with Swedish floor wax. A highly important comrade gets up to greet you from behind his light-colored Finnish desk; you discuss vital questions with him—questions whose resolution may lead to a lucky break for you or to a dirty trick for your enemies.

And there is another simple reason why folks are in a holiday mood. He has shined shoes and she has brand new pumps. He is clean-shaven and she has been to the hairdresser. He wears a white shirt, a quiet necktie, and a handsome imported suit, preferably dark gray, while she sports a *krimplen* synthetic-fiber skirt and a blouse made in Czechoslovakia.

Men in uniform come and go—the military, the militia, the law; they make a good impression here, but you can't help thinking that to put everyone into uniform would be going too far. In the first place, the guards would no longer stand out. In the second place, trench coats and boots are a thing of the past. Between Party bureaucrats and other groups, such as scholars, writers, and cultural workers, the lines of distinction are becoming blurred. Comrades can travel abroad. We have no objection to taking the best that the progressive culture of the West has to offer. Everything about Man must be beautiful.

Our editorial office—our God-saved office, I'd like to add—is located two blocks away from Smolny, across the street from the Tauride Palace, where the Higher Party School (HPS) is housed. An office with only about fifteen employees cannot very well have its own mess facilities,

yet one does have to eat from time to time. There is no
place to go in the neighborhood, except for a *pirozhki* bar,
and food like that won't keep you going for very long. The
disadvantageous location gives our chiefs a trump card for
high-level negotiations, winning access for us to one of
two canteens—either the one at Smolny, in the years when
we are lucky, or, less lucky, at the HPS in the Tauride. Considering our modest status, we do not really have a right to
this fabulous privilege. It fell to our lot unmerited, fortui-
tously, as it were, under chance circumstances and with
certain restrictions. First of all, we must not show up earlier than one-thirty, which means eating up what is left after the main contingent has finished. Second, we are categorically forbidden to use the store.

Rumor has it that you can buy anything you want there.
In the Tauride, the store is right next to the dining room,
while the one at Smolny is tucked away somewhere in the
remoter depths. To be admitted to the store is an inestima-
ble privilege: It frees you from the hopeless chore of making the routine shopping rounds and from standing in
those long lines which a friend of mine so aptly terms a
school of hatred.

However, as I have said, the store is off-limits to us, and
we have given our gentlemen's agreement to stay away:
There is not enough to go around. To some extent we can
compensate for that restriction by patronizing the snack
bar, where the kindly girl at the counter (who is eager to
fulfill the plan quotas) may sell us hard-to-get items over
and above our regular portions of snacks or dessert. For a
list of such items, I refer the reader to the first page, above.

Once they temporarily deprived us of our feeding
trough. We were punished after two female Marxism-
Leninism teachers complained to the manager that "outsi-
ders with long hair and beards took the last frankfurters in
the snack bar." The business manager of the HPS is an im-
pressive-looking character named Pashayev, who used to
run errands for Tolstikov. He reminded the persons who
interceded on our behalf that, while he was always happy
to oblige a group of creative people, the comrades should
nevertheless appreciate his situation.

Yes, we must understand. Our relationships are delicate.
After all, this is not China. As Simon Leys writes, China

has strict rules as to the hierarchy of eating privileges: An official of sufficient rank, a revolutionary-cadre leader, is "he who eats meat." But in our country everything is done by nuance, by subtle hint and inference, and everyone is expected to understand.

Yet not everyone does understand. Not every time. Many people, including comrades in positions of responsibility, display a lack of understanding. I can recall some amazing scenes. Once, close to the New Year, when everybody wants a holiday spread and when, in the words of the poet, "the food stores are crowded and muddy," I was walking through the movie-famed hall at Smolny. At the guard post where extras under Romm and Yutkevich used to roll out the Maxim gun and where People's Artist Shchukin ran sideways playing pocket pool as he went, I witnessed the following genre picture in the manner of the lesser Dutch masters: *Red-headed Lady with Geese and Soldier*.

The red-headed lady, N.S., received her schooling at a physical-education *tekhnikum*. Now she occupies the position of ideological secretary in the Dzerzhinsky district Party committee. Her duties include pulling the Leningrad Writers' Union up to the proper level of ideological maturity and artistic mastery, telling the Hermitage Museum what to hang and what to store away in the reserves to gather dust, and issuing instructions to the Maliy Opera Theater—just what instructions I don't know, perhaps as to whether the ballet dancers should pirouette to the right or to the left.

On this occasion she was having an argument with a guard. With one hand she was showing him her Party card, and with the other she held two dead geese by their wrinkled necks. The guard said: "That is not allowed. It is forbidden to carry unwrapped food products out of Smolny." And he added in a confidential tone: "Folks will see who's taking out what. That's bad. You should have a carryall or a briefcase for this type of thing. Why don't you go back to the store and ask Valya for some big bags."

This is not China. The rungs in the hierarchy have not been hewn by the bureaucrat's ax; rather, they have been shaped casually, artistically, with here a delicate touch and there a gentle hint.

As everyone knows, even in the shabbiest district center the local restaurant, formerly a teahouse, has one special room that is a little cleaner than the others. In this room the Komsomol, the executive committee, and maybe the Party committee, too, forgather for their revelries.

But not all those who frequent the special room can count on getting the same kind of service, since that depends on the treatment extended by local tradition to the various ranks. A few years ago, accompanied by the photographer Lev Polyakov, I visited Guryev. It is the filthiest town on the planet—a town, by the way, that supplies black caviar to prosperous gourmets throughout the world. The Komsomol chief decided to entertain us in the Party committee room of the local restaurant. We were served *besh barmak*, a regional specialty. The mutton was piping hot and unusually good; the vodka was chilled and not too bad. As the meal progressed, we noticed that our host was becoming irritated. Then he exploded. His face darkened, as though he had been grossly insulted, and he began to yell in Kazakh at the waitress, who snapped back at him rudely.

The cook entered from the kitchen, glistening with the sort of fatness that comes from years of eating choice lamb and drinking green tea. He calmed our host down. The quarrel abated; the waitress went out and returned with a tray full of cups. The cups contained bouillon—fragrant, tasty, and invigorating, like the broth in Hauff's fairy tale, *Der Zwerg Nase*. The Komsomol chief drank his bouillon and told us the reason for his outburst: "With *besh barmak*, the most important thing is the bouillon. The bouillon makes all the difference in the *besh barmak*." And with a nod in the direction of the kitchen he added: "That cook thinks that we Komsomol people are fools. He serves bouillon to the Party committee, but when the Komsomol shows up he drinks the bouillon himself."

So Guryev is a town where the real chiefs are the ones who get bouillon with their *besh barmak*.

The dried-apricot pies baked at Smolny are delicious. And furthermore, dried apricots are good for you if you have high blood pressure.

Every day they bake a fresh batch, and the pies left over

from the day before are delivered to the Tauride Palace,
two blocks away, where the cadres of tomorrow are nur-
tured and nourished. Young people have strong teeth. Bit-
ing into a tender pie is a privilege, too.

In our educational system, the Higher Party School
ranks on a level with the universities. But the students here
are special. They have already had a whiff, however faint,
of the heady air of power, and as a result they cannot take
their temporary student status too seriously. Judging by
their suits, you might think they were regular *apparatchiki*.
But the fact that they are not required to prepare questions,
to draft directives, or to vent attitudes, and so on, causes
them to behave in the mockingly lighthearted manner affected by *nomenklatura* VIPs who are ill-at-ease on vacation,
who are embarrassed by such frivolous activities as hunt-
ing and fishing.

The bell rings and the lecture is over. The HPS students
swarm into the echo-filled lavatory of the former State
Duma, where in the old days Deputies Purishkevich and
Malinovsky relieved themselves without so much as a
glance at each other. The students, flexing their shoulder
muscles above the urinals, exchange the latest news on
such topics as political economy, hockey, and Zionist intrigues. This ex-parliamentary facility is more heavily fre-
quented than the men's room at Smolny, because the Tauride snack bar sells *bier*, whereas the one at Smolny is
strictly dry. Making *bier* available to the HPS students is a
playful way of indicating that their student status is not all
that serious and they might as well have fun.

In the marble washroom, near the basins, there is a large
table. On several occasions I found my colleague Valyora
busy at this table. Valyora is a writer of prose, and he works
in the same office as I. He is a monster, an individualist
who couldn't care less about the collective. He flies in the
face of convention. Yet at the same time he is also a devoted family man.

Do you know what this man does? Not only does he feed
his bearded face at the HPS (my beard is a lot smaller, and
even so it gets me into trouble); not only does he dress pro-
vocatively (Valyora is a big dandy: from a writer's trip to
France he returned with a bright pink necktie and shoes to
match; he wears a navy-blue blazer bought on the black

market, with gold buttons, and wine-colored trousers tailored in the Litfond shop—this against a background of gray HPS jackets with East German mottling); but to top it all he has the crust to walk into the store! Simple as that, he just walks in. And he buys anything he wants. He knows that they won't yell at him or throw him out. But it never occurs to this parasite that the entire collective could have their passes revoked.

He buys up a whole pile of bags, cans, and packages. He has plenty of money. He wrote an artistic biography of Yemelyan Yaroslavsky, proving that it was Yemelyan who thought up the name *Pravda* for the newspaper. "Ingenious, wasn't it?" He complains that the editors deleted a human-interest item in a quote from the prison diaries: Yemelyan noted that he was worried about masturbating.

At the table in the washroom, Valyora packs his purchases in polyethylene wrappings and stuffs them into what he calls a sports bag—just right for carrying barbells. Into a little plastic bag he puts some fresh beef liver that is wrapped in a loose blood-smeared piece of paper; this he holds away from himself so as not to get spots on his blazer. His fingers are covered with blood.

One day I ran into another fancy dresser, a doctor whom I had known when he was still a medical student. One word led to another, and he told me about his amazing career.

He had a rough time of it after graduating. An outpatient clinic in a village. Giving enemas to old women, making out death certificates, having drunkards throw up all over him. Plus abortions and more abortions. Finally he succeeded in getting into postgraduate study. He went in heavily for socially useful activities. He joined the Party. And would you believe it, on the strength of his résumé he landed a job in a special polyclinic!

"Sverdlovka?"

"Well, yes, generally speaking, only my office is in the residence on Kamenny Ostrov. There they fixed up some old townhouses and put fences around them, converting them into sort of country homes in the city where overworked chiefs could relax in style. In short, they really have a ball. A palatial restroom is installed next to the banquet hall. All the equipment is Finnish, and there is even a bidet! Everything was planned down to the last detail. Anyone who has overindulged and goes to relieve himself, getting soiled in the process, can leave the restroom via a separate exit leading straight to the lounges and the bedrooms. The restroom has a dispensary for comrades who get sick and need medical help. But obviously your run-of-the-mill Hippocrates won't get billeted in a setup like that. First, you must be a postgrad. Second, you must be a Party member. Third, you must have a flawless record. It's the kind of sinecure I never dreamed of."

"Lots of patients?"

"No, the work is a pushover. Maybe sometimes you give a guy an aspirin, or a sniff of ammonia, before you put him to bed. Nighty-night. But at least it's not your routine drunkards from the Moscow railroad station who have to be soberized. These people really relax in style. They tell jokes and they sing."

"What do they sing?"

"Different things. Folk songs. Soviet songs. By the way, their best singer is Romanov. He has a velvet-smooth tenor voice and he sings real heart-warming numbers—sailor songs like 'Wide Lies the Sea' and 'Farewell Beloved City.' His talent took him places. He had been running errands for some district Party committee, but being a sociable type with a big repertory, he made friends in high places and did well for himself. . . . I sit there and write my doctoral thesis and listen to music. I drink all the French cognac I want, and I gorge myself on the food."

Old Bolshevik Lazurkina made a speech at a Leningrad Party conference. She's the one who had startled the Twenty-second Congress by claiming to have held post-humous consultations with Lenin. Resuming her attack on behalf of the Old Guard, she criticized the comrades in the regional committee most harshly for having set up polyclinics, kindergartens, and so forth. She went too far, and Comrade Tolstikov cut her short: "In our country, nearly every enterprise and installation has its own canteen, polyclinic, and kindergarten. Why shouldn't the children of Party workers, like anyone else, be able to attend their own kindergartens?"

The old lady was silent. Perhaps the rules allowed her no rebuttal. She could easily have launched into demagogic comparisons. For example, she might have pointed out that there is about as much resemblance between the Smolny kindergarten and that of any old Red Cork factory as there is between the Smolny polyclinic or Sverdlovka hospital ("parquet floors, well-screened doctors") and the ordinary ones, where people line up at dawn to get a number, or between the above-mentioned canteens and a factory mess (potato and beet salad—"twenty kopeks there and back").

Nor will you often find postgrad medical students working as lavatory attendants.

It was just before a holiday. I rode in a taxi with a merry driver. Things were being offered for sale all over town, and my driver, getting more and more excited, kept telling me to look:

"See that line, with nothing but old women? They are waiting for onions . . . At Yeliseyevsky there are some good package deals: two cans of saury, a bottle of export vodka, and you are required to buy half a kilo of granulated sugar. That always comes in handy at home . . . And did you hear what happened on Vasilyevsky? You know the store on the such-and-such line, three steps down? They got in a shipment of red caviar, two kilos for the whole store. That happens only once a year. The salespeople didn't have a chance. The manager and her assistant divided it all up between themselves. Then they quarreled, and the manager struck the other woman with a bread knife. Just missed her heart by this much."

An earnest-looking woman was walking leisurely down the sidewalk, her arms weighted down with huge shopping nets. Around her neck was a wreath of rolls of toilet paper. My driver leaned out of the taxi almost to the waist: "Hey, lady, where did you get the toilet paper? Or did you have it dry-cleaned?"

We rode on. The taxi driver said: "Me, I have no caviar problem. My wife's sister works in the Smolny snack bar. They have to write off the leftover sandwiches after three days. The caviar is still good, even though it's a little dried out on top. My sister-in-law scrapes the caviar into a can and throws away the bread. We always have a can of caviar ready in the icebox."

We are not starving, thank God. But you have to be resourceful to get enough to eat. In Moscow and Leningrad the situation is tolerable, but the provinces are another story. For some reason I keep remembering a marble counter with a MEAT sign still hanging over it. The counter was cluttered with dusty bottles of fruit and berry wine. An unforgettable sight in a town that in the old days was famous for its meat and milk.

I had a friend who, when he was still working with us, refused to take advantage of our fabulous privilege. At lunch time, hat pulled down low and beard wrapped in a scarf, he would take a long bus ride to a place that served *pelmeni*—the Siberian ravioli that inspired a poet to say: "*Pelmeni* roll around in your belly like billiard balls."

My friend said: "They don't humiliate me there. This is my *act*." He always spoke that last word in italics.

A taxi driver with a can of Smolny scrapings left over from the day before yesterday . . .

An ideological secretary with geese . . .

Prose-writer Valyora in the lavatory, with a chunk of liver in a blood-smeared piece of paper . . .

An elderly writer whom I like very much once said to me: "I should love to write one more little book, summing everything up—a book about human dignity."

So would I like to write such a book. So would I!

Along the Glass Wall

You can live all your life inside the Soviet State without once running up against it. But you always know it's there. You can't forget it, because it is drummed into your mind from childhood on. It is the Glass Wall.

The term, borrowed from Zamyatin's *We*, is most probably unfamiliar to the average Soviet citizen. It would tend to make him think of some Soviet journalistic cliché of the routine sort: "Sleeplessly they watch, by day and by night, over the borders of our Motherland"; "a reliable cordon";

"the frontier is sealed!" All these well-worn little words repeated through the years erect the Glass Wall in your consciousness—a feeling that one-sixth of the globe is hopelessly fenced off from the rest of the world and the rest of humanity.

One of the foremost figures in Soviet mythology is the border guard with his dog. He protects the homeland paradise from the universal evil that is raging outside, looking for any loophole through which to sneak in so as to harm us and do us dirt. For decades now, Soviet children have been reading in their schoolbooks the saga of the heroic border trooper Karatsup and his faithful hound Indus. Only, in the 1950s, when the Soviet State became friendly with India, this dog changed his name to the somewhat puzzling Ingus.

The border-troop supermen in grade-school texts and movies gallop and shoot like cowboys, crush their enemies with karate tricks like samurai. While so engaged, they do not forget to display the high moral and political qualities of Soviet man: To date, not a single peroxide blonde sent out by world imperialism has yet succeeded in seducing a brave young Russian soldier.

Before I went to school I knew nothing about nationalities, the way most children don't know anything about that.

I was brought up in the Russian language, among Russians. On Pushkin, Lermontov, and Nekrasov. On Russian fairy tales in good solid prewar versions.

I didn't live with my own grandmother, but with somebody else's, and I loved her very much. This grandmother of mine had an icon above her bed. She prayed for me when I was sick. She sang songs, she told me stories, and she recited proverbs: I don't know just how genuinely folk those were. Petersburg sayings. Bourgeois.

I knew almost none of the Soviet literary trash, except maybe those songs against the Fascists that I heard over the radio and sang along with.

The school I attended still used the old name "Peterschule." That pre-victory year, in those big airy intermissions and assembly halls, somehow the good old spirit of the gymnasium came suddenly to life. Or maybe it only seemed that way. A portrait of Wagner with tilted beret over the piano; happy morning sounds of a march by Weber during calisthenics. I was in the first grade and I liked it there a lot.

One day I was going down the broad staircase when an older boy slid past me down the banister, jumped off, and blocked my path. With all the awe common to a first-grader I looked up at the dashing scholar. He was wearing big flannel ski pants. He looked at me and asked:

"Are you a kike?"

"I guess I am," I replied, though I really did not know.

"Anybody'd see that by your ugly face," snapped the boy, catching me in his primitive trap. He slid down the rest of the way, leaving me in that trap for years to come.

It is true that I did not know. Sometimes I thought I was a kike and sometimes I thought I wasn't.

Till one day it was time to realize that there was no answer to this question, because it wasn't a question. The question requires no answer; it cannot even be asked. Because I am only I and nothing else.

That guy can go on sliding down till he wears a hole in the seat of his ski pants.

When I was ten and going on eleven, the winter of 'forty-eight, when the papers printed disgusting cartoons of Jews with the caption "passportless cosmopolite," when it came to the point where even my father was called passportless by the little mongrels who always ran out ahead, I understood a lot more.

I can still remember our street: the Malodetskoselsky Prospekt, still cobblestoned, its February slush glistening in the light of the street lamps. And I remember what, from a distance, looked to me like a strange dance.

Two crimson-faced types, happily drunk, were trampling on an old man and kicking him into the mud. He writhed and screamed. His screams were actually friendly:

"Hey you guys, what are you doing? You're wrong, I am not a Jew!"

They worked him over and over with their feet.

"Hey, you guys . . ."

These incidents made me immune through childhood,

adolescence, and youth. For me, the tragically foolish question of *why* did not arise, when certain higher schools were closed to me and, despite my silver medal, I had almost no direct access to others—no way, that is, without my parents making the rounds of people they knew, begging and cajoling. Not for me, after university graduation, were the coveted jobs in big cities. It was not for me to travel abroad, even at my own expense. A friend of mine who got ahead by toeing the Komsomol line gave me the word: "After all, our country is Russia, and it should be represented abroad by people with Russian names." He did quite a bit of representing himself, even though he had a Ukrainian name on the order of Sidorenko.

But from an early age I thought of all that as part of the Glass Wall, which could be disregarded.

I even considered myself really lucky when I landed a job outside the pale of ubiquitous official anti-Semitism. I went to work in the editorial office of a children's magazine, where most of the employees were old maids of both sexes, in no way resembling those bullies who had trampled on the old man. There, at any rate for several years in a row, there was no talk of refusing to publish an author "because of his name"—the kind of talk so commonly heard in other editorial offices.

Then along came a new chief, the last one I worked under, who showed how tough he was by setting things aright. First he fired the most talented and hard-working editor, who had no bad marks against him and whose desk was literally groaning under the weight of letters of praise and commendations. No doubt about it, there could be only one reason for this man's dismissal from the features department: A person with an unsuitable name could not hold a position of ideological responsibility. And if he did hold such a position, that meant a mistake had been made which must be rectified.

Our maidenly colleagues, up until then, had had only good things to say about that editor, who had always stood up for them. Now they did not let out a peep of protest, and upon reflection they even seconded the Party line.

After that, names began to be crossed off, a calculation was made of the percentage of writers with Russian names, and so on.

I signed off on some poems by the well-known poet Ovsey Driz, who by that time was already dead. The chief struck out the words "from the Hebrew." It came out simply as "translated by So-and-so."

"Wait a minute, this is ridiculous," I said. "You can't do this. A translation has to be from some other language." But I was beating down an open door.

The chief was proud of his reputation as an intelligent and open man, as though it were merely by accident that he occupied an elite Party slot. He decided to have a frank talk with me. For some reason he took all the receivers off the phones, then closed the door to his office, sat down beside me, and asked:

"What do you think of Solzhenitsyn?"

This was so unexpected, so out of place, and so provocative that I was taken aback. But since he fired the question at me head-on, and I did not want to lie, I said: "I like him."

"Well, I think he is a genius!" whispered my boss confidentially, with feeling. "But I don't go around shouting that from the rooftop."

That man violated so many moral precepts that I see no reason to keep quiet about the incident. Besides, I am bound by no promises. Offhand, the incident may look trivial, but it shows what ugliness can result from the silent noninvolvement and the "rejection of lies" that are recommended to intellectuals.

God, how bored I was!

The day the Germans attacked the U.S.S.R., my father, who had been exempted from military service on medical grounds, enlisted in the people's volunteer corps. He saw combat in the first days of summer, led what was left of his battalion out of encirclement through the marshes, was wounded, earned medals for bravery (which even at that time were not exactly showered onto people with Jewish names), and wrote poems during the Leningrad blockade that still bring tears to the eyes of those who lived through it.

After the war he was branded a cosmopolite, and he escaped from final reprisal only by fleeing to another city. Here he began life anew. Tirelessly he worked at his writing, producing a large number of popular songs and poems, books, and plays for children.

Two years ago, on the quay near the Writers' House of
Creativity in Koktebel, he saw a young writer beating a
dog to death with a stick. Not just beating it, but killing it.
The hound had barked at his five-year-old boy. My father
walked up to the man with the stick.

"What are you staring at me for?" snarled this Neander-
thal (Valentin Soloukhin, a prose writer, dragged from the
provinces to Moscow for meritorious service of some kind
and given the job of senior editor in one of the central publishing houses).

"I was curious to look at a real live Fascist," said my father. "I haven't seen one since the war."

The other man cursed back at him: "You sat out the war
in Tashkent, you humanist bastards."

The literary community held my father back and would
not let him have it out with the scoundrel. The literary
community, as a rule favorably disposed toward animals,
wrote an angry statement to the board of the Writers'
Union and arranged for a column to appear in *Nedelya*.

From this column an uninitiated reader could learn that
in a southern resort a young man, whose occupation involved raising the level of morality, beat up a dog and was
rude to an elderly man who called him to task. The statement was handled by the literary general Ilyin in person.
"We will punish him properly," said the general.

And he kept his word. The writer received a reprimand.
From then on Valentin would have to beat out the brains of
dogs where nobody could see, and swear at Jews where
nobody could hear.

All that autumn, before he went to the hospital, my father was kept awake nights by the telephone. "This is
Black September speaking," came a voice over the line,
with what was supposed to sound like a foreign accent.
"We'll get you." Followed by real Russian obscenities.

My father does not agree with my views in many respects. But I could not help thinking about the fate of his
grandchildren in that country.

I am reading *Iz-pod glyb* (From Under the Rubble).
A fine book, a strong book. A book for the strong in
mind and spirit, a book that demolishes false idols and
prompts the soul to seek straight paths.

There is one stumbling-block, however, that every author faces, and that is the difficulty of deciding to whom his sermon is addressed. Hence the revival, with a vengeance, of the century-old debate over definition of the concepts *intelligentsia* and *people.*

Is it really that important?

One thing is beyond dispute. There are individual and unique human souls, created in His image and likeness. The sermon is for them and is about them.

The boldest have taken up this theme, but even they end up prescribing ways for everybody to crowd into the Kingdom of God together.

Yet it is said that the Kingdom is within us.

And that is not all. Surely it will apply to our children as to all children of man in every age: "Cursed is the ground for thy sake; in sorrow shalt thou eat of it all the days of thy life." (Genesis 3:17.)

Aren't our prophets performing an eschatologically inadmissible substitution when they foretell the Kingdom of God in spatial and temporal forms?

The Kingdom of God in Russia? On Madagascar? In Israel? In California? In 1984? In 3976? Tomorrow? Yesterday?

Surely these questions can be answered: Everywhere and nowhere, yesterday and today, there and here, always and never.

They go out of their way to avoid Chaadayev and Pecherin. Isn't that a timid way for men to act?

It seems to me that this is the virtue that challenges our courage: always to know that we do not deserve the Kingdom of God or eternal bliss, and not to lose heart; always to know that our suffering is not a chance bitter lot and someone else's fault, but rather our own fault and at the same time a necessary condition of our being.

Therefore there is no Kingdom of God other than that which we shall build within ourselves by Sisyphean labor; there is no temple wherein we may be consoled save the one we shall strive to elevate within ourselves.

And no homeland is given to us—except perhaps as the P.B. (place of birth) when we fill out forms—unless we find our way to it through our own soul.

In the light of this courageous and honest self-knowledge, the question of whether to leave Russia or not to leave can be solved on a practically mundane level, depending on your personal indebtedness toward those close to you.

If there is so much as a dog who needs you and whom you cannot take with you, stay. If there is not a living soul who absolutely needs your exclusive presence in Russia, then flee from that deathly boredom. And if you can save someone near to you from that falsehood and unfreedom, all the more reason to flee!

A direct opportunity to escape over the border is a happy possibility for a few lucky people. But there are other ways, difficult ways, of escape inside Russia, of internal reclusion. But under no circumstances, as our bitter experience has shown, by way of compromises and silent submission.

In the days of total terror, when any attempt to struggle means sacrificing oneself, who will assume the responsibility of calling for self-sacrifice? There have always been heroes and martyrs and there will always be. But they have always been and will always be exceptions, for the call to self-sacrifice has to come from lips that are not human.

The same is true of the call to creativity. Let us suppose that any one of our living national geniuses—Solzhenitsyn, say or Brodsky—were to take a canister of gasoline and some matches and make a human torch of himself in Red Square or on the Vasilyevsky Island point. Wouldn't that be a terrible violation of the exhortation contained in the parable of the wicked and slothful servant who hid his talent in the earth?

It was not meekness that moved these artists, or the many other Russians who in other circumstances proved their fearlessness when they left the homeland.

All references to the circumstances accompanying their departures are unconvincing in the final analysis, and might even cast a shadow on glorious names. For there can be no determinant circumstances in the sacrificial life of a great artist. Circumstances work toward manifestation of the instinct of self-preservation. Here the responsibility is of a higher order, hence untranslatable into the language of reasons and circumstances, as they are answerable not to limited human reason, but only to God.

Flight, pious reclusion, and salvation are an old Russian

tradition. There is nothing shameful about that. We are not running off to an operatic hermitage to walk under the fountains. We are fleeing into poverty, into solitude, into eternal doubts for the sake of a chance to preserve our living souls.

"A Ruble for the Lot!"

Here is a legend that Soviet propagandists suck on and salivate over like a lollipop: The constant shortage of books in the U.S.S.R. is splendid proof of how the life of the mind, the intellectual personality, has flourished under the Soviet regime. "At a bookstore in Moscow, where a line of people stood waiting to buy Spinoza . . ." cooed Vera Inber sweetly, and the press cannibals picked up the quote: You see! For Spinoza our people stand in line yet, for Spinoza!

Not that Spinoza is the only thing Soviet citizens have to stand in line for. They stand in line for meat and potatoes, for oranges, for toothpaste and toilet paper, for their number in line at the doctor's office, for renting a boat on a holiday, and so on to infinity. And for books, too, of course, when there is hope of obtaining real food for the mind.

A booklover today who looks over the list of what publishers promise under the plan in the way of forthcoming titles will be filled with hopeless longing. What a tempting choice: classics from all the way back; the biggest names in foreign literature; even such writers as Mandelstam, Voloshin, Klyuyev, and others that have been banned for years. But the booklover knows that none of these works will ever show up on the shelves of a bookstore.

If one or two copies do happen to find their way to the store, they will spend a while in the manager's safe before beginning their rounds on the barter system: to the manager of the nearest delicatessen for some smoked salmon, or maybe to the manager of the department store for a pair of Italian sandals. Then a few copies will be distributed among special shops at the regional Party Committee level and upwards—restricted shops with guards and document checks—thence to adorn with their beautiful bindings the beautiful Finnish and Rumanian furniture in the apartments of the Soviet elite.

And some copies of Russian books, so desperately needed in Russia, will travel to other countries.

Still, the real booklover will not give in to black despair, for he knows that in spite of eternal persecution the eternally indestructible and inexhaustible Black Bookmarket goes on.

The black market in books has everything that Soviet publishers have put out in the past ten or fifteen years. You can even order an old book, which you will receive after a while—for a solid sum, to be sure.

It would be unfair to many of my black-market acquaintances to use the term speculator to designate a person who brings a book to the black market. These persons are for the most part well educated: readers, writers, scholars, and collectors. They are less concerned with acquiring a wanted volume at fabulous price than with making a trade, the way stamp collectors do, for example.

However, while the intellectuals determine the business climate on the black market, by their tastes and interests, the people who really run it are the "book sharks" who see to a continuous flow of merchandise. (Not to be confused with the "book beetles" of lower rank—the secondhand buyers who grab up orphaned libraries, intercept books from people on the way to the dealer, and do a little pilfering on the side.)

Geographically speaking, the big-city book markets lead a nomadic life. Today they are in the main square for everyone to see; tomorrow, after the customary raid by the militia, they move to the edge of town—preferably to a place with crossroads, so that the police wagon cannot come up on them unexpectedly. Good military strategy.

Take Semyen Semyenovich, a big shot among the sharks. In the winter he wears a good-looking fur-lined jacket (an item which is also hard to get); in the summer he sports an elegant English blazer with the emblem of an exotic yacht club on it. He hops around and hovers over the suitcase that serves him as a sales counter. He knows his business and has the flair of an artist for different types of customers. With an elderly university lady he will discuss the relative merits of Proust translations, the prewar Frank and the newer Lyubimov. He will pat a little boy on the head: "What do you want, sonny, Ray Bradbury? No, I don't need your money. Just you look at home and see if maybe there aren't some nice old books nobody needs." He will treat a retired colonel to a few select obscenities, thereby getting him to purchase the coveted *Memoirs* of Zhukov for twenty rubles. In the meantime his spies, whose task is to buy for a pittance, flit among the crowd to make a killing off inexperienced newcomers.

But that booty is not Semyen Semyenovich's main source of book supply. The authorities carefully recorded precise distribution data for the Mandelstam volume in the Poet's Library series. Semyen Semyenovich, however, has all the Mandelstam you want, and what is more, he had it before the print run was officially terminated. If you discount a possible miracle factor, there remains a trustworthy connection to the printing shop—with benefits both ways.

Semyen Semyenovich always carries a good stock of foreign hard-to-gets, from Agatha Christie paperbacks to slick monographs from Skira and Rizzoli. Meanwhile people wait and wait for books mailed to them from abroad. Naturally. Customs and postal officials don't earn much (unless again you add the miracle factor).

Actually, even legal book dealers don't always resort to the going barter system. They have personal requirements, too. And that is where Semyen Semyenovich conveniently comes in.

He does not hit customers head on with his prices. His replies tend to be allegorical, as for instance: ten "nominals," twenty "nominals," which means thirteen rubles or twenty-six rubles, instead of one ruble thirty kopeks as indicated on the cover of the book.

When in a still more playful frame of mind he converts to another standard: "How much do you want for Plutarch, Volume II?" "Seven rubles," he replies. The customer has to realize he means seventy. Since the customer is an intellectual, Semyen's price list does to some degree reflect a proper hierarchy of spiritual values. He wants a lot of money for the Literary Monuments academic editions, for Greek and Roman literature, and for Russian poetry published in the copiously annotated Poet's Library series.

Each of three Montaigne volumes costs eighty rubles if you get it from him. Fifty rubles for a volume of Pasternak or Tsvetayeva. Twenty-five for Plautus comedies.

Given the fact that Semyen Semyenovich, in the capacity of an anarchistic businessman in a socialist environment, keeps his finger to the wind instead of following State Price Committee directives, he can screw his prices up faster than Saudi Arabians selling oil. One or two books can cost the monthly salary of an engineer, a doctor, or a teacher.

But the engineer, the doctor, and the teacher bring Semyen the rubles they have earned on overtime, by hook and crook, or by marrying for money. And what they buy from this elegant peddler is "neither Blücher nor my stupid lord" (and not even so much the suspenseful Agatha Christie). They buy Pushkin and Gogol, Goethe and Thomas Mann, Plutarch, Rembrandt, and Chagall, and the fabulously expensive Montaigne.

I remember one Sunday when they announced advanced subscriptions on something, a Lermontov edition, I believe.

Crowds and cries, screams and police whistles all round our bookstore. I went over and listened. "Some oddball padlocked himself with a chain to the bookstore to be first in the morning . . . The Party committee said all copies have to go to the activists at the factory. The activists showed up with wire-cutters, but the people stood up for that oddball. He really wanted those books!"

I shrugged my shoulders and went to the black market. The sun was shining on the beautiful bindings and Semyen Semyenovich was squinting. He was in a good mood.

"How much do you want for the La Rochefoucauld?" I asked him.

"A ruble takes the lot!"

Names That Open Doors

Everywhere you go these days, in every town and every branch of industry, you run across names that invariably work wonders. They are not necessarily the names of Party bosses, the first secretaries of regional or local Party committees.

For instance, in the little oil town where I went to work

after graduation, the magic name was Zabrodotsky. He was the chief engineer of the petroleum administration, an energetic little Caesar in those parts.

"Zabrodotsky gave the order!" "Zabrodotsky's instructions." "Zabrodotsky says to do it." "By request of Zabrodotsky!" "Zabrodotsky sent me!" "Zabrodotsky has issued a V.S." (This deferentially playful abbreviation stands for Valuable Suggestion.)

Anyone able to wield one of these phrases could count on getting some of the best deals in town: an assignment to work on a drilling team where the plan was overfulfilled and the pay therefore high; a flat in a new building, complete with bathroom and toilet; three kilograms of oranges under the counter, at the local *gastronom* store; or even a travel order to the mainland before expiration of contract.

I recall having had this open-sesame name at my disposal on one occasion, and I used it foolishly. At the supply room I drew two dirty old mattresses so that we might sleep easier on the hard couches in our editorial office.

Late one evening a colleague and I flew into Lugansk. Known as Voroshilovgrad for many years, the city had only recently reverted to its original name. In the lobby of the main hotel we saw the typical scene. A desperate crowd was storming the reception desk, where a sign proclaimed the same old story: *No Vacancies*. People bombarded the female manager with their travel orders and credentials, holding up their howling infants and flashing their medical certificates. A luxurious Georgian, who stood somewhat apart, cast hypnotic glances at the unapproachable woman at the desk, the while he patted the bulging wallet in the inside pocket of his cheviot woolen jacket. But all in vain.

I, too, waved my travel orders hopelessly in the air, while my companion calmly bought a local newspaper at the stand, went off to one side and began to read.

"Well," I said, "I guess we'll have to spread your newspaper on a bench and spend the night in the square."

Suddenly my friend threw the paper aside, shouldered his way through the crowd, and, drawing himself up full height in front of the manager, he asked: "Did you get the call from Kuznetsov in Moscow to reserve a double room?"

"Just a minute, I'll check." She quickly thumbed through her papers. "I'm sorry, there is no record here. Maybe the

girl on duty before me misplaced the order. Hey, Gapa,
take these comrades up to the semi-deluxe."

The crowd fell into a respectful silence.

In the "semi-deluxe," which belonged to the regional
Party committee, my comrade laid his newspaper carefully
on the mahogany table. It could come in handy later. From
this paper he had picked out the magic name which then
he had used in a less than legitimate way. It appeared in an
item on the front page: "The audience heard a long speech
by the first secretary of the Lugansk regional Party committee, Comrade Kuznetsov." So we used the name; so
what? We hadn't said that Kuznetsov had ordered a room
for us, we only asked whether there had been a call from
him. And as for Moscow—well, we really came from Moscow, didn't we? Without us the room would have remained
empty, at least that night.

Jewish Names

He did not read books, as a rule, but he always paid attention to authors' names. He picked up a volume from the table and read the cover. "Shklovsky. A Jew."

"What makes you think so?"

"Do you think Jewish names have to be Kogàn, Shapiro,
or Shusterman-Freyerman? Oh no, my friend! All of those
Minskys and Pinskys, Belinskys and Krychevskys, those
Berdichevskys and Shklovskys and Ostrovskys—"

"Now wait a minute. Are Belinsky and Ostrovsky necessarily Jewish?"

"What else?" he snapped.

Numbers

The morning was already hot. We jumped into a battered
car and drove out into the countryside around Lgov, a
quiet old southern Russian town. So remote and demoted
was Lgov that even so unimportant a guest as myself merited two escorts—an elderly guide from the pioneer house
and the stoop-shouldered chief of the municipal telephone
exchange, who let us have his official vehicle for the occasion.

The guide pointed out the main tourist attraction. This was a supposedly Gothic tower, resembling an ancient pump-house, in the overgrown garden of Prince Baryatinsky's home where that romantically inclined nobleman had kept his illustrious prisoner Shamil.

Then the guide began to recite something about a grandson, either of the prince himself or of the estate manager, who had returned in his old age to have a look at the familiar surroundings.

We rode on, past fields alive with crickets. The choppy asphalt road crossed a wide strip of superhighway. "Only thirty-two kilometers," said the phone chief, "to Kalinovka. Where Nikita came from. They built that road in one week, just before his visit."

And he went on, without letting the guide recover the conversational initiative: "They installed automatic telephone service in our area last winter. All the bigwigs quarreled over the numbers."

"How so?"

"I had a hard time trying to please everybody. I gave out numbers by rank and title. The first secretary got 4-12, naturally."

"Why is that?" I asked. He chuckled resonantly, snapping a skinny finger against his huge Adam's apple. It came to me in a flash: "Of course, four rubles and twelve kopeks is the price of a bottle of cheap cognac." (That is what it cost in those days.)

"The second secretary got 3-12." A bottle of Stolichnaya!

"Number 2-87 went to the chairman of the district Soviet executive committee." A bottle of Moskovskaya.

"The militia chief asked me to save 1-49 for him." The price of a fourth of vodka.

"And what number did you assign to yourself?"

"I'm just an ordinary guy. Zero-22, a glass of beer!"

Ghostwriters at Work

Even in the Soviet press there is occasional mention of deals involving theses and doctoral dissertations. Demand begets supply. The powers that be pay in kind, so to speak, for dissertations: with apartments and promotions. Sometimes the writing is done simply for money. There are plenty of customers in the rich central Asian and Transcaucasian republics. Those ladies and gentlemen, who have enough to eat and wear, enough houses and cars, feel the need of adorning their names with an extra degree or two, a title here and there.

When my friend N. had to have money to buy a co-op flat, he took on two ghostwriting jobs at the same time: memoirs for an old general and a doctoral dissertation for a woman in the town of Mary. Her subject was "Problems of the Development of the Soviet Historical Novel in Turkistan."

Before a small circle of friends, N. read aloud from a letter he had received from his client. " 'Dear N.! The first chapter of our work'—note the tactful first-person plural—'was discussed by the faculty and given a high rating. They decided that it should be read at the board meeting of the local Writers' Union. They advise us to have a look at the following books.' " She concluded with a list of historical novels by Turkmen writers.

A certain author, present in the group when this letter was read, had another suggestion: "It would be more interesting for you to get together with the people who actually wrote those Turkmen novels."

The Ideal Soviet Writer:
Konstantin Simonov (1915–1979)— A Summing Up

BY MARK POPOVSKY

Translated by Albert C. and Tanya Schmidt

From *Kontinent* No. XIV, 1978

On the fifth of September, 1979, the *Literaturnaya Gazeta* devoted an entire page to the death of Konstantin Simonov. From the various articles, Soviet readers learned that Simonov was a "strong, handsome, noble person" (Eduardas Mezhelaitis), that he was a "genuine Party man" (Alek-

MARK ALEKSANDROVICH POPOVSKY *was born in Odessa in 1922. He attended an army medical school and the Army Medical Academy in Leningrad. He lived through the Leningrad siege. A medic in the war, he advanced with the Soviet Army as far as Breslau (Wroclaw). After the war he graduated by correspondence from the philological faculty of the University of Moscow. He published over five hundred items in the Soviet press; in the U.S.S.R. he has to his credit fourteen books, including biography and reportage (*When a Doctor Dreams; The Destiny of Doctor Khavkin; The Map of Human Suffering; People Among People; Panacea, Daughter of Asclepius; The Thousand Days of Academician Vavilov; and others). Member of Writers' Union since 1961. In the spring of 1977 he notified the Secretariat of the Union of his resignation in connection with the persecution of L. Kopelev and V. Kornilov. Emigrated to the U.S.A. in October 1977. Among his books published in the West are* Guided Science *(in four languages);* The Life and Times of Voino-Yasenetsky, Archbishop-Surgeon. *Participated as author and publisher in the first two issues of the* samizdat *historical collection* Remembering.

sandr Krivitsky), and that he was a "tirelessly active public figure" (Irakly Abashidze). Aleksey Surkov, in his article, pointed out that Simonov "managed to keep his finger on the pulse of the times whenever history took an important turn" (sic!). The writers met with complete agreement on the part of comrade Brezhnev, as well as Comrades Andropov, Grishin, Gromyko, Kirillin, and Kosygin, who affixed their signatures in alphabetical order to the combined Party and government obituary. They added that the deceased "exerted every effort toward the noble struggle for peace" and that his poems "inspired heroic deeds and instilled unshakable faith in victory."

It would be an exaggeration to say that the newspaper provided its readers with an overabundance of information on the life and work of this famous poet and writer. But the readers will not complain, for they realize that by Soviet tradition a man in Simonov's position has as great a right to secrecy as he does to a state funeral. On the hierarchical ladder of Soviet officialdom he occupied a rung higher than that of a minister; therefore, commemorative statements concerning him may not and cannot exceed the formal boundaries of official panegyrics.

And yet there are many aspects of Simonov's life that are important and of considerable interest to the world he left behind. Not so much the fact, recalled by Surkov, that over forty years ago the poet "received his baptism of fire in the sultry Mongolian steppe at the Khalkhyn-Gol River." Nor is it so interesting to know that during World War II Simonov rode in a submarine and aboard a bomber. In those days lots of people were flying and sailing. It is far more worthwhile to inquire into the secret of Simonov's success over the years at remaining the favorite of three Soviet dictators one after another, and to learn why he nonetheless enjoyed the reputation among the Moscow intelligentsia of being a liberal. What was his opinion of himself? What were the real activities of this poet and bureaucrat, this diplomat-playwright, this writer-politician? It is essential to clarify these questions, inasmuch as the official Soviet legend is now being supplemented with Simonov myths in the West. In the reminiscences by Madame Um-el-Banin on the subject of Bunin (*Vremya i My* No. 41), Simonov emerges as a knight without fear or reproach: He is intelligent and handsome and noble. One senses an analogous degree of admiration on the part of my friend and colleague Anatoly Gladilin in his article published by *Russkaya Mysl* on September 13, 1979.[1] Not satisfied with dubbing Simonov the Soviet Hemingway (both writers, we are told, created the same kind of heroes: courageous and solitary), Gladilin has proposed the theory that this highly placed Party functionary lived a double life. Gladilin hypothesizes thus: "All of a sudden, a few years from now, a new unpublished book by Konstantin Simonov will appear —a book he wrote for the desk drawer, as they say, and one in which he was able to display his literary gifts to the fullest. This, then, may well mark the surprise beginning of Konstantin Simonov's posthumous glory as a writer." I shall return to this theory presently, as well as to other theories advanced by my contemporaries in their attempts to unravel the "secret" of Simonov's liberal reputation and luck in the line of work. But first I should like to mention an incident I witnessed at an early stage in my journalistic career.

I.

In the autumn of 1949 I submitted my first piece to the *Literaturnaya Gazeta*. They printed it, and I became a regular contributor to the science department of the paper. The *"Literaturka,"* as we called it, in those days was a place where you could breathe more freely than in any of the other Soviet newspaper offices. Then as now, it served in the Party propaganda system as a show-window aimed at the West. It was assigned the role of disseminating intellectual disinformation or something like that. To be sure, we young journalists who had been through the war and were testing our prowess in the business of writing gave no thought to the paper's function in that respect. We were happy to be published, to reach a wide audience, to be sent out on assignment all over the country as long as we

[1] *Vremya i My* is a monthly periodical formerly published in Tel Aviv, now published in New York. *Russkaya Mysl* is an émigré weekly newspaper published in Paris.

thought up interesting and entertaining subjects for our articles. From these trips we tried to bring back as many stories of "socialist achievements" as possible, for despite its privileged status the *Literaturka*, like any other Soviet newspaper, was required to report only successes and accomplishments.

We were proud to be part of the *Literaturnaya Gazeta*, the country's most interesting and widely read newspaper. We even regarded it as the most decent and the most truthful. This optical illusion can be explained to some degree by the fact that Konstantin Simonov became the paper's editor in 1950. All the members of the staff adored him. They loved him as a poet, as a war hero, as a strikingly handsome man, and as a chief who knew how to joke with his colleagues and who responded with a smile to other people's jokes. When he rejected a manuscript, he never hurt the journalist's feelings; when he praised a piece of work he invariably underscored the author's personal merits. We liked the way he rolled his r's and we liked his sparse manly gestures. Most of all, however, he earned our deference by making such a dazzling career. The first time he had been appointed to the editorship of the *Literaturnaya Gazeta* was in 1938, when he was only twenty-three years old! His example went to many a head: You never know.

So there we were, working for Simonov. The weather outside was as vile as could be. It was the end of the 1940s: Mass arrests of the so-called *povtorniki* were taking place, and a wave of official anti-Semitism rolled over the land. Our food, our clothing, and our housing were meager in the extreme. Work alone compensated for the hardships of life. Not a day passed but that anti-Semitic feuilletons appeared in the other newspapers—yet not in ours. In other editorial offices people were being arrested, fired, or chased away, while in ours a businesslike atmosphere prevailed, calm and congenial. That was the advantage of having a favorite of Comrade Stalin as our editor!

Suddenly, in the space of a single hour, everything changed. It happened in January or February of 1953. That morning Simonov strode as usual down the editorial corridor, under the rapturous gaze of typists, female editors, and charwomen. He told his secretary to get the whole staff together for a special meeting. When all were assembled he smiled and pulled his pet crack: "Be seated, fellow irkers." He rolled his r's, as always. He paused for a moment while everybody took their seats and quieted down. Then he began to speak in his customary half-joking, half-serious manner: "It is not quite clear to me, my friends, whether we have a feuilleton department in this paper or not. Do we or don't we? And who is in charge of it? Where is the production from that department? Ah, Rudolf Bershadsky runs it. And where is he? He's not a member of the editorial staff? Well, get that Bershadsky in here."

Rudolf Bershadsky, head of the feuilleton department, was a Jew and a Communist, a man of limited mental capacity and orthodox to the marrow of his bones. With a slight limp, resulting from a wartime injury, he entered the office. By the time he showed up, Simonov had already made his point clear: The editorial office was infiltrated by persons who were maliciously interfering with exposure of the roots of bourgeois nationalism. (He neglected to mention precisely which nation he had in mind.) Having wormed their way into the confidence of the newspaper's management, the persons in question were stalling publication of important coverage and undermining a serious Party measure.

What followed was an interrogation of Bershadsky, who was frightened to death. The head of the feuilleton department swore up and down that he, a front-line combat officer, had nothing to do with any kind of nationalism and that he was hardly even Jewish. If feuilletons is what you want, be my guest, as many as you like, only up to now they never gave me any room on the page. And the order never came down. In touching on the latter point he got it across that he had operated under the direct orders of the editor-in-chief. But no one paid any attention to that. The staff members noted in the minutes that there had been a slackening of vigilance in the editorial office, and that bourgeois nationalism had reared its ugly head in the department of feuilletons, but that it had been exposed and nipped in the bud.

Within the next several days Bershadsky was expelled from the Party, dismissed from his job, and placed under arrest. In the pages of *Literaturnaya Gazeta* there appeared, one after the other, two virulent anti-Semitic feuilletons, no different at all from the sort of thing being printed at the time by *Pravda*, *Izvestia*, *Krokodil*, and other Party publications.[2]

We, the young employees and writers of the *Literaturka*, were deeply shocked. We were not children, we were not naïve, and we knew pretty well how the machinery worked in those types of offices. It was plain to see that somewhere on high (right up at the top!) it had been noticed that the *Literaturnaya Gazeta* was not keeping in step, was not lending its weight to the anti-Semitic campaign unleashed by the Central Committee. They barked an order at Simonov. A victim had to be found immediately; he found one, and he performed the sacrifice. He did exactly what others would have done in his position—others like Vadim Kozhevnikov, the editor of the magazine *Znamya*, or Yevgeny Popovkin, the editor of the journal *Moskva*. If those men had betrayed a colleague, no one would have been surprised. As sure as one and one make two, a chief editor must be ready to sacrifice a subordinate in order to save his own skin. But—Simonov! Our Konstantin Mikhailovich!

We might not have been so stunned had we known that handling jobs like that was no novelty for our chief. Many years later I heard an eye-witness account of how the civil execution of Mikhail Zoshchenko was staged in Leningrad in the fall of 1946. That event figures in Soviet history under the code heading "party decree concerning the journals *Zvezda* and *Leningrad*." The decree is studied in Soviet schools to this day. But here are some details which you probably won't find in the textbooks.

The task of twisting arms was entrusted to Druzin and other Leningrad literary bosses. From Moscow, Simonov was sent in as reinforcement. It was a big responsibility and no failure would be tolerated. As always in such cases, Moscow demanded "active mass participation." Leningrad writers were required to "express their indignation" and to vote in favor of expelling Zoshchenko from the Writers' Union. All members of that organization were obliged to

²Grigoriy Svirsky describes this episode in more detail in his book *Na Lobnom Meste* (London: Novaya Literaturnaya Biblioteka, 1979), pp. 87–88.

attend the mock trial in the Dom Literatorov. Zoshchenko himself was summoned to be present. The Leningrad speaker, appointed by the regional Party committee, painted in the blackest colors a public and professional portrait of the renegade writer. To highlight Zoshchenko's essential decadence, and incidentally to whip up the audience into a state of white fury, the speaker—I think it was Druzin—said that during the war Zoshchenko had spent his days as an officer sitting in the rear instead of doing battle with the Hitlerites.

The truth of the matter is that Zoshchenko had not been sitting in the rear, rather, he had been in besieged Leningrad where he nearly starved to death. But he did not bring that up, nor did he discuss his literary views when his turn came to speak. He simply stated that he had not been drafted into the Soviet Army, owing to poor health: in World War I he was poisoned by gas, wounded, and evacuated from the front as an invalid. For his bravery in combat he was decorated with the Cross of Saint George. Having made this brief statement, he left the platform. There was silence in the hall, yet one had the impression that a bomb had been dropped. If it was untrue that Zoshchenko had sat out the war in the rear, perhaps the other charges brought against him were equally false. The members of the presidium were seized with panic. They knew full well what the regional Party committee would do to them if they botched the Central Committee's operation. All hopes were pinned on Simonov.

He mounted the platform. He was dressed in his military uniform, resplendent with ribbons and medals. In all his martial and literary glory he symbolized all that was noblest and best in the war that had so recently ended. Instead of talking about Zoshchenko he rolled out his favorite topic: camaraderie at the front. And somehow he succeeded in putting things in such a way that all the people in the hall were old wartime buddies and only Zoshchenko was the outsider, who got carried away, stuffed his head full of wrong ideas, and had now sunk to treason. Maintaining a tone of warm soldierly solemnity he spoke of the need for Party discipline and professional rigor, pointing out that Stalin's Central Committee, from its lofty elevation, had a better overview of the general welfare than any one of us whose horizons were limited by narrow personal interests. And if the Stalinist Central Committee made such a decision, then that's how it is; we should consider ourselves privileged to be living at this happy time, when everything is clear, when everything is just and correct. In concluding his remarks, the Moscow envoy dropped the flowery language and declared that the recalcitrant are on dangerous ground, and that the Party has many ways and means of pulling them back into line if they understand no other language.

After such a speech, the Leningrad writers had no choice but to surrender, to raise their hands in favor of ousting the renegade Zoshchenko. The vote was unanimous. The Party people reported to Moscow and everything was fine. Thus began for Mikhail Mikhailovich Zoshchenko a long period of poverty and neglect. In 1953 we were unaware of how Simonov had accomplished his Party assignment in 1946. Indeed, how were we to know? Episodes of this nature are not reported in the press or in encyclopedias, and the literature textbooks are mum.

II.

Shortly after Stalin's death, during the so-called thaw period, Ilya Ehrenburg made this remark to a friend of mine: "Konstantin Mikhailovich has weak sphincters. He always lets go a second too soon." In medical terms the sphincters are the muscular mechanisms controlling evacuation from rectum and bladder. Ehrenburg had in mind the 1953 incident involving Bershadsky; what he was really saying was that while Simonov had perhaps wished to preserve decency, he had been unable to do so, unable to refrain from producing anti-Semitic feuilletons. Only a month or two remained until the death of Stalin and the end of the "doctors' plot." But his sphincters let him down.

I believe that Ehrenburg, himself a rather devoted servant of Stalin, was being unfair. Obviously a person has to make some sort of effort if he wants to maintain a level of decency. The young Simonov, however, had set himself life-goals of an entirely different order. I knew his mother, an elderly lady of noble origins who loved to talk about her education at the Smolny Institute for aristocratic young ladies. I also knew his stepfather, a retired general who had served with the rank of colonel in the Russian army during World War I. Konstantin was adopted at the age of three by his stepfather. The parents were decent folk in the prerevolutionary sense of the term, that is to say, they professed the simple virtues without which, as they saw it, life could not be lived. To violators the house closed its doors, and no one shook their hand. In that system of values, treachery was regarded as a supremely disgraceful and criminal affair. In the early 1930s the boy rejected the "bourgeois views" of his parents. During the period of collectivization and industrialization, he left home and lived for several years in factory and student dormitories. In 1937, a fateful year for many millions of people, Konstantin Simonov attracted the notice of Stalin himself. He was treated kindly, and from then on he remained a Kremlin favorite regardless of who happened to be in power.

Simonov published thousands of pages of wordy prose and hundreds of pages of journals. But nowhere does he say a word about his first steps in the corridors of power. I do not think this can be attributed to modesty on his part. It is unthinkable that a man could gain Stalin's confidence in 1937 and be named head of the *Literaturnaya Gazeta* in 1938 without doing something specific. We do not know precisely what Simonov did to win the leader's trust. But we do know that every official writer singled out for distinction in the 1930s had to pay for it. Fadeyev put his signature to "assessments" of persons who were tossed into prison. Ilya Ilf and Yevgeny Petrov composed stories on commission in which they lampooned the Russian intelligentsia. Ilya Ehrenburg spent most of his time abroad, corrupting the minds of Western intellectuals, while Fedin and Katayev stayed at home and betrayed their friends and neighbors. Vishnevsky, Lavrenev, Pavlenko, and Gorbatov collaborated openly with the Cheka-GPU-NKVD-KGB. I repeat: We are ignorant as to exactly what Simonov did in order to join the group of literary figures who basked in the warmth of Stalin's smile. We do know for certain, however, that in the seven years from 1942 to 1949 he received five Stalin Prizes for his writings. The only man who held more such awards than he was Yakovlev, the designer of

military aircraft. The monetary portion of those prizes
amounted to a million rubles. And earnings from books,
motion pictures, and stage plays were even greater than
that.

Furthermore, having become Stalin's *Landsknecht*, Simonov never betrayed him, nor did he ever betray Stalin's
successors. My choice of the term *Landsknecht* is not intended to cast aspersions on the memory of the poet. Quite
the contrary. When a medieval mercenary sold his skills,
his soldierly craft, and his arms to his overlord, he considered that everything including his own life was fully compensated by the royal wage. Indeed, the *Landsknecht* was
paid well, and in return for the money the Swabian mercenaries, for example, swore absolute fidelity to the lord who
hired them. They did not break faith: They stood fast in
battle and did not go over to the enemy. Simonov inherited
this tradition from his predecessors-in-arms. He was grateful to the leaders for his medals and awards, for multivol-
ume editions of his works, for Stalin prizes and Lenin
prizes, for cars and country houses, for special rations from
the Central Committee and official trips abroad at government expense. He was generously rewarded, he found the
remuneration equitable, and he served faithfully.

In his prose and poetry we find no departure from the
Party line. Or, more precisely, from whatever line the
Party bosses chose to lay down at any given time. Simonov
realized early that in the Soviet climate a thaw is a temporary and unreliable thing: In Russia, freezing weather is
the norm. Simonov set his course by the cold spells,
thereby avoiding mistakes. When Ehrenburg published
The Thaw in 1954, Simonov disregarded the current political uncertainties and fired off a whole round at the book—
six special articles in the *Literaturnaya Gazeta*. From the
standpoint of his own career he proved to be right. Another true servant of the throne, Boris Slutsky, gave vent to
his genuine feelings after Stalin's death by publishing several anti-Stalinist poems. The young Yevgeny Yevtush-
enko went full speed ahead, gambling heavily on the anti-
Stalinist theme. But Simonov's last farewell to the departed
leader and benefactor was a tortuous yet well-intentioned
poem entitled "The Way You Taught," in which the author
solemnly swears continued allegiance to Stalin and to his

"iron Central Committee." The iron Central Committee took note of that protestation. Appointed by Stalin to candidacy for membership in the Central Committee in 1952, Konstantin Simonov held that position—a high one for a writer—until 1956; thereafter, to the end of his days, he was a member of the Central Auditing Commission of the Communist Party of the Soviet Union and a deputy of the Supreme Soviet.

It should be remembered that it was much harder to serve as a *Landsknecht* in the mid-twentieth century than in the fifteenth or sixteenth century. In those earlier times the armed mercenary took the oath only for the term of contract—from three months to a year. For the rest of the time he was free to do and think as he pleased. And in his off-duty hours the hired soldier was at liberty to go to church, to visit the tavern or the brothel, to get drunk or fall in love, to follow his own true inclinations. We live in a different age. Konstantin Simonov served the Soviet leaders for over forty successive years without a moment's respite. I saw him at meetings, in his private office, at the party celebrating Victory Day, at his colleagues' funerals, and he always stuck to his role. His role, his image, was that of a faithful soldier of the Party.

Simonov fashioned for himself the mask of an old trooper, a good guy without any say-so. His was not a very colorful act. It consisted of an impassive expression of the face, softened on occasion with the smile of a simple soldier, and a ready collection of coarse jokes. Now and then he would trot out some nostalgic lines on the order of "Remember, Alyosha, the road to Smolensk . . ." Also part of the picture was his upright bearing, plus attractive gray hair and a heavy gait suggestive to onlookers of leather belts and creaking boots. It was not a very complicated bag of tricks, but Simonov handled it to perfection. None of the people I knew in Moscow ever saw him with his mask off or his psychological uniform unbuttoned. His act was not for the benefit of us plain folk, but rather for the grandees of the Central Committee. They really liked that pose of a loyal soldier-poet. It was their ideal of what every intellectual should be: plenty of spiritual gifts dressed in khaki of military cut. As for Simonov himself, after wearing that mask for well-nigh forty years it fit him so closely that he

probably could no longer tell which of his actions were
natural and which were part of the pose. He spent his
whole life on the stage, as it were, always starring in the
same role.

When other hirelings proved to be disloyal, Simonov got
mad. After the bloody Hungarian events of 1956, Howard
Fast, the American writer, became disillusioned with Communist ideals and published articles exposing the movement. Simonov was ordered to teach the defector a lesson.
Literaturnaya Gazeta came out with a long article, rather wa-
tery and hardly convincing, in which Simonov made a big
show of lighting into Howard Fast like a punching-bag.
But one passage in the piece conveyed to the reader the
genuinely impassioned indignation felt by the author. Fu-
riously, Simonov reported that, while Soviet publishing
houses do not normally pay foreign authors, they did pay
Fast for his works published in the U.S.S.R. They paid him
in dollars (!!) and a tidy sum at that. This ungrateful person
responded to the solicitude shown to him by our Party and
government by going over to the reactionary camp. Simonov was evidently most upset by this display of immorality
on the part of Fast.

After the death of Stalin it was no longer so easy to serve:
Discipline weakened in the lower ranks, and in the upper
there was no unity. The loyal soldier Simonov loved order.
Everything must go through the proper channels. As editor of *Novy Mir*, in 1956, he published Dudintsev's novel
Not by Bread Alone in that journal. The slant of the novel in
question corresponded altogether to the position taken by
Nikita Khrushchev at the Twentieth Party Congress. Khrushchev exposed Stalin, repeating over and over again that
the Party was not afraid to look truth in the eye and that
exposing the personality cult would only strengthen the
Party. Simonov was convinced that in publishing the Dudintsev novel he was not departing one iota from the
wishes of the new boss. At meetings where the novel came
under discussion, Konstantin Mikhailovich liked to talk
about the "publisher's noble courage," which he put on a
par with the writer's courage. In point of fact, no particular
courage was demanded either of Simonov the editor or of
Dudintsev the author. It should rather be termed a case of
collusion between the two.

On the "advice" of Simonov, Dudintsev added a fourth part to the novel. The reader had learned that the hero, a talented inventor who had proposed a useful innovation for Soviet industry, had been slandered and arrested; now the author composed a sequel depicting a series of highly improbable events. The very same investigating officer who had run the hero into jail suddenly realized that the man was innocent, and began to fight—under Stalin, mind you—for his release from prison camp. This phony plot twisted things to make it appear as though the scientist's personal enemies bore sole responsibility for his troubles. The honorable Party investigator cleared the whole matter up and rescued the hero. Owing to the efforts of the author and of Editor Simonov, the novel *Not by Bread Alone* fit neatly into the socialist-realism category and was thus suitable to be printed in *Novy Mir*. It is interesting to note that some years later, in the 1960s, the novel was published in book form, but Soviet readers this time paid no attention whatsoever to this best-seller of the 1950s.

In 1956 a group of Stalinists in the Central Committee sought ways of curtailing Khrushchev's debunking activities. They picked on Dudintsev's book as their target, saying in effect: "You see what happens! After all those anti-Stalinist speeches, even the writers are getting unruly." Simonov, as one admitted into higher councils, kept closely abreast of the discussion. At some point he realized that Khrushchev had lost ground to his opponents and that his anti-Stalinist zeal was abating. At points like that a ritual sacrifice must quickly be found. If the Central Committee is always right, that means someone else is wrong, and that that someone else must be promptly punished. Simonov sensed exactly when the right moment had arrived. The 1953 scenario was replayed in the editorial office of *Novy Mir*. As he had done before at the *Literaturnaya Gazeta*, Simonov called a staff meeting. In a tone of amazement he posed the question: Who is it that allowed Dudintsev's politically illiterate and weak piece of writing to be printed in the magazine? (He loved the word "political" and knew how to use it.) For several years following that editorial meeting, Vladimir Dudintsev was blackballed from the literary world, deprived of his earnings, maligned and insulted, and reduced to a state of utter nullity.

What astounded people at the time was not the treacherous deed alone, but also the fact that the editor-in-chief of *Novy Mir* calculated precisely the moment at which he should disown his writer. And he made it just in time, for a second later the thunder from on high would surely have descended upon him with a crash.

It is unlikely that Simonov received a special command to strike at Dudintsev. It was said of him that he had intuition. But, as Moscow journalists jokingly put it, "information is the mother of intuition." Simonov did have a very good nose for politics, but the important thing is that from Stalinist days onward he had cronies in the Central Committee who supplied him with confidential information. Being well informed kept him out of trouble on many an occasion. Ehrenburg was wrong: Simonov's sphincters worked fine. He proved this once again when the authorities decided to ruin Boris Pasternak.

III.

Pasternak's novel *Doktor Zhivago* lay around the *Novy Mir* office for a long time. Simonov read the manuscript and promised the author that, if he would do a little more work on it, it would be published. But Simonov was in no hurry to publish the novel. He waited to see which way the wind would blow in the upper spheres, to see whether Khrushchev would continue his Stalinoclastic activities or order an about-face. The unforeseen happened, however. The manuscript found its way to the West and the Italians printed it. Khrushchev had a fit. Simonov had to sit right down and pen a long letter to Pasternak. The letter was published in the *Literaturnaya Gazeta* and subsequently appeared in *Novy Mir* No. 11, 1958. Everyone reading this long-winded epistle realized that it was not really addressed to Pasternak, rather, that it was intended as a justificatory document exonerating Simonov and his editorial staff. What the letter said, in essence, was this:

". . . The basic idea of your novel is the assertion that the October Revolution, the civil war, and the social changes resulting therefrom brought the nation nothing but suffering, and that the Russian intelligentsia was physically or morally annihilated. . . . As persons who hold a view diametrically opposed to yours, we naturally believe that there can be no question of publishing your novel in the pages of the journal *Novy Mir*."

Simonov's letter made the point that it was neither the Central Committee nor the censors who had rejected the novel, but that the editors themselves refused to publish it. Thus, the authorities were divested of responsibility for the ensuing scandal, and that was what they wanted more than anything. There were two opposing opinions about Pasternak's book among the literati, it was as simple as that. And the authorities had nothing to do with it. For the friendly service rendered, Simonov was pardoned by the Party bosses for his transgression. Events developed rapidly: Pasternak's book won the Nobel Prize; Central Committee propagandists once again set about stirring up popular wrath against the intelligentsia, and the *Novy Mir* affair got lost in the shuffle.

Treachery upon treachery: Zoshchenko, Bershadsky, Dudintsev, Pasternak. How many more victims were there whose names we do not know? During the period when Simonov held a high post in the Writers' Union, dozens of the members of that organization were expelled, arrested, and worked over. So how did Simonov get the reputation of being a liberal? Leftist leanings were ascribed to him by the entire Moscow world of literature, theater, and cinema; only the people in Leningrad were more cautious after the Zoshchenko business. Even so severe an analyst as Solzhenitsyn ranked Simonov among the liberals. In his book *The Oak and the Calf* Solzhenitsyn describes a meeting of the secretariat of the U.S.S.R. Writers' Union on September 22, 1967, at which almost all those present demanded a ban on the printing of his books; Solzhenitsyn mentions the independent behavior of Salynsky and Simonov, and comments: "They are not quite enemies, they are halfway on our side." This from Solzhenitsyn was a rather favorable judgment.

What, then, was the reason for Simonov's liberal reputation? Konstantin Mikhailovich had been struggling to win such a reputation for a long time—as early as the time when Leonid Leonov and Valentin Katayev, giving no thought to their own literary future, wrote novels on such required themes as Soviet power and Russian forests in the Lysenko perspective, or the time when Bubennov and Babayevsky were idolized and the novel *Alitet Takes to the Mountains* was considered a Soviet classic. Then it still appeared as though the long night of Stalinism would never end. It was the end of the 1940s, and the farsighted Simonov could already see, as he did in the early 1950s, the simple truth: The literature of socialist realism was not literature at all, it was not an art but rather a heap of well-paid trash. All the Stalinist troubadours like Dolmatovsky, Babayevsky, Sofronov, and their ilk would perish under that trash heap, their names forgotten. And Simonov's own name too would be buried among them. In the 1940s, when Stalin was still alive and when his own fame was at its zenith, Simonov had the perspicacity to foresee his own fateful end. This insight gave him pause.

He was not about to give up butter and caviar for his bread. Yet it is true that man does not live by bread alone. Over and above the good things of life, Russians have always had a deep-seated need to be respected. It is a need felt by a people who have suffered humiliation for centuries, and you will hear it from the lips of every drunkard in the land: "Do you respect me? I respect you." Konstantin Simonov desired to gain respect for himself. It was a rare commodity, and his colleagues could not even dream of obtaining it. What he wanted was not the deference due to his position, he wanted to be genuinely respected as a human being. He, the hireling, wanted to be sincerely respected by his colleagues as well as by future generations, and to go down in Soviet social and literary history as a decent man.

But for all that, as I have said, he was not ready to give up his lucrative position at court. Nor was it in his nature to become a split literary personality—as was the case with so many writers in the 1960s and 1970s who wrote one type of thing for publication and quite another for the desk drawer. These intellectual games did not suit Simonov in his well-rehearsed role of loyal soldier. Moreover, he was smart enough to know that God had not given him the kind of talent that wins readers and posthumous honors. His books would not save him from that inevitable trashheap; by writing poems of comfort and consolation, on the

order of "Wait for Me and I'll Return," he could not hope
to wash away the dirt of the epoch. The only thing left for
him to do was to invent and construct a second biography
for himself, the biography of a writer who is decent and
who struggles in the grip of duty and of service to the
czars.

That second biography was composed carefully over a
long period, without losing a day's work. On the one hand,
at the height of the cold war Simonov was sent to America
by direct order of Stalin; he wrote the propagandistic play
The Russian Question and an equally propagandistic collection of poems, winning the Stalin Prizes in 1947 and 1949.
Every day his picture, complete with medals and awards,
appeared in the newspapers. At the same time, however,
he put the initial touches to the alternate portrait of himself. Aleksandr Borshchagovsky was particularly hard hit
by the openly anti-Semitic persecution of a group of theater critics in the late 1940s (Yuzovsky, Borshchagovsky,
Danin, and others). He was deprived of his daily bread and
forced out of his flat. Simonov did not come to the defense
of Borshchagovsky and the other Jewish writers—his job
would not permit that. But when the heads stopped rolling, Simonov took five thousand rubles from his own millions and lent the sum to the unfortunate Borshchagovsky
as an advance on a new novel.

The news of his philanthropic act quickly spread
throughout Moscow. It was something out of the ordinary.
The capital's frightened intellectuals immediately raised
Simonov to the status of a noble personality. He feared no
reprimand from the authorities for his gesture, since he
knew that the hounded Borshchagovsky would write exactly what was expected of him. Indeed, two years later
there appeared a gigantic novel telling of how the British,
in the Crimean war, sent a naval contingent to the Russian
Far East and how the Russian people heroically repulsed
the attack. Borshchagovsky's novel, entitled *The Russian
Flag*, did not differ greatly in ideological slant from Simonov's *The Russian Question*. This was precisely the sort of
work called for by the Central Committee in the cold-war
period. The authorities were satisfied; Borshchagovsky,
forgiven, was contented; but it was Simonov who earned
the fattest dividends: He had firmly established his image
as a noble and responsive person, a friend of the underdog.

More than once, on subsequent occasions, he resorted to the same stratagem. However, he did not provide financial assistance to anyone and everyone. His aid always had an element of the unexpected about it, being invariably aimed at creating a sensation. In 1958, the talented poet and writer Aleksandr Yashin was forced to go hungry. Of peasant stock, Yashin offended the powers that be by publishing a story entitled "Levers" in the *Literaturnaya Moskva* collection, dealing with peasants who joined the Party, became reduced to a state of stupidity, and were nothing more than levers and cogs in the state machine. As was his wont, Simonov refrained from standing up on behalf of his persecuted colleague, but when he later learned that Yashin's family was destitute he gave the poet's wife a thousand rubles. Again the literary world was abuzz with whispers of admiration and amazement. The old men among the silent minority in the Writers' Union exchanged significant glances and chalked up to Simonov one more A for good behavior.

More often than not, Simonov used his official position rather than his personal fortune: He printed Dudintsev, he promised to publish Pasternak's novel, and put out another two or three smaller works of a nonbanal character. I remember especially an article by Vladimir Pomerantsev, "On Sincerity in Literature," published during the Simonov tenure in *Novy Mir* (1955). There were rumors (rumors, rumors . . .) that Simonov was the one who succeeded in getting approval for publication of the novel *The Master and Margarita* in the review *Moskva*. Thus, his fame as a liberal continued to grow. Then, whenever he would commit the next act of treachery, or veer sharply to the right in keeping with the party line, there were always plenty of people ready to sympathize with him: "Poor Simonov, there goes the Central Committee twisting his arm again."

In the mid-1960s, the discussion in the press concerning pen names brought Simonov considerable success. In an article, "With Lowered Visor," Mikhail Sholokhov publicly declared that an honest writer needs no pseudonym, that an honest writer will not conceal his name from the reader. Such a declaration, in the 1960s, had an anachronistic ring. Sholokhov wanted to revive the postwar years and the ill-famed campaign against "rootless cosmopolites."

But at that particular moment, for tactical reasons, the anti-Semitic angle found no resonance in the Central Committee. Simonov profited by the interval of indecision to publish in *Komsomolskaya Pravda* an article in defense of authors writing under assumed names. He mentioned the pseudonyms of revolutionary leaders and noms de plume of such writers as Pushkin, Gorky, and Saltykov-Shchedrin, adding coyly that he, too, Konstantin Simonov, in a manner of speaking, was operating under a pen name—for his real first name was Kirill. I remember how gratefully Moscow's intellectuals received this little article. Compared to what rabid-rightist journals like *Ogonek*, *Oktyabr*, and *Molodaya Gvardiya* were splashing across their pages in those days, the piece on pen names looked like a gem of liberalism. No wonder Solzhenitsyn referred to Simonov as being "halfway on our side."

To be sure, Konstantin Mikhailovich's liberal reputation sometimes sank to a very low ebb. While the arrest of Bershadsky and the 1953 anti-Semitic feuilletons were written off as inevitable, and the double-cross of Dudintsev aroused disputes as well as sympathy for *Novy Mir*'s editor, the whole Pasternak affair was plain for all to see. In literary circles there was talk of "Simonov tactics." People passed around by word of mouth the acid crack made by Mikhail Svetlov: "Simonov is a decent guy. When he does you dirt, he is not happy about it."

After the Pasternak affair the silent minority, whose affections were so important to Simonov, no longer found any excuse for him. It was a small group of persons, totally unorganized, including Paustovsky, Kaverin, Vasily Grossman, Tvardovsky, A. Bek, Stepan Zlobin, K. Chukovsky, two or three other writers, and a few directors. In the 1950s, the pre-Sakharov and pre-Solzhenitsyn period, the silent minority served as a moral tuning fork for a Russia that was beginning to use its brains. They were listened to; they served as a model for young intellectuals. Having lost the respect of these old hands as a result of the Pasternak affair, Simonov realized that his alternate biography was in serious trouble: Today, these people—the conscience of an age—are making public opinion, and tomorrow they will sit down and write their memoirs. He must win back the good will of the silent ones. Simonov sat down and began to think.

Casually and as though on the spur of the moment, he would drop a few complaints into his conversations with the more important writers, saying that he was sick and tired of petty literary quarrels and the pressure from on high. He was careful, when hinting at that pressure, to give no names or details. To hell with it all! He would move to the backwoods and concentrate on literature alone. In a manly tone of voice—the tone that suited him so well, that of a person who has seen and comprehended many things—he would say to his colleagues: "A writer should write. All else is of the devil!" Of that "all else" there was a great deal: In addition to several public and Party positions, Simonov was also the deputy secretary-general of the U.S.S.R. Writers' Union and editor-in-chief of *Novy Mir*. He took leave of the magazine only, immediately landed a good job as *Pravda* correspondent for Central Asia, and departed for Tashkent.

It is a three-hour flight from Tashkent to Moscow. But for several years Simonov played at living in the backwoods. He did not even go to the Third Writers' Congress. "A writer should write!" And it must be admitted that the trick worked perfectly. I recall commiserative conversations about the poor exile "who did the Party's dirty work in the Pasternak affair," who wanted everything to work out for the best, "but those bastards in the Central Committee . . ."

A year or a year and a half after Pasternak's death, Simonov returned, when talk about the great poet's tragedy had died down. The *Pravda* correspondent was welcomed most cordially back in the capital: He soon became a member of the Auditing Commission of the Central Committee of the Communist Party of the Soviet Union.

IV.

Seventy years ago Lenin praised Gorky's novel *Mother*. "A very timely book," he wrote. When they came to power, the Bolsheviks gradually created a timely literature, the sole function of which consists in providing a timely response to the orders issued by the country's rulers. The ax fell on those who did not learn how to write "timely"

books: Babel, Bulgakov, Zoshchenko, Platonov, Mandelstam, Akhmatova, Pasternak. Simonov began with sincere
lyrical poems, quickly got the drift, and recycled himself
accordingly. Several publishing houses put out his works
every year. And whatever the genre he worked in, his
books have always been timely in that they always
matched the political requirements of the day.

Was he a man of talent? It is difficult to say. The laws and
criteria of "timely literature" are so different from literary
criteria per se that any comparison between them is as impossible as between a cigarette-pack design and a Rembrandt canvas. The fate and function differ in each case.
The plays *The Foreign Shadow* and *The Russian Question* cannot be judged by the ordinary rules of drama, if only because the author himself did not look at them from that
viewpoint. The same can be said about numerous collec-
tions of Simonov's poetry, including the little volume
Friends and Enemies. The latter work is closer to the world of
diplomatic notes and newspaper quips from the era of Stalin and Truman than to the spheres inhabited by the
muses.

It is even harder to see how future literary historians will
handle Simonov's war novels. Konstantin Mikhailovich
did not write his own novels. He dictated the text into a recorder and handed over hundreds and thousands of meters
of tape either to his literary secretary or to his coauthor
Yevgeny Vorobyev. The latter, a mediocre Moscow writer,
was authorized to produce finished literary works from
that balderdash. Several of my acquaintances had to edit
those manuscripts. According to them, the text read onto
the tape often made no sense, the plot was disjointed and
fell apart; by the end of a book the blond hero would start
sprouting wavy pitch-black hair; soft little goatskin boots
on a heroine's feet would suddenly begin to squeak and to
click heels. Whenever the editors would come with their
puzzled questions, Simonov brushed them off with a brief
"Ask Vorobyev." Vorobyev performed his wizardry over
the hair and the boots, combing and snipping here, nailing
and hammering there, and sent the whole thing to the
printer's where it came out in a million copies. For my part,
I see no point in analyzing this kind of synthetic literature.

Let me qualify: The trouble with Simonov's war novels is

not that he dictated them onto tape for them to be written
by someone else. When all is said and done, they are his
novels, and he alone is responsible for them. The irremedi-
able shortcoming of these books is the author's utter lack of
any clear-cut moral approach to the events he describes.
You can invent a plot, you can develop it and carry it
through to a denouement, but you cannot simulate a writer's conscience or feign the true feelings of an author.
Without conscience there is no literature nor will there
arise a spark of genuine trust between the book and its
reader. Whereas the Belorussian writer Vasil Bykov reveals
to the reader, in his every line, the tragic truth of war, Simonov is basically indifferent to past tragedy. His reminiscences serve merely to irritate and reopen old battle
wounds, to suggest to veterans who may still feel the
throbbing pain that he, the writer, sympathizes with them
and understands their nostalgia and bitterness. Here and
there in the provinces you may find an old soldier who
will fall for this kind of false compassion, but it is already
apparent that these books will not long outlive their author. As for Simonov's published diaries, the absence of
sincerity renders them totally worthless. A woman editor I
knew, who had the job of reading those diaries, once
quoted to me a line from somebody's poem, sighing as she
spoke: "To know so many words, and all for telling lies!"

Simonov liked to talk about his special affinity for the
subject of war. For several decades he clung to that theme,
piling up sequels and ramifications to his novels. Yet there
is no dedication or love in any of it. Nothing but calculation.

An author of war books, unlike his colleague who han-
dles contemporary themes, is relieved of the burdensome
necessity of explaining to his readers the ugliness of the
post-Stalin era. He can pretend that over the past thirty-
odd years nothing of any particular significance has happened in the country. This is a very convenient stance,
safely shielding the writer from the watchful eye of literary censors. The war theme enabled Konstantin Simonov
to maintain contact with his readers and editors these past
thirty years without the slightest worry.

In the Soviet Union the war theme is always timely. In
fact, it is the very cornerstone of "timely" literature—the

most profitable, the best meal ticket. Whoever masters the art of producing timely books will never go hungry. There is only one drawback to this kind of activity: It kills the soul and destroys talent. Even the least gifted of writers, as a general rule, loves his people. And he has the power to distinguish authentic art from fakery. But now and then, in the course of my life, I have come across fellow writers who were outspokenly indifferent to their craft. Invariably, they were masters of timely literature.

I ran into one of these men in the hall of a House of Creativity outside of Moscow. He was a renowned writer of children's books. He emerged from his room in slippers and wrinkled pajama pants and ambled in the direction of the cafeteria, for it was lunchtime. Pausing at the head of the stairs, he stretched his prematurely obese body and said sadly: "What a colossal bore. Am I sick of all those tiny tots of mine!" He was referring not to his own offspring, but rather to his fictitious characters—little country boys and country girls. This colleague of mine won a Stalin Prize in the early 1950s for a story about young pioneers on the collective farm. What he wrote was revoltingly untrue to life; he himself was as fully aware of this as anyone else; he detested the young heroes who had made him famous as well as the profession that was his bread and butter. Miserable and emptied out, he made no bones of the fact that the only thing about writing that interested him was his salary.

I had a second encounter, one which on the face of it might seem to have nothing in common with the first, yet which left me with exactly the same impression. In the Central Writers' House at Moscow a commemorative evening was held in honor of Mikhail Bulgakov (1891–1940). The masterworks of this supreme artist, hounded in his lifetime and doomed to die in poverty, were brought back to light and began to be published. The authorities hastily declared Bulgakov to have been one of their own Soviet kind. Be that as it may, the occasion was a real celebration for me and my friends. Actors read excerpts from Bulgakov's magnificent prose, and people who had known him recalled jokes and pranks by the genius who wrote *The Master and Margarita*. Only one person remained unmoved throughout the evening, and he was the chairman of the proceedings: Konstantin Simonov. As usual, he had been charged with handling a potentially explosive situation, and he did his best to dampen the enthusiasm in the audience. From his introductory remarks one gathered that, indeed, there had lived in Moscow a writer named Bulgakov, who lived his life and then died of natural causes. The Party and the government took good care of his papers, and now some of the things that the author had been unable to publish were being printed. Konstantin Mikhailovich uttered all of this in a cavernous voice as he looked over the assembled heads with his cadaverous eyes. In the same tone of voice and with the same look he presented each number on the program. Everyone noticed his demeanor. "Evidently he has instructions to ruin our mood," said a woman next to me. "Nothing of the kind," replied her companion, "Simonov has simply had his fill of all these literary games." At intermission I overheard a remark by an elderly writer: "Seems like Mikhail Bulgakov looks more alive today than Konstantin Simonov." The man with him shrugged his shoulders: "What do you expect him to do? It's already past nine o'clock, and Kostya is still on the job."

V.

To the end of his days Simonov remained in the Party fold. He vacationed at the exclusive Central Committee rest homes; he received medical treatment at the Kremlin hospital; he attended conferences to which common mortals were denied access. But his true value as international agent and seductive propagandist diminished year by year to the vanishing point. Time was when Konstantin Mikhailovich traveled abroad in high style. Right after the war he was sent to France for the express purpose of persuading Bunin to return to the U.S.S.R. He did not succeed in luring Bunin, but he did catch some small fry. Most of those Russian repatriates of the late 1940s ended up in prison camps. Later too, in the 1950s, the Soviet regime capitalized successfully upon Simonov's pseudoliberalism. This went on until genuine liberals and authentic dissidents left for the West and spoke out for human rights. In the 1960s came a rising tide of information on what Soviet life was really like, and Simonov the errand boy lost his appeal among Western audiences.

His literary glory dwindled as well. For a while his works were much translated. Red and pink academic intellectuals in Paris and Brussels, London and Washington plowed through Simonov's books to find explanations for Soviet war victories and postwar tragedies. But then Europe and America became acquainted with the poems of Okudzhava and Galich, the prose of Sinyavsky, Daniel, Belinkov, Voynovich, Nadezhda Mandelstam, and Georgy Vladimov; and Simonov's literary star paled and faded out. To top it all, along came Solzhenitsyn with a bang. One might say that Simonov's fame abroad as an interpreter of Russian truth perished a good ten years before the man himself went to his grave.

The Soviet authorities have a panic fear of funerals. The nearness of death and the reality of a higher power above Party and government mitigate the citizen's fear of the regime. When a prominent person dies, a leading artist or writer, the situation is fraught with explosive potential. The authorities are aware of this, and so they surround the public funerals with heavy police contingents. But State Security has other methods, too. The obsequies are accompanied by empty speeches from trusted orators and by a flood of hypocritical articles in the newspapers. The purpose of all this prolixity is to stifle any real feelings toward the deceased. The bureaucrats do their best to let the cement of their rhetoric—polished up to look like bronze—harden as quickly as possible, so that no one among the living may take advantage of the sad occasion to speak truthful words at the graveside.

In this regard the funeral of Konstantin Simonov was much like any other official undertaking of the same order. His rank entitled him to burial in the Novodevichye cemetery, with a strictly prescribed ceremony. However, in his last will and testament the poet requested that his remains be placed alongside the tomb of his mother in the German cemetery. His wish was not granted. Everything had to be so arranged that idle tongues should not wag: The loyal soldier's last farewell must be accompanied by volleys of rifle fire and volleys of oratory. Nor would any deviation be permitted in the press coverage. "He entered the auditorium at the Polytechnic Institute, threw off the army overcoat that still reeked of gunpowder and battleground dust, and mounted the platform—young, handsome and extraordinarily stern." Thus, in the standard prose of the day, wrote Eduardas Mezhelaitis. He is describing not a man but a monument. This is what was required of him.

It is interesting to note that in his own lifetime Simonov had the task of carrying out analogous operations in the Writers' Union. He buried Paustovsky, Ehrenburg, Aleksandr Bek, and many others, always maneuvering skillfully among the subsurface reefs. In the last years of his life, Konstantin Paustovsky had addressed numerous letters of protest to the authorities; yet in Simonov's speeches this writer was portrayed as an artist of the purest water, the creator of bucolic aquarelles. The tortuous career of Ilya Ehrenburg was rendered incredibly straight and smooth in the obituary treatment.

I believe that Simonov enjoyed handling these delicate assignments. Funerals of prominent colleagues helped him to bolster his own public image. For nearly ten years Aleksandr Bek tried to have his novel *The Last Assignment* published. He died without having ever seen the book in print —a fact impossible to gloss over at the funeral: The manuscript had made the rounds and a lot of people had read it. Simonov evaluated the situation correctly. He devoted practically the entirety of his speech to what he called this wonderful book. "Sleep in peace, dear Aleksandr Alfredovich," he intoned over Bek's coffin in the Oak Room of the Central Writers' House. "We will publish your work whatever the cost!" Of course nobody in the Soviet Union intended to put out a book exposing high-level Stalinist officials, but after the funeral Simonov was on top of the world. Showered with thanks and congratulations, he saw his reputation go up again by several points. The unpublished Bek novel found its way abroad and was printed in 1971 in *Posev*.

In the Soviet tradition we are in the habit of classifying historical figures as either liberals or reactionaries. Neither label fits Konstantin Simonov. I would not go so far as to say that he preferred the clamp-down periods to the brief thaws. It is quite possible that in the depth of his soul he preferred the more liberal atmosphere when it happened to prevail. It is easier to play the part of a "noble gentleman" when the weather is pleasant—and it is safer. Furthermore, each time that the clouds over Russia began to disperse somewhat, none was so quick as Simonov to proclaim the good news to the public. In that context they used to say in Moscow: "Simonov is always the first to run out into the cleared minefield." (Also quoted in Svirsky's book, cited above.)

No, our hero cannot rightly be called a reactionary. He simply made no distinction between just and unjust causes involved in the operations entrusted to him. He went where he was told to go and he axed whomsoever he was told to ax. Then, after the next armistice, he would give the defeated side to understand that he was just a plain old soldier. ("If something goes wrong, what can we do? We do what our country tells us to.")[3] And that anyone else in his position would have hit even harder.

It cannot be said that Simonov was an immoral man. Rather, his public conduct did not figure within a context of the concepts of ethics or morals. He regarded as superfluous the notion that ethics must take precedence over immediate utility. "I have no need of that hypothesis," he might have said, in the words of the astronomer Laplace. Even when he seemed to be doing good, his conscience was a nonparticipant. His ethical scales were permanently rusty.

Here we might bring the story of our hero to a close. But there is one more touch to be added to the portrait—a small incident I recently heard about from a former Kiev journalist now living in the West. He was on assignment in Odessa in 1972. He was given a hotel room to share with an elderly accountant from Smela. The accountant was a quiet man who loved good books. He complained that in Smela he was unable to obtain the works of his favorite authors, Bulgakov and Akhmatova. The roommates got to like each other, shared the traditional half-liter bottle, and talked about the books of those two writers. Somehow the name Simonov came up in the conversation. "A complex character," said the accountant with a frown. "You met him?"

[3]This is a line from an Okudzhava song.—TRANS.

"No, but in a manner of speaking I had a run-in with him."
It turned out that the old man liked Simonov's early poems
and also his articles, which he clipped from the newspapers. In 1948 or 1949 he came upon a piece in which Simonov befouled Tito as a traitor and bloody Fascist dog.
Simonov described having flown to see the Yugoslav partisans; he recalled the combat losses at the time, and concluded that Tito had betrayed the cause of the Yugoslav
people by joining the imperialist camp. This was one of
many articles reflecting Stalin's hatred toward the independent Yugoslav ruler.

Some years later, Khrushchev made his peace with Tito,
and in the same newspaper, *Pravda*, another Simonov article appeared. Again he wrote about his trip to the partisans, but this time he expressed his enthusiasm over Tito
the great popular leader and genuine Leninist Communist.
Comparing the two articles, the accountant from Smela
was depressed. His disillusionment prompted him to do an
ill-considered thing: He put both clippings into an enve-
lope and mailed them to Simonov in Moscow, along with a
note asking in which of the two articles the writer had spoken the truth—when he called Tito a Fascist dog, or now,
when he called him a genuine Communist and Yugoslav
hero. The letter was an outcry from a man whose feelings
had been hurt. Still, the accountant was sufficiently astute
as to leave his letter unsigned. Nor did he include a return
address. What's more, he mailed the letter not in his home
town but in Kiev when he was there on a job.

Nonetheless he got an answer. Half a year later, the accountant was summoned to the regional KGB office at
Cherkassy. He was questioned by the chief, a lieutenant
colonel, who placed the unfortunate letter on the desk in
front of him. "Did you write to Simonov?" "Yes, that is my
letter." "Why did you have to do that?" "I wanted to know
the truth." Apparently the Cherkassy lieutenant colonel
took a liking to the provincial booklover, and the year was
1958, when the tendency was in the liberal direction: Their
conversation was altogether cordial.

"My dear friend," said the lieutenant colonel, "I beg of
you, don't ever again write anything of this kind. Right
now we are not putting people into the pokey for such an-
tics, but I can't guarantee what may happen in the future.

Go back to your Smela, my friend, and shut up." The kind-hearted officer volunteered, further, the information that Moscow had issued strict orders to seek out the writer of the letter in question. Simonov himself had insisted upon such a search. And, although it took quite a while to comb through the fifty million inhabitants of the Ukraine, the glorious security organs had accomplished their mission and were now serving a solemn warning upon the writer of the letter.

"That is the type of guy he is, Konstantin Mikhailovich Simonov," the accountant concluded his tale. "And now you see who his friends were. He was angry because someone knew about his bad conscience. If times had been different, they would have cooked my goose under Article 58, and I would have done a good ten years on account of that letter."

Thus ended the conversation in the Odessa hotel, as reported to me by my journalist friend.

Optimistically, one might share Gladilin's hope that a secret Simonov book will turn up one of these days, a novel replete with truthfulness and talent. Or Schönfeld's presumption, spelled out in *Russkaya Mysl* (October 18, 1979), that "Simonov . . . was always torn between wanting to be a liberal and not deviating from the compulsory Party line." But the real and true life story of Konstantin Simonov, recently brought to a close by the passage of time, leaves no room for illusions. The man was not torn or divided in any way whatsoever. He was an integral whole, a complete Soviet person. The ideal Soviet writer.

Concert for Trumpet and Orchestra

BY ANATOLY GLADILIN

Translated by George Bailey

From *Kontinent* No. XII
(German edition), 1979

It is not a story, not a novel, and not a sketch
either . . . it is simply a solo for bassoon with
orchestra—describe it that way.
—V. Katayev, "The Dice"

Dark chords of the string instruments sound in deep octaves. Shovels swing rhythmically. The infantry is digging in—deeper and deeper. Cellos in echeloned defense positions. Hide yourselves from the evil powers of the cold world! The foremost fortified lines of the violins sob weariedly. The violas deliver short, sharp salvos. The self-

---

ANATOLY GLADILIN *was born in Moscow in 1935. He studied in 1954–58 at the Gorky Institute for Literature. His first short story, "The Chronicles of the Times of Victor Polgursky" was published in the magazine* Junost *in 1956. In 1959 the story "The Brig Hoists Its Sails" was published, in 1962 "The Eternal Business Trip," in 1965 a volume of stories,* The First Day of the New Year. *Ten of Gladilin's books were published in Russia. The others were published in the West and are available in the Soviet Union only as* samizdat. *Among these are the novel* Prognosis for Tomorrow *and the collection of stories* Rehearsal on Friday, *from which this satire is taken. In 1976 Gladilin emigrated to the West. He lives in Paris.*

propelled gun, the piano, creeps on minor passages into cover. Dull and forlorn in the distance boom the howitzers of the bass fiddles and the tubas.

And suddenly the trumpets whirl high into the heavens. A battle formation mounts the attack. Our fighter planes are already overhead. The infantry goes over the top. The violas overtake the violins. The cellos form into assault columns. The piano rushes ahead with major acceleration. Large-caliber brass shoots point-blank. Quite out of breath, the harpist–field nurse hurries to the scene. The drummer beats the bass drum. Victory is near.

And all this because the trumpet was committed to the attack.

Over the lower octaves of the strings floats the high tone of the trumpet and imparts the sensation of forgotten, prehistoric happiness. My God, how fortunate are those who can understand this harmony! One could say that they enjoy paradisaic bliss without effort or exertion. And all this for only a ruble or one ruble fifty, the price of a ticket of admission.

Incidentally, also in the matter of harmony, order must prevail. For us professional musicians it is the system of the seven keys, C, D, E, F, G, A, B—on the note paper, *"doremifasolati . . .* the kitten is in the ta-xi . . ."* It is also the minor or major series, with cavalry attacks in B minor, and this, that is . . . Incidentally, regard the ABC of musical notes yourself: For my part I have long since noticed that all the notes of a certain octave have made their way forcefully into my life. I wake up in the key of A. I fall asleep in the key of C, in the lower register. My wife gets on my nerves in the key of D. A lecture on international subjects ends obligatorily in the key of F major. When during our rehearsals, for example, instead of the finale of the Fifth Symphony something like a battle between Russians and Kabardinians emerges, then the concertmaster raps on the music stand and says in a reproachful key of E: "Comrades, aren't you ashamed of yourselves?" The keys of G and H are the voices of my children. I am probably not alone with my idiosyncrasies; I remember a visit at Petruchov's—the first violin—"French horn" Shengelaya told a couple of amusing stories and everybody laughed except "Countertenor" Sadovkin, who just sat there with his eyes tight shut

and wagging his head. "What's wrong with you?" someone asked him, and he, as though he had been startled out
of sleep, measured us all with a glance from his moist blue
eyes and said: "What a pure A note that girl just produced!"

A dissonance develops when people don't understand
each other. I have a very busy young man in front of me.
He is talking into two telephones at the same time, giving
his secretary directions, and also listening to my stuttering.
I am thinking of a rehearsal, he—about foreign climes. He
assembles the complement of artists for guest appearances
abroad, and I, in my old dandruff-speckled jacket, do not
harmonize at all, I do not belong in the picture, I am not
appropriate. He looks at me with irritation. He has a typical
loser in front of him. Good God, how fed up he is with it!
Thank God I am not unemployed and I have a home of my
own, a roof over my head. What more can I ask? Anyone
can see that . . . that I can hang around here mumbling all
day and nothing will come of it. I just rob busy people of
their precious time. I just scrape the prongs of a fork on
plate glass. And that is dissonance.

A great many people of my sort come to him. Presumably they all resemble one another. A ready, well-practiced
smile. The would-be ingratiating glance. A certain inclination to humor (at one's own expense, to be sure). Very
obliging. Prepared at any moment to acknowledge the superiority and profundity of this silly-ass power broker.
And what is all this for? To stir his sympathy, to touch him,
to awaken his compassion, to wrap him around one's little
finger? No, it won't work. Because if this good-for-nothing
understands anything at all, then he senses your secret in-
most desire to spit into the official, red-tape expression on
his face.

This type of bureaucrat is turned out in carbon copies,
stamped into being in the stillness of mysterious official
chambers at whose doors scruffy secretary-dogs are
chained. They don't bark, they don't bite, but they don't let
anybody in either.

But even if he knows all about your secret desire, he can
be perfectly sure that you will never dare to act on it. They
will take you to task and you will thank them for it; they
will make fun of you in a polite way (in a just barely polite
way, as the rules of the game stipulate) and it is you who
will make the apologies.

But after all, you are the trumpeter!

"When the trumpeter mounts over Krakow with his trumpet."

Mounts!

The archangel announces the Day of Judgment with the blast of his trumpet. The people will hold their ears so as not to hear it and stare into their television screens. But there on the television screen, instead of an athletic contest they will see one of the horses of the Apocalypse. And it could be that, just a moment before he takes his trumpet in his hand, the archangel will call me and ask me to advise him, I mean ask me to tell him which note to begin on, how to carry the melody, and whether to blow a high A—after all, the archangel will not permit himself to make a mess of it.

The archangel knows that in our profession, too, everything is a question of technique.

I am a trumpeter, and the theme of the trumpet is the calling of mankind, his destiny, the only motif that can pierce the soundproof wall of our "best of all worlds." We must listen to this melody or lose ourselves.

The trumpet—the trumpet is our conscience, but we hide the trumpet in its case. We must awaken mankind, but instead we blow soap bubbles of dance music into the air. Fate plays with mankind. That is a biblical truth. And man plays the trumpet. That is a small anecdote from the club smoking room.

All that is true. It is true because it is not given to us to blow the alarm signal. We guard the herd and call them to drink with melodic trills. The shepherds' flutes are calling. And we ourselves are a "herd." We, too, are shepherded. We are let out to pasture in specially designated meadows where the grass is thin. And we accept this state of affairs as habitual and naturally given. The mutiny in us does not amount to a protest against the fact of our being shepherded. No, we are dissatisfied only with bad shepherds! We would prefer to be guarded by vegetarians. Then in a trice we would be quiet. An idyll.

But there won't be any of that. Well, all right, we say, but if you have to slaughter some self-assuredly bleating ram for supper, then do it quietly, somewhere off on the side-lines, while you explain if need be to the onlookers that it is being done for their own security. It is desirable at such times to show us openings to new pastures, new vistas. That always makes for distraction. Then we will accept the whole business as a matter of natural need. Why, certainly —we will even sign an address of thanks. Wolves and sheep united! And we wish you good appetite.

To put it briefly, Victor Nikolayevich Samorodov suits me personally just fine.

He has talent, a cool head, he is a bureaucrat by profession, he needs no specially constructed armor or even metal in his voice. He is a diamond in the rough and a born leader.

Victor Nikolayevich is a colonel. In 1948 he was detached for political indoctrination and instruction to our orchestra from the tank corps.

Allegro moderato. An abbreviated table of contents: The tops of large, shady trees rustle in the wind. In the same stream of air the banners of allied armies flutter and whip. The heroine approaches an empty bench at the fountain. She is wearing a white-and-rose-colored dress. She sits down, smoothing the creases in her dress. She seeks out her lecture notes and quietly lights a cigarette. The birds chirp as softly as the waters of the fountain fall. In the middle of the fountain stands the statue of the great leader of the people, head erect, the right arm outstretched, and a powerful stream of water gushing from his mouth.

We often perform under the direction of guest conductors, both domestic and foreign. During the concert we follow every movement of the conductor. He swings his arms, he lowers his head, he raises his eyebrows—and the orchestra reacts with great sensitivity.

We are, for that matter, an obedient instrument, we are under the direction of the conductor. The guest director harvests the applause and is gone. *Bon voyage!* We have been rented out for the occasion, so to speak. After all, we have our own conductor. His name is on all the posters. He accepts all congratulatory messages and on ceremonial occasions he speaks "in the name of all." He directs the production of most of the concerts, selects the repertoire and determines the personnel policy, makes up the so-called "face" of the orchestra. He puts us through our paces like a schoolmaster (he even gives us homework) at rehearsals. He arranges competitions—but here he is no longer the absolute ruler. Talent and qualifications certainly have their significance, but the forms for personal-history statements are also important. And these fall within the jurisdiction of Victor Nikolayevich Samorodov. The repertoire is actually also subject to his control. For he will say, for example: "Not that I would presume to give you any advice, dear maestro, but lately an unhealthy inclination toward Western music has manifested itself in our ranks. We ought to take something from the Russian classics or something contemporary, Soviet, optimistic, something thoroughly in the folk tradition."

There are various kinds of chief conductors. Some of them open the door to the office of the Minister of Culture with their feet, and in the presence of such *grand seigneurs* Samorodov takes care to remain in the background. But chief conductors come and go: I myself have survived eight of them. Samorodov stays.

Samorodov makes recommendations, gives guidelines for our conduct abroad, decides who participates at guest appearances, sets the value of the prizes in competitions, and determines who gets how much for what. You can go to the chief conductor with some sort of request and he will promise you heaven and earth. And then he forgets all about it. Well, what can you expect from him, anyway? After all, he is a creative artist.

But if Samorodov says "Yes," then it means "Yes"; if he says "No," then there is no point in complaining. Because the chief is the chief, all right, but the master of the *domaine* is Samorodov.

I can still remember how I managed to get an apartment. My turn had long since come up. I had collected a full bushel of certificates (including recommendations from the nerve clinic and the fire department), but the executive committee kept putting it off. I went to the chief conductor, and he even took the trouble to telephone to the committee in my presence. Of course the committee promised to expedite the matter and see it through to a successful conclusion (after all, the chief conductor is a People's Artist and a Meritorious Artist of the Soviet Union), and still nothing changed. It was only then that I turned to Samorodov and told him the whole story.

"Victor Nikolayevich," I said, "please telephone the executive committee. I have small children and in our room there is hardly space to move in, and the neighbor dumps her garbage into our soup."

Samorodov laughed, then he said: "Telephoning doesn't help. I am an old functionary and I know how to handle this sort of thing. I'll write a letter. The letter will go to the executive committee. There is also a functionary on the executive committee. He will know that I have a copy of the letter. A piece of paper is a serious thing. You cannot get away from it."

He composed the letter and within a week I had the authorization to occupy an apartment.

On one occasion I became involved in an unpleasant affair, and, as always, at the worst possible time. There was one of the regular competitions for places in the orchestra. I was supposed to be promoted from *artist* to *soloist*. I was qualified in every way for the promotion and the question was practically decided, when an "amoral" relationship between the second violin (Vatrushkin) and the French horn (Mrs. Shengelaya) came to light. Actually it was their personal affair, but these days it is not so simple. Moral turpitude needs a private place. Both these people had families. Vatrushkin and I were friends—we had both served in the same unit in the army. And so it was that Vatrushkin asked me to help him. So from time to time I gave them the key to my apartment (my wife and children had gone to the country for the summer). Then the whole story became known and there was a terrific ruckus. Shengelaya's husband had a discussion with Vatrushkin on the street and put him in the hospital. Local Party headquarters met in session to deal with the matter: "Where did the two meet?" "At Kotyonotchkin's place." "Oho, so Kotyonotchkin was an accessory!" So it was all over with my promotion. I was even excluded from the competition.

Once again I ran to Samorodov to complain and cry. With the promotion to soloist I would have received a raise. My wife had already planned to buy a coat with the extra money, and had signed up for the eventual purchase of a frigidaire. How could I explain this to my wife? She could even become suspicious of me, and then it would be all over with the healthy Soviet family.

"Good," said Samorodov. "Get your papers together, we will bulldoze this one through."

I come to the chief. He is sitting there with Samorodov and leafing through my file. Samorodov reports: "This is the way it is, Kotyonotchkin requests that he be promoted to soloist. But I can't do anything, because if I give my endorsement, you, dear Alexander Alexandrovich, will ask me what justification I have for giving it. According to the law, the matter falls within the jurisdiction of the competition committee, which, however, will not meet again for the next two years." The chief agrees: That's the way it is, he personally has nothing against promoting me, but the law is the law—after all, we live in a democracy.

I stand there like a fool, I understand that they are right, and I am on the verge of a nervous breakdown. O.K. The law is the law, but why did you, Victor Nikolayevich, make me any promises, then? Why this scorn?

Samorodov continues: "I'd like to help Kotyonotchkin, but I don't see any way." Alexander Alexandrovich agrees with him again—so it is, he doesn't see any way either.

Samorodov begins again: "I'd like to help Kotyonotchkin, but . . ."

And they kept at it, back and forth, for a long time; I was practically in a state of collapse. I thought, well, I'll just slam the door shut and disappear. But then all of a sudden the chief caught on.

"All right," he says. "Since Victor Nikolayevich wants it that way, I'll do it."

Samorodov, quite naturally, is astounded: How, by what means?

"By way of an exception," says the chief. "We have a precedent in the case of Morozov."

'Well," said Samorodov, "if you give your sanction then I'll put my signature to it."

It was only then that I understood everything. The inspector had not put one over on me. He is simply a sly old fox. He just didn't want to accept the responsibility. He really knows his way around in our friendly little creative collective. There would have been caterwauling, Samorodov would have been accused of favoritism. As it is, they haven't got a thing on him.

Once during a general meeting the first violin, Petukhov, came out against Samorodov. He spoke to the point, and he was nasty. He talked about administration, about the suppression of every form of criticism, about unjustified interference in the repertoire. Since there were people from the Ministry present, we thought that something against Samorodov was in the works. After all, Petukhov is the first violinist, and besides, he is a very careful fellow, so he must have smelled something. Petukhov spoke, his audience applauded approvingly, and Samorodov sat through it all very quietly. To be sure, I noticed that at one point Samorodov whispered something to the secretary, who trotted out—tack, tack, tack—on her high heels, and then trotted back in—tack, tack, tack—with a thin folder which she gave to Victor Nikolayevich. Petukhov finished his speech and walked away proudly from the speakers' platform. Samorodov took the floor.

Criticism, he says, is good. Certain isolated mistakes, he says, have been noticed and we will study how to correct them. However, the attention of the comrades should be directed to the personality of Petukhov himself. Petukhov is a very talented musician, but . . . And Samorodov begins leafing through the papers in the thin folder and then reads certain items out loud: Petukhov has not paid his debts to the amount of 200 rubles to the Fund for Mutual Assistance of the collective for three years. Last summer he was arrested by the militia for brawling in a restaurant while in a state of inebriation. During a tour in France Petukhov kept to his room in the hotel while the whole collective went to the Père Lachaise cemetery to put flowers on the memorial wall of the murdered communards. He pleaded indisposition and then ran into a striptease bar in the rue Molière. In his youth Petukhov had a criminal record for blackmarketing in canned food at the Tishinsky market, a fact which Petukhov had never seen fit to mention in his personal-history statements. As a student he had been bound over because of a relationship with a minor schoolgirl . . .

At this point the audience became unruly. Catcalls were heard: kick the rascal out of the orchestra, kick him out of the civil service. The people's culture must have representatives with clean hands!

We all thought: Well, now Petukhov is finished. There

goes our first violinist to the devil, and then he could play rhapsodies à la Dunajevsky before the late show in movie houses for the rest of his life. But then, just as the Petukhov case was to be decided at a higher level of the bureaucracy, Samorodov—of all people—intervened on his behalf.

Only some time later did I comprehend that it would have been senseless to fire Petukhov. As it was, he was a man with a broken back. In future he would be as soft as butter—easily manageable. It would cost a lot of effort and trouble to bring a new violinist to such a pass!

My life is a concert. I put on a white tie and tails that are like the rear end of a commercial jetliner and for three hours I fly to the heights of pure art—a dark angel with swept-back wings breaking the sound barrier (and simultaneously a royal penguin, white breast and all). But what happens with me outside the concert hall is an intermission that lasts too long. I mosey around the apartment in an old, faded woolen sweater, cook soup on the gas stove, feed the children when they come home from school, and play on my trumpet. Scales and études. "*Doremifasolati . . . the kitten sits in the ta-xi.*" What a soft, downy little kitten. It wagged its tail and then ran off to warmer climes. And now we repeat in a higher register. About eight hours a day. Polishing up the technique. Monotonous but also soothing. Scales and études are my intimate friends. We know everything about each other, we don't have to put on airs, search for highfalutin words, or pretend to be somebody we are not. This is my habitual company. In this circle my life goes by. *The Loneliness of the Long-Distance Runner*, I have read this book, too. I have forgotten what it was all about, but one thing in it I do remember: In order to clock a good time, a runner must run about two hundred kilometers every week. Whether you want to or not—you must. One has to keep in shape. For that reason the long-distance runner is lonely. It's understandable. Who will run thirty kilometers a day with him willingly, just to keep him company, in rain or snow, and at varying speeds? To run in competition in a huge stadium—that, too, is a concert. Such occasions of high ceremony occur only twice a month. On all the rest of the days there is nothing but open-field running, intensive training. My racetrack is my life. For whole days at a time I play one and the same thing on the trumpet; I keep in shape that way. But when in concert (to revert to the terminology of athletics) I can lap the opposition. Even the dumbest bogtrotter yells "Bravo!" when he hears my solo.

In the beginning our neighbors in the apartment house looked at me with hatred burning in their eyes. Some of them moved out, but those who remained became accustomed to the trumpet. My family became accustomed to it as well. For my wife my monotonous passages on the trumpet are nothing more than the sound of traffic on the street. She no longer notices the one or the other. My children have adopted a condescending attitude toward me. Certainly, the fathers of other children come home from work with new jokes, turn on the television and help them with their homework. But I, for my part, am rather a dull person. I play the trumpet. Practice, practice—they know the pieces as well as I do. But then, I am still the father. The breadwinner. The head of the family. One must respect me, or at least pretend that one respects me—and obey. Evenings, off to the concert. I have forgotten what "I will" means. I only know the word "I must." Thirty kilometers of open-field running, rain or shine. That is my duty. It is said that musicians are dull people. But how should one not become dull in such a profession? It is as though we live in a lethargic sleep and come awake for only three hours during the day, when the concert begins. Freely and lightly we float up into the sky, teach people to dream, teach people to be human beings. And then back to the same old thing—scales, études, rehearsing the piece, the loneliness of the long-distance runner. The pain in the chest, that is the usual thing in our profession, and the eternal aftertaste from the brass mouthpiece.

I seldom dream during the night. A thick black curtain, and the light is turned off. But then if dreams come even so, then in my dreams I am always playing the trumpet.

Anyway, it would be wrong to complain. Playing the trumpet is the only skill I have.

Andante cantabile. Abbreviated table of contents: Once upon a time a great Russian composer lay abed and surrendered himself to pleasant thoughts. Suddenly there was a

knock at the door. "What do you want, Archipka?" asked
the composer in a very dissatisfied voice, because everybody in the house knew that the composer was not only
disposed to play the Sybarite during the mornings, but that
he also composed then—yes, yes, the note paper lay on the
night table and the pen stood upright in the inkwell near
the mirror—the morning is not the worst time of the day to
work, when one still has a clear head. "Sir," said Archipka
behind the door, "a Count from the Royal Opera has come
to visit you." The composer uttered a brief curse, threw on
his dressing gown, and went into the salon. And indeed,
there in one of the chairs the deputy director of the Royal
Opera, Count N., had made himself comfortable. "In what
way can I be of service to you, Your Highness," asked the
composer, and in the tone of this question even a less musical ear would have detected a trace of dissatisfaction and
embarrassment. The composer was dissatisfied because the
reasons for the early visit of the titled servitor of the muses
were well known to him. The contractual deadline for the
delivery of the new opera had come and gone and the composer had hardly completed half of the assigned work. His
embarrassment, on the other hand, was explained by the
fact that there was a lady in his bedroom at the time; and
the liaison with this lady he was by no means desirous of
allowing to become known, and especially not to the
Count. This personage rose to his feet, bowed superciliously, and proceeded to parade his magnificent uniform,
complete with ceremonial dagger, the length and breadth
of the room. Graciously and discreetly he hinted to the
composer that the public, so to speak, was waiting for the
new opera, that the time allowed by contract had expired,
and that the administration had the legal right to demand
the return of the advance to the full amount. The Count
talked and talked, but it seemed to the composer that His
Highness cast curious glances in the direction of the bedroom—and especially when the sound of a breaking bottle
was heard coming from the bedroom. It was imperative
that the composer do something and quickly to remedy a
situation that was growing more embarrassing by the minute. And then an idea worthy of genius came to him. He
told the Count that he very much appreciated his administrative talents, but took leave to assume that the Count was

less familiar with the problems of the creative process. The opera was not yet finished because the composer would have to return to his native village, to be present at a peasant wedding in order to take in the songs and the dances, to listen to music in a country inn, etc., etc. "Why such complications?" asked the Count, with a little more readiness than was called for. "Because, my dear Count, music is created by the people, and we, the composers, only do the arranging!" The Count fell silent in the presence of this revelation and, bowing, quickly took his leave. The composer sighed in deep relief, but after the passage of time, in a hundred years or so, there appeared in a huge spread in one of the major newspapers the mighty quotation "Music is created by the people, and we, the composers . . ." and so on as reported. Later this saw provided the bases for a hundred and twenty dissertations, while the number of doctoral candidates was well over two thousand. This quotation wandered from one book to the next, from one article to the next, and for a long time after, artists painted these words on placards in the local people's clubhouses. They were to be found engraved on the façades of music schools and in the foyers of conservatories and philharmonic halls. In the stillness of great and stately official residences hit-tune composers hastily threw together and transformed Brazilian dances (Negro folk music) into optimistic marches for the air force. But behind opaque windows in a frosty fog the epoch of the "basis" and the "superstructure" was taking form.

I fell flat on my face, thanks to the machinations of American imperialism, during the tour of the Cleveland Symphony Orchestra. We were playing in the Chaikovsky Hall at the time and we had been warned that we would be receiving illustrious guests. Naturally we took pains to look and do our best. The audience applauded a full twenty minutes, and in answer to the calls for encores we performed a piece by Gluck. And then, when I had already put my trumpet away in its case, Sadovkin rushes into the dressing room. "Lyosha," he calls, "pick up your feet and lay them down—into the director's office!" I rush up there, understanding nothing, and find the room crammed with people. They are handing around glasses full of champagne and somebody says sandwiches are on the way.

Plenty of comrades from the Ministry and also from the administration are there. I take a closer look: Of our people, only the chief, Samorodov, and Petukhov, the first violinist, are there. What am I doing here, I ask myself, surely Sadovkin was pulling my leg, because the cynosure is a potbellied American in a striped suit. Behind him there are other people of foreign origin. Interpreters are trilling like nightingales. I finally catch on, Sadovkin is a bastard—this is a reception for the bosses! I try to navigate my way to the exit, and then Samorodov calls my name. Now it looks bad. Of course he has noticed that I sneaked a glass of champagne. All right, it's not my fault, I'll report everything word for word and Sadovkin will not be able to deny it. Then suddenly Samorodov throws his arms around me as if I were his best friend, smiles at me sweetly, and drags me to the potbellied American in the striped suit. "Here he is," he says, "Alexei Yakovlevich Kotyonotchkin, the trumpeter whose solo you liked so much." To this the interpreters translate "Fridli-bridli-trulala!" and then suddenly shut up as if they had an attack of the hiccups. Everybody is staring at me. I see that the eyes of our comrade leaders are covered with a moist film, the kind that comes with the state of well-being after a fine meal, and you can feel the smile in the air. The potbelly in the striped suit, however, extends his hand to me and says something like "Kurli-murli-please," and then a sporty type, a young man I don't know, whispers in my ear that the impresario of the Cleveland Orchestra would like to drink to my health. They pour me a glass of champagne and I throw a glance at Samorodov, but Victor Nikolayevich nods his head and winks at me. "Thank you," I say (and I am myself astonished at my piping, hesitant tone of voice), "Thank you, but I would suggest that we drink to art, art which binds all the peace-loving peoples of the world together!" The smile that lurked in the room flew upwards; you could hear the rustling of the wings. Our chief appeared as if he had dropped out of the ceiling: "May I, Kotyonotchkin, drink to your health?" We drank, emptying our glasses nonchalantly. I feel that it is time for me to make myself scarce. But the potbelly in the striped suit gives me no peace and is obviously bent on continuing the provocation.

"How much do you earn?" he asks.

I answer.

Question:

"Apparently the interpreter has made a mistake. The sum he mentioned you must receive for every performance and not, as I understood him to say, as a month's salary."

And the smile is again floating in the room, like a migratory bird, but this time it is motionless, frozen stiff.

Oh, you thick-bellied, striped bastard. You ought better to be sitting in a restaurant, ladling in the caviar, but no—instead you prefer to misuse Russian hospitality, you would rather spy, stick your nose into our affairs. But this particular act doesn't work with me, this time you are up against the wrong customer!

I answer:

"I don't understand your question. We Soviet musicians are not interested in money. We are in the service of art."

And suddenly all the migratory birds in the room began to twitter and beat their wings, as happy as though a storm had just passed. Our chief looked at me with devoted dog's eyes. "Come on, Kotyonotchkin, let us drink to the health of your charming wife!" I look around again at Samorodov, but he looks as satisfied as though he were sitting in pine-scented foam bath. We emptied another glass of champagne, each of us, but just as I was trying to get hold of a sandwich, the potbelly in the striped suit buttonholes me and, speaking Russian in a pure Odessan dialect, says:

"Tell me, Lyosha, what are you doing here? You have no trouble at all hitting the *so* while our Smith Johns can't reach *re* without getting the hiccups. Why don't we see you in Europe?"

I must admit that his Odessan dialect knocked me for a loop. Instead of giving him the brush-off he deserved, I stuttered and said: "There was a time when even Dakschitzer was afraid of competition from me, and I would like very much to go to Western Europe, since . . . the Ministry of Culture . . . maybe they will organize a tour, and anyway—music is international, you know . . ."

Suddenly I came to my senses—too late! The little birds were struck dumb, only the interpreters were chirping, right in front of my nose was the back of my chief, and in the corner stood Samorodov, the smile frozen on his face, his eyes like glass.

* * *

A foggy morning. Rain drops rap on the windowpanes while Samorodov paces the floor of his office.

"Certainly," said Samorodov, "in the West a trumpeter earns ten times more than he does here. That is a fact. But why is this so? Naturally, it is because ten other musicians are unemployed and doomed to death by starvation. But here you are not threatened by the spectre of unemployment. Incidentally, yes, we are going to have a new competition for promotions in the orchestra . . . I don't know how the jury . . . Apropos, the American impresario is not a musician at all, he is a well-known spy. The State Department sends such types to the socialist countries in order to make contact with unstable elements."

"Victor Nikolayevich," I implore him, "this confounded spy played a dirty trick on me—he set me up, prevented me from eating anything, and I, well, after the concert my head is as empty as my stomach, and that 'gentleman' kept refilling my glass with champagne and putting pressure on my psyche."

"Yes," sighs Samorodov, "the methods of the enemy secret services are many and various and insidious. Do you know how much the CIA pays for an espionage assignment?"

"Victor Nikolayevich, I have never missed a political-indoctrination course!"

"Incidentally, some of our comrades will soon go to Canada to sign a treaty for cultural exchange. It will include performances in various cities. Undoubtedly the concerts will be a great success. Socialist art is continually conquering new fields and gaining more and more recognition. But from time to time, intoxicated by the applause of the public, we forget to exercise the necessary vigilance. And anyway, who in Canada has the possibility of attending a performance of the philharmonic? The proletariat has no money to pay for admission tickets. Do you see what I am getting at?"

"Victor Nikolayevich, if you mean that one seminar, then I swear to you—I was sick! I brought you the doctor's certificate myself. I was running a high fever—"

"But we believe you, Kotyonotchkin; you have been selected for guest appearances, too. In the Uzbek Socialist Soviet republic. A tour that carries a great deal of responsibility with it."

And then there follow the usual bald lies in the newspaper under the heading "The Whole World Applauds." But how can the whole world applaud? The concept "the whole world" certainly includes a billion Chinese, Indians, and Pakistanis. They are all dying of starvation too! They don't have time to applaud. And not every worker in the civilized West has the means of acquiring a ticket of admission. . . .

New York, Ottawa, Hamburg, Kyoto, Port of Spain, Nantes, Saragossa, Rabat, Detroit, Havana, Singapore, Melbourne, Honolulu, Mar del Plata, Wellington, Manila—what wonderful cities there are in this world!

And the islands—Phoenix, Fiji—such places do not exist even in dreams! Brussels, Antwerp, Vienna, Geneva, Baghdad, Karachi, Boston, Buffalo, Sacramento, Montevideo, Buenos Aires—none of these places is very far away, five or ten hours flight time, no more. So let me go there, for God's sake, I won't stay there! I just want to run around the streets a bit and have a look. I don't even need any money —everything I earn in hard currency I'll give to the State. And I won't need an interpreter—even the wild tribes on the Upper Amazon understand music.

The existence of biological life has not been scientifically established on any of the planets. But they would sooner send me to the constellation of Cassiopeia than allow me to cross a State border, all of which are so closely guarded by soldiers in green uniforms with small, yellow, brilliantly polished buttons. Chromoxide is the best polish for buttons. . . .

"The gentleman with the shaggy mustache,"[1] said Sadovkin, "acted wisely when he prevented people from crossing the borders. Why, I was once in London, and after that it took me about two years to come to terms with myself again. Every night in my dreams I was walking along Piccadilly. No, it's better to stay home."

"Of course," I said to this. "On the other side of the border all you can do is become confused. But here at home,

[1]The reference is to Stalin.

why, you and I can drink half a liter of vodka, cry our eyes out together, and the next morning early, as usual, quietly bring the bottles back, and everything is in order. But in the West, they say, absolute isolation is the rule. There is nobody with whom you can go drinking with."

Not long ago I went to a reception hosted by Samorodov and I made my plea to him the moment I crossed the threshold of his office: "Victor Nikolayevich, soon the tour of guest appearances in Sierra Leone will be coming up. They will be nominating candidates . . ."

"Excuse me, Kotyonotchkin," replied Samorodov, looking at me sternly over his spectacles, "have we ever given you a bad efficiency report?"

"Never, Victor Nikolayevich. They were always very positive. But at the last moment, when the list of participants was finally set, for some reason my name was invariably missing."

"The Ministry is always cutting expenses. There is nothing we can do . . . apparently there's a shortage of hard currency. . . ."

"Victor Nikolayevich, understand me correctly. I make no claim against the Ministry and certainly not against you. But I am an old man. You spend three months filling out the necessary papers, collecting certificates, a superfluous strain on the nerves, you are in a constant uproar. And all for what? What good comes of all the unnecessary excitement? I ought rather to go on vacation and relax completely, put in for an extended cure in good time. After all, they will abbreviate the list of participants this time, too—you said so yourself, we are in a bad way as far as hard currency is concerned."

"Have a seat, Alexei Yakovlevich. Do you smoke? Please have a cigarette. Yes, it's true, we are no longer young, and we don't take care of ourselves, watch our health the way we should. And it is high time we did. How is your health, anyway? You haven't been looking all that well lately. But no, no—by no means take retirement. You and I will have to work a little longer. But one must take care of oneself. I have been thinking about it for some time already: Why shouldn't you apply for a cure in a sanatorium? In Kislovodsk, for example? Not a bad thing, that."

"To Kislovodsk? Not a chance! There, everything is always booked up."

"Why not give it a try, anyway? We will support your application. You can fill out your application right here and now with me."

"Victor Nikolayevich, a trip like that eats a big hole in the pocket. What, I should go to a spa and my family remains here without any money? I am afraid nothing will come of this."

"Specify in your application that you desire to take the cure gratis—at the expense of the trade union."

"But that would be embarrassing. The comrades would say, how come Kotyonotchkin rates such privileges. How would I justify it?"

"Just let that be my worry. Do you understand? All right —fill out the form. We want to make sure that the best musicians in our orchestra are well looked after. Incidentally, Sierra Leone has a very muggy climate, I can't recommend it, it has a very high humidity."

"Kotyonotchkin was lucky," said Petukhov, the first violin, afterward. "We can feed ourselves on frogs and other garbage, but he relaxes while he takes the famous waters of Kislovodsk."

"Treat yourself to one less pullover," I retorted. "Otherwise you will come down with stomach ulcers, if you eat only canned food."

Finale. Moderato e grazioso. Synopsis: I noticed that the bombardment had ceased, when I felt the raindrops on my back. Yes, it was a mild autumn rain. The rays of the sun glittered on the moist grass, on the leaves, on the wet green cabin of a truck that had been blown over on its side by an explosion. And suddenly I heard the command: "Orchestra to me!" In the middle of the highway, next to a huge shell hole, stood Colonel Sherbakov, and behind him two soldiers with the flag. We crept shyly out from behind the bushes, glancing fearfully up at the sky to where the Junkers had just now shaved the tops off the trees. "Unpack the instruments," commanded the colonel, "and play a march!" In the air that seemed to be deaf from the incredible stillness, the first notes of the march, "The Farewell of a Slavic Girl," sounded—*tu-tu, tu-tu, tu-tu, tu-tu* . . . Vasya Axelratorov played the alto part on the tuba with professional aplomb. *Ta-taa, ta-ta-taa, ta-taa, ta-ta-taa!* my trumpet

pierced the heights. I am alive, I am alive, I thought to myself. For a while there it really looked like they had done
me in, once and for all. But no, I am on my feet, I am alive!
And it even seems that I am all in one piece, that they
didn't wound me, the bastards. So thought I and my trumpet sang—on its own, independent from me, as though it
had suddenly acquired a life of its own. Out of the dead,
maimed woods our boys crept forth, shaking and brushing
off the dirt, cursing wildly, and then lining up in formation. Ten kilometers further to the left our regiment was
surrounded by German tanks—but many of us would
never know that.

Through the show window of the workshop I see how
the clockmaker, with his black monocle–magnifying glass
stuck to his eye, undertakes to solve the mystery of time.
And when one day the curtain closes behind me (the
smooth curtain that closes horizontally in the crema-
torium) and I rise up directly to the archangel in that super-
quick, noiseless elevator (the latest thing: it comes from
Finland, and the very first day it was in use someone wrote
"Misha is a dope" on the wall), then this archangel will of
course ask (maybe it will be Mikhail Israelevich): "Tell me,
Kotyonotchkin, were you satisfied with your life?"

And in the sad Semitic eyes of the archangel I shall see
openly expressed disappointment.

"Ah, Kotyonotchkin," the archangel will sigh, "you
were a born trumpeter, we placed such high hopes in you!"

"Place your hopes in God, but keep your eyes peeled,"[2] I
shall answer. "After all, my salary didn't fall to me from
heaven, and he who pays calls the tune. To whom should I
have prayed, then?"

To Samorodov, to our dear Victor Nikolayevich!

I am a trumpeter. When the concert is over, I go out onto
the street. I am an insignificant person and it is only with
notes that I know my way around. But from all sides I am
pressed by the militia and society, by the apartment-house
management and the neighborhood court of honor, ministries and trade unions, executive committees and the city
council, the community chest and schools, the laundry,
dry-cleaning, the book of civil law, political indoctrina-

[2]A Russian proverb.

tion, the press and television, kindergarten and enemy propaganda, the aggressive NATO Alliance, Chinese dogmatists, economic reform and Morganism-Mendelism, Modernism, Abstractionism, Revisionism, Apoliticism, Amoralism, Diurnalism, Productivism (but no meat in the shops), Speculativism, Sexualism, Deficitism, Solialism, Alcoholism, and still many other -isms—there are so many —and here I am all alone! Who is going to help me get out of this mess, who will open my eyes, who will make out a certificate for me, send my child to a special school, make it possible for me to take the cure, make out an application to the apartment-house management? Let us assume that some drunk starts a free-for-all in a trolley bus and I am drawn into it, who will protect me from having charges brought against me, reserve a bed for me in the hospital, gain admittance to the distribution point for me, have a telephone installed for me, teach me the necessary wiles, console me, and act with a certain amount of tenderness toward me? Only Samorodov, dear Victor Nikolayevich. All my hopes are pinned on him.

I was not allowed to go abroad. And rightly so. What sense would it have made to send me out there? Oistrach and Rostropovich were there many times—and the result? The confounded West was not in the least shaken. And I myself am not all that stable a person. So Victor Nikolayevich saved me from losing my integrity.

I have a weakness for alcohol, and suppose some blonde had lured me up to her apartment after a couple of drinks in order to besmirch the honor of a Soviet man. After that sort of thing there is no way to save yourself from humiliation in the public meetings at home. No, Victor Nikolayevich kept watch: Praise and thanks be unto him!

When the time comes, Samorodov will see to it that I get a pension. And when I die, my family won't have to worry about anything, Victor Nikolayevich will get a niche for my urn, will organize a memorial service and see to it that I get a dignified obituary. And all this, just think of it, will be paid for by the State. All these convenient arrangements cannot be valued highly enough!

God forbid that Samorodov should be taken from us. There is no telling what would go on here if such were the case. The young cadres are arrogant. You can't expect *them* to meet you halfway, with understanding and compassion. They haven't had time to build themselves *dachas* yet. Victor Nikolayevich has all that behind him. And for all that he never even stole anything: Others steal as though it were the last day of creation. A great many inspectors have managed to get themselves the title "People's Artist" (even though they can't even read notes), but Samorodov is smart, he doesn't make an exhibition of himself, he has his rank, honestly come by: colonel. They say that he keeps his epaulets to this day in a safe.

If a new inspector were to take Samorodov's place, then he would only be interested in making a career; but the career of an inspector, as everybody knows, depends on his being able to ferret out, to expose, to see through the so-called secret modernists and sycophants and put them through the wringer. And then there would begin a nerve-wracking disquiet and intrigue again in the collective, and all our rehearsals would go to the devil, and certain people would be on the carpet all the time. Samorodov, on the other hand, has grown into his position, is satisfied with his job, and therefore is only interested in the orchestra's working as it should and won't make any unnecessary fuss.

And if one of our people were to be appointed inspector, it would be still worse. A violinist would give all the privileges to the strings, a horn player would only look after his own, a drummer would have only marches in the repertoire, and the conductor would raise regular hell with everybody. Samorodov, however, stands apart from all cliques and groups, for him we are all alike.

This is the reason why, whenever I see that familiar figure at the other end of the corridor, I always rush joyfully along and greet him with all my heart: "Good health to you, Victor Nikolayevich!"

Three Fragments
Chapters from a Book

BY ERNST NEIZVESTNY

Translated by Edward Van Der Rhoer

From *Kontinent* No. XXI, 1979

I. Red Men and Green Men

Once my friend—no small official of the Central Committee—came to my assistance by obtaining an airplane ticket in his ticket office, which was impossible to do in a normal ticket office in that day. He asked me to come at the close of work to the Staraya Ploshchad' (Old Square), to the Central Committee building, since he might be delayed.

That is also what happened. The work day concluded and people poured out of the doors. My friend was not among them, and since it was necessary to wait and, if possible, not to be bored, I began to observe the single brain of the country tumbling out of the cells of offices and disintegrating into separate persons.

Unexpectedly for me, however, I noticed that this great number of people was not perceived by me as an ordinary crowd which possessed a personalized diversity. This sated herd was uniform. Before me there passed test-tube clones completely devoid of individual features. The difference in weight and size had no significance.

ERNST IOSIFOVICH NEIZVESTNY *is an outstanding modern sculptor. He was born in 1926 in Sverdlovsk, graduated from the Surikov Art Institute, and emigrated in 1976 to the U.S.A. This is his first appearance as a writer of prose.*

Such an enormous quantity of nonindividual masks, cos-
tumes, and gestures literally stunned me. Nevertheless, I
began gradually to differentiate among them. I observed
that these people, released from work and dumped out by
elevators from the upper stories into the street, did differ,
not personally but as groups, like two varieties of the same
species. For my own convenience, I designated them as the
"red men" and the "green men."

As a rule, the "red men" represented the peasant type of
people (a type of rude peasant, not the agreeable and aristocratic *muzhik*). Good suits look ridiculous on them; pince-
nez, eyeglasses—everything as if for a masquerade, stolen,
belonging to someone else. They have been somehow
oddly and unnaturally fattened. They are not simply stout
people, which would be normal—no, these people have
obviously grown fat on a diet that is unnatural for them.
They seem as if they have betrayed their genotype. It is apparent that by heredity they were fated to work in the
fresh air and that their ancestors from one generation to
the next had been occupied with physical labor. Torn out
of their normal destiny, set down in offices, they become
just as ridiculous as house borzois. These people are
"red men" in the literal sense of the term. Their full-
bloodedness is unnatural and does not give an impression
of health. On their cheeks there appears an exaggerated
crimson blush. They do not know what to do with their
queer hands, which have grown unaccustomed to work,
swollen, dead, reminiscent of fins. Their flesh, nourished
by a diet with too many calories and not benefited by useful activity, has expanded: Everything about them is large
—cheeks, eyebrows, ears, stomachs, thighs, buttocks. They
get into cars as if their male genitalia interfere with them,
but at the same time they do not lose their grotesque dignity. Everything points to the fact that *they* are the bosses.

Then there are the "green men." At first it is difficult to
distinguish them in this homogeneous crowd. Looking
closely, however, you notice that some of the clones possess greater imagination in gestures and manners, and just
from this it is evident that they are something like trans-
planted intellectuals who will never succeed in achieving
the innate perfection of the "red men." No matter how
much you try to conceal the fact, obviously you come from

a university, from journalists, philosophers, or from some sort of historians there—in general, a place from which a real person cannot come under any circumstances. And even if such people are sufficiently red, the eyes that are red *from work* shatter the harmony, thereby sharply distinguishing them from the eyes of the "red men" which, undimmed by any dream, remain limpid. Even without looking at any secret rosters, it is clear that the "green men" belong to the advisory staff. They, the "green men," have an obviously ravaged look (which does not mean, of course, that the "red men" drink less).

In comparison with the stony mien of the "red men," they, the "green men," are lively and high-strung. Against the cinnamon color of the "red men," they are rather pale, insufficiently red, although they eat the same food, but that food does not benefit them.

The "red man" is so triumphantly fair and calm because he has been created in order to adopt an irreproachable decision. He belongs to that breed of Soviet untouchables who can do anything—let the harvest rot, buy up output which is of no use to anybody, suffer losses anywhere and everywhere—but they are always unruffled because they do not make mistakes. According to social laws, they simply cannot be mistaken. This irresponsibility of a whole social stratum, which is unprecedented in history, constitutes its greatest achievement, and it is perfectly clear that they would sooner derail the whole world than waive even a tiny share of their astonishing and delightful irresponsibility.

With impunity, they can spit on and defile the scientific trends and discoveries that are most important to the country as well as the products of literature and art that represent the pride of the nation.

And as soon as life has shown their wrongness and demonstrated the rightness of the people and ideas persecuted by them, they—the very same ones, not others—will attend and deliver speeches at anniversaries and funerals of the martyrs of culture and art.

They appropriate for themselves the merits of those who have been tortured, and give each other awards for the accomplishments of people whom they murdered.

They decorate one another with rattling medals and other regalia.

They congratulate each other with prizes.

They admire one another.

They are tongue-tied—but they talk without stopping. They alone talk, the others remain silent. They control radio and television, newspapers, movies.

All the others have only one occupation: to stick to them and thank them for at least not taking away the air up to now.

They demand that all people without exception admire them.

They are content—and justified in their contentment: When they say, "Life has become better, life has become more joyful, comrades"—they do not lie. Where, when, in which epoch could people possessing such qualities receive so much? Without paying in the process, for stupidity and boorishness, negligence and wastefulness—and simply for the general and manifest ugliness of their personality?

History is not an innocent maiden, it has known many villains and sadists, but it has never known, I think, so many totally untalented conquerors.

Since the "red men" by nature are without sin, in principle no allusion to their competence becomes necessary. Besides, if they must be elected, there can be only one of the two simplest alternatives: YES and NO. The YES and NO are worked out by the advisory staff, and the YES and NO are equally scientifically established. Moreover, by the laws of group irresponsibility, by laws of the apparatus of which they are a part, the "red men" do not function individually, and as soon as some definite quantity of "red men" react with YES or NO, the decision has been made.

The unity and equal mediocrity of the "red men" guarantee their stability, whatever happens to the country due to their group will or group lethargy. Any movement of such an enormous body, of such an enormous mass, as the U.S.S.R., engenders an event, called or appearing to be historic, which is endowed with a meaning that the numerous culprits responsible for this event did not even dream of.

On the strength of the world's reaction to any half-drowsy, semiconscious move of theirs, the "red men" experience a real feeling of the significance and correctness of their decisions. Until he is fired, a "red man" is always a winner. Time passes, events unfold, and merely sitting in his office chair is already a victory for the "red man." Victors are not placed on trial.

Imagine that General A. won a battle on the basis of his plan. That more or less automatically establishes that General B.'s plan was poor and faulty. But why? Nobody tried out General B.'s plan—perhaps it was expedient, perhaps it was optimal! History cannot be repeated, however, and General A. will remain a victor forever while General B. is a failure.

Thus the "red men" never make mistakes, only the "green men" make mistakes. The "green men" are those who must convert the mumbling of the "red men" into articulate speech. Those who must guess their wishes but formulate them in such a way that the collective brain will recognize the formulations as their own, as if the "red men" themselves had created them. Monstrous work, thankless, sleepless—and, above all, according to the antlike laws of the apparatus, it ceases to be creative.

One "green man," casting his own phrase into a heap of phrases of other "green men," loses it; afterward all of them together thumb over the material, and in this common porridge no one knows any longer where his thoughts and phrases begin and end. I do not know whether their work makes any real sense, but when I listen to the addresses of the chief "red men," it is perfectly obvious to me that the words they cannot pronounce were inserted by the "green men," but the general sense, of course, reflects the interests of the "red men."

The "green men" suffer from a great number of organizational complexes. It always seems to them that they are better than the "red men" and know what must be done for the latter's success and prosperity, although this is naturally incorrect, since the "red men" remain the greatest masters when it comes to a knowledge of their own profit!

Even when they sometimes acquire significant influence, the "green men" still remain the pariahs of the Party, although this may be imperceptible to the outside observer. The "red men"—even when they are provincial, even when they have a lower official rank—behave superciliously toward the "green men" because the mode of their reddish life and their careers are based on normal laws: from the primary Party cell to the transcendental party heights. They, the "red men," form an inner party. They are predestined from heaven to rule all people, animals, forests, rivers, mountains, and the past and future of the country. And, of course, the external party. If "green men" ever mature to the level of the "red men," it can only be by means of gigantic nervous expenditure, by means of renunciation of many of their personal attachments and intellectual claims.

The "red men" are tranquil. In contrast to the "green men," they are incapable of making an analysis of social conditions, of which they constitute an element. They do not have to have doubts and there is no need to renounce anything, they simply live and make careers by right of being "red men." To be sure, one cannot think that "red men" are always and necessarily more stupid than "green men." Reflection linked to great erudition is still not intelligence. Nevertheless, before he can perform a base deed, a "green man" must find a theoretical justification for it. Historical determinism, dialectics, and worn-out dogmas no longer give him the possibility of calculating the effectiveness of the sacrifices offered on the altar of progress—he searches for new dogmas but alas! strikes on old ones: the state, nation, empire, etc., etc. He is sorrowful because a pessimist is nothing more than a well-informed optimist. Information engenders a cornucopia of ideas which, even if they rapidly pass by, nevertheless leave marks on the soul. A liberal pose, dinner-table gallantry, and cynicism are no salvation. Certainly in the time free from work one can drink, and this does happen.

Simple everyday cynicism is not even necessary for the composure and self-assurance of a "red man." He acts without bothering with theories—only in accordance with what is best for him. He always avoids a discomforting situation. The amoeba flees from a drop of sulphuric acid without knowing anything about it. An amoeba knows nothing about chemistry. The "red men" proceed from the simplest premises. All their philosophy can be reduced to the proverb, "The fish seeks in the depths but man seeks where it is best." They make careers because they know: The higher you go, the better you live, the less you work, and the less your responsibility.

It is difficult for the "green man," especially when he has any pretensions to some sort of remaining illusions or his own personality. They find themselves inside the apparatus like a complex being inside a primitive but powerful and enormous one-celled creature which temporarily tolerates for its own biological requirements some qualities of the "green men." Nevertheless, sooner or later this gigantic amoeba absorbs them into its own tissue or simply ejects them. Similarly, society, intent on converting itself into a homogeneous, undifferentiated mass, ejects everything that is distinct from the daily, compulsory grayness prescribed by law—into prison, emigration, or a culture of the catacombs. The "green men" and nimble cynic-intellectuals are only a temporary deviation necessitated by tactics. In the evolving situation it is clear that what is most simple characterizes this system.

Most improbable for normal human consciousness is the elementariness of a great number of personal desires constituting a social phenomenon which sets this machine in motion. The scale of aftereffects engenders an illusion of complexity and twists scientific and pseudoscientific theories as well as terms, analyses, and arguments, to impose on the world such a refined picture that one simply marvels. Why does an army of intellectuals try without fail to portray as a giant a rapist who contrives to violate the world in the most crude and vulgar way? Evidently one does not at all wish to confess that we are often raped by ordinary, dull-witted pygmies. The bottom of the national body conquers the top—not, however, in the positive sense of a carnival but in the most literal sense. The hind part has spread out and, remaining the hind part, occupied the place of everything else, and so the pithecanthropus conquers man, the rat the pithecanthropus, and the louse the rat. . . .

Thus I stood and fantasized at the doors of the world's most enormous office building, and I grew sorry for the "green men" who were wasting their often outstanding intellect and talent in this awful game of beads, and I could visualize them at the point of grunting and going about on all fours; I almost physically felt how this gray, gray building sucked them dry day by day, imperceptibly, taking away mind, initiative, talent, and, above all, human dignity.

A man with a very red, full-blooded face detached himself from the faceless crowd, and at first I failed to recognize my friend—he was just like all of them. But at a distance I already knew: This was a . . . "green man."

Moscow, 1974

II. The Merry Little Pigs

The anthropomorphic nature of contemporary Soviet representatives of government, ideology, and culture very often deludes Western people—and not only Westerners. These functionaries often occupy rather high official positions, if they are not at the very top of the ladder. Well-disposed Westerners who meet such people are greatly encouraged by the knowledge of languages and literature as well as pleasant, informal freedom of thought of their by no means old interlocutors (as a rule, these are middle-aged people). Many Western observers see in this a sign of the changes allegedly taking place in the ruling apparatus.

Without being a captive to such an illusion but lacking any prejudice, I became friendly with some of the people who belonged to this category. It became clear to me very quickly that to link any hope of a change in the structure of the ruling apparatus to the presence there of such personalities, however outstanding, is groundless. These personalities are more likely to change in the direction required by the apparatus than the reverse. Moreover, it would be strange to think that the operation of a machine could be changed by being inside it and performing a separate function similar to that of a tiny, automatically replaceable component of a cybernetic machine.

Indeed, the system represents a machine, a rebuilt machine. The points occupied by persons are pits or holes within the machine so that the point operates and not the person located there. A person can create a microcoloring within this chamber, but the system itself runs according to the laws of machinery, and anyone who seeks personally to affect it flies out of the machine or is destroyed by it.

Now, I believe, the machine has been more rebuilt than in the times of Stalin and Khrushchev. That is why it is so colorless and stable and surprisingly tedious. The operation of this machine may beggar the imagination, but, if analyzed, it turns out to be elementary. For clarity, the following example may be given. Imagine a queue. In this queue there stand a general and a poet, a child and a locksmith, an artist and a beauty, a professor and a housemaid. But, you see, personal qualities, biographies, destinies, and characters do not make a queue. A queue is depersonalized; what makes it occurs in the intervals between people—the space and air between those standing in front and behind composes the social contract which makes the queue take shape.

Roughly the same situation has arisen in today's Soviet society. No one personally decides anything, everything "shakes down." A question rises to the top, goes off to one side, and moves downward—i.e., the decision passes through all the so-called interested instances, is ventilated, settled, clarified, again ventilated—and by certain combinative laws a procedure is established and a decision adopted, having come into being in the interim.

But it remains an oligarchy of functionaries—not a movement toward democracy, as many would like it to be. After all, Stalinism is not simply a whim or mistake of Stalin. It is a historically shaped situation in which the control function is such that cardinal changes cannot result from within the apparatus. To be sure, one functionary cannot now seize another and throw him into a torture chamber, but all of them together can do this with anybody; and if they do not put him in jail, they can persecute and slander him and force him to emigrate or die. Terrorism continues—the personal terrorism of Stalin has merely been replaced by the terrorism of the machine, of which he is considered the creator. Of course, the work of Sovietologists, who seek to figure out the course of events based on an evaluation of the leaders' personal qualities, is interesting but hardly relevant without an understanding that this is not the main thing. The main riddle lies in the principles of this fantastic machine, where, in essence, there are no personalities and no brain center in the sense that one customarily thinks of it. In this way unity and security are coordinated, the dream of the modern apparatus of power. Therefore this system is so stable, so unchangeable.

An amoeba whose vital centers are everywhere and no-where.

Since people with civilized manners are parts of the machine of terror, evidently it is necessary to view *their function* within the control apparatus. This inevitably leads us to the conclusion that so long as they still have not been dismissed from work and appear in the capacity of intelligent, elegant, and supposedly free-thinking interlocutors, it only means that they are *essential* to the machine in *this capacity* today; but it does not and cannot attest to any basic changes. The practical effect of their actions does not diverge from the goals of their coarse teachers, who go around in the jackets of the first Stalin five-year plans and not only are unable to speak "foreign" languages but even their native Russian language.

These clumsy old men with the masks of good-natured average citizens, these cannibals afraid of their own wives, have not until now learned the words "communism" and "socialism" (apparently they survived the Stalin purges by virtue of this), but their "communisms" and "socialisms" proved to be enough to hold the world by the throat. Their elegant disciples, translating "socialism" and "communism" into all the languages of the world, trilling all the beauties of a hermetic culture, all the latest geopolitical terms, thus trying to look like liberals, serve (and it could not be otherwise) "communism" and "socialism" in the elementary police version of their teachers and mentors. But withal, they sincerely wish to look like liberals. They conduct cultured, open-minded conversations with enjoyment, they wish to be discriminating connoisseurs of art—they particularly love gifts from officially condemned artists, they collect condemned literature and music. (I myself listened with amazement to songs of the prohibited Galich in the apartment of one of Brezhnev's assistants. But all of this is done, of course, in the complete absence of any free thinking in their practical affairs.)

Here the genius of hypocrisy widely and freely spread its wings. As with any widespread phenomenon, there are many reasons for it. For the moment we should note a psychological reason, by no means the most idle one. All of this crowd are prisoners of a dual internal situation. On the one hand they have received the rights and privileges of the Russian nobility and merchant class (in the peculiar Party version, of course). They possess an incredibly high standard of living (by modern, and now, I think, by world scales): rations, *dachas*, services, comparatively great freedom of movement (in any case, in terms of cultural exchange with foreign countries they represent only themselves), information. In comparison with the "legal" privileges of the nobility and the merchant class, their privileges are literally illegal and therefore conspiratorial, hidden from the people. Not one of them has a constitutional justification. This creates, if only at first, some psychological awkwardness in relation to the intellectual circles from which these people frequently come. The teaching in school and in the institute was built, you see, on a respect for the traditions of the Decembrists, Chaadaev, Radishchev, and Herzen, on the traditions of Russian love of freedom. While the Moloch of revolution spilled blood, while the struggle with opponents and enemies of the people was in progress, in the chaos of deaths and wars it could appear that everything, including property inequality (naturally temporary), was justified by the dialectics of history.

Now everyone sees that *the God of revolutionary liberties in Russia is dead*. The Soviet leadership has become a closed supersect cut off once and for all from the tasks which gave birth to it, and having only one aim: the satisfaction of its own constantly growing demands and the perpetual prolongation of its existence. To sufficiently literate people it is clear that the very impenetrability, ossification, and impossibility of creative work within the framework of this sect, the impossibility of changes in it from within—for its social function is such that it cannot change without destroying itself—all this testifies to the reactionary character of this social process's development.

Nevertheless, the *nouveaux riches* of the party elite, children of the Twentieth Congress,[1] who, on the whole, have just initiated their careers, are accustomed to a liberal, though limited, pose so attractive to tender hearts. This

[1] It was at the Twentieth Party Congress, in February 1956, that Khrushchev made his famous secret speech denouncing the crimes of Stalin.—ED.

pose evoked a liberal grimace in poetry, literature, and films and placed an indelible seal of duplicity on a whole generation of so-called cultural workers.

The creative intelligentsia particularly cultivated this duplicity. After Stalin's death something came to light and was realized. The conquerors were worse than the conquered, the murder victims and the damned became models of excellence, and in the social consciousness the murderers were transformed from officially designated geniuses into what they had been from the very beginning: into dung. Since suffering, as it turned out, was the destiny of geniuses, while worldly success was the destiny of dung, it became fashionable to suffer. In Russia, in Pushkin's words, people are only able to love the dead. For that reason, the most involved Soviet intellectuals, sitting with black caviar and real Russian vodka (available only to foreigners, the government, and *them*) in beautiful apartments and *dachas*, weep crocodile tears—as if *they* are the ones whom others insult and oppress rather than being insulters and oppressors themselves. They wish to be martyrs, not being such. They desire the glory of the Decembrists who ended on the gallows, and simultaneously wish to spend their lives comfortably and pleasantly. If a foreign guest overflowing with a benevolent sort of blissful ignorance happens to find himself in their midst, it may seem to him that he is present at a conspiratorial meeting of real fighters and dissidents. But if you look into the souls of the respective personages, their secret dream is plainly revealed: to be the head of the KGB but have the international glory and prestige of Sakharov and Solzhenitsyn.

Naturally, they can no longer attain great reality, but, in terms of domestic theater lavishly sported by the state, they replace real problems with imaginary ones and, with the aid of foreign dupes, create an appearance of social life, an appearance of relative freedom of speech—and, by a fictitious formulation of problems, hold up a colorful veil before the ugliness of a system that strives toward the annihilation of any creative individuality.

Nevertheless, in their time, in the times of the Khrushchev thaw, the struggle seemed socially meaningful to the fighters of the "right" and the "left." And then some! How the gray liberal banners fluttered, how the cast-iron foreheads of the old but still tough pterodactyls resisted them! There are no words to describe the turbulent feelings and, for example, the scope of the battle of the freaks from the Union of Artists with the monsters from the Academy of Arts! How their fiery hearts throbbed (and the hearts of freaks and monsters are located, as we know from ancient literature, by the posterior openings)! You cannot begin to imagine the atmosphere of those battles!

Yes, history made an indecent noise, as Pantagruel did in former times, and begot freaks and monsters. Time now plays the role of Panurge and contracts marriage between them, and as a result so many insects have come into the world. That historical battle was waged for the holy of holies—for the key to the safe where the money lay. And it became clear *who* was more important for the state treasury, the grays who came from black or the grays from white. Who was worthier to be the executioner of the spirit abiding in art. The dispute also assumed theoretical proportions. "What is socialist realism"—"mucus with sugar" or "mucus with salt"? The scientific question was resolved as to how a murderer should look in our days—frightening or gentle. For some time the artistic, creative milieu looked like a mixed ensemble of trained beasts of prey: pterodactyls, hyenas, and crab-lice. In the end the liberal "merry pigs" conquered them all—temporarily. Why temporarily? Because by natural social laws they themselves very quickly turned into pterodactyls. They proved that torturers can be made into Cézannes, Hemingways, and Kafkas without detriment to ideology. They proved that one can lick the backsides of the powers that be though better qualified and receiving less pay; they proved that they have a better nose for an enemy and greater speed in pursuit of the enemy. As one of them used to say: "I don't like this work, we have to look closely at it, most probably there is something anti-Soviet in it." Bitter cynicism. Pitiful cynicism.

I think that a circle of such people has already become a spontaneously developed institution, taken over as a weapon by the state. Quite like hard-currency stores, hard-currency whores; like comfortable leprosariums for the reception and seduction of foreigners, where big-bosomed women interpreters are permitted to imitate not only freedom of opinion but of customs before the happily surprised guests; where national minorities speak in all the languages of the country about liberty, and dance, and sing for foreign currency—which is so necessary to the state—to do what they have long since ceased to do in their native villages; where there is even a Jewish magazine.

In the atmosphere of falsehood and camouflage there has appeared a certain cynical fraternity into which a simple-minded strangler, a Stalinist pterodactyl in chrome boots, no longer fits: He is inconvenient in the unfolding situation. A place can be found for him in the provinces, but under no circumstances in the façade which confronts the European and world arena.

People of this fraternity are ubiquitous—from the politician to the declaimer of stage verse. They are "scientists," "journalists," "doctors," "film workers," and "artists," indispensable participants in international congresses, embassy guests, irreplaceable "lions" of fashionable gatherings and receptions at which foreigners are present. They recognize one another by some sort of scent, by the cynicism—"we are of the same blood, you and I"; and the more two-faced you are, the more quickly you change your mask, the more you are one of them, the more you are valued in this cordial company.

Superficially these people make careers in defiance of old Soviet laws. Precisely owing to their duplicity. No one, however, should be deceived; they are necessary now. Such is the real international situation, it amounts to a commitment.

In a certain social situation, some of them, perhaps, would adopt a real position as free-thinking liberals—when society encouraged them to do so and if it proved to be advantageous to them personally. Nevertheless, time is working against them. The cynical fraternity of double-thinkers, like a mold that came forth in a climate of thaw and détente, is a sort of experiment, no more than the pubescence of the Soviet functionary. It is youthful masturbation. Such self-indulgence is tolerated only up to a certain level. If, however, the real career begins—not in secondary but in leading roles—then duplicity is no longer possible. Even have a lobotomy, but be like your elders: Laugh sincerely when everyone laughs; drink and sing what everyone drinks and sings; eat what all the others eat; and grunt when everyone grunts. Then the youthful features harden, the fine lips of a laughing mouth form a rigid and haughty slit, and a genuinely fixed social expression, not a mobile changing mask, adorns your hardened, set physiognomy. You abandon the "advisory staff" and enter the inner sanctum. You have turned from a "green man" into a "red man."

III. The Courtyard

Prospekt Mira 41. An ordinary day. Morning.

Ninka stole a valuable brooch from her mother and swapped it for a half-liter.

Her brother Nikolai drove home in a huge motor truck. The line for which he worked as a driver allowed him to park the truck in the courtyard due to his illness: he was a drunk.

Welders from the factory next door tried to sell me heavy welding equipment taken from their own state enterprise. Unable to sell it, they abandoned it on the spot, in my courtyard, so as not to have to go very far, and began to beg for five rubles. Finally convinced that I did not have the money, they asked for the bottles that stood in the window, in the hope of returning them, getting the deposit, and curing their hangovers with more alcohol.

Bottles, tubes, vials, shots, dead soldiers, jars, bowls . . . the Moscow courtyard begins its life with thoughts about the bottle. Citizens and comrades search for money to get some of the hair of the dog that bit them. One cannot do without the accustomed morning dose of alcohol—it is impossible to begin work with shaky hands. The courtyard is dying of thirst—it is tormented with the hangover syndrome. This syndrome has given birth to numerous stories —amusing and tragic. Strictly speaking, the whole history of the courtyard and the whole biography of its inhabitants lie in the events connected with getting drunk or the tormenting desire to cure a hangover with more alcohol. All conversations revolved around bottles. Time became flat and stopped in an alcoholic delirium: There was no "yesterday" and no "tomorrow," there was only—"First three of us shared a bottle; true, I'd already had about two hundred grams to start with—well, not two hundred, almost three hundred; then we had another bottle, and after eight hundred each we became friends. So Vas'ka says, let's have some rotgut, but for me it could be piss, just if it goes around. . . ."

". . . Your pants are full from laughing, I tell him, and he says to me, the milk still hasn't dried on your mouth. . . ."

". . . Ninka, though, is scum—you don't see her at all, she just lies there day and night. . . ."

". . . God be with her. . . ."

". . . Ah, we're living again. . . ."

". . . My uncle has the highest principles. . . ."

". . . Semyen, what else can you think of? . . ."

". . . But we've—got to go—in a stall! . . ."

". . . flapping our wings like eagles. . . ."

". . . not being able to stand on our pins? . . ."

". . . No, brother, no, that's not cultured: Go away and pee culturally, have some sense, but as to people: culture is crap. . . ."

". . . they say that the cook was fired from his job. For what, boys? He mixed the hot cereal with his cock.—Ha, ha, ha!—that's something to laugh about—fill your pants. . . ."

". . . Here's Sen'ka with the alcohol, his is the best of all, and I'm not against the denatured stuff, only you have to know how to handle it, brothers, thus—let it stand so the mud settles to the bottom—crust of bread in the glass—drink it up, like nectar, eat the crust—tastes so pure in the mouth. . . ."

". . . took a bottle, if they give it to you, take it; if they fight, run away. . . ."

". . . I have a mother-in-law, boys, a mother-in-law—never pass the mother-in-law's house without something, I stick my cock in the window or show her my ass. . . ."

". . . but I tell you, you're wrong. . . ."

". . . it's always like that with us. . . ."

". . . still a long way, brothers, to Communism. . . ."

". . . you respect me—I respect you. . . ."

". . . they us, I him, we you—you us. . . ."

". . . We had a little fight, first I hit him, then he hit me. . . ."

". . . What's a wedding without a glass, a Jew without a car, a binge without Ivan, what's·Ivan without a cunt. . . ."

". . . Ah, your Tartar mug!—what? Armenian? As for me, you could be a Chinaman, just so you have a bottle. . . ."

". . . Ah, flying like doves, laughing—well, it's enough, boys, time to go to work. . . ."

With my peculiar interests, sculpture, Dante, the Bible, and music, and poetry, I was submerged in a softened—not good and not evil—half-idiotic society of the street where my studio was situated. Not on the outskirts and not in a slum, only eight minutes from the Kremlin.

I tried to create impenetrability, isolation, my sort of bathysphere, but that was possible only within myself. I had need of many things—bronze, nails, boards, plaster, clay, stone, etc., etc. I, a sculptor cut off from official orders, had no opportunity for many years to receive such materials from the state, the only repository of such blessings. For that reason I was a potential buyer in the unofficial market —and I became a center of attraction and a victim of hangover intrigues, and for that reason the whole avid mass of the population laid at my feet anything that they could— for the most part, articles and mechanisms that were useless to me.

What the population did not offer to barter for a bottle! Yet the same population consisted in no way of criminals, but of workers and employees who could not satisfy their thirst on their scanty pay and hence dragged everything possible from their plants and offices. I was offered women's brassieres and panties in short supply; Czech audio tapes; chopped meat for *pirozhki*; sophisticated electronic gear; a tame rabbit; Japanese contraceptives with whiskers; boat motors; gold foil stolen by restorers of Kremlin churches; low shoes of excellent leather without soles; belts without buckles and buckles without belts; scarce instant coffee; electronic tubes for television sets; icons; typeface; precious type metal; cellophane tape; toilet paper; tripods for movie cameras; badges intended only for foreigners; all kinds of junk stolen from the house: curtains, stools, stands, ladies' stockings, shawls, cameras, gold coins, ginseng root, morphine from a drugstore, syringes, bandages, iodine—and all of this for a bottle. . . .

Sometimes there would be a bottle of expensive and evidently stolen cognac in exchange for a larger quantity of vodka. Incidentally, it is interesting that the unlucky merchants could spend hours trying to talk me into buying an article that was of no use to me, but when I proposed that one of them should help me with some work and at the same time earn more than it was possible to make in such dealings, this was taken as an insult. With no regard for his own or my time, the merchant, who was dying of thirst, instead of earning in twenty minutes the sum needed for a bottle, would spend an hour trying to convince me that I desperately, vitally needed, say, can-openers—no less than sixty of them.

The haggling came down to the following:

I: Beat it, I don't need that.

HE: No, Ernst, you don't understand, the openers are top quality, and all sixty for the price of a bottle. . . .

I: Beat it, you're bothering me.

HE: No, you'll see, what can-openers, absolutely new!

At times it came to a scuffle, very often the merchants had to be thrown out through the door, but, alas! they would climb in the window. The inhabitants of the courtyard realized that there were moments when I could offer no resistance and turn them down. For example, one catches sight of a foreign automobile—that means there is an important guest, so you force your way through the door with a loud crash, "Ernst, give me enough for a bottle!" So I buy the stuff and give him the money—what else is there to do? The foreigner would not understand, you see, if I started to punch someone before his eyes! How much ingenuity, fearlessness, wit, and absurdity had been engendered by the desire to get a bottle immediately—*immediately*, this second; as the saying goes, you must have it here and now!

While on a spree, Zhen'ka pinned a girl he knew in a telephone booth and took the unfortunate's watch—obviously not for the purpose of keeping track of the swift passage of time, but to swap it for a bottle. Regrettably, he did not quite succeed in completing the barter and getting drunk, for a policeman who ran up in response to the screams of the distressed girl nabbed him in ten steps. Zhen'ka, still suffering from a hangover, got off, as they say, with a light scare; the collective interceded for him because he sometimes appeared on the honor roll as a shock worker of Communist labor. He received only three years, but in the courtyard everybody was certain that he would get an early release, and anyway Zhen'ka would not perish in a camp—he was a good locksmith, so everything would be all right with the bottle: There the bosses desperately needed good workers because they depended on such people for their own bottles.

Then a pensioner brings a package of carbon paper and paper clips—enough to last a good office for a year—and all of it for a bottle. But if you bargain—you will get it for a ruble. I did not own a typewriter and had nothing to fasten, but I felt sorry for the old man, and so I offered him a deal: If he took his wares and went away at once, I would give him three rubles. He agreed, but he wanted a drink right away, so he asked for a favor: Let the stuff stay with me, and he would pick it up later. After leaving behind an enormous package, which blocked my foyer completely, he did not concern himself with it subsequently and failed to take it away, and as a result I had to throw it in his hole. Poor fellow, he had a wife who worked in an office, but there was nothing to steal in such a place other than office supplies, therefore every day she carried home carbon paper and paper clips to be bought from her husband, but, alas, they were unmarketable goods!

And really, everyone said that "Sergeyich had bad luck with his wife," other people had goods that were much more marketable! For example, one businessman prospered greatly for a while, bringing the most delicious jam from a state enterprise. His business, however, was somewhat ruined after he went on a binge and good-naturedly confided the secret of his mode of transport: He had sewn himself cellophane underpants with ties below, so that the jam, poured inside the underpants around his legs and intimate parts, where it was hidden from the gaze of the building guards, would not flow out. Many people, including myself, stopped buying his product out of excessive fastidiousness, while many others did not, eating it as is or boiling it in order to kill microbes that might get into the jam from the entrepreneur's various intimate places.

Outside the studio window there was a racket. It came

from the sons of my assistant, a nice, nondrinking engineer, again declaring war on their aged, sick mama. The two morons, ranging in age from thirty-five to thirty-eight years, brought her into the courtyard, in the snow, on a mattress and kept her there, bare except for a nightgown, demanding of the old lady that she give them a bottle of port wine that she had hidden from them somewhere. The neighbors did not interfere, fearing the big oafs. I did not interfere either, because I realized that it was useless. On one occasion I had called the police, but when they arrived, Mama denied having been beaten up by her sons—she was afraid they would be put in jail. Nevertheless, it appeared to me and my assistant that the old lady had no reason to be afraid: There was a certain mutual understanding and even collusion between this pair and a police that also eagerly wanted a bottle.

But look, look!—today the persistent and stubborn old lady conquered her strong sons with only the strength of her spirit: She did not surrender in spite of the temperature and the torture inflicted on her by her sons; and the spectators hanging out the windows saw the weary oafs, oppressed by failure and sick of working to no purpose, abandon Mama in the middle of the courtyard and go off, bent over, to seek their luck elsewhere.

The courtyard followed them with a gaze in which there were mixed feelings: One pitied them, knowing full well what a problem they were having with their hangover, but at the same time felt sorry for the battered mother. True, some—mostly men—said: "Why was the old lady so stubborn? They'll still get it some other place. If she had given it to them, that would have been the end of it. Why does she grudge them a bottle?"

Oh bottle, bottle—symbol of life, around which everything revolves—oh bottle, the measure of everything: This costs so-and-so many bottles, that costs so-and-so much. . . . How the courtyard would have envied some Arab sheik if it knew how many bottles he could buy for the oil he sells! Unfortunately, oil in its pure form, as is known, is not drinkable.

A gang of workers, who broke into a neighboring house, discovered in the cellar a huge bottle of something—but of what? A delegation came to me, as a local intellectual and,

besides, a drinker, to do them a favor and determine
whether or not one should drink it. Although, however, I
had a higher education and although I sometimes took a
drink, I still could not tell them, so I advised them to go to a
pharmacy. But a far more simple and direct method was
found: They went to a bar and located a volunteer, who
possessed the daring of a kamikaze; they told him the
whole story openly and honestly and proposed that he
taste it, promising that, if he did not die first, he could
share in the binge until the end on an equal basis with his
companions. No sooner said than done. Right in front of
my studio windows there gathered this avid gang led by
the bold taster, who drank down at a gulp a glass of the suspicious liquid smelling (pleasantly enough) of alcohol. His
impatient drinking companions ascertained with joy that
instantaneous death did not ensue, and the drink, whatever it was called, "cuddled up" or "lay on crystal." Simply
and merrily.

What they drank in that courtyard! Denatured alcohol
under the name "Blue Light," and varnish, into which salt
was strewn so that the stickiest part went to the bottom, as
well as triple eau de cologne, toothpaste diluted in water,
valerian, and a mouthwash of a repulsive violet color—
never mind, it was O.K. Well, not always.

On the very bins in front of my window two men died,
trying to ease their hangovers with something that was not
very beneficial to the health, and the whole courtyard
wondered why Pet'ka died at once, while the cook, Pet'ka's
friend, who did not come from our courtyard but a neighboring one, suffered agony for several hours. People came
to the conclusion that the cook always ate anyway and
therefore there was something in his stomach that prevented him from being burned right away, but the poor
devil Pet'ka generally did not eat much, and when he
drank did not eat at all, and for that reason the fluid "went
right through his stomach."

The same thing happened to old man Zubanin, father of
my caster, Sergei Zubanin. There was something on hand
to drink, it is true, but the old man in his tipsy state confused one bottle with another; moreover, he drank right
out of the neck, and it was such a powerful preparation
that, when it reached his gullet, before he knew where he
was, it flowed out from below and spilled on the floor.

Much—too much—could be said apropos of this. Zuban-in's brother also died, not because he drank anything bad but simply because, getting drunk, he grew angry and boasted that he could lift more than ten men (he was a freight handler). They loaded it on him and—well, he was crushed.

Ah, much could be said on this subject! And all of it happened at Prospekt Mira 41, Building 4.

My fellow countrymen know that not a single word of mine is untrue and that they have had similar experiences, or if they have not had them, acquaintances have. If a mistrustful foreigner does not believe it, let him ask his correspondents to go to that address and ask if all this happened or not, and how Vladimir Petrov's sons are doing, what took place with Ninka and her brother as well as the chauffeur Kol'koi, and what happened to the group of my friends the welders headed by the foreman Papanei, taking seven hundred grams of port wine per head as if it were a compulsory school breakfast—they will be told of other things as well. Perhaps they will hear about the two old women—an astonishing Russian tale:

Once upon a time there were two sisters. Both were not beautiful young girls but pensioners. One was paralyzed, while the other remained rather spry. And this other—the rather spry one—took care of the household, went to collect the pensions, and shopped, but the first sister, because of her paralysis, simply lay there and could not move. They had no social life, nobody came to see them—there was no sense in it anyway, they would not have served anything for a hangover.

They lived without being too unhappy in their five meters and had already forgotten about the time they made an application to be placed on the list for an apartment. Luck came their way unexpectedly, giving them the apartment for which they had waited thirty years. But the old women balked; for some reason, they did not wish to leave. The active one would not admit an inspector to their home, using as a pretext the fact this could disturb her paralyzed sister. The house became empty, windows were being knocked out in neighboring apartments, and the gas and electricity began to be disconnected, but the old women still would not move out. The bellicose ambulatory woman simply said: "I'll scratch the face of anyone who comes onto our territory—whether it's the janitor or a policeman."

In the end, however, the time came to tear down the house, and then, despite the old woman's screams, a policeman and the janitor burst in anyway, together with one very important citizen from the district soviet. The smell in the room was very bad, obviously the room had not been aired out for thirty years—approximately as long as they had been waiting for an apartment. They had not aired the room, probably thinking: We'll get a new place and be able to breathe.

But, as it turned out, that was not the problem. It turned out that for many years past there lay on the bed a withered mummy. It turned out that, afraid to lose the pension for two after her sister's death, the ambulatory woman mummified her and slept beside her for a good many years. An astonishing scientific feat of this old woman: Up to now scientists are still trying to guess the secret of mummification; people say that Lenin is not a mummy but a dummy, yet in her case the sister did not decompose! And the old woman's self-control was also astonishing—to live with a corpse and sleep with a corpse for so many years! . . .

Even I, accustomed and hardened to such things, was somewhat shaken by this story. Be envious, Hitchcock!

Nevertheless, the inhabitants of the courtyard took a simple view of the affair: You can't live on one pension, you'd die; so what's better, to live with a corpse or become one yourself? That's the way. . . . Necessity dances, necessity jumps, necessity sings songs. . . .

New York, 1977

The Political Advantages of Destitution

BY IGOR YEFIMOV-MOSKOVIT

Translated by Edward Van Der Rhoer

From Kontinent No. XX, 1979

1. "Richer Every Year"

Soviet propaganda has changed many slogans in sixty years. But the slogan "Raise the material well-being of laboring people" remained practically unchanged and was not once replaced by Stalin, Khrushchev, or Brezhnev. Before each holiday, after every Party congress or plenum, there is only one thing to be heard:

Raise!

Still higher!

To an unprecedented height!

The Party solemnly pledges that the present generation of Soviet people will live under Communism!

IGOR YEFIMOV-MOSKOVIT *was born in 1937 in Moscow. From 1965 to 1978 he was a member of the Leningrad section of the Writers' Union. He has published about ten volumes of prose. Among them:* Tauride Garden; The Female Laboratory Assistant; Cast Off Every Yoke. *His philosophical work* Practical Metaphysics *(written under the pseudonym of Andrei Moskovit) appeared in* samizdat *beginning in 1971. Excerpts from it have been published in the magazine* Grani *No. 87–88, 1973. Another work of a historic-philosophical trend,* Metapolitics, *written under the same pseudonym, appeared in* samizdat *in 1974, and in 1978 was put out in book form by an American publishing house, Strathcona Publishing Company. At the present time he is living in the United States.*

Although everyone knows that in the last twenty years no real improvement has taken place in the lives of Soviet citizens, the proclamation itself has not usually been called into question. After all, the reasons for its nonfulfillment are so obvious: the incurable sores and ailments of the planned economy, the low qualifications of economic leaders imposed by the Party, excessive expenditures for defense, gigantic growth of the bureaucratic Party machinery. Therefore it is customarily accepted that, at least in regard to this slogan, propaganda does not lie. Presumably the regime would like to raise the standard of living but simply does not know how to do it.

And really, if the people began to live a little better, could this somehow injure the all-powerful Party bureaucracy which rules over them? Seemingly it would be easier to rule over a satisfied people and their labor output would certainly grow. If the labor output grew, there would be an increase in the volume of efficient production and, accordingly, in that of its most important branch—arms; military deliveries would expand all over the world; international influence would be strengthened. Reasoning logically, we must come to the conclusion that the Party bureaucracy's very love of power and striving for world hegemony would impel it to take steps for improvement of the economic machine. If a by-product of this improvement happened to be an increase in the people's welfare, this could not arouse the slightest dissatisfaction on the part of the Kremlin rulers.

What seems self-evident according to criteria of traditional political thought, however, often turns out to be untrue by the criteria of Communist doublethink. From this viewpoint, interesting results can be obtained from an analysis of those efforts to increase labor productivity undertaken in the country during the past five years at the initiative of the ruling hierarchy and urgently propagandized in the central press, on radio and television, in reports, lectures, and seminars.

Among the salvage pontoons placed under the ship of the Soviet economy in the seventies, we shall distinguish three basic types and examine the fate of each of them.

2. First Pontoon—Contractual Method

It was originally employed in construction under the designation "Brigadier Zlobin's method." According to this concept, a team of workers is allowed to take a contract on the erection of a whole house from the laying of the foundation to the interior finishing. The team receives the stipulated pay only after delivery of the house to a commission. If it succeeds in doing this in a half year—excellent. In four months—all the better for it. Thus the amount of a worker's monthly pay turned out to be directly dependent on the effectiveness and quality of his labor.

At first the method achieved astounding results. There was of course nothing new about it, in old Russia the *artel'* (cooperative) has existed from time immemorial. In the *artel'* everyone is in plain sight of one another, there is no possibility of deceiving all its members as any boss can be deceived. Thus lazy and incompetent persons simply cannot survive in the contractual team—they would not be tolerated there.

The new initiative was intensely propagandized, the campaign swiftly gathered strength. The Party leadership demanded general application of the "contract." For example, such decrees were issued: "Managers who cannot ensure the shift of thirty percent of the teams to the self-supporting [i.e., contractual] method are not qualified for the positions they occupy." (*Literaturnaya Gazeta*, March 2, 1977.) Efforts were made to carry over the contract from construction to other branches of industry. An analogous method had long existed in agriculture under the name "accord" and now also started to receive general application. A field team was assigned machines, land, and seed, and the final accounting with it took place in the fall according to the harvest which had been collected. Here, too, the accord teams contrived to extract from the hectare nearly twice as much grain as normal teams working in neighboring fields by the usual conditions of operational pay: separately for plowing, sowing, harrowing, and reaping.

The only trouble was that neither the contractual nor the accord teams could for some reason take hold. It was incomprehensible who prevented them from becoming the

rule rather than the exception. The new method promised
the workers larger pay, the management demanded its extension, but people persistently preferred to work in the
old way, and the number of self-supporting teams only increased on paper.

Finally in 1977 there filtered into the newspapers admis-
sions which revealed the real reason. As it happened, the
administrations of enterprises found themselves somehow
between two fires. On the one hand, all of them—construction bosses, factory directors, and *kolkhoz* chairmen—
were faced with demands for an increase in the number of
contract teams. But on the other hand, they were also
called upon to fulfill the plan still more strictly. Planned
tasks are always assigned to excess, but machinery, raw materials, and labor are not adequately supplied, and production figures are checked, as a rule, not by real results but by
quarterly and annual indicators.

At the end of every quarter the telephone rings in the
industrial manager's office and the voice of the regional
Party Committee secretary screams something like the following: "Hey, what's the idea, you're messing up the plan
again? Underfulfillment on ten targets . . . What does it
mean, 'no people, no machinery'? Are you a Communist or
a jerk? See that you catch up with the plan by tomorrow.
You'll answer for it with your Party card!" So the manager,
in feverish pursuit of additional resources and labor reserves, rushes first of all to the place where they can be
found, where the situation is most favorable—the sectors
of the self-supporting teams. He takes away from them cement, bricks, and metal materials as well as people and
transfers everything to the "hot" targets, promising to provide compensation for everything later, yet never able to
keep his promise. In exactly the same way, on the collective farms it becomes necessary above all to account to the
authorities in the very dust of the harvest for the quantity
of harvested hectares. Therefore, at the critical moment
chairmen take away combines from the accord teams and
curtail the supply of fuel in order to harvest the fields of
backward teams, even if the crop there is only equal in
weight to the seeds which had been sown.

Thus both the construction workers and the agricultural-
machine operators taking part in the propagandized initia-

tives very quickly become convinced that their strenuous and often overtime labor will not bring them any real increase in pay but simply plug the holes in the picture of plan indicators. Working by the usual methods, they will always at least receive pay for enforced idleness, while with the contractual methods, not fulfilling the conditions of the agreement by the fault of the administration, they may be left by and large without a penny. All this "initiative" is reduced to nothing more than another trick of management to squeeze out of them surplus free labor. Therefore it became more and more difficult to drive them into contract teams. The system proved to be incapable of organizing labor in the *artel'* form, and all the threatening orders and loud appeals remained powerless.

3. Second Pontoon—Peasants' Private Plots

The 1969 population census showed that up to then about one half of the U.S.S.R.'s citizens lived in villages and settlements. It was not a secret to anyone that the potato occupies the central place in the rural resident's ration. Thus it feeds not only people but fowl and livestock. Peasants never buy it in store, they grow it on their private plots. At the same time, private plots may not exceed 0.15 hectares per family and, accordingly, constitute about 1.5 percent of all cultivated land in the country.

All of this was known, and nevertheless many were astonished when *Literaturnaya Gazeta* (dated May 11, 1977) published statistics from the handbook *The Political Economy of the U.S.S.R.* It became clear that on this 1.5 percent of the land worked by manual labor there grew 60 percent of potatoes as well as 34 percent of vegetables, and it produced 40 percent of the eggs and supported 18 percent of the All-Union stock of sheep, 18 percent of pigs, 33 percent of cows, and 80 percent of goats.

Publication of these statistics signaled the inauguration of a newspaper campaign in support of private plots. There appeared articles asserting that peasants had no place to buy seed and seedlings for their plots and gardens, no place to obtain fertilizer, that they faced enormous difficulties in the procurement and processing of feed for livestock, with materials for hothouse culture, for mechanical irrigation, while no one even dreamed about small agricultural machinery. It was said that all these deficiencies needed to be corrected and every possible assistance should be given to people who contrived to produce on 1.5 percent of the land one third of the agricultural production. In some articles the most daring authors permitted themselves to say that those who engaged in trade with their surplus products at the market were not at all necessarily accursed private operators and speculators but might be to some extent people useful to society.

But precisely this last marketing problem was recalled most rarely of all, in passing, or for the most part continued to be ignored. The functionaries of the propaganda apparatus sensed with the instinct of many years' experience that here lurked the danger, the stumbling block, of the new campaign. Because it was one thing for a person who worked on a collective or state farm or in a workshop to busy himself in free time on his plot and insure his food supply for the whole year, thus relieving the authorities of any concern about feeding him. And it was quite another thing when the same person began to trade openly and freely with his surplus produce. At this moment he approached close to the line beyond which commenced the most unacceptable thing of all—economic independence from the authorities.

Markets in the central part of the country exist only in large cities. Even in regional centers they have already been reduced to such a pitiful condition that something can be bought there only in the first hours after their opening (they are open only one or two days a week). Every obstacle is placed in the way of peasants seeking to bring produce to the market: They are denied transportation, they are required each time to present a special certificate from the village soviet, and as tradesmen they have to pay supplementary taxes. There exist cooperative organizations which are responsible for the task of buying up the peasants' surplus produce. Their staffs, however, are so small in number that they can buy up only an insignificant part and, of course, do so only at extortionary, monopolistic prices. Therefore enormous amounts of fruits, berries, vegetables, and other quickly spoiled products perish in the villages while they are vainly awaited in the cities by millions of purchasers.

Those peasant families in which only the old people can work on the private plots have difficulty in supplying themselves with foodstuffs and do not think of engaging in trade. In many families, however, health and age permit people to labor much more strenuously in field work, and they could produce much more if they knew that their labor would not be wasted and they could sell the surplus. When from one year to the next they see that cucumbers are left to yellow in the beds because there is a shortage of barrels for pickling, that tomatoes rot on the bushes and return to the soil as pink juice, that apples every autumn must be fed to pigs, they drop their hands, and, naturally, the desire to work disappears.

Although the campaign in support of private plots continues, it bears in itself the same insuperable contradiction as the struggle for self-supporting teams and hence is doomed to failure. People will not labor more energetically on their plots, not because they do not have the strength (they could find the strength), but simply because this extra work will not bring them any visible results. Their connection with possible consumers has been forcibly severed; therefore, as before, they will only attempt to provide for themselves and their families—nothing more.

4. Third Pontoon—Administrative Reform

In the last period the greatest hopes have been placed in this pontoon. In truth, it is still in the stage of design and elaboration, but at least one has been permitted to state aloud that the reform of 1965 did not bring the desired results and that the system of centralized planning and regulation requires recurrent alterations.

This was where it began!

Economists, factory directors, planners, and ministerial workers began saying that things could no longer continue in the same way. Estimating fulfillment of the plan of an enterprise by aggregate costs of finished products inevitably pushes the administration toward the output of expensive products to the detriment of cheap ones. The valuation

by aggregate weight artificially brings about heavier machines and equipment. A plant which attempts to use
cheap raw materials is automatically numbered among
backward plants because the price of its products thereby
diminishes. A factory thinking of modernizing its equipment almost certainly will disrupt fulfillment of the plan
because it must shut down lines and sections for retooling.
Centralized planning does not react in time to fluctuations
in demand, and therefore the production of nearly all consumer goods is doomed to jump forever out of the frying
pan of shortages into the fire of oversupply.

What, however, can be proposed instead of the existing
system?

At this point the friendly chorus becomes silent and an
incomprehensible dissonance begins.

"The activity of enterprises should be assessed first of all
by the rates of growth," says one voice. (*Literaturnaya Gazeta*, February 16, 1977.)

"I think that achievements should be reflected in the index of capital productivity," responds another. (*Literaturnaya Gazeta*, May 18, 1977.)

"It is essential to make valuations not in rubles and tons
but in standard rubles and standard hours," asserts Doctor
of Economic Sciences D. Valovoi. (*Pravda*, November
10–12, 1977.)

"There is an old indicator tested by life: Pure profit,"
maintains Member-Correspondent of the Academy of Sciences L. Bunich. (*Literaturnaya Gazeta*, August 3, 1977.)

"It is necessary that what is advantageous to the state
will always be advantageous to any enterprise and to the
individual worker," profoundly notes Academician A. G.
Aganbegyan (*Literaturnaya Gazeta*, May 4, 1977), failing to
specify how such a miracle can be achieved.

Only rarely amid the newspaper clamor there can be
heard the voices of skeptics who admit that, regardless of
which index is considered primary, factories will quickly
readjust to it and put out not those goods which are desperately needed by the consumer but those which will favorably affect the index. Rates of growth? Then all will begin to
grow at any price and increase production of even nonessential goods. Capital productivity? They will then work
their equipment to the limit and generally discontinue

technological modernization. Pure profit? They will try to induce ministries and committees to raise the selling price of their products. And the latter will meet their wishes, since bad indices of enterprises are taken as bad work on the part of the relevant ministry. After all, who wants to join the bad or backward ones?

5. The Abominable Market

All the enumerated campaigns appear at first glance to have a different direction and various reasons for their failure. But if we try to avoid getting lost in details, we shall see that all of them, after wandering for a short time over devious paths, sooner or later come up against one and the same wall.

What are contract and accord teams? This is an attempt to avoid payment for labor according to wage scales applicable to the whole country and begin to pay for labor in a differentiated way, based on its real result. In other words, to open the labor market for at least some professions where true ability, skill, and energy can be recompensed as they deserve.

What are the peasants' private plots? This is a tiny part of native soil whose harvest is not entirely collected by the state but is left to a significant degree for those who raised it. But any effort to enlarge the volume of production in this sector of agriculture must inevitably be linked to an expansion of the network of markets where the products can reach the consumer.

Finally, all the endless, highly intelligent talk of economists about "perfection of the system of administration of socialist production" through its many years of futility clearly testifies to one thing: Centralized planning is not capable of rationally managing a national economy under the conditions existing in an industrialized era. Only the introduction (if only to a minor degree) of market relations among enterprises can improve the production of goods and broaden the sphere of services.

Thus we see that the wall against which all efforts for economic reforms wind up is everywhere one and the same: the market.

Yet why are Communists in such haste, wherever they come to power, to do away with the market? What makes them so afraid of it? After all, it is not necessarily private but also collective owners who can participate in the market, as already is the case with all nationalized enterprises in the West. Indeed, all the market terminology—supplier, customer, price, profit, revenues, profitability—has been preserved for enterprises in countries of the Communist bloc. Then why not fill it at least to some degree with real content?

There is not the slightest doubt that, preserving a complete monopoly of political, administrative, and judicial power, intervening in the domestic market as the most powerful purchaser and regulator of prices, the Party bureaucracy could derive enormous benefit from a broadening of the sphere of market relations in the country. The miraculous experience of NEP[1] resurrecting in three or four years an economy ruined by civil war completely confirms this. Then why does the Party leadership paralyze even its own reforms as soon as it sees that their implementation would lead to a partial revival of the market?

The answer to this question cannot be found as long as one remains in the sphere of pure logic. Only the special properties of Communist rule can explain the paradox of its irrational hatred toward the market.

Communism is, above all, the theory and practice of seizure and retention of power. Its strength lies in the fact that it has renounced a view of power as a means of insuring order and the rule of law in society and worshiped power as such, converting it into an end in itself. The flourishing or impoverishment of the state is not viewed by Communists as criteria against which to measure a regime's worth. For them the only criteria are: solidity, totality, and indestructibility, and at what price this is achieved remains unimportant.

[1]The NEP (New Economic Policy), adopted by Lenin in 1921 as a pragmatic measure to restore production, permitted private enterprise in agriculture, light industry, and distribution; the "commanding heights" were retained by the state. Capital and technicians were also obtained from abroad. When Stalin consolidated his power in 1928, it was replaced by the first Five-Year Plan.—ED.

It is precisely this approach which explains the senseless (at first glance) outbreaks of terror convulsing the Communist state from time to time. Mass destruction of peaceful and loyal citizens is a realization of the regime's instinct, a demonstration of the alienation and opposition of the Party bureaucracy in relation to the rest of society, aimed at inculcating society with mystical horror before the holders of power. Regular outbreaks of inner-Party terror—so-called purges—are the destruction of that part of the Communists among whom worship of the idol of power has weakened, who have fallen under bourgeois influence—that is, begun to experience alarm about the fate of society as a whole.

Attaining complete power in all spheres of social life, the Party bureaucracy takes in its hands economic power as well. Control of the economy is the main possibility and excuse enabling millions of Party officials to give a graphic, day-by-day demonstration of their power. To relinquish some share of control to the market would mean giving up a significant share of power, in other words, to go against the bureaucracy's greatest instinct—putting it bluntly, against its very nature.

How can the chairman of a collective farm installed by the Party tolerate accord teams, which cannot be deprived of equipment, which cannot be dispatched now here, now there in order to carry out the regional party committee's latest directive? How can a factory director or the chief of a construction division reconcile himself to the "contract," to those insolent, self-important workhorses who burst into the office, pound their fists on the desk, demand raw materials, tools, machines because, look here, you can't let them stand idle like the others—this hits them in their pocket?

What about the regional administration in an agricultural region, which must see to it that the population assigned to the land diligently labors in the collective-farm fields? It knows very well that if the market were permitted to operate in settlements and hamlets, half the people would spit on the meager state-farm pay and make a living from their garden plots.

And the Party bosses in the cities who appoint the factory and plant directors as well as the chiefs of shops and

laboratories? They also understand very well that the introduction of elements of market regulation, the fulfillment in a real sense of concepts like "remunerativeness"
and "profitability" would entail a weakening of their
power. For in that case it would be necessary in making
appointments to executive posts, to take into account the
candidate's capabilities and energy and not just his principles, obedience, and the position which he has occupied in
the hierarchy. Thus the idea might get about that the Party
is not all-powerful and that it is prepared to retreat before
some sort of unprincipled profitability—before the deviation of "economism," as this is called by the Maoists in
China.

Holding in its hands not only the regime but also all the
media of mass propaganda, the Party bureaucracy seeks to
instill in society the same aversion toward the market
which it experiences itself. Many years' abuse, defamation,
and harassment have brought about a situation in which
trade in agricultural regions came to be seen not only as
half forbidden but repellent. Even in large cities, where
markets give city dwellers the possibility of obtaining first-
class products, one often has to listen to open abuse and
cursing addressed to "market speculators."

Incidentally, it is a curious psychological phenomenon
—the abuse is so sincere one feels at once that more than
propaganda is involved. Nor is it only the high prices that
shock the purchaser, accustomed to artificially reduced
store prices for potatoes, bread, meat, butter, and sausage.
And not only the fact that the absence of legal protection
for private trade frightens honest and law-abiding citizens
away from engaging in it and leaves it open to determined
and not very scrupulous operators. No, in addition to all
this, people instinctively feel that ordinary market trading
is some sort of relapse from the usual order of their lives,
an isolation from the accustomed course of things, due to
the fact that it alone has acquired something unique in the
conditions of victorious socialism—independence from
the regime. Scanty, temporary and confined within economic limits—but independence all the same. Unable to
recognize the nature of the mixed feeling of alarm, suspicion, and envy toward the phenomenon of independence,
the buyer, who takes home from the market early radishes,

tomatoes, strawberries, and pomegranates which no store can offer him, hisses through his teeth the all-explanatory "Oh-h, damned speculators."

Theoretical disputes about the significance of the market in economic life have not ceased, it seems, since the time of Adam Smith. By now everyone seems to agree that complete supremacy of market relations in society is fraught with uneven redistribution of capital, monopolization, crises, the growth of unemployment, and political instability. Social shocks experienced by many countries in the nineteenth and twentieth centuries evoked the powerful growth of socialist ideas and movements seeking some way or other to control the market element. In developed states the governments received broad powers for coping with dangerous, near-crisis situations.

For Communists, however, the dangers of the market economy are only a pretext for a struggle against it, a propaganda trick. Wherever they come to power they inflict upon the economy of the country such chaos and devastation that, in comparison with it, any capitalist crisis appears to be child's play. No, their hatred and irreconcilability arise solely from the fact that the market is always a guarantee of independence. The market is simply inconceivable without a free buyer who meets there with a free seller. But freedom is precisely what cannot be permitted under any guise.

While the wave of nationalizations at present sweeping over Europe under the pressure of leftist movements lowers, of course, the effectiveness of production, it still does not mean a complete fall into an economic abyss. Seventy to eighty percent of industrial capacity can be nationalized in a country, but all is not lost so long as free exchange of goods and services has not been abolished. Nationalized enterprises which have access to the internal and external market continue to concern themselves with profitability, with the competitive edge of their products. Due to the existence of a free press, those which begin to operate at a loss immediately become known to the public. The government may replace their managers with more capable and energetic people, find means for modernization and reorganization, or even denationalize them.

The Communists' advent to power is another matter. In

an ideological sense, Communism is a system which exploits the individual's dissatisfaction with material inequality, the competitive struggle and all its oppressive aspects. Therefore, entirely consistently, it sees its task in the extermination of all types of open competition in society. It is unimportant whether Communists come to power by means of an armed revolt or through victory in elections. Without fail, they begin with suppression of political competition, destruction of all forms of political activity in the country even to the extent of local self-government, and end with destruction of competition in the economic sphere—abolition of the market.

6. Convenient Poverty and Dangerous Prosperity

In the Communist world there of course exist gradations. Aversion to the market economy has not resulted in its complete destruction everywhere. In any case, Poland, Hungary, and Czechoslovakia differ greatly from China, Cuba, and Cambodia. In Yugoslavia the market is open to such a degree that she cannot be considered a real Communist state at all.

Let us try now to imagine that in the Soviet Union the Party bureaucracy had matured to the point where it was able to overcome its irrational hatred of citizens' economic independence and had enlarged the market's scope of operations. To what would this lead?

Yes, labor productivity in many spheres of the national economy would immediately increase. It would become easier to obtain food, clothing, housing, and services. A resurrected NEP would open up enormous reserves of the people's labor, business, and intellectual energies that have no outlet under the present forms of organization of the economy. But it is very doubtful that these changes would lead to a strengthening of the Party bureaucracy's power.

After all, man is so constituted that he cannot stop desiring to improve his situation. As long as his life is filled by standing in endless queues, running to stores, the patching and repair of low-quality goods, and the search for some additional meters of living space, he simply does not possess the strength to think about anything else. But relieve him of these tormenting daily cares—and he will want more. He will begin to notice his social and political disfranchisement and feel burdened by his position as a state serf. From here it is only one step to the ripening of opposition—that is, to the appearance of a threat to the uncontrolled rule of the Communist Party of the Soviet Union.

The low level of welfare makes it easy to manipulate manpower resources. By offering supplementary pay for remote regions, one can transfer great armies of workers into the construction of rocket bases, fortifications, oil and gas wells, gold mines, hydroelectric stations, and strategic railroads. By paying the graduate of a military academy twice as much as a young engineer, one can without difficulty staff the officer cadres of an army of ten million. But just try to improve people's living conditions, and they will value more greatly rest, health, and comfort. It will become harder to pull them away from their home towns and send them to an uninhabited wilderness in order to "strengthen the defensive might of the state."

The material inequality existing in the country between the Party summit and the mass of the population has been painstakingly and successfully concealed. The inequality brought about by the difference in the supply of various cities and regions (first, second, third categories) does not strike the eyes of people until they are allowed to come to the big centers and hunt for goods with which provincial stores are never even supplied. But in case of an expansion of the market sphere the inequality will begin to appear in much sharper and clearer forms. Some regions, enterprises, organizations, and individual producers will begin to enrich themselves more quickly than the others, and this will certainly lead to a sharp aggravation of social and national differences, to open manifestation of hatred and hostility, to outbreaks of violence. Maintaining order in society will become immeasurably harder, the centrifugal forces rending the Soviet empire will acquire from material inequality a new source of energy. Once again the monopoly of political power will be threatened.

Finally, universal poverty simplifies to the utmost the problem of insuring the loyalty of the Party apparatus itself. With the chronic shortage of the most elementary

goods and services, any Party functionary can be made
happy with a pass to a closed restaurant, a separate apartment, a telephone, a special clinic, or a trip abroad. A reduction of the shortage of goods and services would result
in a huge rise in the costs of the bureaucratic Party machine or an unprecedented growth of bribery and corrup-
tion. This was what happened in the period of NEP, and
this is also now the case in the republics of the Caucasus
and Central Asia, where market relations in their perverted underground form are more widespread than in
other parts of the state. (In Azerbaijan and Georgia in the
sixties the purchase of jobs and services of officials went so
far that it became necessary to renovate the whole Party
apparatus, beginning with the first secretaries, replacing
them with ranking officers of the local KGB.)

Perhaps it would be a psychological simplification to
consider that the Politburo, announcing another campaign
for a rise in labor productivity and improvement of the
people's well-being, is consciously and cunningly dissem-
bling. No, it behaves in the process like a starving shark
which has gobbled up all the fish in a lagoon and decided
to feed on land creatures, but on its first attempt to crawl
up on the shore it felt the stones tearing its belly, the gills
burning from dry air, the tail thrashing about uselessly—
that is, it recognized that it was denied this quarry.

Thus even those levels of the Party bureaucracy which
were capable of overcoming irrational hatred of the market
and sparks of independence in the citizenry would be convinced very quickly that the changes that were economi-
cally advantageous to the country and people were politically disadvantageous to the ruling summit, and they too
would turn the ship of the national economy onto its former course.

7. Export of Destitution

Sometimes one is obliged to hear that the low level of production deprives Communist countries of the advantage of
foreign trade. Because of their low quality, the goods are
not in demand on the foreign market and hence their share
of world commodity circulation is not great.

Presumably this comforting illusion exists only because of the impossibility of obtaining exact figures. Reliable data on the world trade of the U.S.S.R. and its satellites come to light only in those areas which relate to trade with industrially developed countries, and here, in fact, the volume is not very great. But the volume of trade with countries of the Third World amounts to no more than an approximation, and this is precisely the area which accounts for the principal export produced by the "fighters for peace"—arms.

In democratic states the sale of sizable shipments of arms must be long prepared, deliberated in the parliament, and has to overcome the opposition of public opinion. In the U.S.S.R. the Politburo can react to a request for arms deliveries almost instantly, organize an airlift within twenty-four hours to any geographic point in the world, and begin to send tanks, guns, explosives, shells, and rockets. Vietnam, Syria, Ethiopia, Angola—we know about them because those arms went into action immediately. But many countries buy Soviet military equipment in good time, and as a rule these purchases are not advertised. It is practically impossible to form an idea of the full volume of the sale of Soviet military equipment to the Third World.

Oil, coal, timber, and other types of raw materials are traditional items of export from the U.S.S.R. There should be added to this some exotic items—trade in vodka, caviar, furs, handicraft wares, canned fish of the expensive sort. Revenues from international tourism are also very large, because the number of Soviet citizens allowed to go abroad is insignificant and they are permitted to exchange for foreign currency a ridiculous amount—ten to twenty rubles. Foreigners coming to the Soviet Union are fleeced to the extent that, for example, the trip from Helsinki to Leningrad costs more than to Italy at the same time. But mainly one should remember that, regardless of the ware on which the Communist countries are making a profit they are always selling in essence one and the same thing—cheap labor.

In *Time* magazine of October 16, 1978, there appeared an article about the appearance on the European market of products from developing countries. Figures were cited on the hourly pay of workers in the textile industry: in Belgium, $8.27; West Germany, $7.32; Italy, $5.15. And next to them: South Korea, $0.45; Hong Kong, $0.35. Such an irregularity in pay had as a result that, say, already in 1977 some 43 percent of cotton goods purchased by Europeans were manufactured in countries of the Third World. Aside from South Korea and Hong Kong, big suppliers included India, Malaysia, Pakistan, Colombia, Brazil, Egypt, and Thailand. Many textile plants in France and Belgium have been forced to close down and thousands of workers found themselves on the street.

In exactly the same way the Soviet Union, with its enormous manpower resources, is groping for ways to invade the world market. The easiest way of all is to accomplish this by buying Western technology—for example, an automobile plant of the Fiat company—and then selling in the West products manufactured with the aid of this technology but costing considerably less. A worker of VAZ-Fiat receives an average of one ruble an hour, about $1.30 at the official rate of exchange or $0.35 in real terms. The Zhiguli car coming off the production line of this factory costs 7,500 rubles in the Soviet Union but is sold under the name of Lada in Europe for five thousand dollars. By the official rate of exchange it works out that trade is being conducted at a loss, but in reality it amounts to an enormous profit because the automobile's real cost price is very low.

Another example—ocean transport. *The Economist* (August 5, 1978) reports that all goods shipped to Soviet ports and shipped out of them are transported on ships under the red flag. These ships offer their services throughout the world at prices distinctly below the average. The Soviet liner *Kazakhstan* regularly makes tourist cruises between New York and the Bermuda islands, and six similar ships with a displacement of 16,600 tons each are being built now in the shipyards of Finland. Cruises in the Baltic, Black, Mediterranean and Caribbean seas will cost a resident of the West 25 percent less if he chooses the ship of a Soviet company. The possibility of such cut rates is assured in the same way: the extreme cheapness of labor in the U.S.S.R.—the labor of oil-industry workers supplying oil, the labor of harbor workers, the labor of seamen. A former captain of the Soviet merchant fleet, V. Lysenko, now re-

ceives on a Swedish liner $933 per month. A Soviet steam-
ship line paid him 160 rubles, that is, $213 according
to the official rate of exchange or four times less by the
real rate.

The extortionary approach of the state is revealed with
particular clarity in the trade involving the work of people
in science and art. Foreign tours of Soviet musicians, dancers, and circus performers assure the U.S.S.R. Ministry of
Finances a regular influx of hard currency. Scientists who
receive foreign prizes or work under contract abroad are
also obligated to turn over all the foreign currency they receive for a pitiful compensation in rubles. In 1973 the
U.S.S.R. signed the Berne convention for protection of authors' rights, and since then the royalty for any literary or
musical work translated or performed in the West is divided in this manner: 85 percent to the state, 15 percent to
the author. Once again not in foreign currency but in rubles. (At best they are paid in coupons for the special
stores.)

The cheap labor of slaves in ancient Rome ruined the
free peasants and turned them into indigent farm laborers.
Slavery in the American southern states heavily weighed
down on free farmers of northern states. Now as well, with
active world trade, a country which knows how to combine
cheap labor with relatively advanced technology can
deliver serious blows to the living standard of developed
countries.

The extreme ineffectiveness of a planned economy, of
course, deprives the Communist bloc of the possibility of
conquering the world market to the degree that, for example, Japan succeeded in doing in recent years. But the fundamental difference lies in the fact that in Japan strike action is permitted and hence there exists a real growth of
wages, and consequently she cannot lower prices on her
goods endlessly. In the Soviet Union, on the other hand,
the real wage can still remain frozen for decades. Therefore
it is worthwhile to overhaul the qualitative production of
some articles, and she will be able to inflict great losses on
the corresponding branches of Western industry, forcing
firms to curtail production and even bringing about the
bankruptcy of some of them.

8. So That the People Will Be Neither Alive nor Dead

There is no argument that for mature Communist regimes industrial ruin or starvation in one's own country cannot be considered desirable phenomena. In such a situation social stability breaks down, there occur disturbances and revolts of the hungry, and military strength weakens. Nevertheless, careful analysis shows that the growth of the people's well-being also conceals quite a number of threats to the Party bureaucracy's power. The ideal arrangement for it is a situation in which the people resemble a person caught in deep water so that only his face remains above the surface. To manage such a person while sitting on his shoulders proves to be very easy, because he will not struggle against the one who is straddling him, due to his fear of choking. But if the bottom under his feet rises and his body comes out of the water at least to his chest, the situation of the rider could become extremely dubious and unenviable.

The whole history of the twentieth century proves that the concepts of "exploiter" and "exploitative class," having been torn out of the context of political demagogy, are devoid of any meaning. No developed state can exist without appropriation in its favor of the surplus share of labor which satisfies requirements of administration, legal procedures, defense, social welfare, education, and so on. In countries which boast of the abolition of "exploitation," this surplus share of labor squeezed out of citizens turns out to be three to four times greater than in countries which preserve in a limited form the principle of private property.

Yes, a market economy, even with a developed system of preventive measures, conceals in itself the danger of getting out of control, the danger of becoming unmanageable. Yes, the unevenness of the distribution of the good things of life under market regulation of the economy can very often cross the boundaries of what is reasonable and just. But if the awareness of these dangers and this injustice impels the present-day Italian, Frenchman, Spaniard, or Portuguese to vote for the party calling for the abolition of the market—for Communists—he must clearly take into account that he is voting not only for the end of political pluralism and social liberty in his country but also for the advent of poverty.

Because all the latest historical experience clearly testifies to one thing: A Communist regime that destroys the market economy as the last refuge of freedom and puts in its place a centralized bureaucracy of planning and controlling officials is not simply incapable of ending poverty and destitution. It also does not wish, and, by its very essence, must not wish, to end them. For poverty and destitution are indispensable conditions for the firmness of the Communists' political power.

The Speech I Would Like to Deliver at My Graveside

BY DAVID DAR

Translated by George Bailey

From *Kontinent* No. XIV, 1978

1.

Today you are burying one of the happiest oldsters in the world. My happiness consisted in the fact that I did not believe in Jean-Jacques Rousseau nor in Karl Marx, nor in Lenin—as though every man has the right to food, work, and happiness, to freedom, equality, and fraternity. When I was born into this world, I made no demands of anyone, set no conditions, and no one promised me anything, just as no one promises anything to a newborn cockroach, or to a newborn puppy or a newborn lion.

Therefore I never asked anything of anybody: neither from nature nor from society, nor from relatives, nor from friends.

And, it may be just for this reason, everything always worked out for me.

DAVID YAKOVLEVICH DAR was born in 1910 in Leningrad. He was first published in 1940. Some twenty books of his, including fiction, essays, and travel reportage, have been published. In the Writers' Union he was the Chairman of the Commission for Cooperation with Young Authors and did everything in his power to help young writers, a fact which led to frequent clashes with the leadership of the Leningrad section of the Writers' Union. He left the U.S.S.R. in 1977 and lives today in Israel.

I was lucky in my youth: I never caught the clap, never got mixed up with a gang of rowdies, never became a drunk.

I was lucky in war: I did not fall in battle, was never taken prisoner, and they did not amputate my wounded leg.

And I was lucky after the war: I was not declared an enemy of the people, my daughter did not become a prostitute, and at the age of sixty I still did not have cancer nor had I suffered a heart attack.

Every evening I said to myself:

"But it is really surprising, if you consider how many unpleasant things could have happened to me today.

"I could have fallen down in front of a streetcar, somebody could have stolen my wallet, the salesgirl in the shop could have been downright nasty. But no—for me, thank God, everything went beautifully. So I was lucky again today!"

And, very satisfied with life, I put my rejected manuscript in the far corner of the bottom drawer, thought over the problem of where to get money for tomorrow, took a gulp of Validol,[1] took a sleeping pill, and, groaning with rheumatism and asthma, composed myself for sleep, rejoicing that I had a roof over my head, a blanket to cover me, a pillow under my head, and my general good fortune.

I ran out of luck only once, and that was yesterday when I died. But even that cannot be considered such a bad stroke of luck. Because even death has its positive side.

In the first place:

Death has freed me forever from the fear of death, and only now, two days later, have I managed to throw off this burden which has so heavily weighed upon me my life long.

In the second place:

I am now better off than you are, even though only because there is no longer anything that can threaten me in life. But you, you are still being threatened by someone's bony finger while I can joke easily about my one single stroke of bad luck, which has already receded into the past and has become, you might say, a hurdle already taken in a

[1]Medication for the heart. —ED.

race already run. But you, for your part, can hardly be inclined to joke about that inevitable calamity which awaits
you in the future and which is so much more terrible than
my calamity, since grief in prospect is always so much
more terrible than grief in review.

From this I draw a very optimistic conclusion: that every
calamity that has happened should be regarded as a stroke
of good fortune. And not only because it has receded into
the past but also because no matter how great it was it cannot happen again.

2.

Among other things, it was just this consideration that
helped me greatly in life, always—from childhood on, or,
more accurately, from the day when I found out that I had
flunked and would have to repeat the sixth grade.

And they flunked me because I had studied badly. Why I
studied badly I don't remember, but I remember very
clearly that I studied so badly that they would have been
justified in throwing me out of school altogether.

On that day I went home well satisfied.

"Why are you so happy?" asked my dear mother after I
had told her that they had flunked me.

"You mean you don't understand?" I asked with astonishment. "Why, they could have thrown me out of school
altogether! Now do you understand how lucky I was?"

But she couldn't understand it. And she never understood it until the day when they finally actually did throw
me out of school. And they threw me out of the ninth
grade because I was rude to our great and glorious biology
teacher in class.

Big, fat, and good natured, he stood before us in the
classroom and, gesturing with his huge, powerful hands,
explained to us gleefully that man was not created in the
image and likeness of God, as it is written in the Bible, but
in the image and likeness of any given mammal—a dog or
a mouse, for example.

Although I do not in the least doubt and did not doubt
then the nonexistence of God and hence the nonexistence
of His image and likeness, I did not at all want Rita

Barkhatova, a delightful girl, whom I walked with every day from school and read poems to on the way, poems I myself had written, and with whom I discussed Kant, Spinoza, and Freud (none of whom I had read), to see in me the likeness of a dog or—especially—a mouse.

To be in the likeness of a mouse seemed to me to be humiliating, the more so since even at the age of sixteen, just as also at the age of sixty, I considered myself a personality unique in its kind, distinguished from all other personalities which have existed in the past, exist now, or will exist after me.

Probably just as you have, I felt that there was a special, incomparable significance to my personality, setting it apart from the world that surrounded me, and only such respect for myself moved me to write poems, discuss Kant, Spinoza, and Freud, and to consider those thoughts which entered my head as worthy of attention.

But what sort of respect can one accord to a mouse? The comparison with a mouse insulted my sense of personal dignity. And of this I courteously informed our great and glorious biology teacher.

But when he gleefully continued to slander me, himself, you, and all other people, with an expression on his face that would lead one to believe he was telling us something pleasant, I considered myself obliged to act in the defense of humanity. By reason of my youthful inexperience I did this so awkwardly that, as you already know, they threw me out of school.

On that day I returned home extraordinarily pleased with life.

"Why are you so happy?" asked my dear mother after I had told her that they had thrown me out of school.

"You mean you don't understand?" I asked. "Why, they could have sent me to reform school for rowdyism, and all they did was kick me out of school. Now do you understand why I was so lucky?"

And Mama, to give her her due, understood my precocious wisdom and waved her hand resignedly, and from that time her life became easy and bright and there was no grief that could cast a shadow over her old age.

But from that time on my youth was overshadowed. Not because they kicked me out of school, but because I be-

lieved our great and glorious biology teacher that man had
been created in the image and likeness of a mouse.

At first I rejoiced over this and considered that you and I
were lucky: If we had been created in the image and likeness of a worm or a cockroach it would have been still
worse.

But later I noticed that, meeting with Rita Barkhatova,
arguing with friends, or even just walking alone along the
street, I somehow for some reason tried to hide from others
that I had been created in the image and likeness of a
mouse.

But it became more and more difficult for me to hide, because I suddenly lost my usual eloquence and somehow
became hectic and rambling and once or twice even tried
to wag the tail I didn't have.

It is true that sometimes still, while composing new
poems, or trying to read a philosophical tract of Hegel, or
astonishing Rita Barkhatova with the remnants of my eloquence, I felt in my immature soul the stirrings of a proud
sense of significance, but—but at that same moment the
thought occurred that perhaps the same proud sense of his
own significance is felt also by the mouse when it succeeds
in making away with a piece of bread from the table. And
with that thought the proud sense receded from my soul,
and I no longer wanted to write poems, or read Hegel, or
astonish Rita Barkhatova with the remnants of my eloquence, nor did I even want to study and work. All I
wanted to do was lie on the couch in my winter coat, listen
to the radio, and make away with a piece of bread from the
table.

I lived on for a time in this way, not studying, not working, not writing poetry, not reading books, not meeting
with Rita Barkhatova, but only lying on the couch all day
in my messy old winter coat and making away from time to
time with a piece of bread from the table. And all the while
I was mulling something over, namely, that apparently the
mouse in whose image and likeness I was created is not
torn by any sort of doubts whatever, since it wags its tail
quite cheerfully all the time. But for me, alas, this kind of
life for some reason or other was less than edifying.

Weighed down by this very sad circumstance, I waited
on one occasion near the school for our great and glorious

teacher, who was making his way home, with his hat pushed back on his head and very much satisfied with life.

I made my excuses to him for what had happened in school and asked: "Tell me, please, doesn't it bother or depress you one little bit that you have been created in the image and likeness of a mouse?"

"Not one little bit," he answered firmly.

"Well, it does bother me," I admitted. "For some reason or other I can't see a personality in a mouse."

"But why should a mouse have a personality?" he asked. "They can live perfectly well without a personality if only there is no cat on the premises."

"But in that case, why is it that, try as I might to live like a mouse, I get very little satisfaction out of it—even though there is no cat in our house?"

"Very simple, little friend," he answered cheerfully. "Because in the harmony of the universe the mouse is predestined to play one role and you another. A mouse is predestined to find a hiding place under the floor, make away with crumbs of bread from the table, and beware of the cat. In fulfilling its predestined function the mouse is perfectly satisfied. On the other hand you, my little friend, are predestined to work, to fall in love, to write poetry, and to beware of evil temptations. And if you fulfill your predestined function in the harmony of the universe, then you can be certain that you will be just as satisfied as the mouse."

3.

Having thanked my great and glorious teacher, I hurried to make arrangements for steady employment, moved to communal quarters, fell in love even more with Rita Barkhatova, started to write not only poetry but also short stories, and, as far as evil temptations are concerned, why, I simply ran away from them as fast as I could in order so doing to fulfill my predestined function in the harmony of the universe and become as satisfied as a mouse.

But I must admit that, although I fulfilled my function one hundred percent, I did not succeed in becoming as satisfied as a mouse. This was because in meeting with Rita Barkhatova and sharing with her my feelings, thoughts, and poems, I suddenly put the following question to myself: But what significance do my feelings, thoughts, and poems have if I fulfill my predestined function in the harmony of the universe in exactly the same way that any mouse fulfills its predestined function in the cellar, or any grain of sand in the desert or any drop of water in the ocean?

And if Rita Barkhatova never knows anything of my feelings or my thoughts or my poems, if nobody ever knows anything about any of them, and even if I die tomorrow—well, then, the harmony of the universe will not in the least be disturbed, since any grain of sand in the desert and any drop of water in the ocean can be replaced by another grain of sand or another drop of water and any mouse can be replaced by another mouse and consequently any person can be replaced by any other person.

But such an interchangeability of all people did not square with my feeling for my own personality and did not do justice to the significance which I assigned to my feelings and compositions. And then, imperceptibly wagging my tail, I hastily took leave of Rita Barkhatova and returned to my communal quarters, turning over in my mind my insignificance in comparison with the grandiose harmony of the universe.

But the commandant of the communal quarters was a vigilant man who, even from afar, would immediately notice if someone or other happened to be thinking of something or other.

"What's this, brother, are you thinking again?" he asked, stopping me in the corridor.

"I'm thinking," I admitted.

"It's clear from the expression on your mug that you're thinking," he said. "I'd be interested to know what there is for you to think about. Let those who work for capitalists think things over. For you and me—and that's the difference—Marx and Engels have done all the thinking and we don't have to trouble our heads about anything now, but just roll up our sleeves and get on with constructing our beautiful future."

He stood in front of me, broad-shouldered, thick-set, and red-faced, like a brick.

"Marx and Engels did all the thinking for you, but not for me," I said.

"How is that?" he asked.

"This is how it is," I answered. "Because when somebody else eats it doesn't do my stomach any good, when somebody else sleeps it doesn't make me any less tired, and when somebody else thinks I still have to think for myself. And this is what I think: It would still certainly be better if I knew that I was created in the image and likeness of God."

"I'd like to know, you fool, just how that would make things any better for you," said the commandant. "Here I am, running this communal home, and I don't get any peace day or night, but I still get paid for it: I can buy myself a beer or go to the movies. But God Almighty has the whole world to look after and what does He get for it. Only prayers. Well, you can't fill your belly with nothing but prayers, brother. But you, you live well, you have no cares or worries. You have, thank God, a good bed with clean sheets, the government provides you with food and drink —you have a fine profession. I don't understand what it is that you lack."

"The feeling of personal dignity," I said. "Of greatness. What sort of greatness can it be if I have been created in the image and likeness of a mouse?"

"Of a mouse?" The commandant was surprised. "What sort of fool told you that a man is created in the image and likeness of a mouse? A man is created in the image and likeness of a brick. Now, there is greatness for you!"

"Of a brick?" I asked. "Are you sure you're not mistaken?"

"When I say a brick, I mean a brick," he answered, and proudly expanded his mighty chest. "Run out and get some beer and I will explain everything to you."

And when I had run out for the beer and we sat in the official commandant's room, he made a regular speech.

"You say that the Lord God created the universe and in this lies his greatness. Let it be so," he said. "But people, too, have created more than a little. They are constructing a grandiose tower of progress and civilization, they have created skyscrapers and airplanes, television and lightning rods, and the tower keeps growing, bringing humanity nearer and nearer to a beautiful future. And this tower is made of bricks, of such bricks as you and I. You and I are standing, as it were, on the shoulders of our forebears, and on you and me our progeny will stand. Recognize yourself as a brick in the grandiose tower. Look from the height of this tower at our forebears below, who are running around without any pants on, dressed in animal hides, and then you will feel your own greatness."

"I'll try to see myself as a brick," I said, "but what about my personality? What good is the personality of a brick?"

"What do you mean?" asked the commandant, drinking the last gulp of his beer. "A personality is the most important thing of all in our business. Why, just think how it would be if my daddy hadn't hided me with a belt. Why, I would probably have been to this day a complete fool. But, thanks to his personality, I am thoroughly civilized human being: I don't belch at table, I use a handkerchief when I blow my nose, and I teach you, you fool, the rules of good sense so that you will be still more civilized. So don't have any doubts about it, follow in the footsteps of your forebears, work as hard as you can for progress and civilization, and then everyone will respect you, and you will be satisfied and at peace with yourself, like a brick in its place in the wall."

Then, finishing his beer, he looked at me with the tired contentment of self-satisfied wisdom. I wished him good night and tried to recognize myself in the likeness of a brick. I won't say that this gave me any particular sense of pride, but somehow or other I was able to come to terms with it: After all, being in the likeness of a brick suited my sense of male dignity better than being in the likeness of a mouse.

4.

I put the advice of the wise commandant conscientiously to practice: to follow in the footsteps of my forebears and to work for progress to the fullest of my youthful strength.

Working for progress didn't turn out to be all that easy. For the progress of science I was a completely useless brick because, as you know, I was a poor student and I had been thrown out of school.

Technical progress also had to get along without any contribution from me for the simple reason that I was never able to distinguish a screw from a washer or a nut from a bolt.

As far as my literary works were concerned, which might have served to further the progress of manners and morals, well, I never once noticed that my friend Vaska Timofeyev, a desperately foul-mouthed drunk who in all his life never read a good book, but who was the only one in the whole commune who recognized my talent—well, then, I never once noticed that Vaska Timofeyev desisted in the least from his use of profanity or refused yet another glass of vodka because of my poems.

Still, despite all these adverse circumstances, I never lost heart. After all, the chief characteristic of a brick is its hardness.

And I really was hard and strong, and following in the footsteps of voluminous bricks purchased in the bookstore called The Old Book, I wrote poem after poem, while nobody saw fit to publish them, and I gradually began to turn into a rather solid and heavy brick so that, espying somewhere or other a still young and unhardened brick, I would even offer to help him: "How about it, sport, shall I share my experience with you and put you in your rightful place in the tower of civilization? Here, pal, scramble up and stand on my shoulders, follow in my footsteps, work for progress, draw nearer to the beautiful future."

But Vaska Timofeyev, who after all had never read even one decent book in all his life but was more and more enthusiastic about my poems, still just as always swore a blue streak and guzzled vodka as though it were water; in short, I was not able to discover any sign whatever of any improvement in his moral character, or in the moral character of mankind at large, for that matter, as a result of my efforts.

And it may be for that very reason, I mean because of Vaska Timofeyev, that I somehow did not succeed in taking pride in the tower of progress and civilization, and that I did not manage to achieve a sense of personal importance because someone else had invented the lightning rod and someone else had written *The Brass Horseman*.[2]

5.

Troubled in my capacity as a solid brick by this circumstance and mulling over what it could be that I lacked in order to be happy, I managed somehow to share my deliberations with Professor Bublik, who, as you are aware, knows everything there is to know, or rather, he knows how everything was, is, and will be—it is only that he does not know why and for what everything was, is, and will be, and because of this his factual and always persuasive knowledge is ranged as it were on the periphery, positioned in the surrounding country, leaving a gaping hole in the middle, the existence of which it is neither possible to prove nor disprove.

"There is something I am unable to understand, dear Professor," I said to him. "What is it that I lack in order to be perfectly happy?"

"Idealism," he answered. "How is it possible to be perfectly happy if you are not struggling for the realization of an ideal?"

"And for what should I struggle?" I asked. "After all, the tower of progress rises higher and higher toward our beautiful future in any case."

"But that is exactly the point. In which direction is the tower mounting and where is this beautiful future located? It is precisely here that you cannot proceed without the battle of ideas. Some think that the tower should be built straight up, because that is where the beautiful future is. Others consider that the tower should be built toward the left. Still others, to the right. And there are even some who think that the tower shouldn't be raised into the air at all, but that it should go down, back into our beautiful past."

"Excellent," I said, "but the direction of progress and civilization doesn't altogether depend on me. What can one man do—especially if he is created in the image and likeness of a brick?"

[2]A long narrative poem by Pushkin.

"Of a brick?" The professor was astonished. "What fool told you that man was created in the image and likeness of a brick? Man was created in the image and likeness of a fraction."

"Of a fraction?" I asked. "Are you sure you're not mistaken?"

"That's right—a fraction," he answered with conviction, "a simple fraction. Here, take me, for example: I am a one-two-hundred-thousandth part of those scholars who consider that it is necessary to turn the tower to the left. One-two-hundred-thousandth—now, isn't that inspiring? But, what is more, I am also a one-three-billionth part of the whole of humanity, which is struggling for a better future. Just imagine: We are three billion. It is simply grandiose! Our power and greatness are in the denominator. Conceive of yourself as in the likeness of a fraction, and your life will become clear and majestic, just as sure as three times five makes fifteen."

"Well, well," I thought to myself, "if the professor is right and we are all created in the image and likeness of a fraction, then we can consider that we have been very lucky, because we could be created in the image and likeness of the extraction of the root or the raising to the nth power—which is something that I am not even capable of imagining. And there is comfort in the circumstance that I began life as a simple fraction, trying to get the feeling of its own dignity in its denominator."

It is true that in considering myself one-quarter part of my family and struggling with our neighbors who had failed to turn out the light in the hall, or in considering myself one-eighth part of the residents of our apartment struggling for the installation of a new bowl in the toilet, I did not experience any special pride, but it was worthwhile considering myself a one-one-hundred-thousandth part of the admirers of Anna Akhmatova and to join in the struggle with the admirers of Ludmilla Tatianichev, or even when I considered myself a one-one-hundred-and-fifty-millionth part of the citizens of my country and dashed into battle with the citizens of another country. I somehow felt that my denominator had lifted me to a giddy height and lent a special significance to my actions and compositions, which carried with them, as it were, not only the sound of my name but also the sound of the names of all the admirers of Anna Akhmatova or of all the citizens of my country.

From time to time a misty recollection of school arithmetic surfaced in my memory, and at such times I would suspect with some bitterness that the greater my denominator, by so much the smaller was the portion made up by my sorry and unchanging numerator, and that therefore the actions and works of a man, created in the image and likeness of a fraction, could be regarded not so much as significant as rather signified as insignificant by his denominator.

But there was no way for me to achieve a feeling of personal dignity except in this denominator, so that insofar as I became accustomed to consider myself as representative, a part or share of something, in thinking of myself I somehow learned not to notice my numerator at all and sort of merge with my denominator.

And insofar as I belonged to humanity, so, at one time or another, I managed to say: "We have already conquered the heavens"—and insofar as I belonged to writers, on one occasion I almost said: "We have already written *The Brothers Karamazov*."

6.

And so, in the role of an insignificant numerator supporting itself on its short legs on a powerful denominator, I lived until my thirtieth year, feeling, as perhaps many of you feel, the agonizing contradiction between the fact that in my own life my personality had such tremendous, grandiose significance, but in the life of mankind as a whole its significance was no greater than that of a mouse in the cellar, of a brick in a tower, or of a numerator over a denominator.

But everything changed on that day when I found myself at the front, facing no-man's-land, squirming in a narrow trench, waiting for the signal to go over the top. It must have been the seventh attack that day, and beyond the parapet of the trench the ground was pitted and heaped by shell holes and the smaller holes made by bul-

lets and soldiers' boots, speckled with the charred stumps
of trees, and almost entirely covered with gray mounds,
some of which still twitched, others moaned, but many had
already grown stiff and become parts of that stark and terrible landscape.

And the most terrible thing was: I understood that these
mounds until just recently had been living people—even
such as I—but this understanding fizzled out on the way
from my consciousness to my heart and for some reason
never reached my heart—did not awaken within it either
sorrow or compassion, as though these mounds on the
earth were not slaughtered human beings but merely dead
ciphers.

Alongside me, almost pressed against me, a young little
soldier awaited the beginning of the attack. He was still a
boy, really. I did not know his name, not even his first
name, I only saw how from under his helmet, on his forehead wet with sweat, a small lock of hair cropped out; his
big, somehow absurd hands, the hands of an adolescent,
kept shaking so much that he could not light a cigarette,
and in his eyes there was such anguish, such helplessness,
such despair, that I almost choked with tenderness and
compassion, and suddenly he seemed to me to be a lonely
and helpless numerator without a denominator.

And when the attack started he did not leave my side for
an instant; when I hit the dirt he hit the dirt alongside me,
when I jumped up, he jumped up, too.

But then at one point he didn't jump up again. I grabbed
him by the hand: The hand was as limp as a rag. I wanted to
lift him up bodily, but all of a sudden I stumbled and fell
full length and then, still holding him, flew into an abyss.

When I returned to consciousness I felt pain. I looked
around and understood that I was lying in a ditch, in
blood, that someone was lying beside me.

And all of a sudden—stronger than the pain or the fear
—an illumination struck me: Only just now I had not existed and here I was again, I lived again and beyond the
time that had been allotted to me, let me be without legs or
arms, let me be lying in a ditch, let me be granted no more
than another minute of life—even this would be a great
happiness simply because my life had returned to me, the
only one that belonged to me, to me alone; and then, too, I

felt that I was not at all in any way a numerator, not a part of something or other, but a whole, indivisible, unreproduceable, that even my pain was mine and only mine, that no words had ever been invented that would enable me to transfer my pain to others.

And this sensation of living my own life as something that could not be fitted into any framework or system of measurement, this sensation of my own life, one fleeting moment of which means more to me than the thousands of years of life of the whole of mankind, dazzled me with such a bright flame of some long-awaited and happy enlightenment that its light lasted me to the end of my days.

Then I plunged again into oblivion, and when I came to, it was already evening and very cold.

I felt that everything was steeped in blood. I stretched toward the one who was lying next to me, touched his stone-hard face, and suddenly a great tenderness toward the young fellow, the impossibility of reconciling myself to his death, wrenched a wolf's howl of grief from my breast.

And again—a sudden illumination, different from the one before, but of such power that it tore to shreds some sort of holy veil within my mind, and I felt that the death of one is more terrible and more frightful than the deaths of thousands and millions, that there are criteria of reason and criteria of feeling, and that previously I had measured the world not by real but by false criteria, by those born of cold and passionless reason and not by living and warm feeling.

I was astounded to discover then what a distorted picture of the world my reason had created, inspiring me with such an absurdity—as though a small mountain which rises before me, and I needs must climb, were smaller than Everest which is remote from me; as though an epidemic, which destroys a whole people, were worse, more terrible, more frightful, than the sickness of one child, raving in fever and delirium.

Let any mother ask her own heart: Isn't it so? And her heart will answer: So it is!

While I choked with grief and pain, my heart hastily whispered to me that by its criteria, the criteria of feeling, one man is more than all mankind, that all the questions which had previously plagued me about the sense and the goal of life were invalid when applied to the whole of humanity, and valid when applied to each and every person. . . .

But I didn't have time to think this through, because once again an abyss opened up under me and everything ended.

Life came back to me the third time gradually: At first out of the darkness the stars appeared overhead, then some sort of purple cloud, as though it were filled full of black blood, and then—the butt-end of a rifle sticking out over the edge of the ditch.

And then, keeping pace with my returning consciousness, the universe, which had only just now been nonexistent for me, assembled. It appeared out of nothing, out of a vacuum, like the first day of creation: the sky, the earth, the dead soldier, my children, my mother, my books...

The universe filled up, as though I myself had created it out of what I knew, felt, remembered, imagined, and suddenly, for the third time that day, a new illumination—not the one that came the first time, nor the one that came the second time, but with as much and perhaps even greater power—filled the rest of my life with an unprecedented clarity.

I saw that the universe in which I live was made by me myself, just as the universe in which every other man lives is made by that man himself. In my universe there exists only that which I know and feel, but whatever I can't figure out or imagine, that doesn't exist for me, because I never met him, never heard or read anything about him—as contradistinct from my magnificent drunk, Vaska Timofeyev, who undoubtedly lives and walks the earth, this most honest and to me loyal friend. And although someone or other may consider him a drunken bum, capable of betraying me for a jigger of vodka, I don't know that, and therefore there is no such drunken bum in my universe, an impostor named Vaska Timofeyev.

I was astounded at the divine power of my creation, astounded that I was able to create planets and stars, earth and oceans, fine stands of trees and rushing brooks, and the inextinguishable lamp of the human spirit, and the loyal friend Vaska Timofeyev, and mountains, and cities, and birds, and my enemies, and wise men and good-for-nothings.

I felt myself to be great and glorious, like God, and with the same magnificent helplessness: Whom could I judge, to whom could I complain, of whom could I ask or demand if everything was created by me and everything existed only in me: my sorrows as well as my joys, my freedom as well as my captivity?

And for everything I alone was responsible: for all good-for-nothings, for all wars, for every lie, for all evil.

And you, will you please forgive me for not having been able to create the universe better: without good-for-nothings, without wars, without lies and evil? This not even the Lord God himself could do, He whom I created by the power of my imagination so that then he could create me in His image and likeness. And He and I really tried hard, believe me.

But, unfortunately, I had no rights, just as He had no rights, but only obligations—and with obligations there is nothing doing.

The obligations were inseparable from me, like hands, like feet or ears, and it didn't matter whether I liked them or not. My whole life long I carried with me the weight of my obligations, expecting no reward for so doing, just as you expect no reward for the fact that all your life you carry your hair on your head and your head on your shoulders.

And it may be that for this reason my burden seemed light and joyful to me. And although it evaporated in the air, just as the smoke from my pipe evaporates, and I knew that within a short time not a trace of it would remain in this world, I also knew that there are in this world three or four people who, inhaling this barely noticeable, slightly scented, and rather bitter bit of smoke, felt themselves in my uncomfortable universe to be just a tiny bit more comfortable and sure of themselves.

And this was enough for me to consider myself a very happy old man, because, by the criteria of my heart, three or four people are more than three or four million people.

PART TWO

Justice?

Notes from the Prisons and Labor Camps

A Visit with Andrei
at the Labor Camp

BY GUZEL AMALRIK

Translated by Alfred C. and Tanya Schmidt

From *Kontinent* No. XI, 1977

Andrei Amalrik was killed in an automobile accident on February 8, 1981, on his way to the
Madrid Conference on Security and Cooperation, an East-West meeting on human-rights and
other issues. The following two selections
are fragments from his life—this account by his
wife, and the next one, by Andrei Amalrik
himself.

In the summer of 1971 I received a letter from the labor
camp. My husband wrote that we would be permitted to
see each other in the coming winter—to spend three whole
days together! All excited, I began preparing for the trip
right away. There is a Russian proverb that says you should
fix up your sleigh in the summer and your wagon in win-

*GUZEL AMALRIK, née Makudinova, was born into a poor Tatar family in
Moscow in 1942. She has described her childhood and family in the book*
Reminiscences of My Childhood. *In 1965 she married Andrei Amalrik, who was in Siberian exile at the time. Together with her husband she
left the Soviet Union in 1976, and now she lives in Utrecht, the Netherlands. An artist by profession, she wrote the present account at Utrecht in
November 1976, five years after the events narrated.*

ter. This was the proper moment for me to heed that maxim, because in Russia you can never get what you need at the time you need it.

Winter came. A twelve-hour flight and there I was, in the dirty little airport at Magadan, only 250 kilometers away from the Talaya settlement, where my Andrei was languishing in camp. Magadan struck me as a gray and foggy place, gloomy and depressing; only the mountains surrounding the town looked beautifully majestic. The Sea of Okhotsk was frozen over, and the wind blew in powerful gusts.

Next morning I took the bus to Talaya. There was only one. Sitting in front of me was a tall thickset man, wearing a dark overcoat with the insignia of the public prosecutor on his cuffs. He exchanged glances with a young couple and frequently turned around to look at me intently. Finally he asked me if I was on my way to meet my husband. Evidently I was riding to Talaya with the public prosecutor himself!

We arrived at the settlement toward evening. In his letter, my husband had given me the address of a girl who would let me stay with her. I wandered at random, lugging my huge bundles and backpack. For a while the only people I passed were military, and I could not bring myself to ask them for directions. I approached a shriveled and wrinkled old woman, who led me uphill past a lane lined with little houses and faceless concrete three-story buildings. My load was terribly heavy, but the old woman trotted on at a lively pace, until at last we reached the communal hostel on the hill. It was a long, narrow structure painted white; people who looked like workers were constantly going in and coming out. Inside the hostel was a long hall, with doors on either side opening into the rooms.

Lena greeted me cordially. Her room was sparsely furnished: two iron beds, a small table, and a slender wardrobe, plus two chairs for which there was hardly enough space. On one of the beds sat a little girl of eight or so, licking her finger and leafing through a book whose pages were already well worn. The child was Lena's little sister; their mother was dead. Lena was twenty-six and unmarried, though to me she seemed an awfully attractive blonde.

Another unmarried young woman named Masha shared the same room, together with her daughter, who was about the same age as Lena's sister. The four of them slept on those two narrow beds. An hour after I came, Masha's friend showed up. He was drunk, and he started pawing her in front of everyone. The little girls, solemn beyond their age, understood what was going on. They huddled on a corner of the bed, playing with dolls and pretending not to notice; every so often they would glance surreptitiously at the couple and whisper between themselves. Then Lena's friend appeared. He was sober. The ten square meters of living space were insufferably crowded, and it was painful to watch those unhappy children and those unfortunate women.

The next day I went to the camp, where I was told that I would not be allowed to see my husband until evening. So I decided to have a look around the village and to visit the famous health resort of Talaya, two kilometers away from the camp. The contrast was shocking. In order to build a resort around the mineral springs, they had first set up a labor camp so that the prisoners could do the construction work. Now that resort employs many of the wives of the camp supervisors. The two girls I was staying with worked there as waitresses, and brought leftover soup and meat home to feed to their children; they were even so clever as to get away with sugar and cookies. Under the clothes in their wardrobe they kept piles of sugar taken from the resort.

I was struck by the contrast between the resort buildings —gaudy palaces, full of columns and grottoes, fountains and a pond—and the pitiful houses in the village with its rough streets strewn with chunks of the local rock.

From the window of the hostel on the hill I looked down and saw an area surrounded by a high barbed-wire fence. This was a wood-processing combine where prisoners worked. They came from the camp in long rank and file with pairs of soldiers and dogs in front and in the rear; clad in quilted jackets and tarpaulin boots, they walked with heads bowed through the freezing cold. It was twenty degrees below zero Centigrade—sometimes the temperature dropped to as low as minus sixty degrees. I ran out of the house and waved my scarf at the prisoners. Some of

them caught sight of me, and the last man in the line
waved his hand back at me. For an instant I thought it was
Andrei, although I knew that he was not supposed to go
out on heavy work details ever since he had come down
with meningitis in prison. A guard began to poke the prisoner in the back with the butt of his rifle, prodding him to
get a move on. The dogs barked loudly. Later I learned that
it was not Andrei. But I think that those prisoners were
pleased to see any woman wave at them from the hillside;
many of them knew that Andrei was expecting a visit from
his wife, and they described me to him: That is how he
learned of my arrival.

As dusk fell, I put my things together and got ready for
the visit. I was tremendously excited. It was almost like
meeting him for the first time, when we were young. Now
we had been separated for nearly a year and a half. How
would he greet me? Would there be any estrangement between us? When you live together, you do not notice
changes of character so readily as you do after long absence. It was with misgivings like this that I approached
the wall of the camp.

First they showed me into the room of the officer on
duty, took my passport and checked it for the marriage reg-
istration, then went through the entire contents of my
backpack and bundles. They even cut the chocolate into
bits to see whether it contained some sort of political proclamation or letters from friends; they also looked for a
tape recorder or camera on me. Suppose I should take a picture of my husband, who had lost twenty kilograms, all
skin and bones, and show it to the outside world! They
found my little bottle of cognac and set it aside, saying that
it was unauthorized. And here I had been so hoping that
we might celebrate the New Year ahead of time with that
token quantity of cognac.

They led me down a hall, through a door that opened
and closed automatically, then down another little hall,
and into a small room with two neatly-made iron beds, a
table, and two chairs. It resembled the girls' room at the
hostel, or any room at all in some village hotel, except that
here there were bars on the tiny window. And I had to pay
for this room, too, as I would in a hotel.

My husband was not in the room. I was confronted, instead, by an elderly woman, all dried out, with an angry expression on her face. My escorts went away; the woman sprang at me like a panther and began to frisk me. She insisted that I undress of my own accord, as much as to say: Don't lose time, you want to see your husband in a hurry, don't you? I refused to undress. Then she simply felt me over, fingering the seams in my clothes; she grabbed my comb and jerked it through my hair, thinking that maybe I was hiding something up there. I thought I was dreaming. Like a sleepwalker, I resisted feebly; she ran the comb through one last time, and apparently convinced herself that she would find nothing of interest in my hair. When I threatened to complain, she snapped back that she was afraid of nobody, that she had been in this place for thirty years, that she knew all the rules and regulations and followed them. She tried to take away my fountain pen and even my eyebrow pencil, but I absolutely refused to give them up.

Finally the old woman left. I was upset and in tears. Expecting Andrei to appear at any moment, I slipped into a lovely French negligee, lit a candle, and spread our old red tablecloth on the table. It was our favorite, though shabby, and I had brought it with me from home. The door opened. There stood the slender figure of my husband—or rather his shadow, he was so thin. He wore a white cap like a clown's hat and gray overalls with a number sewed on. We flew into each other's arms. I had the feeling we had never been apart, but the sight of his face jolted me back to reality: He was terribly emaciated and covered with pimples from lack of vitamins.

Those three days were a dream for us. We did not want to think how quickly the time would pass. With the delicious things I had brought from Moscow I tried to fatten Andrei up a little bit. I did the cooking right there in the room on an electric hot plate, but my husband was practically unable to eat. After the first supper he was so ill that the very next day the camp doctor had to be summoned to give him a shot. I will have a word to say later about that female doctor.

I was very excited. Three days was not enough time for all the news we had to share. I tried to write down on paper everything important I had to tell him, and we talked under the blanket, for we knew that the room was bugged. Andrei also wrote a long letter to his Dutch friend Karel van het Rewe, describing how he had been transported across Siberia as a sick man. It would be up to me to smuggle this letter out and send it to Holland.

When we parted, I gave Andrei some warm underwear. I also wanted to leave him a pair of shorts, into the waistband of which I had sewn a few ten-ruble notes, so that he would have the means to buy smuggled-in food at the camp. But he declined to keep the shorts, explaining that when they searched him after our visit they would certainly discover the money and confiscate it.

They came and took Andrei away. I was left alone. Suddenly an officer and two women entered the room. One of them was the old woman who had searched me. She was employed at the camp as a censor, reading the prisoners' mail. The other, a younger woman, was the doctor who had examined Andrei. She wore a white smock and gynecological gloves. The officer said that these women would rapidly look through my things and then release me. He walked out. The women got busy on the clothing, checked every seam, and were delighted at finding the money sewn into the shorts. The old woman, throwing hostile glances at me, turned to her partner and said: "People like this ought to be shot, nobody would miss them!" To me she added: "We work hard and never go anywhere, we make a contribution to the State, while all you do is spread slander, you anti-Soviets. Your husband is getting off light. If it were up to me, I'd let him rot here." I was silent and I gritted my teeth. Then, unable to hold back, I called her an old Fascist.

After my belongings had been inspected, the women asked me to undress, but I refused. I was not an inmate of the camp, hence not obliged to strip and be searched. The woman with the rubber gloves was ready. I began to scream at them and demanded to see the public prosecutor. Grinning insolently, they sat down at the table where my husband and I had breakfasted that morning. One woman said to the other: "I feel like a cup of tea." The doctor kept her rubber gloves on while drinking her tea and even took a piece of sugar without removing them.

Two hours passed. I kept repeating that, however long

they might detain me, I would not allow myself to be searched and would speak only with the prosecutor. Two more hours went by, and I was hungry. I still had a lot of good things left to eat, because the prisoners were not permitted to take food back with them after a visit. I ate, and the women looked at me with envy: They drank their tea with plain dry bread. I then dozed for a spell, which made them so furious that they began to quarrel with each other. The doctor said crossly: "My work day is over, my son is already back from school, and I'm not home yet!"

At that point I had to step out for a moment, but they would not let me go. They brought a bucket, placed it in the middle of the room, and said: "We aren't men, go ahead, don't mind us." Praying silently to all the saints that I would not accidentally drop Andrei's papers, which I had so carefully hidden, I succeeded in relieving myself right under the watchful gaze of those two pairs of eyes. The women appeared to relax somewhat. One of them left the room and returned ten minutes later with the public prosecutor for the Magadan region. He was the man who had been on the bus with me, yet all the while they had been trying to tell me that there was no prosecutor here.

The prosecutor greeted me like an old acquaintance. After listening to me attentively, he gave the order for my release, but only on condition that I report to the camp commander. On my way through the hall I ran into the young couple who had also been on the bus. When they saw me they retreated into one of the rooms. Later I learned that KGB agents had arrived on the scene to stay for the entire length of my visit: Perhaps these two were the agents.

The camp commander rose from his desk and walked up to me with a smile. That surprised me. Usually the chief remains seated, eyes the visitor with a cold stare, mutters a greeting through his teeth, and proceeds with formal questioning. But this chief politely inquired about my meeting with my husband. I began to tell him about the six-hour search. He asked how it happened that a pair of men's shorts was found among my effects, with money sewn into the seam. Keeping myself under control, I replied: "What makes you think those shorts were meant for my husband? They were not found on him. They are my shorts, and I sewed the money in so as not to lose it while I was traveling." I doubt that he believed me, but he did not bring up the matter again. Subsequently, my husband submitted a complaint, and they had to return the money.

The commander asked whether I was acquainted with Solzhenitsyn and why he wrote only about the horrors, painting everything black. Don't we have our brighter side, too? I asked him if he had read Solzhenitsyn's books.

"I have only read *One Day in the Life of Ivan Denisovich*. A very interesting story."

"Then how can you say that he writes only horrible things, if all you have read is one story of his?"

"I have read the reviews in the newspapers, and I have no reason to disbelieve them."

That was the end of our discussion of Solzhenitsyn. The commander stood up. Taking a fountain pen from his pocket, he said it was a Korean pen and that he was giving it to me as a present. In a fairly friendly manner he showed me to the door, smiling as before. Perhaps he was simply being clever with me, fearing that once back in Moscow I might complain about the way I was treated here; or perhaps he really sympathized with me. I had the impression that his job was beginning to be too much for him. And indeed, he was relieved of his duties shortly thereafter.

Freedom at last! It was already dark outside, and there was a moon. I was in a state of agitation. After I had walked barely three hundred meters, I instinctively turned around and went back to the camp. I walked up to the headquarters building, looked into the lighted window, and saw my husband. He was standing and arguing with the duty officer. I rapped on the window and shouted through the transom that everything was all right, that they had held me for six hours but now I was fine. "Take care of yourself, and be sure to wear the cap I brought you." Andrei was terribly happy to see me. He had been worried about me and now he felt better. We said good-bye over and over again through the window, until the officer rudely interrupted our excited cries, slammed the transom shut, and drew the curtain.

Calmly I walked back to the village. I was on my way back to Magadan and Moscow. Later I gave Andrei's letter to friends who took it to Holland, and Karel van het Rewe still has that letter in his strongbox.

From the Notes
of a Revolutionary

BY ANDREI AMALRIK

Translated by Edward Van Der Rhoer

From *Kontinent* No. XIV (German edition),
1980

A slight feeling of hunger and lack of money are familiar to many young writers and artists, but in our case these were scarcely linked to any hope—our life style constituted a challenge to the system, which does not regard hunger alone as in any sense an adequate punishment.

ANDREI AMALRIK was born in 1938 in Moscow. He was expelled in 1963 from Moscow University because he advocated a point of view opposed to official historiography in his dissertation, "The Normans and Kievan Russia." Thereafter Amalrik worked as a construction worker, film technician, proofreader, and postman, among other things. On the side, he wrote stage plays that were never actually performed but cost him sixteen months of Siberian exile. He describes his experiences in exile in the book Involuntary Journey to Siberia. *On May 20, 1970, he was again arrested on account of his essay, "Will the Soviet Union Survive Until 1984?" which had become famous, and was sentenced on November 12, 1970, in Sverdlovsk, due to "slander of the Soviet state and social order" (Paragraph 190), to three years in a labor camp, which he served in the remote Northeast. In 1976 he emigrated with his wife Guzel. After sojourns in the Netherlands and the U.S.A., he lived as a free-lance writer in France. He was killed in an automobile accident in February 1981 on his way to the Madrid Conference.*

We lived at that time in a large apartment occupied by various parties on Vakhtangov Street nearly in the middle of the Arbat. From an anteroom in which a dim lamp burned—the neighbors kept shutting it off on grounds of economy—an L-shaped, narrow corridor led by the kitchen, where laundry was drying in the smoke and old women with bored faces stood at their tables, past the bathroom in which a woman neighbor was washing laundry while lowering her head into the trough and extending into the corridor her broad rear end covered by blue flannel underpants, past a curtain under which suitcases bulged, past large and small doors, past little cupboards lining the wall—and finally this corridor ended at the door of our room.

If you opened the door, however, you would hit a grand piano. The grand piano took up half of our room, although neither Guzel nor I knew how to play it. It came to me as an inheritance from an aunt, a singer, and was about as useful to me as an elephant to a poor Indian. Moreover, it was completely wrecked, only a couple of lunatics occasionally played it: Guzel's sister and the painter Sveryev, and—in truth—they elicited from it magnificent sounds, Sveryev often doing so even with his head. Aside from the grand piano, there stood in the room a sofa, a clothes cupboard, a writing desk, and the remains of a buffet that Grandmother and Grandfather had purchased at the time of their marriage in 1905, in the year of the first Russian revolution. Later, as our financial position began to improve a little, we built a large wooden bookcase to replace the buffet. While I was in prison, one of Guzel's friends, Susanna Jacobi, wrote an article in *The New York Times Magazine* about me and, evidently wishing to show the precariousness of our life, mentioned a "rickety bookcase." I liked the article, but as soon as I came to the place about the bookcase I was on the point of writing a reply: I took pride in it, it had been constructed according to my own design, and I figured that Soviet power would grow shaky and collapse before my bookcase did. We made a present of the bookcase and the grand piano to our friend Yuri Orlov before we flew abroad, and it now stands unshakably in his home, but—alas—while I write these lines he is locked up in Lefortovo prison.[1]

At first we possessed only two chairs. On the back of one of them I nailed a strip to which I attached a tin can, and in this way there came into being an easel on which Guzel did some beautiful portraits. Unfortunately, she was able to work only in sunny weather: From the room one looked out into a dusky shaft of a backyard of the Arbat, on whose ground there was a men's toilet. People used to make a little fun of us, especially the foreigners, because we, who lacked even a dining table, filled half the room with a useless grand piano. But precisely its lack of any utility and its beauty, together with the pictures, the old books, the grandfather clock, and some cobweblike dried plants on the cupboard, lent our room an atmosphere like that in a fairy tale. I felt this particularly strongly when I returned home from many years in exile.

Our apartment formed, so to speak, a microcosm of the Soviet world. Directly behind the entrance door there lived an older Jewish couple. The husband, a major, worked in a nebulous institution but cautiously expressed his enthusiasm for Israel. The wife mainly concerned herself with preparation of the midday meal for her husband, behaving deferentially toward the influential neighbors and benevolently toward the others. Guzel learned from her how to prepare excellent Jewish fish dishes. An old Communist, as squat as a mushroom and with a rasping voice, seldom came out of his room, but his wife made up for it by reigning in the kitchen, a tall, vigorous person. Guzel thought of her at once when she read Gabriel García Marquez's book, *One Hundred Years of Solitude*. She always emphasized her devotion to the Soviet regime and was very proud of the fact that her son was a public prosecutor; incidentally, he had been fired for accepting bribes. She spent hours on the telephone discussing the book she had just read or the film she had last seen. This would have even been childishly touching if there had been more than a single telephone for all the residents. If one passed her room, one could hear the BBC, Radio Deutsche Welle, or

[1]The KGB investigation prison in Moscow, where Orlov was held until his deportation to the Perm camp.—TRANS.

the Voice of America; the old man expressed the view that
it was necessary to know one's enemy, besides, listening to
foreign radios was the favorite pastime of Soviet pensioners. This happened to end badly for him: After he heard
that this or that dissident had been arrested, another
placed in a psychiatric clinic, still another exiled from
Moscow, he suddenly became obsessed, as he was being
transported to a little house in the country, with the idea
that he was being exiled from Moscow, and cried and kept
repeating: "Of all people, me, me, who honorably served
Soviet power all my life." He died soon afterward.

Across the way there lived a mother, an old lady with
sunken mouth, and her forty-year-old daughter. The
mother had moved in from a village long ago, but she still
retained some bad rural habits, while the daughter was the
manager of a bakery. In the next room there lived a purple-
faced man who had married a woman from a health resort
in the south in the hope that he could live summers with
her, but she had married him because she expected him to
obtain a residence permit in Moscow for her. But since they
distrusted one another and the one did not want to help
the other to obtain a residence permit, this marriage was
breaking up before our eyes. A little farther on there was
the room of an acidulous lady of seventy, the widow of a
colonel, and thus the apartment became a battlefield of
ambition—who was more important: the widow of a colonel or the wife of a major (if only a major, but a living one
just the same), the manager of a bakery or the mother of a
public prosecutor (if only a former one, but a public prosecutor is still not the same as a baker)?

And last but not least there lived directly next to us two
women without any social inferiority complex: the emaciated and bony Olya, forty-five years old, and her aunt,
whom she called "Grandmother." Olya's under-age son
was in jail because of his participation in a gang rape.
When Olya got drunk—this happened nearly every day—
she turned up a tape to full volume and yelled, pounding
her fist on the table: "Grandmother, I drink, I booze!"
"Bah, bah, bah!" answered the grandmother. Toward the
end of the tape the music became somewhat softer and a
firm male voice imitated the intonation of a radio announcer and said: "This music has been recorded for Olya

Vorontsova by the senior operator of the motion-picture theater 'Scene'!" "Did you hear, Grandmother, this is for me, the music!" yelled Olya, and in reply you heard: "Bah —bah—bah!" A little later they were assigned another apartment, and a worker couple—the fat Tanya with the slender Vanya—moved in instead of the acidulous lady.

Guzel worked very energetically, she rapped with a shoebrush on the canvas so that the chair shook, and worked out a unique style of her own—in some ways she followed her teacher Vassili Sitnikov, in some ways Vladimir Weysberg, but in drawing and in the emotional perception of nature she was closest to Modigliani and van Dongen, whose pictures we only knew at that time from reproductions. What Guzel painted was so far removed from Socialist Realism that she had no chance, and not even the wish, to be admitted into the Union of Artists and to receive official commissions. The first picture Guzel sold was a portrait of the wife of a correspondent whom I visited at Ginzburg's wish. It seemed that they hesitated rather long to buy this portrait: The portrait was really good, and for us it was almost a question of life and death, because we were completely penniless at the time; and after we received sixty-six dollars we felt like tremendous Croesuses. First of all, we bought a lovely jersey suit for Guzel: before that she had worn the discarded clothes of her friends.

It was foreigners above all who began to order portraits from Guzel from time to time. I owned a small collection of works by young painters that I had assembled before my first exile. They had turned over a part of the pictures to me for sale, and I did sell some of them—a circumstance that provided a certain help to us. The rulers rejected the uncanonized art, there were hardly any rich collectors, and the foreign colony in Moscow represented essentially the only market. There were several reasons why painting came into fashion among Moscow foreigners. In the first place, the low prices in Moscow made paintings accessible to those who would not have been able to buy the paintings of good artists in their own homeland. Secondly, many people in a foreign land would like to acquire something characteristic of this land and yet relatively rare; thus foreigners purchased, for example, Russian icons as readily as the pictures of contemporary painters. Thirdly, the unofficial art reflected the foreigners' hopes for a "liberalization" of the Soviet system. An art that contained the element of protest and still was permitted by the authorities was the best evidence for such a liberalization....

I wished to be a guest of foreigners and to invite them to my home, to associate with them as if we were just the same type of people they were and they were the same type of people we were. Although this will strike many Americans and Europeans as a commonplace—how can one deal with people otherwise?—I introduced, strictly speaking, a regular revolution. The word "foreigner" has been and is endowed with a mystical sense in Russia—and at that it is not only a question of the barriers erected by the state but also the ingrained tradition of isolation and the inferiority complex upon which the Soviet regime has imposed the form of ideological exclusivity.

Foreigners in the Soviet Union also have begun to regard themselves as beings of a special sort—most of them have promptly accepted the rules laid down by the authorities. Many have managed to live for years in Russia or to undertake long journeys without even meeting a single Russian except for the officials who accompany them. And then books are written about Russia in which they cite as the worst shortcomings the unusually long delay in getting a waiter in a restaurant, or a garbage pile outside a window. Accordingly these empirical data were generalized and the theory of convergence emerged.

After I had begun the "revolution in relations," I was not only confronted with my exile to Siberia but also with a rumor that was actually circulated by the foreigners themselves, according to which I was a KGB agent. When in 1976 in New York I received the Prize of the League of Human Rights, I listened with pleasure to Pavel Litvinov,[2] who spoke first of all not about my books but about the fact that I was the first to begin this unofficial process of communication and by this very means made mutual understanding possible. Ginzburg had the same thing in view when he said that I knew how to "deal with foreigners."

[2]A well-known civil-rights activist now living in the U.S.

* * *

(After the Trial of November 11, 1970:)

One experiences a sentence almost like a new arrest. Moreover, I was faced with a move to a strange cell—the convicted are immediately moved, and this also resembles a new arrest. But to my relief I was brought back to the old one, where Zhenya awaited me with impatience.

The next day Shveisky[3] said that he had appealed to the Supreme Court of the U.S.S.R.; since, however, I had refused to recognize the court proceedings, I decided that I myself would make no appeal against the verdict. In response to the question whether he could transmit the text of my final statement to Guzel, Shveisky answered with a determined "No." So there remained only one last chance: another meeting with Guzel. When I was brought to my attorney, I imagined at first that I was being conducted to her, and while I spoke with Shveisky the final statement literally stuck in my teeth.[4] Early that morning I had sharpened a pencil with a razor blade I had secretly put away, and copied my statements to the court in tiny letters, folded up the slip of paper very tightly, wrapped it in cellophane, and tied it through the middle with a thread—this produced a little capsule I concealed in my mouth and kept there the whole time in order to become used to it and speak naturally. I wrote down the whole of it on an ordinary sheet of paper and hid it in my pants—I hoped that this sheet would be found during the search before our meeting and that my jailers would be satisfied. I had intentionally crumpled it up so as to pretend that I had no intention of passing it to my wife but to retain it for toilet paper. And I actually remained calm when I was brought to the examining magistrate or to the public prosecutor, to my enemies, but before my meeting with Guzel and my attorney I had abdominal cramps.

I could not copy everything without Zhenya noticing it —he could have betrayed me when I was brought to my attorney or now as well, when I was again immediately

[3]Amalrik's attorney, who also defended V. Bukovsky in 1972.— TRANS.

[4]A figure of speech corresponding in Russian to the German "zum Hals heraushängen" (to be fed up with, be sick of).—TRANS.

torney or now as well, when I was again immediately
called out. Two guards searched me, detected the paper
under my rear waistband, and carried it out with satisfied
faces into the neighboring room. Then I was led to the visiting room and caught sight of Guzel. Zhenya had not betrayed me!

We were placed at opposite ends of a long table and
warned that we were not allowed to kiss or to touch one
another. An impenetrable metal barrier ran under the table, at the end sat two women attendants who attentively
listened to and watched everything. But at least we saw
one another and could speak to each other. Such conversations always began in somewhat confused circumstances,
one wanted to talk about something important but only
brought forth banalities. I wanted to know whether Guzel
had been left in peace during this month. And she told
how, before her departure for Sverdlovsk, she had been
followed by a black car from which someone called out to
her: "Guzel, just look out, it will get still worse!" It seemed
to me that we still had a lot of time ahead of us; usually, visiting time lasted up to two hours, but not even twenty minutes had passed when an attendant said: "Visiting time has
expired!" And although we started to argue, it was clear
that this was useless. They were already pulling us in different directions, and then Guzel and I embraced and
kissed one another while we leaned forward over the
broad table with the attendants hanging onto us. And
while I kissed her, I tried to push the cellophane container
with my tongue between her lips—the thought of it had
not left me throughout our whole meeting. But Guzel did
not understand me, she saw the kiss only as an expression
of tenderness and love in parting—and the container
nearly fell onto the table. Guzel, however, caught it and
quickly stuck it into her mouth.

"She has swallowed—swallowed something!" cried both
attendants.

"Swallow it, baby, and pass it off!" I was barely able to
call out. I had no doubt that they were capable of pulling
my message out of her mouth but would never go to the extreme of cutting open her stomach. I heard Guzel answer
the attendants in a calm voice that she had not swallowed
anything but that, because of excitement, saliva had
dripped out of her mouth.

For months I repeated my speech by heart because I intended, if it had been confiscated from Guzel after all or if it was dissolved in her stomach, I would dictate it anew to her during a personal meeting in the camp. Guzel related later that her throat had dried up so much as a result of excitement she absolutely could not at first get the capsule down but ultimately, while convulsively choking, managed to swallow it. And then a doctor turned up, and Guzel really was overcome by the fear that she would be subjected to an operation and began excitedly to repeat her version of the dripping saliva. The doctor listened to her irresolutely and with a slightly ironical smile, and went away with the words that medicine could not do anything in this case. After Guzel was held for about two hours, she was set free.

"We already thought that they had arrested you." Lena, who had waited with a friend in the vicinity of the prison, rushed toward her with these words. "Did you get the final statement? Yes? Where is it?"

"Here it is," said Guzel, pointing to her stomach.

Concerned that my speech would not long remain there, they rushed to the nearest restaurant. Under the astonished gazes of people at the neighboring table, Guzel mixed vodka with port wine, peppered the mixture, and drank up two glasses of it. When she grew nauseated, she went with tottering steps to the toilet: "At the first attempt nothing came out, but I gathered all my strength, and I was choked again—and, oh joy, the undamaged container lay in the sink, so well packed that only a single word had been obliterated."

And Even Our Tears

BY ARMAND MALOUMIAN

Translated by Edward Van Der Rhoer

From *Kontinent* No. XX, 1979

In the world of concentration camps, where the soul is laid bare, the varnish of upbringing and education flies off like enamel from a dropped bowl. Anyone who has gone through the KGB's rolling mill, through corporal and spiritual suffering, is capable of appraising and measuring a person with the first and only glance because only the catalyst called "Gulag life" makes it possible to detect unerringly the difference between good and bad people and arrive at a choice. Hunger, cold, fear, horrible crowding, and exhausting, killing labor alone can perhaps reveal the true worth of a human being.

If in the era of Gulag it was extremely complicated to remain Don Quixote, I encountered him none the less.

Wasn't he really a knight, like Cervantes' hero? One of

ARMAND MALOUMIAN *was born in 1928 in Marseilles into a family of Armenian refugees who settled in France after the massacre of the Armenians in Turkey in 1915. In 1944 he lied about his age and joined the Second Armored Division of General Leclerc. In 1947 he moved with his family to Soviet Armenia, where his father, an eminent specialist in athletic traumatology, was offered a professorship in medicine. Vastly disappointed in the Armenian version of Soviet reality, the Maloumian family soon discovered that it was not free to return to France. Efforts to contact the French embassy resulted in prosecution by the Soviet authorities. Armand was arrested on charges of espionage and treason. The family managed to return to France only in 1954. Armand was released two years later, after having spent eight years in Soviet prisons and concentration camps.*

those amazing people who devote their lives to the defense of widows and orphans, who struggle on behalf of truth, justice, purity, who are seeking...Don Quixote's grave?

When Vladimir Maximov asked me to write about our mutual friend, I realized that I would not be able to write a funeral eulogy to a great writer whom Russia has lost: That has already been done, and done beautifully.[1] Besides, that is not at all in my character.

Yuriy Dombrovsky is dead.

His work will live. His undeniable talent will be subjected to careful analysis and criticism, it will be evaluated. His books will enter world literature through the front door.

As far as I am concerned, I prefer to acquaint readers with the *zek* (prisoner), with a man, with my friend.

Enemies? Oh, yes, he had them. Intolerance and folly of the human sort. The only two eternal "subjects," as he used to say. He could not bear the cowardice and groveling of those who submitted to any humiliation in order to survive.

For Yuriy there existed two sorts of *zeks* in the camps— those capable of struggle and others "awaiting freedom through amnesty." (He used the acronym of this expression: ASS.)

I bestowed three nicknames on this tall, angular fellow: Raven, Nose, and Don Quixote. He really bore some resemblance to a raven: eyes sunk deep in the sockets, caution, intelligence, and natural leanness accentuated by the "shaped haircut" that was obligatory in the "rest homes" and by the blue caps issued to us. I must confess that he was not very fond of this nickname, which reminded him of the "Black Maria" (in which prisoners were transported) and the raven of fables.

"Nose"? His was expressive, solid, of impressive dimensions. Yuriy greatly liked the famous tirade of Cyrano de Bergerac I recited to him in a punitive cell, and every time

---

[1]Dombrovsky died of a heart attack in Moscow in 1978. His book *La Faculté de L'Inutile* appeared in France in 1979 when it received the prize as the best foreign book of the year. The eulogy was written by Jean Cathalé in the course of his review of the book on that occasion.

we got into an argument with the State Security types and "Nose" wanted to give me a sign that it was his turn to speak, he made the gesture of Rostand's hero and said: "I am the last to get the message. . . ."

Nevertheless, "Don Quixote" fitted him best of all. His humaneness, simplicity, and sensitivity were hidden beneath the mask of a grumbler; he possessed great intellect, humor as sharp as a Toledo blade, the nobility and pride of a Spanish grandee. But his height and leanness, which have already been mentioned, made him resemble a windmill, like those with which he had resolved to fight—all he needed to do was to raise his arms, and the illusion would have been complete.

In revenge he gave me the nickname "Duval"—based on the character of Dumas *fils* with whom I shared a name and . . . Koch's bacillus (he from Marguerite Gautier, I from the sixth tuberculosis barrack).

"Vorkuta!"

"Norilsk!"

At the sound of the watchword that the names of those two concentration-camp complexes have become, after heroic and unforgettable revolts, glass is shattered and doors fly off their hinges under the blows of planks. The Taishet punitive cell block 601 is captured in its turn by *zeks.* The guard force runs away, although we assure them that none will come to any harm. Turmoil and commotion, with the clamor of an Oriental bazaar, reign in the punitive cell block. Prisoners wander from one barrack to the other. A group of thieves "by law" come toward us to congratulate us on our victory over the "bitches" (trusties). There are also several people of the 58th, and above their heads there rises up one that strongly resembles a crow, surrounded by sparrows and pigeons. The "head" comes close to me, warmly squeezes my hand, and introduces himself:

"Yuriy Osipovich Dombrovsky, an enemy of the people by grace of the Kremlin charlatans, by profession an old camp inmate. Happy to be that and to make your acquaintance in this *dacha.*"

"Armand Jean-Baptiste Maloumian, a traitor to the homeland that was never mine, by the grace of 'the Mustache' and the manipulations of State Security alchemists."

"You're French?"

"Yes. From Paris. At the present time I'm resting at a health resort on a twenty-five-year pass. My profession is to be irreconcilable."

One of the criminals asks me:

"How did you land here?"

"Permit me, sir, said Dombrovsky, with special emphasis on the *s* and winking with the edge of his eye, "permit me, sir, to speak with my brothers of the 58th.[2] In our days, in our time of hanging heads and concerted silence, it is absolutely incredible to meet *zeks* that have organized a political strike, beaten up 'bitches,' and smashed windows and doors in the punitive cell block. Good heavens, what an age! And what will become of all those blabbers, *provocateurs*, and their bosses?"

That's how we became acquainted, and if there are people in this world that make friends at their first meeting and for all their lives, then Yuriy undoubtedly was one of them.

Now I reproach myself for not describing Yuriy during his lifetime in *Sons of Gulag*. All because of that damned fear of causing trouble for those "who were there."

I met him again when I found myself for three weeks in the same punitive cell block 601, then later in the BUR [*barak usilennovo rezhima*, disciplinary barrack] where I spent two weeks, in Taishet, in a transit camp. As you might have noticed, our periodic meetings occurred in places of a "privileged" nature, which could be called seminars for "model" *zeks*.

We slept six in a room (designed for two), a circumstance that was almost luxurious by Gulag standards. It was summer, holiday time, hot weather, and the air in the room was saturated with the sweet smell of the slop bucket and the exhalations of six bodies. Opening my eyes from time to time, I saw Raven, enthroned on the slop bucket like Job on a heap of his own excrement and just as indigent, conversing with an Estonian from Tartu, Ewald B. I heard him quote Kierkegaard, Jaspers, and Heidegger.

"Look, Armand has woken up. Did you have nice dreams, old man?"

---

[2]People convicted under Article 58 of the R.S.F.S.R. Criminal Code relating to "counterrevolutionary crime."

"No. Nonexistence. Hearing you mention those names, I waited until you spoke of 'existence' so as to make the transition to existentialism and Sartre, representing nonexistence."

"True, I was just about to go on to that, although I don't bear any special love toward him and his kind, who, with their writings and thoughtless positions, assist the very people that are burying us. With his 'man is liberty without any link to a divine being,' he nicely subscribes to the Kremlin's general line."

"I beg you, Don Quixote, leave that salon nihilist to his fate."

"Well spoken, but Sartre's influence on the flower of modern youth will not be reduced by such a thing. And that's serious. He is doing a lot of harm, for every sneeze of his is translated into fifteen languages. Returning to our conversation,"—he turned again to Ewald—"the definition of semantics I have given you is quite scholastic, for in our days, from the Marxist perspective, even the study of the origins of a word changes according to political necessity."

"Precisely, Nose—according to the camp in which it is used, a word may either lose its meaning completely or acquire the opposite sense."

"What do you mean to say by that, Armand?"

"For example, one and the same man may be an 'intelligence officer' for the country that sends him and a 'spy' for the country in which he operates. Meanwhile, his functions are not at all changed by that."

"You hit it. Just so. A terrorist becomes a 'fighter of the people's army of liberation,' an executioner becomes an 'executive,' a deserter is a 'high-principled ally,' a criminal 'socially close,' a traitor a 'genuine patriot,' but you, my dear Armand, who fought against Nazism, you are called a 'fascist' by people that use *their* methods."

"Do me a favor, Yuriy, say what you think of the piquant redundancy 'people's democracy.' "

"Yes, it's really savory. But I think there is an explanation for it. The rulers of these countries know perfectly well that their regimes are not in the least democracies, but wish to persuade the whole world that they are popular. In addition, they don't know Greek, and encyclopedias are reactionary. The mischief of the century—the concentration camp—has become a 'camp for work reeducation.' And our brothers restore to the ITL [*ispravitel'no-trudoviye lageri*, corrective labor camps] their real meaning—*istrebitel'no-trudoviye lageri* [extermination labor camps]."

"How right you are, Don Quixote! Since then, everything has continued in the same spirit: Revolts of workers in East Berlin, Budapest, and Prague became 'fascist onslaughts,' the free world is the 'camp of warmongers,' NATO is the 'army of mercenary revanchists,' the troops of the Warsaw Pact are 'guarantors of peace,' the Wall of Shame is the 'Wall of Peace.' 'Socialism' constructed paradise on earth and, in order to protect the elect against temptation, surrounded it with barbed wire, watch towers, and a curtain—whether the curtain is iron, silk, bamboo, or of reeds."

We encountered one another again—this time for several months—in Hospital No. 2 in Novo-Chunka, where there was a transit camp for the ones whom Khrushchev and Bulganin released—not, as some think, because they had a higher sense of justice, and not due to pangs of conscience, not out of humanity, but out of necessity. The "contingent of prisoners" was unproductive and unsuitably employed, while numerous mutinies and strikes in the camps threatened to merge into a general insurrection.

Our meeting was joyful and moving, although Raven did not belong to the class of people that are called effusive. He very rarely bestowed on anyone real confidence, but those who knew him and merited his friendship were aware of the value he placed on that concept. And if I was proud to be called his friend, he was proud to be called mine.

One of Yuriy's characteristics was his erudition. He corresponded with his mother in Latin. That became the occasion for a most amusing scene that took place in the office of the "godfather" from the MVD, whither I and three of our other comrades escorted Yuriy, in accordance with a rule that we had laid down at that time.

"What's this?—you too, Dombrovsky, are participating in this comedy—going with a retinue when you are called in by an officer of State Security? You're not from Vorkuta, as far as I know!"

"No, and that's what I regret most of all about my career as a *zek*, God knows to whom I owe that debt. I would have liked to see how the Moscow command was forced to send a delegation of forty high-level officials, led by the Procurator General of the U.S.S.R. and the Deputy Minister of Internal affairs, to conduct negotiations with striking political prisoners."

"What a joke!"

"A joke? But your Kremlin bosses must have thought differently if they sent Rudenko and Maslennikov with a letter signed by Voroshilov and Pegov and giving them the right to act in the name of the Soviet government and take essential measures on the spot—a letter that they were forced to show the *zeks* at the very outset of negotiations."

"Nonsense!"

"Then why do you allow four prisoners to accompany me and be present during this conversation? Do you call that a comedy? If political prisoners had established this rule earlier, you would have been long since out of work, Comrade Godfather, you would have had to earn your bread by the sweat of your brow, which, as I realize, you still have not had to do."

"That's enough, Dombrovsky. Stop being rude. I called you not to make speeches here but to translate this letter for me, it's written in a foreign language."

"In Latin."

"Well, well—in Latin. Translate it."

"I categorically refuse, Citizen Chief. I have never been your accomplice, making it easier for you to do your . . . work."

"I'll confine you [*tebya*], Dombrovsky."

"In English the address 'thou' is only used to God and in poetry. Two areas that are absolutely unknown to you. Therefore I didn't hear your words."

"What has English got to do with it? *You're* a Russian, or what?"

"Russian. But not Soviet. And in general I intend to become a British subject, for in that country you only have contact with gentlemen, who respect others, their personal life, correspondence. Normal aspects of life that are, of course, unknown to you."

"You think that if you're freed and this . . . rea . . . reha . . . rebili . . ."

"Just a little more effort, Comrade Chief. You have learned a new word to add to the five you already know: 'denunciation,' 'affidavit,' 'stool pigeon,' 'provocation,' and 'sentence.' *Rehabilitation*—is that sufficiently clear?"

"All right, if you don't want to translate it, I'll ask one of the others. . . . Look, you're a priest, you must know Latin?" he said, addressing Father K., a Pole from Krakow.

"I don't know the Russian language."

"If you don't know Russian, what are you doing here?"

"I am giving them the support of the Church."

". . ." (A masterly checkmate had occurred.)

"Well, just wait, you'll have time to learn Russian in jail. You, Morozov."[3]

"I—know Latin! What's with you, Chief, are there flies in your head? I can hardly write my own name. You should open a new case of sabotage against those who put me in jail and prevented me from learning Latin, which is so necessary to you today in order to learn strategic secrets that the prisoner Dombrovsky, despite early release and rehabilitation, continues to transmit to his mother."

"O.K., O.K., Morozov. But you, despite being freed, still haven't been rea—amnestied. Just wait a little bit."

"I've been waiting ten years already. My term has been extended from one phone call to the next so that I don't even have any pants to take off now."

"What about you, B., you're a student of phi . . . lo . . . lol . . . ?"

"Yes, Chief."

"Translate it."

"Bandera people don't cooperate with you."

"Ten days—do you hear?—ten days in the lockup!"

"That would surprise me very much. I have been taken off work, so I am no longer on the camp list. You see only my shadow now, in reality I'm not here."

"It's no use asking you, Maloumian, of course. As always, you answer 'no.' "

"Yes, for the first time I agree with you: I say 'no.' "

[3]Semyen Morozov, my good and courageous comrade, who took part in all the battles, was killed three days after his liberation, by two "bitches" from the railroad gang we manhandled in the transit camp at Taishet.

"I know, I know. You're taking advantage of the lack of discipline and the present liberalism, but that won't last long. You still have a long time to serve here. Wait, I'll do a nice thing to you!"

"Another one?"

The furious "godfather" lowered his head, thought a little, then suddenly broke into laughter, and shouted to the messenger:

"Korneichuk!"

"At your command, Comrade Chief!"

"Find Gusev, the chief doctor, for me as soon as possible!"

"Yes, Comrade Chief."

Captain Mel'nik smoked a "Kazbek," inhaled with enjoyment, and looked at us all with an ironic glance.

"You think you're the most clever, you ragged bums, more clever than everybody. You decided to wrap an old Chekist around your finger. Think about it . . . if you can. Incomprehensible? Camp infirmary equals doctor equals Latin!"

Satisfied with his deduction, he began to laugh self-confidently.

"What elegant dialectics," Yuriy said rapturously, adding: "The namesake of your messenger undoubtedly lost his wings[4] . . . . he has been plucked by you."

Into the office came the chief doctor, Gusev, a man who was not unkind; a nice fellow but not a courageous man. Moreover, he was also a bad surgeon—a combination of qualities permitting him to fill the position of a civilian chief doctor in a hospital for prisoners.

"Good day, Comrade Captain. You asked for me?"

Gusev surveyed our group with alarm. A complaint? In the present circumstances it is dangerous. A denunciation? That is not like these five. We see by his face that he has become a little calmer. The vodka he had drunk before he answered the godfather's summons has begun to have its effect. Ninety-proof spirits with slightly sweetened water has a double value: first of all, for the alcoholic content, secondly, for costing nothing, since it was intended for the treatment of *zeks*.

[4]He had in mind A. Korneichuk, author of the play *Wings*.

"Hello, doctor. Please translate this letter written in Latin for me."

"But . . ."

"You're a doctor, so you must know Latin."

Alcohol had obviously put Gusev in a state of exceptional good humor, so that he lost all caution. He was in that state of euphoria illustrated by two proverbs: "What a sober man thinks, a drunken man says," and "When a man is drunk, the world lies at his feet."

"Latin? Not particularly. Why, is it very necessary?"

We laughed with all our hearts—except for Captain Mel'nik, of course. Even Gusek smiled, as if he had played a good trick on the godfather.

"What, are you serious, Doctor? Are you joking? You know Latin, you must know Latin!"

"Ah! Badly, very badly. Awfully."

"But still . . ."

"Several purely medical terms, but the rest . . ."

So Yuriy's Latin letter was not translated. I doubt that the "little relative" left it in the dossier without a translation—that would have served as proof that the godfather's performance of his responsibilities was poor.

On December 13, 1978, together with N. Gorbanevskaya, V. Maximov, V. Bukovsky, and V. Delon, I was at the showing of a film about Chinese concentration-camp "life" whose central character was half-French, half-Chinese: Jean Pascalini. Like connoisseurs, we judged this suffering, this abasement of human dignity, the Machiavellianism of "self-criticism" turned into collective informing—all this reminded us of our own experience.

Have we not escaped from the "labor camps" or the psychiatric hospitals? And had the impudence, at that, not to perish but to become a "living reproach" in order to interfere with those who, even today, in spite of everything, continue to sing the Internationale—in short, to be, as Communists shamefacedly say, victims of "separate misunderstandings"? Leaving aside everything that separates me from Communists, I must confess that I share with them one common point of contact: They, like me, suffer from absolute and impenetrable deafness; only in my case it is physical, the result of numerous traumas, while theirs is moral.

The close-ups of the film showed the tormented, broken, sick Pascalini and his comrades, who secretly brought him food and medicines and said: "You must leave here so that you can tell the free world what you've seen here."

How much there was in common between his sufferings and mine! A Frenchman like myself, arrested for that alone, suffering torments in order to remain as such. . . . And, feeling close to me the warm presence of my dissident friends, seeing those frames, I was suddenly transported to Eastern Siberia twenty-five years earlier, to the sixth barrack, where I struggled against illness and the outcome of the struggle was still not at all clear. From time to time I emerged from nonexistence only to be submerged an instant later still deeper in it.

Between two surging waves of consciousness I notice Dr. Ts. and, behind him, Don Quixote, Leonid B. and Marian D. Doctor Ts. says to me, smiling:

"Your friends obtained antibiotics and fresh fruit for you."

Each time I floated to the surface, I see Don Quixote's anxious face. He wipes the perspiration off my forehead and gives me sour milk—found by I don't know what miracle—to drink.

"Duval, you can't, you mustn't do this. You have to fight, you haven't the right to die. You must live to return to France someday and testify on behalf of those who can't, don't know how, or don't want to testify."

I stayed alive and began to recover and, despite prohibition of the "godfather" of visits to me under threat of the lockup, my striker comrades constantly brought me food or sweets, obtained by barter with unescorted convicts for clothes, even a bottle of Crimean wine "to make your blood thicker," as Vitya K——ov said. The lifegiving warmth of friendship lengthened the intervals between pain, and it was clear that friendship was indestructible as long as such people existed in the world.

Every hour Raven appeared with news of the great number of freed, rehabilitated, work-released, and repatriated foreigners....In short, a great shift. A great shift, alas, in barracks overfilled with seriously ill prisoners, physically and morally broken, gathered together from the camps scattered throughout the region in order to die in this hospital, incapable of making any use of their "liberation."

"Duval, I have good news. And still another piece of news that's not so good."

"Begin with the good news, Raven. It's never late to hear the bad news."

"Peter M. wrote me a letter from Moscow. He's already there. Many of our freed people are passing through Moscow, he goes to the station whenever trains come from our parts—exactly on time, like a Swiss railroad schedule. He met Sasha A., Mitya B., and many others."

"Tremendous! God willing, they'll be out for a long time! And the not such good news?"

"That brute Voronin, the vile informer—he has been rehabilitated. He leaves with the next group."

My neighbors listen to us and comment about the news. Among them there are two Hungarians, a Japanese, and two Koreans. These are all boys on whom you can count in the fight against "everything that is Communism." Their hatred toward the U.S.S.R. is so great that they unfortunately lump together the Soviet with the Russian, Russia with the U.S.S.R., like many people in the West, and because of this they do not like to speak Russian—except with such fellows as Yuriy, who belongs to the numerous sons of Russia capable of inspiring love in those who see their duty in hatred.

"What, Voronin? He—free?" says the Japanese. "He in same car with me, my people cut off his head."

"How many of our brothers have perished because of such villains, these Judases? How many victims altogether are there on the conscience of this system? Will we never really learn this?" says Morozov and sadly shakes his head.

"Of course we'll learn," says Yuriy. "Each of us can do simple calculation with the aid of ordinary arithmetic . . . and data published officially: The population of the country in 1917 amounted to something like 140 million people. Statistics give the average rate of demographic growth of the Union as 1.7 percent. If we multiply 140 million by 1.7, it comes to 2,380,000. Between 1917 and 1940 there were 23 years. Multiply 2,380,000 by 23, and we get 54,740,000; add that to 140 million—the total is 194,740,000. Such is the size of the population in 1940."

"Why 1940?" asks Kim.

"Because in the years 1939–40 numerous territories and

countries were added to the Union. By grace of Stalin and with the complicity of Hitler (not to speak of the powerlessness of the West to prevent this), the population of all these territories became Soviet—that yields something like 20 million. Therefore all of this together amounts to 214,740,000. Is that clear?"

"Just so. Now, we multiply 214,740,000 by 1.7 and get 3,650,580 new citizens per year. From 1940 to the current year, 1955, there were 15 years; multiply them by 3,650,580, and we get 54,758,700; add that to 214,740,000 and we get the grand total—269,498,700, let's say a population of 270 million. But you, as well as I, have read in the newspapers that the population of this country is two hundred million."

A cold sweat came out on all our foreheads. We were struck dumb by this simple logic.

"Yuriy," said Morozov with a trembling voice, "there's a shortage of seventy million. Seventy million dead. Seventy million," he repeated.

"Yes, Semyen. Centainly there was a war that carried off twenty million of our people. Certainly there was an emigration at the time of the revolution, as well as all those who stayed in the West in 1945. But that shouldn't amount to more than five million. Of course, as the years pass, the Kremlin will increase, inflate even the figures for wartime losses, so as to account for the 'missing,' since the calculations we have just made could be made by anyone. Nevertheless, there's no getting away from the fact that forty-five million human lives—direct victims of Lenin, Stalin, and their accomplice-heirs who now rule over us—are unaccounted for. Such is the tragic outcome of the hope that existed at the dawn of their October Revolution. There are also fifteen million of us in camps and exile now. The record of Communism is so monstrous, the number of its victims expressed in such astronomical terms that no one is willing to believe it when we talk about the subject."[5]

"The Russians are to blame," said Shanya T., a Hungarian.

"No, old man, you're mistaken," said Yuriy gently and

[5]As we now know, these figures were "modest," if one can express oneself in this way.

sadly, putting an arm around his shoulders. "You're mistaken," he repeated, "you're not right, and you hurt us—
Semyen, Volodya, Petya, and me: We are Russians and
proud of it. Don't forget the horrors of Nazism—yet not all
Germans were Nazis, and not all Nazis were Germans. The
crimes of Communism here and everywhere exceed in
scale all that has existed in ancient and modern history. For
that very reason, I want you to remember that not all
Russians were Communists, and not all Communists were
Russians."

Well, in the past twenty-three years—from the very minute on February 17, 1956, when I passed through Branden-
burg Gate in a car on which the little tricolor flag of the
French Consulate in West Berlin fluttered—I have not
ceased to say that, Don Quixote! . . .

Sitting in the mortuary—one of the extremely rare
places where it was possible to talk without fear of being
overheard—Don Quixote sorted out his notes and letters.
On the next day he was leaving the camp. I felt something
unusual in Raven. An awkwardness, almost shame of a
man departing for "freedom" in relation to someone remaining in jail. Our meeting was understandably sad: Two
good friends were parting, what awaited both of them in
the future? I was of course happy for him, and yet—a man
is weak as well as sinful!—I felt some envy, and that made
me blush.

Ivan M., out of breath, ran in and blurted out:

"Armand, the godfather's messenger is looking all over
for you."

"Which messenger? From the MVD or the MGB?"

"The MGB."

"A dirty trick is in the offing. Well, so let's get ready to
go into the arena. Poor Nose, even on the eve of your liberation it's still not possible to have peace."

"I have alerted," said Ivan, "Petya, Volodya, Semyen
Morozov and, in Yuriy's place, Marian G. to go with you.
They're waiting for you in front of the mess hall."

"Thank you, Vanya, it's good that you thought of alert-
ing Marian."

"What's this—in place of me?" said Yuriy. "As far as I
know, I'm still here. I'll go with Armand. There can't be

any talk of missing my turn.[6] It's simply inconceivable that I shouldn't participate in the last 'debates' with our 'friends.' "

"I beg you, Don Quixote, leave Rosinante in the stable. Tomorrow you'll be free, you can't permit yourself such lack of caution. This isn't a godfather from the MVD, but from the MGB, so it's much more serious and dangerous, especially for you."

"The prosecutor states that I have been set free and rehabilitated. Therefore I'm a 'citizen' who enjoys all rights . . . or, let's say, nearly all. And my duty as a citizen of a country in which 'man breathes so freely' is to express my profound disagreement with these . . . gentlemen."

"Listen, Yuriy, stop this! I left you—" Ivan began.

"Enough, *caballero!* Am I to understand by this that if you were in my place you wouldn't venture to accompany Armand to the godfather? I know you too well—you and Duval. Well, O.K., we won't make our friends and the gentlemen from the MGB wait."

"Yuriy! . . ."

"No. Let's go. And don't forget, Duval— 'the last to get the message . . .' "

None of Ivan's requests, none of my efforts to reason with him shook his resolve. A real Aragon donkey.

Despite the heat, I donned Ivan's warm jacket—in case I went into a cell at once—poured some *makhorka* tobacco into my pockets and tucked away newspaper for rolling cigarettes, three footcloths, and some matches. Two pieces of lead concealed in the innersoles of my boots would allow me to send notes to my friends. I swallowed a piece of bread with the remains of food in Ivan's mess tin and three lumps of sugar. Now I was ready—until the next "banquet."

We go to the godfather. The door is open. First we see Lieutenant Yashchuk seated behind his desk. Next to him stands the camp's chief bookkeeper, a civilian. A little farther off, some unknown major sits on a stool. The major is perhaps from the operations department of Ozerlag, his physiognomy is completely suitable. Probably on a special

[6]Each person assumed the duty of accompanying any of the prisoners summoned to the godfather for a week at a time.

mission. But why is the chief bookkeeper present? This does not presage anything good.

"Greetings, Maloumian. Come in, come in," says the godfather with a great cordiality that does not at all tally with his person.

"Did you call me, Comrade Chief?"

"Yes. Look, you're always yelling about illegality and protesting over everything and nothing, but this time you won't be able to accuse the MGB of only causing you trouble!"

"?!?"

"There, take a good look. That's a money order for two hundred rubles from the French Embassy in Moscow. Well, what do you say about that? You don't believe it, eh? Just take it and read what it says."

He gives me the money order. My heart beats madly. A money order from my embassy! My parents have taken action. The embassy knows where I am and is giving me a signal. All of my being is overflowing with joy. I read aloud in a slightly trembling voice: "The Embassy of France, Moscow, Bol'shaya Yakimanka . . ."

The major gets up from the stool and comes over to me:

"You're French?"

"As if you didn't know. Incidentally, it's confirmed by the money order."

"Perhaps it is. Or perhaps it shows you're a French intelligence agent. Otherwise why would the French Embassy suddenly send money to you, a prisoner?"

"Stop, Comrade Chief. Keep your shabby tricks for naïve novices and not for such 'educated' people as myself."

I hold the money order with both hands like a dog hanging with his teeth onto a bone. I even fail to hear what else the major is saying. "Embassy," "Moscow," and "France" whirl in my head.

"Take this and sign for it," the chief bookkeeper says to me, holding out a one-hundred-ruble and two fifty-ruble notes. "And sign here too," he adds, "for notification of the delivery—that you actually received two hundred rubles in your own hands."

Affixing my signature, I suddenly realize that in this way the embassy will receive confirmation of my arrest and confinement and satisfy itself that, on the date in question, I was alive.

"Let me see it, Armand," Yuriy says earnestly.

I hand him the notice. He reads it and suddenly *kisses it with deference.*

"What's with you, Dombrovsky? Have you gone crazy, or what?" asks the godfather.

"It will be useful for you to know that you always kiss a lady's hand. But France is a lady, and a great one. She has taught us Russians and, incidentally, other peoples, what Liberty is. I felt obliged to render her this homage."

Yuriy left the camp the next morning. I escorted him to the gate and embraced him and other liberated comrades for the last time. They were already outside the zone, and the duty officer placed checks on the list. And just like the first time I saw him, I saw his head above all the heads, the head of a raven surrounded by sparrows and pigeons.

Before the gate closed behind them, Don Quixote turned around and shouted "Brothers! Armand! The door ajar, we are departing and breaking all our chains. The world must find out, and if some of us lose our lives on this road, others must follow it to the end. The whole truth must be told about what happened and is still happening here—all of it, with nothing held back. We must conquer fear and break the silence in order to build a just and reliable future. Farewell, Duval! Farewell, brothers!"

He bowed to us and stood at attention with lowered head, tears falling from his eyes onto the Siberian earth, which had already soaked up so much blood....

I never again saw Yuriy Osipovich Dombrovsky or heard his voice.

May you be damned! With your prisons you destroyed the right to live in hope—for this wonderful man, in addition to millions of others. You even stole from us the tears with which to weep for him.

I would like to bow at his grave and chisel on the tombstone:

HERE LIES YURIY
WHO FOUND DON QUIXOTE'S GRAVE,
FOR IN IT HE NOW RESTS.

The Face of Inhumanity

BY LYDIA CHUKOVSKAYA

Translated by Catherine A. Fitzpatrick

From *Kontinent* No. VII, 1976

Mustafa Dzhemilev was sentenced on April 14, 1976, in the city of Omsk.

Why in Omsk? Because Mustafa was serving out his latest sentence in a prison camp not far from Omsk. That's one reason. And because Omsk is a city which offers great conveniences for conducting any open trial: It is closed tight to foreigners. That's the second reason. In Omsk, far away from the eyes of journalists, it is easier to make a choice between whom to let in and whom to leave by the door. A similar sorting-out process occurs in all cities in our country—why, even in Moscow. Although in Moscow you can't avoid making noise. But in Omsk? Who there is going to care about the Tatar Mustafa Dzhemilev? He is as much of an alien among the local inhabitants as cypresses are alien to the taiga that surrounds Omsk.

However, the authorities did not succeed in holding the trial of Mustafa Dzhemilev in utter silence and emptiness. It is not for nothing that Dzhemilev has spent a quarter of

Born in 1907 as the daughter of the famous children's writer and literary critic Kornei Chukovskaya, Lydia Chukovskaya became famous in her own right as a staunch dissident, publicly protesting the prosecution of Sinyavsky and Daniel, defending Solzhenitsyn and Sakharov among others. For this her book The Deserted House *(written in 1940 and bitterly attacking Stalin) was forbidden publication in the Soviet Union (it was published in the West after Stalin's death). She herself was expelled from the Writers' Union in 1974.*

his life in prison or labor camps (eight years—and he is only thirty-three years old). Three times the trial was postponed, and three times Dzhemilev's kinsmen and friends flew thousands of miles to Omsk. And they even flew in the fourth time—from Uzbekistan, from the Ukraine, from Orel, from Moscow—all of sixteen people—but no place could be found for them in the courtroom. At first no one was allowed in, and then only members of the immediate family, and then even they were not allowed to stay throughout the whole trial.

Figure it out for yourself: What are relatives and friends doing at a trial, anyway? This isn't the kind of public a court ought to have. Step back, citizens, don't interfere with our work. Citizens, this courtroom isn't made of rubber. There will never be enough room for all of you. You can see for yourselves how many people there are. (After all, this isn't just any trial, this is an open trial, a public trial, and how can we have a public trial without any public?) We're observing the law, we have brought in our own special, hand-picked public through the back door, well in advance. Visitors must sit behind the door.

His mother? Well, all right, we suppose we could let his mother in. She is his mother, after all, and we're humanists. How could we not let his mother in? Could we really not do that? When we have to, we'll let someone in, and when we have to, we'll take someone out. Well, all right, let his brothers and sisters in, too, but the rest of them must stay behind the door. And if they start kicking up a fuss, there'll be bruises and trips to the police station in store for them. They're interfering with the work of the court! That same "public" we brought in beforehand is capable of twisting your arms behind your back and dragging you down the corridor. They know their job, they're professionals, they're used to this kind of work.

Why am I writing about the trial of Mustafa Dzhemilev? Am I hoping to help him? No. But at this trial, the features of inhumanity were so clearly visible that it would be a sin not to describe them. I'll begin with the end. It is the sacred right of every accused person, whoever he may be, to say his last word, to appeal to the heart and mind of the judge for the last time, and to call on his sense of fairness, duty, and honor. The right of the defendant to give his last speech, be it long or short, is protected by law in all the countries of the world. It is protected by Soviet law as well —on paper. In reality, however, the accused rarely gets the opportunity to finish saying his piece through, especially in cases where he is not busy refuting cleverly woven accusations, but is using his last speech to substantiate the main point of his thoughts, and the primary reason behind his actions.

The judge did not let Mustafa Dzhemilev have his last word, but rather stopped him short. This is not only a crime against the law, but a crime against humanity.

Dzhemilev stood before the court after being on a hunger strike for ten months. "Stood" is not really the appropriate word here. He did not have the strength left to stand. When answering the questions of the judge, the procurator, and the defense attorney, he somehow managed to raise himself up from the dock, with guards supporting him on both sides. But it was even harder for him to speak than it was to stand. He moved his lips and spoke in a rasping voice. Each word was torture, physical torture, because for ten months he had been force-fed through a tube so that he would not die of starvation. A tube stuck down his throat every day could not help but scratch his larynx. And besides this, Mustafa was seriously ill. He had diseases of the heart and stomach and atrophy of the liver.

But the judge had an atrophy of human feelings. He was a well-fed man who could not understand a hungry person; he was a healthy man who could not understand a sick man; he was a judge whose magistrate's chair had all four legs firmly planted on the platform of the KGB. He was an inhumane man, capable of calmly cutting short the last speech of an accused man, knowing that it might very well be the next to last speech spoken by Mustafa on this earth.

"Don't stop him from speaking," begged Mustafa's brother. The judge had him removed from the courtroom, just as he had had his sister removed for "disturbance of order."

Order?

Oh, when will that order be disturbed that allows the authorities in the Soviet Union to silence those who speak?

The Constitution of the U.S.S.R. guarantees citizens freedom of speech. The law also guarantees this, but there are

two formulas, limitless in their emptiness and capacity—
"anti-Soviet propaganda" and "anti-Soviet slander"—
which insure the annihilation of both this freedom of
speech and the person speaking, in one fell swoop, regardless of whether he is speaking the truth or lying. If he is
revealing something which the authorities are concealing,
let him be silent. As the proverb has it, "Whatever hurts a
person, that is what he will talk about." What is hurting
Mustafa Dzhemilev is the Crimea. And that is what he talks
about. The Tatars, who were forcibly and shamelessly
evicted from the Crimea in 1944, want to return to the Crimea, to the land they loved and cultivated. Why must the
authorities necessarily hear "anti-Soviet propaganda" in
Dzhemilev's peaceful speech, and not a natural appeal for
an open, loud, public discussion of a festering, burning issue? Why was it necessary to force the pain back within,
and force the man into the grave? Why is it in general that
every active thought born in real pain is anti-Soviet? The
concept of "anti-Soviet activity" is just as ambiguous as it is
elastic. It is truly an insatiable maw, devouring people's
thoughts and lives, hundreds and thousands of lives, without a sound, without a trace, and all in vain.

Now the fate of another person concerns me besides the
fate of Dzhemilev, someone who is also involved in Mustafa's trial. His name is Dvoryansky, and he is twenty-six
years old. The whole trial was really resting on him, on his
testimonies. Dvoryansky is also an inmate, but I do not
even know whether he is a criminal or a political prisoner.
I don't even know anything about his past life before
prison camp, but to think of what lies ahead for him makes
my hair stand on end.

Dzhemilev was sentenced for "anti-Soviet propaganda,"
which he supposedly continued to carry on while serving
his term in a prison not far from Omsk. Who was it that
heard those unlawful words from him? Dvoryansky. A
new investigation into Dzhemilev's case was begun while
he was still serving his latest sentence, when only three
days remained before his release. That's how it happens.
The gates of the prison are just about to open before you,
but it's useless to count the hours, you'll never see freedom, because a new case is being brought against you. It
was in protest against this deliberate, sophisticated form of
mockery that Dzhemilev declared a hunger strike.

But this did not help. He was force-fed through a tube, and on April 14, half alive, he was brought into court. And here, a miracle happened—I cannot call what happened otherwise. The witness Dvoryansky, the very same person on whose testimonies the whole renewed case rested, drew himself up manfully to his full height, and in a full, manful voice announced to the court that the testimonies which he had given against Dzhemilev during the investigation were all lies. (Most likely it is in this way that a man comes out of shelter to face a hail of bullets.) Dvoryansky announced that the false testimonies he had given during the investigation had been made under pressure. All sorts of methods were used—promises, the punishment cell, and threats. He resisted and was dragged off to the punishment cell five times. If you give testimony against Dzhemilev, we'll get you closer to home, we'll shorten your sentence. If you don't give testimony, harm will come to you and your family, and you'll have only yourself to blame. And that is why he gave false witness against Dzhemilev. But now he was announcing that he had heard nothing from Mustafa that defamed the Soviet system.

I do not know what kind of person Dvoryansky was before, but at the trial he behaved like a real human being. A valiant human being. But did the judge behave like a human being?

I am not a lawyer, but even without having a law-school education, just on the basis of simple common sense, I know exactly what the judge was obligated to do in this case. He should have released Dzhemilev immediately. After all, hadn't the accusation fallen apart? He should have immediately begun a case against the investigators who had wrung the false testimonies out of Dvoryansky.

But this could only have happened if the court judged the case according to justice and law. Then Dvoryansky's announcement would have changed everything. But the court judged the case according to injustice and illegality and, most importantly, according to an instruction which had been previously handed down from higher-ups.

Did I see that instruction? No, I did not. No one ever sees those kinds of instructions—we just suffer their consequences. The court passed sentence on Mustafa Dzhemilev: two and a half years of strict-regime corrective labor camp for anti-Soviet propaganda. Two and a half years, plus another three days for the three days which remained from his previous sentence.

The court also handed down a "special decision" to bring to trial...who do you think? The investigators who had extorted false testimonies from Dvoryansky? No, it was Dvoryansky himself who was to be brought to trial. For what? For giving false testimonies. So. But which false testimonies? The ones that he gave during the investigation in prison camp? No, the testimonies he gave in court. There you have it—the face of inhumanity.

TRANSLATOR'S NOTE

In December of 1977, after having served ten months in prison on a hunger strike, Mustafa Dzhemilev was released, in extremely poor condition.

Following his release from prison, he was kept under house arrest for six months. At the end of this period, he should have obtained the right to come and go freely and even visit his parents. But on February 8, 1979, Mustafa was once again arrested by the KGB just outside the border city of Tashkent, on a charge of violating passport laws. On March 6, after another unjust trial without any evidence for the defense, Dzhemilev was sentenced to four years of exile.

At the present time Dzhemilev is serving out his term of exile in Yakutia, U.S.S.R. He has recently married and his wife is with him.

The Beginning of Charter 77

BY VACLAV HAVEL

Translated by George Bailey

From *Kontinent* No. XIV (German
edition), 1980

After the Soviet invasion of Czechoslovakia in 1968 and after the inauguration of the Husak regime, the whole of Czechoslovak society entered a long period of total depression, apathy, and weariness without hope. To be sure, even in this period there were people who were moved to bid defiance to the totalitarian power which had established itself in our country. Indeed, in the early seventies there was a whole series of political trials. But neither these attempts

---

VACLAV HAVEL was born in 1936 in Prague. Because of his bourgeois origins his educational opportunities were severely restricted. He worked first as a taxi driver but managed to get his high-school diploma by going to night school. He studied for two years at the Technical University in Prague, but he was not admitted to the faculty of Art History or the faculty of Theater Science. His penchant for the stage brought him to the Theater on the Strand in Prague, where he began as a stagehand and advanced by degrees to playwright. It was in this theater that his plays The Garden Party, The Message, *and* Complicated Possibilities for Concentration, *which are now well known throughout the West, were first produced. As an active advocate of the "Prague Spring," Havel was forced to leave Prague after the Soviet invasion of Czechoslovakia in 1968. As a spokesman for Charter 77, he was arrested and held for three months in 1977 and then given a suspended sentence of fourteen months. In 1979, after months in investigatory arrest, he was sentenced to four and a half years in prison. Since then he has refused, apparently repeatedly, the offer of Czech authorities that he emigrate to the West.*

at defiance nor the political trials met with the response in our society or abroad which they deserved. Nonetheless, it was in the attempts of these people who thus preserved such shreds of hope as we had in 1968 that the authentic roots of Charter 77 lay.

In the mid-seventies in certain strata of our society, especially among the intellectuals, free and independent thinking again began to make itself known. At that time, for example, there appeared the well-known Petlice Edition, a *samizdat* edition of *belles lettres*, which today numbers at least 170 volumes. At the same time other cultural initiatives were mounted. These, however, were confined to a small circle of people and so achieved only local significance.

Until that time no attempt at any broader coordination had been made, nor had there been any common effort— there was no solidarity between various isolated groups which sought their own independent way toward freedom of expression, of reaction to events, and hence in their own way to a certain kind of political activity.

It is interesting that the first decisive impulse to the overcoming of the isolation of these various groups which had existed in our country since 1973–74 came from the famous court trial of the rock group Plastic People of the Universe.

I will try to explain how it was that this trial, of all things, played the role of coordinator and led to the further development of political consciousness in Czechoslovakia.

This was not the first time that this had happened. We know of similar situations from the fifties when there was such a moment and society began to move—not as a result of a confrontation with a defeated opponent, that is, with those who had already been eliminated from public life, but a moment when a newly established regime came into conflict with the new generation, with young people who were without a political past, without any political experience of their own. Exactly such a moment arrived when the prosecution of the rock group Plastic People and their followers began. The rock group Plastic People of the Universe was formed at the end of the sixties after the dissolution of the Primitive Group, but became especially active at the beginning of the seventies. It was then that their non-

conformism led to their being prohibited by court order
from appearing in public. Thereafter they played only at
private parties, at wedding receptions, and on festive occasions in the homes of their various friends. The group had
a rather large circle of fans and was, in fact, for a long time
the only rock group in existence which was authentic in
the sense that it was unconventional and independent,
played the music that it liked, and thus freely expressed
the feelings of young people about life. This group and the
whole movement which it represented was called the
Czech musical underground by its spiritual leader, Ivan Ji-
rouse.

In the spring of 1976 this group found itself in direct
confrontation with the regime. Some nineteen musicians
and fans of the group were arrested, bound over, and had
formal charges brought against them. At that time in our
country there still existed various groups of "dissidents,"
as they are called in the West—we don't particularly like
the term, but that is irrelevant here—these were people
who had been active in 1968 and were consequently from
the very beginning of the Husak regime the targets of un-
remitting attacks by the propaganda office and the police.
Between these dissidents and the movement of young musicians, which was so drastically suppressed by the regime
in the spring of 1976, there existed until this time no contact whatever.

But precisely at the time when the young musicians were
so drastically deprived of their freedom the situation began to change. A very interesting process was set in motion
—the various groups suddenly became aware of the phenomenon of the indivisibility of freedom: They recognized
that the attack against the young and unknown musicians
was a surrogate for an attack against all those in our country who had still not completely resigned, who had not yet
subordinated themselves, and that certain writers and politicians were spared the worst only because their names
were well known. They understood that these young people had been arrested only because they were unknown
and it could therefore be assumed that their persecution
could be carried on without any reverberations at home or
abroad.

At that moment they realized that the blow against the

musicians was in reality aimed at one and all, that the most important thing of all was under attack—freedom of opinion and the right to live according to individual taste—and that for this reason the young musicians would have to be defended.

I was personally in the fortunate position of being able to follow the trial closely because I organized the various protests in favor of the Plastic People of the Universe, I wrote protest notes and collected signatures. So I was able to follow with my own eyes the interesting process of the formation of awareness, as for example when it became clear to Professor Jan Patocka that freedom to conduct his phenomenological researches was the exact equivalent of the freedom of this rock music, although the latter was by no means important to him personally. I saw how various writers and politicians became aware of this fact.

Then something happened which the regime did not expect. The regime had believed that sentencing several long-haired disturbers of the peace could be accomplished without creating a scandal, so that the entire matter could be dealt with and the danger to the regime because of the popularity of the rock group among the younger generation averted. I shall not describe all the ins and outs of the prosecution of the young musicians: The number of those formally accused gradually grew smaller and it was clear that concessions were being made by the regime. Finally the trial took place. It became an *affaire*, a political scandal, which was the last thing the regime wanted but was now obliged to deal with.

In the corridors of the court building where the four chief representatives of the rock-music movement were finally sentenced one saw the first appearance of Charter 77. A wide variety of people were involved: twenty-year-old long-haired youths, former members of the Communist Party of Czechoslovakia, leading art theoreticians, critics, professors, writers, and many others. There was gathered there an entire cross-section of the human material from which Charter 77 was later to emerge.

The further development of the movement was almost automatic. We met three times at general sessions with representatives of groups that had theretofore been completely isolated, with former politicians (Jiri Hájek, Zdenek

Mlynar) with writers (Ludvik Vaculik, Pavel Kohout) and with several other people. At these meetings the spectrum of opinions of Charter 77 was already propounded: from the musical underground through Communists to Trotskyists, from various writers and mavericks to Catholics and Protestants.

There was another event that must not be left out of consideration: In the autumn of 1976 Czechoslovakia became a party to the international pacts on human rights, which were then ratified by our parliament. In the most natural way it was shown that the basic human rights which were anchored in these pacts were exactly the same things that united these various groups and made up the platform, the common ground on which we all stood.

So it was that the first proclamation of Charter 77 came about. It concerned itself with the confrontation of these pacts, legally anchored in Czechoslovakia, and the reality of our totalitarian society.

When at the very beginning of Charter 77 we were collecting signatures for the proclamation, which we then meant to hand over to the state authorities, we were not at all sure that it would be possible to create a lasting association capable of actively defending human rights. In the course of our attempt to deliver these signatures to the authorities on January 6, 1977, we were arrested by the police and bound over.

Our greatest satisfaction—and what was for me particularly surprising—in those weeks between our first public appearance and my arrest as one of the three main spokesmen of Charter 77, lay in the fact that the first 250 signatories of Charter 77 did not understand their act as limited to that occasion alone (which would have been no small achievement in itself) but as precisely what it was meant to be: the beginning of a continuing activity.

Beginning at that time, Charter 77 has now existed more than two and a half years, having published twenty-four documents, communiqués, protests, letters, and interventions for various people. Other initiatives have developed within the framework of Charter 77, for example VONS (the Committee for the Defense of Unjustly Prosecuted), the Fund for Citizen's Aid, and others.

What in the beginning was only a dream has become

reality. The reality is severe. Not only because we are daily confronted with the police, because all signatories and especially the active ones are subjected to unceasing persecution. Our reality is also difficult because a closed association like Charter 77 must always ask itself, again and again, whether what it is doing really makes any sense, whether it has not become too isolated from the public or become too radical, whether it has not chosen a path that is unacceptable to the majority in our society.

These are the complications and problems of our work, but however great they may be, Charter 77 lives, moves forward, and works, it is what from the very beginning we wanted it to be. And this in itself is a great change, a significant event in our country in this decade.

PART THREE

Out of the Frying Pan

The Emigrant Experience in the West

The Saga
of the Rhinoceroses

BY VLADIMIR MAXIMOV

Translated by Ludmilla Thorne

From *Kontinent* No. XIX, 1978

For Eugène Ionesco

1.

We are sitting with him in the cluttered yet very tidy study
of his apartment on the Boulevard Montparnasse. His gray,
slightly bulging eyes bear a glint of ever-present surprise

VLADIMIR MAXIMOV *was born in 1932 in Moscow, the son of a factory
worker. He left home at the age of twelve and roamed the length and
breadth of the Soviet Union as one of the legion of adolescent hoboes called*
bezprizorniki *(without guardian). He spent some three years in a deten-
tion camp for such young vagrants, but for the most part made his way as
an occasional laborer, particularly as a bricklayer. He was first published
at the age of eighteen in a provincial newspaper, where he became a staff
reporter. Less than ten years later his stories were being published in the
Moscow press. He was well known as a promising young writer and became famous with the publication of his novella,* The Ballad of Savva.
His major novel, The Seven Days of Creation, *like his subsequent novels, among them* Quarantine *and* Farewell from Nowhere, *have been
published in several European languages, but not in the Soviet Union or its
satellites. He was expelled from the Writers' Union in 1972 and allowed to
emigrate in 1974. Maximov is the cofounder (with Andrei Sakharov and
Alexander Solzhenitsyn), publisher, and editor-in-chief of the magazine*
Kontinent.

and radiate a soft childlike expression, which lives and exists independently of his sharply chiseled face, touched by age. A white toga with a crimson-colored border would be more befitting to this face than a sweater—which, actually, also looks regal on him. From time to time he lazily takes a sip of straight whiskey on the rocks, and, without interrupting, silently listens to my verbose complaints about the spiritual deafness, ideological narrow-mindedness, and herdlike instinct of the Western intellectual elite.

"Out of the frying pan into the fire," I exclaim with anger. Was it worth it to let our feet carry us away from a state dictatorship, only to become the whipping boys of a dictatorship of social snobbery? In a certain sense, everything is the same: the censorship, the divisions between "us" and "them," and the boycotts by publishers and critics. It is conformity in reverse, presented under the guise of respectable democracy. And the method used to carry on the polemics also long ago became familiar, after all of the soul-searching conversations that were held in the offices on the Old Square.[1] You would give them certain concrete facts, and they would respond with generalities about the oppressed peoples of Africa and the class struggle.

My host wearily lowers his heavy eyelids, and the invisible toga with the crimson border drapes downward, in majestic folds. He has heard all of this dozens, and perhaps even hundreds, of times before, from that very same populous desert which had spread itself around him, and once again, as dozens or hundreds of times before, he can offer no help and has practically nothing to say.

"Oh, Monsieur Maximov, Monsieur Maximov," he says, as I'm enveloped by an infantlike trust, oozing from under his drooping eyelids. "There is no class struggle in nature. For hundreds of years there has been only one mortal struggle in the world, that between the *grande* and the *petite bourgeoisie,* and, for the benefit of their own material and spiritual well-being, they have used in this struggle all of the remaining classes, along with their ideas, and after achieving victory, they abandoned them to fate's mercy.

"With its false teeth the *bourgeoisie* has ground up and

---

[1]This is the address of the Central Committee of the Communist Party of the Soviet Union in Moscow.—TRANS.

utilized for its own benefit all of the most outstanding and sacred achievements attained by humanity through suffering—such as liberty, culture, and religion. Throughout history, a person has had to possess courage and a conscience in order to retain his individuality. Unfortunately, the *bourgeois* does not have either of these. The only thing that he has is his teeth and the animalistic ability to adapt.

"The *bourgeoisie* is an order, a Mafia, an *internationale*, and, if you like, the *bourgeois* shopkeeper and the *bourgeois* intellectual do not differ in any way from the *bourgeois* revolutionary or the *bourgeois Parteigenosse*. Perhaps you have noticed that, in spite of all the political and national differences, they are quick to find a common language—the financial manipulators and yesterday's expropriators, the snobs from Saint-Germain-des-Prés and Moscow's official esthetes dressed in civilian clothing, the humanist with the cocked Kalashnikov machine gun and the Uganda cannibal, done up in a field marshal's regalia, as well as our president, smacking of the liberal aristocrat, and the Vietnamese executioner who has not as yet cleansed his hands of his countrymen's blood. They are a multitude, and their name is legion."

As he once again lowers his eyes, I suddenly perceive the mounting sounds of countless trampling hooves coming from afar. The stomping grows and intensifies, it becomes ever stronger, until I'm completely engulfed by its force. Wildly snorting and grunting, emitting the tart aroma of frenzied sweat, and spraying a mixture of saliva and foam in its path, a predatory, cruel, aggressive herd stampedes through my powerless soul. Their eyes are suspended in a bloody fog; their coarse horns stand readily poised. At first distinct bodies cannot be defined amidst the solid wall of groans and stomps, but gradually, out of the cacophony of chaotic sounds, something begins to emerge, something dimly resembling human speech. . . .

2.

He's a professor. An intellectual. At one time he was even an attaché in a dingy banana republic. He's progressive to the very tips of his chewed-off fingernails. An expensive little cigarette dangles out of his sensuous lips; his hand, carelessly flung to the side, holds a glass of champagne. When he speaks, he lazily stretches himself, as if to say that anything you may impart is elementary and is already known to him.

"Have you read the *Gulag*?" I ask him. (Our conversation revolves around Russia.)

"No," he answers, looking askance, with an absent-minded gaze, his cigarette ashes falling on the lapel of his tuxedo, "and I don't intend to. I have my own opinion, and please don't try to confuse me with your facts."

Then, forgetting all about me, he drifts in the direction of his gaze, toward a newer and obviously more desirable object. The intellectual's snorting nostrils flare, in anticipation of his prey, and I distinctly hear his rhinoceros skin rustling with confidence, underneath his tuxedo.

This one is different. Open and unpretentious, he's really one of us. He will give you the shirt off his back, but luckily there's not much to give, because everything he has is invested and, for greater safety, it's all invested in his wife's name. He's dressed in carefully worn-out jeans, although, given his age and the size of his little paunch, he ought to be wearing a warm robe and house slippers. He's thoughtfully disarrayed and uncombed; his face is in a consistently unshaven state, as if his beard's growth had temporarily stopped dead in its tracks. His enlightened soul is simulated each morning by a gifted barber.

He works for a super-leading, super-modern magazine with devastating ideas and an inclination toward homosexuality. He runs around Paris with great intensity, blithely not noticing anything or anyone around him.

"Hello," I stop him. "Yesterday someone translated an article for me from your magazine about a respected professor who, according to your journal, allegedly collaborated with the occupying forces, but knowledgeable Frenchmen assert that he was an active member of the Resistance. Please do me a favor and explain."

Like a kindly grandfather, he slaps me on the back with an air of contempt, as if I were his slow-witted grandchild, and says: "Don't worry, he's such a right-wing scoundrel that anything can be said about him. *Adieu!*" Then, with incredible determination, he flies off, nimbly skipping along the sidewalk, his rubber hooves made by Bally.

This one I had just met. Quiet and stealthy, a perpetual half-smile hovers over his formless and, as we say in Russian, womanly face. His eyes are morose and unblinking—like calf eyes, to use another Russian expression. He's famous. He's recognized. He's established. And so on, and so forth. He's also well known for his selective support of, and weakness for, social terrorism.

Time and again I implored him to say something at the forthcoming P.E.N. club meeting in Belgrade on behalf of Vladimir Bukovsky, who at the time was critically ill at Vladimir Prison.

"Yes, yes," he mumbled with his dissipated lips, "of course, but you must not get all caught up just in your own problems. In the world there is a great deal of suffering and grief, besides your own. To an Indian woman with many children, you can't explain her poverty in terms of the Gulag. Or look, for example, what is happening in Chile, not to speak of South Africa...."

"God," I start to reproach myself, "why do you keep imposing your own sore points on this man? His heart is bleeding for all of the minorities. Sitting in his luxurious apartment, with his grieving soul, why should he care for our concerns, when bloodthirsty plantation owners are depriving unfortunate Papuans of their fair share of coconuts? Have a heart, Maximov!"

"Yes," I sigh sympathetically, trying to share at least a part of my host's grief. "It's really awful. Take, for example, also the East Germans, who are fleeing to the West. They are being shot down like rabbits. How can this be!"

The man changes radically. His soft, womanly face turns to stone, his calf's eyes reflect cold remoteness. "And why are they fleeing? This problem should be resolved around the negotiating table, or by means of diplomatic channels. And in general, the most dangerous form of violence remains, nonetheless, exploitation. Material wealth must first be justly distributed. You yourself are a Christian." Saying this, he even flings himself against the back of the chair on which he's sitting, believing that his argument is surely beyond reproach. "After all, Christ also first shared his bread."

His hardened, heated glance reflects self-confident triumph. And this creature, whose head had turned to stone, could not possibly fathom that the Son of God shared his *own* bread, and *voluntarily*, whereas he not only longs to share someone else's bread, but also means to do it with the aid of automatic weapons and handcuffs.

This one started talking to me himself, with the obvious goal of placing the neophyte under siege, thereby putting him in his place and teaching him some sense. Barely having seated himself at the table in a small restaurant in the rue du Bac, he hastens to shock me with a challenging postulate:

"Why are you constantly harping on truth, truth! If there's a right to truth, then there must also exist the right to falsehood." To him, this argument seems to be overwhelmingly disarming. Come to think of it, Smerdyakov was impressed by this very same argument, but it's just that the man sitting across from me didn't bother reading *The Brothers Karamazov* very thoroughly. Or perhaps he didn't even bother looking at it. In my opinion, he didn't have to: He doesn't read books, he writes them. And besides, he's in charge of the East European department of a respectable, pro-totalitarian newspaper. Before that, he had been a correspondent in Moscow. But as a true heir of the original dynasty of rhinoceroses, he forgot nothing and learned nothing. He repeats the dregs of Smerdyakov's and Goebbels's conclusions, but is convinced that he's mapping uncharted territory.

And speaking of Dr. Goebbels, another figure featured in this parody also had a connection to this former doctor. Currently he is the chief editor of a popular boulevard weekly publication of pink orientation, but in 1945—that is, right before the collapse of the Third Reich—he worked in a department headed by the above-cited doctor and called for the merciless annihilation of all those who opposed Hitler. Now he specializes in exposing Russian and East European dissidents, accusing them of being reactionaries and of being sympathetic to fascism.

One must admit that this is a most piquant metamorphosis! Could my father, who died in the battle near Smolensk, or my uncle, who lost a good third of his extremities in that war, ever believe that thirty years later their killers, faithful apprentices of Hitler, would be teaching their own children lessons in morality? Such are the times!

This one is a friend of his, and he's also his drinking partner. The man in question is the publishing director of a respectable business enterprise with conservative leanings. In the past he was an unsuccessful writer. But in business he did all right. He openly flirts with pro-Soviet intellectuals, and himself provided a picture-perfect image of an SS officer. He's always in the company of women of a certain kind. He loves the beautiful life, which he copies from bad movies of the 1930s, by parading about with his walking cane and monocle.

"The situation is complex," I tell him, for I was worried about the events that were taking place in Portugal. "If things continue this way, a dictatorship of the right or left is inevitable."

"Why a dictatorship of the right?" He looks at me with a fixed glaze, not concealing the fact that he's deriding me, as if to say, "Here, take that!" Then he bows theatrically and takes off to dine with a recently released Hitler crony, with whom he must conduct his next bit of business.

This pair found itself in a kind of familylike situation. They wound up there quite by accident—a friend had invited them. Both are quick and very much "with it." At first they look around and listen to what is being said. Gradually, they begin to put in a word here and there, thus slowly working themselves into the milieu. He's a doctor, about to retire, she's a housewife, but obviously with certain demands, being a part of the emancipated lot. The group is primarily Russian, and quite naturally, the discussion revolves around our "cursed" subjects.

After becoming completely acclimated and having heard many of our stories, each one more unending than the other, he thrusts his sharp little face toward the middle of the table and says: "It's not true! Like all émigrés, you are not objective. My brother's business constantly takes him to Moscow and he has never come across anything like that. You haven't been in the West long enough, and see everything through rose-colored glasses, but here things happen which are far more despicable than your famous Gulag."

"For example?"

"For example, the inhuman persecution of homosexuals!" he answers, angrily jutting his stubborn nose in the direction of the others, with the approving nod of his emancipated other half. "And the criminal limitations imposed on the mentally ill are there for everyone to see, but society remains silent. That's worth something, don't you think?"

Of course it is! It would also be worth something to lock you up for a while—you four-legged creature, who has become incensed by the sheer overabundance of food. You should try spending some time in a camp of enforced regime, where mentally ill people who are given no care whatsoever will make a passive homosexual out of you, so that you can then fight for your ideals of sexual freedom with the aid of your own rear end. But in the meantime, hop on, Mr. Rhinoceros, away from medicine!

Here's another example with the same rhinoceros nature, someone of indefinite age, sex, and even nationality. Either she's a Frenchified Russian, or a Russified Frenchwoman. She represents in her person the complete unity of form and content: Nature has endowed her with everything, in the same way that God has endowed the turtle.

She has run the gamut from the twisting, purposeful path of French Communist Party membership to serving Soviet intelligence. She acts either as the secretary or the informer of a committee of either physicists, chemists, or dentists. The committee, however, has nothing to do with physics, chemistry, or the preparation of dentures, but deals exclusively with Human Rights, and in a masochistic vein at that. When the Party-madam is delicately asked about the fascinating metamorphosis of her public career, she focuses her victorious fish-colored eyes on the curious questioner and answers:

"Dialectics!"

It would be interesting to know ahead of time which dialectical maneuver she plans to use when she will finally be brought to the questioning stall. There she will stand with a ring pierced through her nostril, and listen as the cases of rhinoceroses-informers—the ones who lived off the Soviet Gestapo's handouts—are heard and decided.

Now for the next one. He's a Nobel Prize winner, along the line of world peace, so to speak. A hawk of the cold war who has transformed himself into a dove of peace. He smoothly meandered from the initial to the final phase of European social democracy's transformation into a servile variant of Eurocommunism. He drinks a little and has a weakness for the opposite sex. With the years he has become increasingly tearful. Out of sheer emotion he has cried onto the lapels of practically all current executioners, from Brezhnev and Castro to Gierek and Idi Amin. He's envious of them: How good they have it, not having to face any sort of opposition, but only solid loyalty!

In answer to the request that he receive and listen to Bukovsky, he carelessly squeezed through his teeth: "Bukovsky is not among my Moscow friends."

That's true. In Moscow, there are other people he talks to, there are others he drinks with, there he has other colleagues. They are the same ones who tortured Russian social democracy to death in the cellars of Lubianka Prison, they are the ones according to whose laws social-democratic activity is equivalent to committing criminal acts, they are the same ones who ordered their German comrades to betray German social democrats to the Gestapo, they are the ones who stand behind East Berlin border guards who shoot their countrymen in the back as they are fleeing to the West. Nice friends you have, you can't deny that!

It happened, it all happened! In the year 1917, on October 24th, that unforgettable Socialist Revolutionary[2] was going crazy in his Winter Palace office! "We are threatened only from the right!" said he. You see, he was threatened by Guchkov and Rodzianko, but on the next day he was forced to flee together with them, and in the same direction. As they say, nostril to nostril, horn to horn.

She's a newspaper siren. An iconoclast from a noble family. In 1945 she was barely able to get out of Eastern Prussia

[2]Alexander Kerensky.

with her title of Countess and her diamonds. She founded a weekly publication and became steeped in new trends. And ever since that time, as the poet aptly stated, she has been "begging for a storm."[3] Out of Russian dissident thinking she accepts only that which smacks of the police.

"Solzhenitsyn and *Kontinent* are deceiving the West," says she. "I have proof from the most reliable sources."

I readily believe this, knowing the circle and quality of her Moscow friends. But where are you going to drag your diamonds this time, when the moment comes when you will also have to run away from these friends, your progressive highness?

A rhinoceros in clerical clothing. It's a vision eliciting little respect, but not lacking in curiosity. He sparkles with worldliness and erudition. He's elegant in his movements and likes to talk. He can grasp any subject and speaks with confidence; he knows what he's talking about. A Christmas-tree garland could easily be woven from the abundance of his quotations and references. He expounds on the idea of historical compromise:

"We are modern human beings and must look into the eyes of political reality. Marxism, like Christianity, has found its way into the human heart, and it is our duty to make room for both of them, side by side."

What can one say? This double-hoofed creature has mastered all of the sciences, he understands everything, even dung. But how he can place the Lord and "political reality" side by side, into one compartment along with Marxism? That you can't pull out of him, not even with pincers. Here he begins to butt, without uttering a word.

And finally we come to an entire herd. The female contingent is inclined either to displaying deep décolletés, or to wearing suggestive pantsuits. The men's clothing interchanges between tuxedos and Mao shirts. We have before us the entire cream of the local radicals. There are no fools here, their conversations are conducted on the highest social level, dealing with such things as Chile, black Africa, the use of terrorism as a form of class struggle—and once

[3]Mikhail Lermontov, *The Sail.*—TRANS.

again, the persecution of homosexuals. It's all as it should be—Parisian chic.

A Czech friend pulled me almost by force into this Baden-Baden cloister of impeccable, fearless knights. Perched on this radical Mount Olympus, among the snow-white herd of martyrs for progress, there are only two black reactionary ravens: he and I.

"Well, brother, there's something that you don't quite understand here," I complain to myself. "People are concerned about others, although they themselves are well-fed and live comfortably. This means that they haven't lost their consciences."

My heart having melted, I make the following suggestion, although with a certain amount of hesitation: "Listen good people, I have some cash on me," say I, "let's make a collection, let's pass the hat, as they say, and send a donation via the Red Cross to our suffering brothers in Africa or in Latin America."

They look at me as if—pardon the expression—I had polluted the air in the room. Of course, they are ready to liberate people, and even more to help them—but not at their own expense.

The herd drives home in their latest Mercedes models. Only two reactionaries hasten to make their way to the bus stop—my Czech friend and I.

Radio news flash: "While riding on a bicycle to his office, the local secretary of the Christian Democratic Party in Pisa was seriously wounded yesterday by two gunshots fired from a speeding car of the Ferrari type."

Such are the metamorphoses of history: Those who have, rebel against those who have not. But this episode concerns those who were among the exploiters. Here, however, I would like to cite an incident about someone who belongs to the exploited class:

A Paris cab driver. He's red-haired, stocky, a little over forty. Somewhat agitated, he looks in my direction and asks:

"Monsieur is a foreigner?"

"Yes, I'm Russian."

"Oh, Russian! You are from the Soviet Union?"

"No, I'm an émigré."

He immediately grows somber. "Yes, of course, I understand, you are probably an intellectual, a collective society
is difficult for you, but on the other hand, the working
man over there has many opportunities. And then there's
free medical service . . . "

"Why don't you move there?" I ask him. "Surely the
French authorities wouldn't place any obstacles in your
way."

He snorts, but remains silent. And I quite understand
him. He's not about to exchange free medical service for
his right to strike and to enjoy his predinner aperitif.

The official meeting hall at Hamburg University. Over
one hundred slumbering beards intermingled with round
curly heads are whistling, bawling, not allowing me to
speak, by chanting:

"Down with socialist imperialism! Down with so-ci-a-list
im-pe-ri-a-lism! Down with so-ci-a-list im-pe-ri-a-lism!"

What sort of connection they found between me and socialist imperialism I couldn't understand, but it seems that
this wasn't important to them. What was important was to
catch the speaker off guard, to get him off balance, crush
him, so to speak, psychologically. It's a familiar signature, a
familiar pattern! And how many such former little boys,
former enthusiasts, former knights of the revolution I had
met along the roads in labor camps, when they stood dirty
and ragged, and had all but lost their human image.

Those who now silently stand behind them, directing
such bacchanalia, are only temporary beams of support,
which will be immediately withdrawn after the taking
over of power. But just try proving this to them now.

At the same time, I'm certain that if you should scratch
their ultra-fashionable beards, underneath you would find
the square jaws of regular storm troopers.

A young philosopher. He's poor. He's emotional. He's
sincere. "Right-wingers scream that democracy is not for
those who speak against it," says he, as his elongated face,
with a surprisingly soft chin, grimaces with erstwhile pain.
"But at your trials in the U.S.S.R., Soviet accusers yell the
very same thing!"

Yes, my boy, you are absolutely correct. But there's one

tiny difference. Democracy here is established and controlled by the voters, but over there it's in the hands of the very same accusers. The difference may indeed seem small, but in my unenlightened opinion, it is quite substantial.

He's a student. Not so long ago, by hook or by crook, he somehow got out of Poland. We are sitting with him on a windowsill in a corridor of Columbia University. He looks at me with the transparent gaze of an albino and bluntly says without a shade of embarrassment:

"America is threatened by fascism!"

They say that someone else's experience doesn't teach you anything. Now it turns out that one's own experiences also don't always teach you any lessons. But on the other hand, who knows what sort of school, institution, or academy he had gone through over there?

An Italian writer. In the Soviet Union he is widely known for a couple of tolerable books and a weakness for Russian food. In some ways he looks a bit like Mussolini, but he doesn't have to shave his head: He is naturally bald. He carries his head as if there were a turban on it.

"What are you trying to tell me," he says with irritation at a reception in honor of two Russian dissident writers, "that in the Soviet Union people are not being published. I'm published!" It's difficult to understand whether in this case one detects more stupidity or cynicism.

Then we have his countryman of a very different kind. He's either the son or the grandson of one of the Duce's former close friends. The man is lean, good-looking, and is tidily dressed, as if he had just stepped out of the dry cleaners. He extends his dry claw to shake hands and with utmost sorrow raises his sclerotic eyes to the ceiling, sighing nostalgically:

"Don't believe these street-cryers. Hitler criminally distorted the bright ideals of fascism!" Then, with the doomed expression of offended virtue on his waxen face, he walks by in the direction of the meeting hall, where an international symposium on Human Rights is being held. It seems that humanism is understood by everyone in his own way.

3.

Stomp, stomp, stomp. Snort. And the saliva mixed with foam fans out. Now they come from all directions, advancing, crashing, forming a complete circle. It should be said, however, that our own native types are of the very same breed, like drops of water reflecting mirror-images of the species that can be found here. There's nothing to be done; it's a process of natural selection, so to speak.

4.

In the past he was a general in the White Army. Although he is now nearing one hundred years of age, in his day he was an eagle, a deft Cossack. The road is all behind him now, from Novocherkassk to Feodosia—framed with gallows. But in his old age, in a state of émigré indigence, he begins to bleed with protective patriotism. There's not a drop of difference between him and the Soviet attaché at the local embassy. They are two columns of a great power, one way or another the blue dream has come true: Half of Europe is under the heel of Russia, there you are!

After a humble meal, the old man bids farewell to the diplomat, who was well trained in his beloved homeland in the line of undercover police work. The elderly host mumbles affectionately through his dentures in the direction of his departing guest: "Well, I'll be . . . there's a patriot for you! He's of our own Cossack stock, not like those scoundrels, how do you call them, those mother . . . those dissidents!"

May God grant them both good health and many years of life. And who knows, maybe we'll be lucky: Perhaps, after sharing a bottle, they will also wind up sharing the same cell, where they can finally dissolve together in the ecstasy of Soviet patriotism.

This one is a poet, playing the frightened little girl, although she's well over forty. There's nothing simple about her. Everything is accompanied by grimaces, distortions, and sighs. She journeys to the cities and villages of the Old and New World, accompanied by her current husband, a gloomy individual from the dregs of Moscow's *beau monde*. She is the one who usually speaks, while he remains silent, looking around, taking stock, following the rule: Business comes first, and pleasure later. After all, work is work.

"I'm far from politics," says she, graciously stretching herself, as if to express the depth of her apolitical nature in the form of plasticity. "My element is poetry."

Perhaps this is so, but nonetheless, it doesn't stop her from leading her bearer of arms to all sorts of émigré meetings, even the most militant kind. But there's a question as to who leads whom.

Her Western kinsmen who share in her rich grazing grounds of graphomania stomp their hooves with great emotion: "Such loftiness! Such purity of soul! Such po-et-ry! Bravo!" And in their eternally petrified heads there is no room for the most obvious consideration: Namely, how is it that this unworldly creature of some forty-odd years with a Soviet passport and a limited French visa is able to cover a third of the Western hemisphere, in the company of her family art critic, the one with an officer's demeanor?

He's a film actor. A director. He's active. An heir of Stanislavsky. He's always either on the verge of going on a drinking binge or getting over one. He's been awarded all sorts of government trinkets, but thirsts for more, and consequently contributes to his country's investigative services by playing the role of the iconoclast. Such work is in all respects beneficial and brings in good money, but it also demands a certain wiliness.

During a press conference in San Francisco he announces: "We don't know and don't wish to know these Carters who receive in the White House some sort of dissident intellectuals." Then comes the crowning film gesture: He cuts the air with his palm, while the elbow moves smoothly to the side. "We are artists and our souls are manifested in peace and friendship, mutually advantageous trade, and SALT II." To sum it up: Whether we're Hindus, or Russians, or whatever, we're all for peace and friendship, hip, hip, hooray!

Naturally, this goose doesn't know—to use his own expression—"any Carters," but he does cite *Pravda* very faithfully, word for word. And the school does leave its mark: When it comes to overachievement, he follows the Stanislavsky method.

He's an orator. A screamer. A civic leader. Whatever you want. With his poems he literally relieves himself. He boils over with virtuous outrage. He exposes and brands people. But whom? Whomever you wish, with the exception of his own official rhinoceroses dressed in civilian clothing. And what? Anything but the cannibalism that takes place in his own country. At the same time he hints, and lets you understand. He makes allusions. On the basis of this poetic marauding he achieved wealth and semiscandalous fame. But his genre has aged, those golden days of handouts have come to an end.

"My fame is slipping away, like water through my fingers," he complains to a friend, drinking away his honorarium in a London pub—an award which he recently earned by exposing the ulcers of capitalism. And his white eyes drain a murky tear: "People are not grateful."

"Die, Denis, but you couldn't say it any better!"[4] However, whether you like it or not, the gratitude is commensurate with the quality of the poet.

He's an *artist*. In Russian this word means "to paint lively." This one paints even too lively. He has already fixed for posterity half a dozen reigning figures and no less than a dozen powerful personages of both sexes, different ages, and various calibers. He works in the manner of icon painting: Lollobrigida is presented as the Virgin Mary, and Brezhnev as Jesus Christ, donning a field marshal's regalia. They say that now he's doing Idi Amin, in a holy-father image, hoping to use his artistic skill in bringing out of a cannibal's face either the features of John the Baptist or Simon the Hermit. It's all done in the spirit of historical compromise, so to speak.

But after completing a recent journey across Europe, the simpleton had suddenly grown sad. He now desires a different kind of fame, pardon the expression, a fame of a heroic nature. Or perhaps the Party bosses have ordered that

[4]This is a reference to the poet Denis Davydov, who used to make this remark after reading his own poetry.

he should yearn for such. Sitting in his Moscow bedroom amidst the furniture of some Ludwig-or-other, he has gathered up on one canvas all past models, so as not to lose anything. And for oppositionary excitement he added the figure of our Savior, a prose writer greatly out of favor with the Soviet regime, and himself. Then he let it circulate in artistic *samizdat*: There you are, you envious rats . . . we can do it as well as you can!

It's not just a painting, but an entire conglomeration, a constellation, a camaraderie, a congress of giants. One could say that here there's not even room for an apple to fall. In this epochal mystery of the twentieth century only Ivan-the-Fool could not find accommodation. Or perhaps such Ivan-the-Fools no longer exist. Perhaps they have all become extinct.

5.

Dear Friends!

More than four years have passed since I arrived in the West. It's time to take stock. Looking back, I must admit with bitter certainty that since my departure from Russia I have lost far more than I have gained. Of course, I'm not speaking of drippy nostalgia, I don't suffer from that. And if my heart does ever start to ache, I have only to scurry to the local kiosk on the Etoile, look through our dear *Pravda*, and my melancholy disappears in a trice!

But how much more difficult for me is the loss of that environment, that is, those people whose fate in one way or another had intertwined with mine; that linguistic element in which my human and literary hearing had been molded; that proud awareness of being right, which comes when a person takes part in a common struggle against a dark and, without doubt, evil force.

That social micro-world which, during the course of several years, we were able to create in our homeland, around us and within us, was ruled by a responsible, fully realized set of moral laws: It was forbidden to kill, to lie, to be false. It was a marvelous island of mutual understanding, where everyone perceived each other from half a word, half a glance, half a hint, and even at a distance. Sometimes we simply remained silent on the telephone (oh, those Soviet telephones!) and for us this silence was far more expressive than the most fiery explanations or speeches.

Consequently, for a person with my makeup and temperament, the first and perhaps the most painful experience in the West was the complete change in the spectra of ethical, esthetic, and political criteria which are accepted here in evaluating people, events, and values. It has turned out that on the whole, everything is possible and permissible. What is black may be called white, and vice versa. Lying and killing is all right when it comes to "executioners," "oppressors," or "agents of imperialism." (By the way, in the opinion of some people your humble servant easily falls into the latter category; thus, who knows what that may lead to?) As to who may be so branded—that is determined in each case by the ideological subjectivity of the judge.

But God forbid, should you ever try, even ever so humbly, to point out certain inconsistencies between such dialectics and the most elementary principles of democracy! You will immediately be accused of obscurantism and be placed in the camp of dire reactionaries. And this, to be sure, will cost you dearly: The majority of doors will immediately be closed to you and gradually you will find yourself in professional and political isolation. The weight of this silent terror has been experienced by practically all those whose names in today's Russia elicit only admiration and gratitude: Orwell, Ionesco, Koestler, Conquest, Marcel, Aron, and many of their fellow thinkers.

I will state here and now: I cannot, I will not, and I have no intention of accepting any sort of political pluralism which includes past, current, or future hangmen, creators of their own Gulags, regardless of how noble their goals may be. For me, the word "communism" has been and remains a synonym for "reactionism" and "fascism." And by saying this, I'm not assuming a publicity posture; I state it as a responsible accusation, for during the course of the past century this word has been associated only with filth and bloodshed, in comparison with which all of Hitler's evil doing now seems to be but a pitiful exercise carried out by hysterical imitators. But if humanity has reached that spiritual and political level as to include also these elements in its pluralism, then why hasn't this same humanity also not found the courage to extend this type of pluralism to Hess, whose crimes don't even come close to those of the others. And yet, Hess is confined at Spandau Prison (and rightly so!), while the others sit in various European parliaments or fly around the world with their idea of "socialism with a human face."

What, then, is the matter?

The answer to this question is disquieting. For this is not merely a case of committing another social mistake, but it is a truly vegetative accommodation on the part of certain "dialectically thinking" intellectuals to political circumstances.

Not only do the new myths allow them to forget their own past quite painlessly by writing off their crimes as having been a part of their philosophical probings, but they also find it beneficial to exploit these myths for their own material gain.

Unfortunately, our own brother doesn't lag far behind; I have in mind, of course, the one who is of a meaner nature but who nonetheless has a good head on his shoulders. Yesterday's religious neophytes, principled opponents of a one-party system and a centralized economy, and former militant Zionists—suddenly become convinced neo-Marxists, advocates of the "third way," and fervent admirers of the PLO.

Writers without books, philosophers without ideas, and politicians without a world view have turned moral elasticity into their professions, after having castrated their memory of the goals and pathos of that selfless movement out of which they came. By considering their genuine or imagined accomplishments in the country which they had left not as obligatory offerings to be made to the continuing struggle, but as a means of receiving nice checks made out in their name, they are ready to use for their own selfish interests all of the tragic contradictions of the contemporary world, such as nationalism, anti-Semitism, and religion. Now it is not uncommon to find that prior to giving an interview about political prisoners or human rights, an émigré voyager crosses his legs and says in a businesslike fashion: "All right, put the money on the barrelhead!"

All of this weighs down your soul with shame, sadness,

and revulsion, to the point of no return. And it's twice as upsetting and disappointing when you find yourself encircled by that angry rhinoceros onslaught, instead of hearing words of support from back home—from those very people you trusted and believed in—you hear only this kind of comment: "Not this, not that, not there."

Could it be possible that over there, behind those walls and the barbed wire where words are drowned out by electronic jamming, it's easier to judge whether things here should be like "that" or like "this"? Would it not be more natural for us to continue our association, as in the past, on the basis of mutual trust and understanding, from half a word, half a glance, half a hint, or even simply at a distance? You are there and we are here.

After all, each one of us has remained the same person that he was at home, with his upward flights (if there were any) and downfalls (if there were such!). We are here with all of our preexistent worthy and unworthy attributes, except that now we have grown much sadder and older.

A wrongful act can be committed because of thoughtlessness or from ill intent by one person, even by someone well known to you, including myself, but standing by me are people whom, I hope, you continue to love: Iosif Brodsky, Volodya Bukovsky, Tolya Gladilin, Natasha Gorbanevskaya, Emma Korzhavin, Erik Neizvestny, and Vika Nekrasov,[5] all of whom have their own personal contacts and attachments. To his very last day, Sasha Galich,[6] a man with a pure soul, also gave us his full support. You must agree that such a group of vastly diverse people could not have conspired to perpetrate the same wrongful act. Yes, people can make mistakes, they can lose self-control, and they can be indecisive, but on the whole, we are pursuing our cause in the name of those very same ideals which united us in our homeland. It is for this that we continue to live and to think. We try to work, as best we can, but at the same time we must defend ourselves on all sides from the merciless attacks of the rhinoceroses.

[5]The author uses the diminutive versions of these individuals' names.—TRANS.
[6]Alexander Galich, a popular Russian émigré poet who sang his verse to the accompaniment of a guitar, and who died in Paris in 1977.

How much easier it would be for us to withstand this incredibly lone struggle if we were made to understand that you are standing behind us, even silently. A vicious encirclement with none of "our own people" standing behind us is fatal for us and you. But if you still do exist, if you are still there and stand waiting, then I feel certain that ultimately, we shall break through to one another.

6.

Horn to horn. Nostril to nostril. Saliva and foam, fanning out. They're breaking through, formation after formation, drawing a circle. And on that tiny disc of land which is still free of their stomping stands a lonely man wearing a sweater, who in my imagination is attired in a white toga with a crimson border. That bit of earth becomes increasingly minuscule and crowded. They encircle him from all sides, squinting with their bloodshot eyes at the doomed, peculiar man, who refuses to yield. Give me your hand, Eugène, we shall fall together beneath their hooves, but we shall not give in. We wish to die as human beings. We who are about to die salute you!

Make way for the rhinoceroses! Make way!

Paris, July 1978

Personal Responsibility
as a General
East-West Problem

Kontinent Round Table Discussion,
Paris, September 15, 1977

Translated by Albert C. and Tanya Schmidt

From Kontinent, No. XIV, 1977

VLADIMIR MAXIMOV: First of all, I would like to thank everyone here today for responding to our invitation. And then, at the request of Andrei Sakharov, I would like to read a document of the greatest current interest. Apart from its news value, this document fits in beautifully with the theme of our round table.

[V. Maximov reads the Letter from Political Prisoners in Perm Camp No. 36:]

ABOUT THE PARTICIPANTS IN THE ROUND TABLE: The well-known playwright Eugène Ionesco and also Vladimir Bukovsky and Ernst Neizvestny are members of Kontinent's *editorial board. Philosopher Alexander Piatigorsky, represented elsewhere in this collection, is a regular contributor to* Kontinent. *Jean-François Revel was until recently editor of the news magazine* L'Express. *André Glucksmann is one of the most prominent of France's young "nouveaux philosophes." Ilios Yannakakis, who is a professor at the University of Lille, was a Greek political émigré in Czechoslovakia, 1949–1968, and has been a Czech political émigré in France since 1968. The older-generation French philosopher Michel Foucault also took part in the discussion but was unwell and dissatisfied with his address, and requested that it not be published.*

The West is faced with making a choice, which cannot be avoided and which will determine not only the political but to a great extent also the moral atmosphere in Europe and in the world. Although this choice is intricately connected to the question of political prisoners and inalienable human rights, it does not pertain simply to the fate of a few hostages held in labor camps and in the "big zone"[1] of evil, force, and falsehood. In reality, we are speaking here primarily about something else: namely, the extent to which liberty and human rights are valued by those who are used to exercising these rights with consistency and confidence.

In plain sight of the entire world, irresponsible leaders of the Communist bloc have cynically scorned their international commitments. In the darkness of closed trials they have been violating their own laws and have been covering up their crimes with false, empty words about serving the people and about the existence of some sort of higher form of democracy.

In its search for unreliable and temporary security and transient political and economic advantages, some of which may be substantive, will the West once again choose not to notice the tyranny, and once again pretend to be simply uninformed and trusting? Will the West again try to gloss over the sharp edges with polite phrases about each of the opposing sides being true to its own social concepts? Will the West consider the military might and evil decisiveness of totalitarian governments as reason enough to allow once again that these criminals will not be tried, but only those who are weaker?

Let's call a spade a spade and ask the following question: Will you be forced to condescend to the commission of crimes because of your conceding posture? Falsehood does not exist without those who believe in it, or at least pretend that they do. Criminals need your acquiescence as much as your dollars; your indifference is as necessary to them as your machinery.

[1]This is an expression used to refer to the entire U.S.S.R. as a labor camp.—TRANS.

On the other hand, the West may find the wisdom to:

—believe that human beings have no higher or more urgent goal than to limit violence and the lying that conceals it;

—insist on morality and equal rights for everyone, for these are the sole guarantees of the secure existence of a world which is now closely bound;

—choose spiritual values instead of daily practical matters, and to defend these values today, rather than tomorrow;

—disregard the momentary contradictions of narrow interests and unify itself on behalf of a greater goal;

—state firmly that someone else's blood and tears are not a matter of their own internal affairs;

—seek solutions to problems which may not be immediately within reach, but are indeed difficult, and try to stop lawlessness at the source, from whence deception and the temptation to commit violence are spread everywhere;

—have enough selfless loyalty to adhere to its moral duty.

That, in essence, is where the choices must be made.

They are trying to convince you that despotism can be peace-loving, and that leaders who have turned lying, slander, and lawless actions into professional careers for thousands of people inside the country, will be honest in carrying out their commitments outside of the country. You are often told: "Be realistic and don't forget how strong we are. Don't drag morality into politics, better leave it for Sunday sermons. Is it realistic to notice things which we are concealing, and to speak about them openly? This can only make détente more difficult."

It is undoubtedly true that making a singular moral choice is indeed not a simple matter in terms of traditional politics.

But if the exchange value in the political game will once again be to the detriment of liberty—someone else's liberty—which your predecessors helped lose for so many people, remember that the disreputable experience of bartering with someone else's liberty inevitably leads to the loss of your own.

ZINOVIY ANTONYUK	PYATRAS PLUMPA
SEMYEN GLUZMAN	EVGEN SVERSTYUK
IGOR KALYNETS	IVAN SVETLYCHNY
SERGEI KOVALEV	BAGRAT SHAKHVERDIAN
VALERIY MARCHENKO	

(Translated by Ludmilla Thorne)

MAXIMOV: This document was received from Russia literally the day before yesterday, and it makes it possible for me to conclude what I say with this brief remark: When my friends and I are asked who we are, whether we are leftists or rightists, we answer thus: We are no further to the left than our hearts, and our hearts are with them—with the authors of this letter.

[V. Maximov yields the chair to N. Gorbanevskaya, who will lead the discussion.]

NATALYA GORBANEVSKAYA: I believe that the theme we have chosen for today's discussion goes far beyond the confines of politics as such, and that when we talk about the problem of personal responsibility we will not engage in mutual recrimination nor will we be patting each other on the back. I am convinced that all those present share the viewpoint of our political prisoners, and that the majority will do everything possible in order that the wishes of our prisoners may attain fulfillment in practice.

[N. Gorbanevskaya reads a speech by Yefrem Yankelevich, who is not among those present at the Round Table. Yankelevich has been an active participant in the human-rights defense movement over the past several years; he has just come out to the West, and at great risk to himself brought the letter from the political prisoners. Yankelevich's speech is written in the form of a letter to the editor-in-chief of Kontinent.]

YEFREM YANKELEVICH: Dear Vladimir Yemelyanovich! The letter from nine political prisoners at Perm is hardly in need of commentary from anyone. However, it is concerned in particular with one aspect of the problem of the personal responsibility of the individual, the problem of moral choice, and I would like to say a few words about that.

Totalitarian socialism has one feature that many people, unfortunately, find attractive. It relieves a person of the necessity for making decisions in concordance with individual ethical values or even with certain general concepts of good and evil. I am sure that in today's discussion there will be a more detailed and more competent treatment of the question of personal moral choices in the ideocratic state. But here I would simply like to say that, nonetheless, no totalitarian despotism is able to deprive a person of that priceless gift which consists in the right to choose between good and evil.

In making their choice, the writers of this letter brought down upon themselves a tragic fate at various times and under various circumstances. As I see it, it was not their intention thereby to assume responsibility for the destinies of their native country and of the world. However, and perhaps for that very reason, they now find themselves among that small number of people who bear such responsibility henceforth. And today no one will think it strange that it is precisely these people, turned into hostages by the inconsistency of some Western governments and by the unprincipled behavior of others, who are speaking of the problems confronting the West and of the roads they envisage as leading to the solution of those problems.

Nine prisoners in the strict-regime camp at Perm are calling upon people in the West to make a moral choice, to choose between freedom and freedom from the necessity of defending that freedom.

I hope that the theme of today's discussion will make it possible to talk about this letter.

[*N. Gorbanevskaya gives the floor to Alexander Piatigorsky, whom she introduces as the only "professional philosopher" among the Russians present.*]

ALEXANDER PIATIGORSKY: First of all, I find it a most unfortunate state of affairs for the management of *Kontinent* to have committed the grave error of inviting me to open this discussion. And to begin with, I should like to clarify, to some extent, my own understanding of my profession. I am a very bad philosopher. And the circumstance that I am the "only philosopher" can hardly serve to explain or justify this low quality.

I would like to start my brief remarks by expressing total disagreement with what has just been said. The reading and all the comments on the letter from the prisoners add up to an attempt to convince the West that it should make a choice. As a representative of that unhappy and wholly degenerated profession, I must say that we not only cannot compel the West to make such a choice on moral grounds, we cannot even request that it do so. The fact of the matter is, in the first place, that on the one hand you have several dozen outstandingly courageous people in Soviet prisons and concentration camps, who have signed their names to these and other letters in which they figure as persons, as separate individuals. For those signatures they have paid with their time, their blood, and their life. On the other hand, they are making a big mistake: The error consists in clinging to belief in an abstraction termed the West and Western man.

In my opinion, there is no such thing as the West and no Western man as such. I see us all as prey to this dreadful misconception, the sources of which go back into Western and Russian philosophy alike. Again, on the one hand you have separate people, yet at the same time there is an impersonal and integral entity known as West or East. And again we hope that the problems for which we have paid and are paying will be solved by somebody else. We say: "The West must do this or that." "The West must understand." "The West must wake up." But I assure you that the West is under no compulsion to do anything whatsoever! "For the entire world to see" is a phrase appearing in this letter. The world cannot see, for the world has no eyes: It is only the individual who has eyes. The world possesses no consciousness. There is no such thing as a collective consciousness.

I know why they write the way they do. But what I cannot understand is why we take it the way we do. "Will the West have wisdom enough?" we read, or "Will the West be sufficiently wise?" At this point I cannot refrain from referring back to a book I have just read by André Glucksmann entitled *The Cook and the Cannibal*. The author writes that that frightful state system deceived the people with the help of philosophy, that this intelligent, freedom-loving and talented people were fooled by the system. When I recall my childhood and my life as a philosopher up until my escape to the West, I am unable to regard myself either as talented or as intelligent. We were fooled because we were fools. Just as the fools were deceived in 1792 and 1793. Just as they are being deceived now and will continue to be deceived. André Glucksmann is very sorry for us; I am not sorry for us.

Now I should like to go on to the next problem, which in my view is the most terrible one of all—the problem of choice. I understand it when wonderfully brave people are being tormented and speak to us about the problem of choice. I can understand that very well. But this problem not only cannot be forced upon others. It cannot be even proposed by given individuals to other individuals. The reason is that we will find ourselves once more imprisoned within the perennial dichotomy of good and evil, which the strong will always discover ways to interpret to their advantage against the weak. In this respect, no culture, whether Western or Eastern, Russian or American or African, will be of any avail.

I believe that the problem of good and evil will remain an utterly hopeless problem as long as it continues to be a problem of the relations between the collective and society, between one person and two persons taken together. I think that the only way to put this problem in its proper perspective, though not necessarily to solve it, will be for each individual to enter into a dialogue on the subject of good and evil with his God rather than with other persons. And I am afraid that the Church itself is as helpless as is the collective to bring about such a communion.

In concluding, permit me to say one more word concerning philosophy. As it happens, we have become accustomed to living in the dualistic world of being and consciousness. This is a disastrous world, wholly dominated—and here I am in complete agreement with Glucksmann—by the basic European philosophical line extending from Plato to Lenin: Every problem is resolved either in favor of consciousness or in favor of being. Either the bald schoolteachers, those degenerates who are teachers of life, annihilate being from the position of consciousness; or else elemental forces will leave them hanging from the lampposts and will destroy consciousness from the standpoint of being. And I believe that we are now living in a curious period where the only possible recourse is for each person to be his own philosopher and pay no attention to other philosophies.

ILIOS YANNAKAKIS: I would like to say that on one point I do not agree with Piatigorsky. Alas, Western man does exist— or, rather, there is such a thing as a Western turn of mind. We who have come out of another world made that discovery, and we were traumatized. For, you should not forget, the truth about Eastern Europe and about the Soviet Union had been known for a long time. But, most astonishingly, the memory of Western man had screened itself off from that truth, refusing to admit the darker aspects which dominate in everyday life. We who have come from the Eastern European countries enjoy a tremendous advantage over a person living in the West: Each one of us traveled his own way, went through his own course of development and occupied definite positions—again, positions that were entirely his own—with respect to the regime, the dominating ideology, and the dominating language. We were fenced in by prohibitions; we had neither sources of information nor the means to acquire knowledge, and yet each tried to grasp the meaning of his own experiences. The result of this was a strange and paradoxical sense of freedom; each one of us, as far as his strength, character, and courage permitted, saw his horizons continually opening out. There, in those open spaces, contact came about among the people whom the West refers to as dissidents or as the dissident phenomenon. These meetings were characterized by mutual tolerance on the part of all concerned, as well as by emphatic insistence on diversity, for we eschew uniformity of opinion.

We held the naïve belief that a Westerner, having at his disposal all avenues of access to information and opportunity for free exchange of words and thoughts, should have a much easier time going through such a process of development than we did. But the occasions have been rare: It is only rarely that people proceeding from different ideological horizons have been able to get together. This is an incontrovertible fact. To deny it would be wrongly to estimate the effort we must make in the West in order that our East European reality may cease to be an exotic article, a luxury item that is purchased when it is in vogue, and may become, instead, a constant source of raw material for thought in the mind of the Westerner when he reflects on his own right to exist. It should become a source of reflection for the person who does not submit to the pressure of established order and routines, of political expediency and ideological phantoms, and who wishes to be the free protagonist in his own history. The tolerance we naturally display toward every individual who goes through his own process of development must become a tolerance possessed by Western man as well. If there is a process of rehabilitation now under way in the West, then it is most definitely a rehabilitation of humanism. To the best of our modest powers we are contributing to that development.

EUGÈNE IONESCO: As far as talk about the West is concerned, it is perfectly clear that the West has accomplished nothing except blunders. It is clear that the real colonization is beginning now, starting with decolonization. In other words, in colonial times cultures were free; spiritual traditions existed; and at a certain moment we even began to hope that the East would be precisely the place where the West would find the sources of perennial wisdom that it had lost. This hope proved vain. Marxism conquered the East, and now the African countries know the high price that must be paid for faith in national independence, since national independence does not signify freedom of the person.

It is difficult to do without ideology. But one must be careful to see that the ideologies retain a direct connection with reality, that they do not become a screen between reality and ourselves. The *nouveaux philosophes*, including Glucksmann who is here today, have demonstrated beautifully to us that ideologies are merely the instruments or the conditions for the enslavement of man. But discussions concerning the enslavement of man invariably involve ideology.

The present moment is favorable to an understanding of reality, an understanding of truth. We have more or less liberated ourselves from a pile of dogmas, including Marxism. The latter is a kind of surrealism, which facilitates the creation—in Alain Besançon's phrase—of "surrealistic societies." We are left without Marxism, and I must say that the consequences of this deprivation are quite heavy. In a book that came out recently, the young French writer Elisabeth Antébi asks this question: How is Western man going to get along without Marxism? For, having lost it, he has at the same time lost all of his points of reference and bearing. I have a friend who is a poet. I respect him very much as a poet, but then he says: "I understand all the mistakes of Marxism and Communism. But what else is there? Where else to go? So I am remaining in that church." Inasmuch as we cannot get along without ideas one way or another, it seems to me personally that it would be better, instead of shuffling around in a void, to resort to the temporary expedient of old philosophies and old religions, whether Christianity or Buddhism or even Western liberalism—which is an evil, of course, but the lesser of evils.

In the final analysis, it is time to learn to distinguish what is good from what is bad. Do we love people or don't we? Do we want to live under terror or do we not? On this level the choice is not between complicated ideologies and philosophies, but between simple and evident realities.

I should like to add that the West has awakened after all. A new philosophical school of thought has appeared; we have already had an opportunity to make its acquaintance. This young school is anti-Marxist, although it proceeds from Marx—or, rather, from a negation of Marx. It is clear that the new philosophy does not want to have teachers with a capital T. But it does have one flaw, very possibly: Is it not perhaps an anti-ideology? Does it not boil down to a simple negation of certain ideological assertions, instead of simply asserting certain fundamental human realities? In other words, I am beginning to have the impression that ideology nonetheless continues to be the source of contemporary anti-ideology; the danger in this anti-ideology, as I see it, is that by growing out of ideology it cannot be a pure

progeny of the facts. The facts have been known to us for a
long time. André Gide, Panait Istrati, Victor Serge, Arthur
Koestler, Raymond Aron, Ferenc Feito, Manes Sperber, and
many others have written about the misery of being Marxist, about the tribulations of Marxist society. And Revel,
who is sitting across from me, has also dealt with this subject. But the act did not go over: These people were not believed. Why not? They were not believed because there existed and there still exist too many different interests
which run contrary to the awakening of humanistic consciousness in the individual.

In 1968, at the time of the occupation of Czechoslovakia,
Czech students protesting against the invasion clashed
with French lefties in the Sixteenth Arrondissement, who
yelled at them: "You are *bourgeois!* What do you know about
it?" The students of West Berlin, in turn, took it into their
heads to travel to Czechoslovakia in order to explain this
phenomenon which the Czechs and the Slovaks were for
some reason unable to understand. That is probably due to
the fact that ideology inspired greater confidence than
reality, as well as to the circumstance that people in the
West had reached a degree of such intense mutual hatred
that they knew everything and yet did not want to know
anything: The end of the world would be preferable
to making the *bourgeoisie* happy or to disappointing
Billancourt.[2]

The French knew what was going on. They had known
for a long time. It would be interesting to figure out why
they are now taking into account that which they shrugged
off earlier. Could the reason be that to become an anti-
leftist you have to go through a leftist stage? That is not the
important thing, however; the issue at hand is the sickness
of American, English, and French thought. As I already
mentioned, quoting Elisabeth Antébi, it is a question of
man having lost his bearings—and also perhaps, I should
hope, of some sort of awakening, of a rebirth of human
compassion and solidarity. Therein consists my hope, my
feeble hope, when I look at the changes taking place in the
West.

Several years ago Maximov said to me: "We will tell

[2]A workers' suburb in Paris.—ED.

about everything. We will tell of what is going on in Russia; we will tell of the camps and the penal colonies; we will tell all—and the West will understand." For the time being, he said to me, the West is still the repository of the conscience of all mankind. My answer to him then was this: "Your efforts will be in vain. Everything you are going to talk about they already know—they simply do not want to take it to heart." Well, I must confess that I was wrong: People really are beginning to take the facts into consideration. But the question is: What is the nature and the depth of their concern? If a Communist government, an anti-humanist government, comes to power—I beg the pardon of the anti-humanists here present, but—I do not know whether they will be able to resist it, whether they will be able to endure the deprivations and whether they will be able to change the face of the world.

There is one more story I forgot to tell. I happened to be present at a conversation between two intellectuals. I say "intellectuals," because intellectuals are not scholars, not sociologists or psychologists, not physicists and not mathematicians. Intellectuals are journalists and people who write novels. Well, these two intellectual novelist-journalists were saying to each other: "It really is terrible, what's going on in the East, but we must not talk about it, so as not to give the *bourgeoisie* cause for rejoicing."

ANDRÉ GLUCKSMANN: It is not easy to speak as a Frenchman, because, as you have been able to observe, the French are very different and, what is more, they cherish their differences. It seems to me that it is important to take that into consideration, since the people in France who adopt a slighting attitude toward the dissidents and their struggle are also very different. At least on the surface: It is significant that a sort of "common program" exists in the realm of foreign policy, which accounts for the fact that the leftists, as well as Giscard d'Estaing, criticize the support rendered to the struggle for human rights—regardless of whether that support comes from the intelligentsia, from various individuals, or from President Carter. But what this proves also is that the dissident movement poses problems that upset traditional patterns, and this somehow permits us to hope that something like the "new philosophy" will exist in the twenty-fourth century—if that century ever dawns, and the outlook for that is not too good. Of all the questions that have been raised here, there is one that strikes me as being particularly serious: Why is it that the information concerning terror in Russia which has been coming in since as early as 1920 took so long to evoke a response in the West, and why has the situation begun to change today? I think there are two reasons for this.

The first reason is the more important: It is the contribution made to our life by the Soviet dissidents, beginning with the greatest of them all—Solzhenitsyn. For it must be said that the new element in what he brought us was not the information about Gulag and its extent, but rather the testimonials concerning resistance to Gulag. In sum I would say that the Russian and East European dissident movement compels us to relinquish our old "reformism-revolution" schematics. For, from everything we can see, the dissidents are no longer focusing their attention on what transpires at the top levels of the state. With the possible exception of the Medvedev brothers, they are not interested in current trends within the Soviet government. And on the other hand, they are not attempting to set up underground organizations for the purpose of overthrowing the regime and seizing power. On the contrary, they are operating as far out in the open as possible, and the human-rights strategy has introduced an entirely new factor as compared with the old methods of waging revolution or reforming the state. I have put this briefly, but I think that is the main point, since it forces us to swing our attention away from what is going on inside the bureaucracies. Criticism of Gulag was always possible in the past, but now we know the main thing, which is what is going on among the people.

And the second point that seems important to me is one on which I am replying in part to Piatigorsky. The only way to understand the dissident phenomenon is to go on the basis of one's own experience. In other words, the choice posed by the Soviet dissidents really cannot be imposed, and in all probability it cannot even be proposed; however, we can approach it ourselves on the basis of our own experience. As far as I personally am concerned, I will say that such an event as May 1968—despite all its ambiguity—made it possible for me and others to arrive at a better appreciation of what the Russian and East European dissident movement offers us. As for the ambiguous character of May 1968, I would like to remind you that the students who took part in that movement were for the most part quite far from being pro-Communist or pro-Soviet in their sympathies; and, even if they were not anti-Communists, then at least they definitely were not Communists. You will recall that the leader of those students applied the epithet of "Stalinist sons of bitches" to the bosses of the Communist Party and the pro-Communist labor union. And he kicked out Aragon, who "had come to bring the support of a poet to the demonstrators," telling him that his gray hairs were smeared with the blood of Soviet concentration-camp inmates.

The primary reason for my own sensitivity to the appeals of the Soviet dissidents dates back to my early years. I was born into a Jewish family that emigrated to France in 1936. At home I always heard conversations in which the question was raised of how little the French understood the tales told by refugees from Nazi Germany. Everyone knows what a high price France had to pay for its incomprehension. Here is an up-to-date example. Yesterday in *Le Monde* I read a statement by a Nobel Prize winner in physics. He said that if he had to choose between America and Russia he would go to the U.S.A. for professional reasons, but he could easily understand if a worker would choose Russia in order to avoid sharing the sad fate of the American unemployed. Everyone is entitled to his own opinion; there is nothing wrong with that; but then doubt is cast over everything that Billancourt stands for—the place where the workers fought for the right to strike and for the right to maintain their own convictions. Indeed, it took several centuries for Western workers to win the right to freedom of movement, the right to leave their employer if they so desired—in a word, the right to be treated as human beings. As we know, none of these freedoms exist in the Soviet Union. And consequently, for a representative of the intelligentsia to state that this can be disregarded constitutes a danger not only toward the support extended to the Soviet dissidents, but also to support for any workers' struggle in France, since every labor movement has been a movement for freedom. To assert that a worker would definitely and naturally prefer Russia to America is simply to nullify three centuries of struggle waged by the workers. Failure to understand the Soviet dissidents implies and entails a failure to understand our own liberties. And this failure is fully as dangerous as the incomprehension manifested by the French in 1937 in the face of what was transpiring in Nazi Germany. This would be true even if the consequences should be less horrendous, as one would like to hope.

A second reason why I respond so readily to the dissidents is as follows. For ten years I attributed tremendous importance to the struggle against colonial wars and racism in the West. And to this date I still consider that struggle to be terribly important, especially in that it enables me to understand the fight against imperialism in Eastern Europe. Let me explain by giving an example. The American blacks demanded application in practice of the rights guaranteed in principle by the Constitution to every citizen of the United States irrespective of the color of his skin. The activists went into the streets to put those rights into effect publicly, "here and now," despite resistance from the police in the Southern states and from the racists. Achieving recognition of rights by putting them into effect "here and now" even at the risk of life and limb is a tactic that is quite familiar to the Soviet dissidents, who have applied it in full force under much more horrible circumstances. As a fighting strategy, effective and self-sacrificing implementation of human rights has attained worldwide dimensions, echoing the civil-rights and free-speech movement in the U.S.A. American Indians are now demanding that the agreements signed in the nineteenth century, granting them benefits and territorial restitutions, be put into effect. These demands are quite similar to those put forward by the Crimean Tatars, with the difference that the Indians may resort to legal action, and obtain court rulings in their favor more often than not.

Thirdly, there was May 1968. It was an ambiguous event, as I have mentioned before; nonetheless it must be numbered among the great spontaneous outbursts on behalf of freedom in the West—analogous to the earlier movement sparked off by the Dreyfus case, for example. Every time such an event occurs, it is followed by a choice, defined by Péguy at the time of the Dreyfus case as the choice between "politicians" and "mystics." At that time, and during the next ten years, Péguy was not yet a Catholic. By mysticism he meant respect for justice—respect, for example, for freedom of the press in the Socialist movement; the latter issue caused conflict, even then, between him and the founding fathers of the Socialist Party in France, including Jaurès. I do not think that this is hard for the Soviet dissidents to understand: At that time it was already known as the Party spirit. On the one hand, the highest ambition of the "politicians" consisted in political careerism within large organizations devoted to the supreme idea of seizing power and determining the destiny of mankind. On the other hand, the spirit of the "mystics" envisaged liberties as being realized by everybody and not as being donated by the State. This essential dualism, as I see it, is rendered clearer and more understandable by the struggle of the dissidents. It shows, if you will, what there is in common between Péguy and Matrëna or Ivan Denisovich.

In conclusion I should like to say that, if we have welcomed the Soviet dissident movement, if our encounter with the dissidents has taken place and all of this is conditioned by our own experience, that means that the phenomenon of Russia cannot be explained in terms of that country's backwardness, as leftist functionaries insist. The intellectual universe of West and East is one and the same. There is only one thing we have to be afraid of—and this does not mean that the Soviet regime is backward, as is claimed by the Communist Ellenstein, the Socialist Atali, and company—namely, that the regime might be ahead of us, by putting into practice a number of ideas on government that are not at all unfamiliar to the West. But let us not be pessimistic. Let us say that in Russia we are confronting an enlarged version of all the same conflicts between ordinary people and the ruling power which occur in France on a smaller scale. On a much smaller scale, fortunately.

JEAN-FRANÇOIS REVEL: First of all, I would like to reassure André Glucksmann: If the Nobel Prize winners think that the working man would prefer to go to the Soviet Union, the working man for his part thinks roughly the same thing about them. Public opinion polls—our new national religion—periodically show that, to the question "Where would you emigrate to, if you had to emigrate?" not more than two percent of the French reply: To the U.S.S.R. This, by the way, is one more indication of what Glucksmann insisted on in his speech—that is, the peculiar gulf that traditionally exists in French culture, as in many other Western cultures, I think, between the ruling class in the state and the population. Unfortunately, it is precisely this ruling element which originates and transmits information, whether it has at its disposal the mass information media, or culture, or politics or economics. In this sense, while Ionesco voices a certain cautious optimism in regard to the consciousness now awakening in the West, I must say that for my part I take a much less confident view of that fact than he and others do, as I believe that we are dealing with a phenomenon that waxes and wanes periodically.

In the beginning of the 1930s, after the destruction and the hunger caused by forcible collectivization, the reputation of the Soviet experiment was decidedly tarnished. But two or three years passed, and that lesson was forgotten. Then the Moscow trials began. Contrary to the generally accepted opinion, the trials were abundantly analyzed and commented upon at that time. One might have thought that the lure of Communism had been conclusively discredited in the West. And the same seemed to be the case after the signing of the Soviet-German pact, and then again at the time of the "doctors' plot" and the trials in Prague, Budapest, and Sofia. Finally, when Khrushchev's secret report was read at the Twentieth Soviet Party Congress, many people thought that a decisive turning point had been reached and that the lesson had at last been learned. Far from it. A few months later, Soviet troops invaded Hungary, and the leftists in France and Italy proved how strong they were. I remember very well how, within a bare six weeks after that deplorable event, they came to life in body and soul as though nothing at all had happened.

André Glucksmann has just cited the example of May 1968, quite correctly stressing the fact that the 1968 movement in France was antitotalitarian in its essence. Two months after it ebbed, that antitotalitarian wave was rein-

forced by an event of the greatest importance—the entry of
Soviet tanks into Prague. But I would like to emphasize
that that same event marked the beginning of an unprecedented growth in the strength of Communist parties in the
West—in Italy and in France. These parties had not experienced such an upswing since the day they were founded.

That is why I think that the phenomenon we are dealing
with is akin to chronic loss of memory. It is caused, in my
opinion, by the constant confusion in people's minds between the right-left antagonism within democratic society,
on the one hand, and the fight against totalitarianism on
the other. The socialist tradition—quite sincerely at the
outset—had identified the Chinese and Soviet totalitarian
regimes with leftist ideas. But the struggle against totalitarianism is neither rightist nor leftist. By definition, it is possible to draw a line between the right and the left only
where democratic conditions prevail. Totalitarianism constitutes a negation of the very possibility of making such a
distinction. Up to now, fidelity to leftist ideas has been tied
to some form of deference toward totalitarian regimes and
fear of criticizing them because they have the reputation of
being leftist. Until we shall be able conclusively to disso-
ciate these intertwined attitudes, we will continue to run
up against instances of the amnesia, or loss of memory, of
which I have just spoken.

And in this context it seems to me that, of all the things
that we are told by Soviet dissidents who are still in the
U.S.S.R. or who are now among us here in the West, the
most important by far is their constant reminder, for the
benefit of our public opinion, that the struggle going on
between freedom and totalitarianism has nothing whatever to do with the left-right conflict within the democratic countries.

ERNST NEIZVESTNY: It is the sculptor's prerogative not to
speak, since his business is to model and carve, and so I do
not wish to philosophize. I would simply like to amuse the
audience by telling some stories, instead of making observations. I will omit all the terrible tales about prisons and
my broken nose and my wounds. I will relate various
things concerning simple life, proceeding from my own
personal experience. I dare to hope that my stories will re-

veal an idea of why we sometimes do not understand each other. Although in principle we should be able to understand each other, because the only word that we all understand and that needs no commentary is the word *death*. But all of the other words have turned out to have double meanings. Evidently, before we converse, it is necessary to compile a new dictionary of concepts which will contain all of the words we operate with.

They have two meanings. The word *freedom* means one thing to us and another thing to you. For example, when in Russia they say, "It is necessary to strengthen legality," all Russia begins to tremble with fear. When they say that it is necessary to develop democracy, housewives begin to burn year-old books. Even such simple words as *theater*, for instance, are completely different. For example, the publisher Albert Skira ordered a book from me about my work, and as a model to follow he sent me a book by Ionesco, whom I respect. The book begins with these words: "I do not remember whether I was two years old or even younger, but I fell in love once and for all with theater and art." And then, before writing my book, I began to think back. Did I fall in love with the theater when I was a child? To me, the words *theater* and *art* were curse words, because in 1937 when my father was brought to trial he said: "This is all theater, a lot of artistic staging." From that time on, from childhood, the word *theater* in my mind was a term of abuse. All the more so in that the real theater was the quintessence of falsehood. Simple Russian people, when they want to say you are lying, say: "Where do you think you are, in the theater?" There you have an illustration of a plain word.

To continue—and I am going only by my personal experience—on the concept of happiness. I believe that happiness is evenly distributed in a person. One half sleeps in the happiness of the slave and the other half in the happiness of liberty. I myself experienced the happiness of the slave. Maybe that was the most delightful feeling in my life. I graduated from a military school [*desantnoye uchilishche*] where the discipline was strict but where there was a problem of choice anyway. For instance, I could go to the latrine when I wanted to. But when they put me on a train and did not say where it was going, I lay down on the bench, and the train left, and I realized that they had liberated me from my will. They were taking me somewhere and they would feed me in time. There is a Russian proverb: "The soldier sleeps but duty goes on." And I experienced a real feeling of happiness. I was totally free. I had obtained the freedom of the slave. That is why I know that the freedom of a slave is equal to the freedom of a free man. And this is where the problem of choice comes in. It is an ancient problem, discussed by Saint Augustine, and Camus, and the Communists, and everybody. And here, too, arises the problem of which my friend Piatigorsky spoke, concerning certain forms of Russian personalism— after all, we do tend to dwell on the idea of personalism. I ask that a distinction be made between the anarchism of Kropotkin and of Bakunin, because in Russia the term *personalism* is equated with the term *anarchism*.

My second story is about the Russian situation, because I am not a doctor writing out prescriptions, but a patient thinking about the problem of his own illness. When I began to study in the philosophy faculty, I suddenly realized how they were teaching us. We knew about Lenin from the writings of Stalin. We knew about Marx from what Lenin had written about him. We knew about Dühring from *Anti-Dühring*. And then some of the students got the idea that they could teach themselves and so a self-education group was formed—a sort of catacomb culture, as it were. The task we set ourselves was not a political one. Our purpose was purely cultural. You can picture intellectual life in Russia as proceeding along two lines. One of these lines may be described as the horizontal, which is socially related culture; but in Russia there is also a vertical culture that has to do with values that are not of the present day. In my conviction, it is only in the center of this cross that the genuine cultural phenomenon appears, where the eternal and the immediate intersect. Dostoyevski is a case in point. But we began to work at vertical culture.

This was not dissidence, but it became dissidence, because in Russia everything that is not official is dissidence. And gradually we got together with the dissidents. Why are we personalists? Because in our country, unlike the West, the religious philosopher is a dissident, and so is the Trotskyite, and the Gestaltist is a dissident, because all of that is culture. And together we stood up against the anti-culture of society. And in order to associate with each other we had to respect personalism and remain friends. We had a common enemy who united us. This phenomenon does not exist in the West. This is why we are sometimes incomprehensible. Perhaps this may serve somewhat as an explanation to Piatigorsky's remarks.

Now I would like to tell a little story about something that happened to me. I have the greatest respect for Sartre. In my studio and at a restaurant I talked with him for about six hours. I cannot repeat that whole six-hour conversation I had with Sartre. So I will tell you how I felt. Imagine that an old camp inmate who has been in prison for thirty years is visited by a representative of the international league of homosexualists, and he tries to persuade him to be a homosexual. The old prisoner listens. Arguments—historical, psychoanalytical, aesthetic, humanistic, social. But the old prisoner does not understand what it is all about. He listens with respect to this intellectual apparatus. But what is it all about? It turns out that the whole thing is about not living with a woman. But he never did; he did not even know that it is possible to live with a woman! Like the character in Molière who learned for the first time that he was speaking prose all along. Because everybody in Russia has to defend his own existence. This is not a theoretical problem, it is a practical problem, it begins in kindergarten.

If I had Solzhenitsyn's talent I would write a terrifying book—not *Gulag Archipelago*, but about a little boy who goes to kindergarten and who can recite more poems about Lenin than anybody else. His mama and papa beg him not to tell anybody about this terrible secret. Because all the other children know only two poems, and the teachers only three, while he knows fifteen. Right away he becomes a social menace. This is the basic tragedy of Russia today. The Gulag Archipelago grows out of this tragedy.

Here is a simple example to explain how that system functions. Here is my friend Piatigorsky, sitting right here. When Piatigorsky decided to leave the country, the Russian intelligentsia began to weep and they all got together in my studio. "How so?" they said. "The only prominent specialist in Buddhism and the Tamil dialects we have today is leaving. How can Russia get along without such an expert?" I replied: "Calm down, my friends. If the government wants to, it will mobilize five hundred thousand Communist youths and, using public funds, it will invite the biggest specialists in the world, and by the law of the greatest numbers it will try to breed another Piatigorsky." In this sense it is a very unique system. And it cannot be evaluated in Western categories.

I would like to conclude my remarks by saying that it is important for us to defend the rights of men wherever they are being violated. As a person with a heavy Russian past, I am naturally interested in Russia, because cancer is always the disease that the other guy has. When you do not have cancer, all discussion of it is theoretical. The main thing is for us to get together, even if only to surmount the terminological barrier.

VLADIMIR BUKOVSKY: After everything that has already been said in this room I do not expect to be able to offer much that is new. But I feel obliged to begin at the point where this evening's discussion began—that is, with the letter from the prisoners. [*He addresses himself primarily to Piatigorsky.*] No matter which way you look at it, I feel closest to those people, the ones who have expressed their "incorrect point of view." Of course, while you are sitting in a concentration camp, it is very difficult to decide just what is meant by the West. The West is some kind of an amorphous quantity that can hand out the technology and pass out the money on loan. But if you ask that quantity, straight out: "Hey you, West, what do you really stand for?" And the answer is: *Not a thing.* To a Soviet person, the West is actually a very dim and vague thing. It gives, but it does not ask for anything. And naturally, all those people sitting behind that barbed wire—they have a very hard time understanding that here in the West there are individual personalities. And what is even more difficult to understand is, here is a person who has come out of the Soviet Union, who is becoming a part of the West, and sure enough he is expressing the Western point of view. Maybe he wants to and maybe he doesn't, maybe he is just dreaming it all or maybe he isn't, but one way or another he is now a part of the West. And where are you going to draw the borderline between us? Tell me, my friend, where is the East and where is the West? Tell me where our compass is. We don't have one.

It seems to me that the people who have really had it hard, who have had it bad and who have been miserable, are the ones who have some kind of a compass, but that compass has no East or West on its markings. Fate planted me into the West, of necessity, straight out of the darkest East. I was absolutely miserable. An incredible number of people in search of scoops tore my soul apart, and all that was left for me to do was to figure out who had what rank by their shoulder insignia. Sometimes the rank matched the man and sometimes it did not. When I was at the U.S. State Department, it suddenly occurred to me that the man responsible for their whole Eastern policy is not the least bit different from the man in charge of the prison where I served my sentence. He was real fat, awfully important, and he looked at me like at some bug crawling across the road. And he knew much better than I did what's good for America and what's good for the Soviet Union. There was nothing I could tell him. And when I was in Germany I met any number of people who are trading with the Soviet Union and selling it their technology, their electronics and steel, their steel-processing technology. They don't want to know what's going to be done with that steel—maybe cannon, maybe tanks. But we're not responsible for that, all we do is just sell steel, we don't know what they're going to do with it. And suddenly I saw it all: They were Soviet people. When I begged them: Do not sell your steel, do not sell your technology, what you are selling is handcuffs for us, they replied: But what can we do? If I don't sell, somebody else will. If the Germans don't sell, the Japanese will; if the Japanese don't sell, the French will, but there is nothing we can do about it. That is exactly what you would hear the Soviets say.

Now tell me, you have talked a great deal about ideology and about philosophy—does that really make any difference at all in a world where you suffocate? It is man who bears the responsibility for everything, whether he is white or black, red or yellow. If he is asked: "Are you now ready to say that you don't want to contribute to violence?" And he answers: "No, I am just trying to make a living and

I have competition to worry about"—then you start seeing the prison guard in him. Because a guard is not a sadist, not a brute, not a murderer. Any one of you could be a potential guard. Yes, any one. [*The speaker addresses V. Nekrasov.*] It won't do you any good to shudder like that, Vitya. You could be one. And don't you forget it.

All of the world's violence is actually based on the unwillingness of the individual to live poorly. No one is going to help you. And your family will be dissatisfied. And your wife will say you are an egotist. And you have children, and you have to feed them, and regardless of what ideology there is in the world it's the ruble that counts. You have to feed milk to the little children and potatoes to the bigger ones. Nobody wants to know anything about such concepts as human responsibility.

I can see no difference between people in the West and people in the East. What's more, I don't believe that there is a difference. I want to see each human being as an individual. The person who got caught with literature in Russia and suddenly forgot about the Universal Declaration of Human Rights. How could he forget that? He read it a thousand times. In our country it is banned as a criminal document. But to him it was accessible from childhood on. The question is not what ideology he believed in—leftist or rightist. The question is whether he is prepared to be a human being, to defend his dignity, regardless of what may happen afterward—even if he does not achieve anything. We will all croak when our time comes. But let's be who we are when we croak.

[*The discussion ends with a tape recording of a speech by Alexander Galich, who had left to perform in Italy.*]

ALEXANDER GALICH: I am very sorry that I cannot be present at the gathering of the editorial board of the magazine *Kontinent* and our French friends. But I hope that this meeting will not be the last of its kind, and that we will see each other again and have a good tête-à-tête chat. I am quite well aware that listening to a speech in tape-recorded form is a wearisome and thankless business, and so I will try to be very brief.

Long ago the ancient Hebrew sage Hillel pronounced

these marvelous words: "If not I, then who? If not now, then when?" We who are gathered here to discuss the problem of personal responsibility as a problem of common concern to East and West might do well to inscribe these words as a motto on our banner: *If not I, then who? If not now, then when?*

We live in an astonishing world, where the concepts "our misfortune" and "your misfortune" have ceased to exist. It has already been sixty years, thirty years, forty years since that misfortune overtook the countries of Eastern Europe, whose totalitarian regime is destroying the intellectual, social, economic, and political life of the citizens of those countries. The same disaster is now right on the threshold of the European states, and it is your business and ours, it is our personal responsibility, to avert that disaster.

I said that we live in an astonishing world. We live in a beautiful world: To convince oneself of that, it often suffices to look out of the window.

We live in a demented world, where people continue to murder each other in the name of what they refer to in their public utterances as a bright future.

We live in an amazing world where hundreds and thousands of people continue to cast their votes in ballot boxes for the same individuals who had repeatedly in the past been caught and exposed as prevaricators and deceivers. And owing to some incomprehensible madness people continue to elect them.

We live in a world where totalitarianism assumes the most varied forms. Here in the West they also have their totalitarianism, which I would call Coca-Cola totalitarianism. The truth is that the so-called mass consumer society has indeed begun to consume canned products, canned art, and canned ideas on a mass scale. Let us say that in order to call oneself a Kantian, it is necessary at least to read the *Critique of Pure Reason*, to study it and to comprehend it. In order to call oneself a Marxist it suffices to memorize four or five formulas—that is also the Coca-Cola dictatorship.

Personal responsibility—where does it begin? I would say that it begins with responsibility for the words we speak or write. Now, a week ago, in the September 7, 1977, issue of the *Literaturnaya Gazeta*, there was an article entitled "For Peoples' Sake" in which the following was written. The topic of discussion is the new Soviet Constitution, and the writer states that this Constitution "guarantees the inviolability of the person and the home of Soviet citizens; freedom of speech, press, assembly and demonstrations; protection of the secrecy of the mails and of telephonic and telegraphic communications. The new Constitution guarantees complete freedom of religion, and it considerably enlarges the legal rights of the citizens. Thus it gives a convincing rebuttal to the campaign being waged in a number of countries concerning violations of human rights in the U.S.S.R." Who do you think wrote these words? You will probably be astounded when I tell you the name of the writer of that article. The writer's name is Maurice Dejean; he was formerly an ambassador of the French Republic to the Soviet Union; and the article was written in Paris. What can you say about responsibility, personal responsibility? Hasn't the time come to stop throwing empty words around? Hasn't the time come to stop trying to be original and cute? Enough! We can see how far all the cuteness has taken us.

This past summer I was invited by Hélène Châtelaine and Armand Gatti to participate in the work of their group at the Avignon Theater Festival. Our work consisted in open rehearsals at which the spectators took part in discussing the outline of the coming play, the outline of the coming performance. And at one of those rehearsals a spectator asked: "Look here, just why are you doing it with us? What are you after?" And Armand Gatti replied to him: "We are after the truth."

I believe that truth is that which is always being sought. The truth, if you will, is a little bit like the horizon: There it is, right in front of you where you can reach it, and yet it is always somewhere up ahead. And in the problem of personal responsibility there is one tremendous temptation. The temptation consists in that someone may take it into his head that he alone knows the truth, the truth in its ultimate dimension, and that by imparting that truth to others he will open for them the road to a happy future. The problem of personal responsibility has its limits. And it is not a good idea to overstep that boundary.

> Do not be afraid of starvation and plague,
> Of prison, or having to beg.
> But do be afraid of the man who will say:
> "I know all the answers today."

A Word About
the Philosophy of
Vladimir Nabokov

BY ALEXANDER PIATIGORSKY

Translated and Revised by the Author

From *Kontinent* No. XV, 1978

For V. V. Ivanov and V. N. Toporov
on the occasion of their fiftieth birthdays.

A word about K. . . . Freudians are no longer around,
I understand, so . . .
    —Vladimir Nabokov, preface to "Última Thule"[1]

ALEXANDER MOYSEYEVICH PIATIGORSKY was born in 1929 in Moscow. He took his doctor's degree in philosophy at the University of Moscow and became a researcher at the Institute for the People of Asia and Africa, then assistant professor at the University of Moscow. In the early sixties he began working with a collective of scientists (Lotman, Ivanov, Toporov) on the development of the basic principles of a new school of semiotics and structuralism. He is the author of a number of monographs and essays on philosophical questions, Hinduism and Buddhism, which have been translated into a number of European languages. Since 1974 he has lived in London, where he works at the School of Oriental and African Studies of London University.

[1]Vladimir Nabokov, *A Russian Beauty and Other Tales* (London: Penguin Books, 1975), p. 139.

This is not in memory of Nabokov. In so short a time no memory can be formed. It is not about his books. Enough has been and will be written about them in due time. And, of course, this is not about his life; enough has been said about it in *Speak, Memory*, and also in the brilliant biographical essay by Andrew Field, *Nabokov: His Life in Part*.[2] Field's masterpiece, which, as if it preconceived the writer's death, has completed the task absolutely necessary for (or before) the end—that of the *estrangement*. That is to say, Nabokov's estrangement from his own emigrant destiny (still, destiny is not life) was already contained in his novels and short stories written in Russian. Future biographers and memoir writers will be desperately trying to return, to insert, to squeeze Nabokov into the emigrant fate and, thereby, to equal themselves to him, or put him nearer themselves. However, Nabokov, if we judge him by his own writings, was never a great lover of company, particularly in serious matters.

I am now going to consider the "most solitary line" of his writings, the line where this estrangement is expressed most strongly—that is, his inner philosophizing, the line in the sense of which each and every conversation has neither a beginning nor an end and goes on to infinity. Or even more exactly: the line which leads a man away from the real cause and pretext of his talk, and estranges him from the facts and circumstances to which the appearance and continuation of his talk are due. Therefore, if somebody says: "Whatever Nabokov wrote of, he wrote only of . . ."—do not believe it! He wrote of what he wrote, but not "only of . . ." ("Only of . . ." means his emigrant destiny, or emigrant destiny in general, or the Russian destiny or anybody else's.) Here we have an endless war between discoverers of truths and searchers for meanings (meaning cannot be discovered or even opened; all one can do is to search for it—Nabokov knew this perfectly well).

Having been quite definitely a modern writer and a man with a completely modern mode of thinking (I mean modern for his own time, of course), Nabokov looked at the modernist world-outlook with the greatest doubts and

[2] Andrew Field, *Nabokov: His Life in Part* (New York: Viking Press, 1977).

completely rejected one of its most important elements—
Freudianism. Why? What were the origins of a stable and
persisting antipathy and even spite toward psychoanalysis
in a man so dynamic, who so clearly understood the
American perception of life as Nabokov did? The answer is
simple and clear as daylight: The hero of Nabokov's *Lolita*,
Humbert Humbert, *himself* knows perfectly well what happens to him. To know it he needs neither Freud nor Jung,
neither Lacan nor Marx, nor angels, nor any other man or
devil. Of course, he understands quite well (like Cincinat
of *Invitation to a Beheading*) that he is already done for (what
a pity!). But all the same, he knows exactly why he got himself into this muddle whence there is only one exit—to the
scaffold or gas chamber. It is quite another point that neither Humbert nor Cincinat could do anything whatever
about it. But this is another matter. In one of his oddest and
strangest short stories, "Ultima Thule," written still in Russian in 1940, Nabokov depicted a man, by name Falter, who
has a *real knowledge*, or Knowledge—but seemingly from
outside, from somewhere completely beyond this world
(not exactly "from above," but quite definitely not from
within), from the sphere where the whole truth of this
world is no more than a particle of sand. Falter himself is,
together with his body and intellect, not more than a one-
billionth fraction of this particle of sand, and he perishes
because of the immensity of this knowledge. The knowledge exists here objectively, but it is acquired in a purely
individual way, while in both Freudianism and Marxism
the knowledge is the objective reality itself, *collectively* acquired, reflected, and transmitted. Physician and patient
already constitute a collective, like investigator and inves-
tigated, executioner and victim, and so on. Nearly in the
same epoch (with the interval of one "generation of writers"), but in a completely different sense and spirit, the heroes of Kafka—Joseph K. and the Land Surveyor—relate to
knowledge. Good God—they simply *do not know*. Well,
speaking generally, perhaps there is somebody over there
who knows, but it is only possible to guess about that. The
ignorance of both of them is only the reverse side of their
guilt (Or its cause: Or consequence? Or primary condition?)
—but in no way a justifying circumstance. Kafka was anti-
Freudian too, but Nabokov regarded Freud just as "Socrates

back-to-front" saying (that is, Socrates saying) "know thyself," or "I know that thou knowest nothing." There is no problem of guilt in Nabokov, neither in the mystical sense nor in the ethical one. Whoever knows will pay, and for his own unhappiness at that. Therefore Humbert Humbert in *Lolita* neither justifies himself nor complains. He simply explains everything as he knows it. Because of that, happiness is not even presupposed as existing like any other final result of one's attempts and tries. Certainly it is enhancing and charming to catch a rare specimen of chrysalis or butterfly, and, without doubt, such occupation is, in a way, a sort of happiness. But it always seems to belong to a time and space other than that where and when I exist at a given moment. Joseph K. and the Land Surveyor justify themselves, complain, and strive toward their aims (in the first case the aim is to prove their innocence). This is not because of ignorance. Nonhappiness is implied here merely as the unattainability of a result.

Perhaps all difference between Nabokov's heroes and those of Kafka is due mainly to this single generation which separates Nabokov from Kafka. Kafka's heroes still exist in society, or more exactly, in the *community*. Through this community unknown forces influence them and act upon them, and toward this they strive, in this they perish. Everything that happens in *The Trial* and *The Castle*, reality and nightmares, good and evil, occurs in a monotheistic world, and even the rejection of God (like, also, episodically committed adulteries) doesn't change anything in the unit and wholeness of this world. The world of Nabokov's knowledge is open to the outside and clearly and precisely dissected and analyzed within itself. There is no community or society whatever. Instead—there is a civilization of things, to which . . . the thought of man is opposed. There is no deep and vague Kafkian counter-position to God at all.

I think that the dualism of Nabokov's world-perception is, first of all, expressed in this constant stressing of the difference between man's thought and the things man-made or in one or the other way humanized. Crudely speaking, all these things might be called "civilization" itself, though this is not entirely true. Not entirely, because civilization is an objective concept, while what differentiates the thought from the thing is usually (though not always), in Nabokov's understanding, something explicitly subjective. This subjectivity is something completely alien in Nabokov's writings. All that is *alien* to thinking is a *thing*. The world of things is, according to Nabokov, much more *dynamic*, however paradoxical it may be, than the world of thought; not only nonliving objects but also everything animated, including the souls of men, are transferred into the world of things when becoming alien to my thinking. Thinking here is much more *static*; it remains itself, evolving (more than developing) according to its own—that is, subjective—laws. Thinking does not change *subjectively*. The only thing that changes is the objective relationship between thinking and things, which depends upon things, not upon thinking. But more about that later. In *Luzhin's Defense*[3] this idea is still present in the so-called "chrysalis" of psychology, in the unbelievably complex interwovenness of Luzhin's and the author's attitudes (one must not mix them up) toward *play*—that is, toward creation understood as play.

Play is aimless, like an analogue of unconscious being, and because of that it is bad. It is play which transforms the genius Luzhin into a monomaniac and his impresario Valentinov into his demon. But Luzhin wants to know play as such, without its outer aims, such as victory, for instance. That is why Valentinov gradually becomes a real demon, for on the one hand he is a devil—seducer (he badly needs Luzhin's victory—that is the aim), on the other hand it is Valentinov who makes Luzhin return to knowledge and awareness of his only reality, that is, *chess*, in its divine and aimless approach to Being. Psychology—here it is Luzhin's monomania—serves only as a sort of shell for the interplay of two impersonal forces—thinking and life. Life wins the personality of the chess player—he commits suicide. But his thinking wins life. He does not give himself to life (like Grigory Skovorodá, according to his epitaph) with his Gnostic-type asceticism. (In general, I think that the main difference between Christian Gnosticism and Christianity consists in their relation to *life*, not to man or to God.) The

[3]*Zashchita Luzhina*, published in the U.S. as *The Defense* (New York: G. P. Putnam's Sons, 1964).—ED.

things of the world surround Luzhin, but he does not understand why and what for; he simply does not try to understand. The things are not inimical to his thinking—if this were so, Nabokov would have been qualified as a romanticist or a psychologist, which was by no means the case. It is thinking itself which *recoils* from the things, but not out of enmity, only out of the alienness of this thinking to the very *nature* of these things. But it is impossible to live in such a way, both in real life and in the novel; because life (to be originated) should in at least one respect get the thinking (beware: the thinking, not the soul—one must be most careful when speaking of Nabokov) related to some ephemeral experience of the world. Luzhin's thinking suddenly sprang upon chess. The chess board and figures became the space of his thinking and the field of his experience. They ceased to be things and became thinking itself. One could include the whole universe in thinking, having thus transformed it into a thing. For Luzhin this one thing, chess, became the whole world. For Humbert Humbert it was Lolita.

The modernism of *Lolita* is beyond any doubt, but this modernism is not in the "reflectivity" of Humbert Humbert and not in the frankness of the erotic scenes. It is already in the first moment of Humbert Humbert's possession of Lolita—the dynamics of this novel, written in the English classical tradition of traveling, are directed toward this very initial moment—when Humbert Humbert finds that "focus of thingness" for his thinking, due to which his thinking itself becomes a true reality for him. Out of this result there is nothing but loss. Escaping and hiding, he catches Lolita as a marvelous butterfly in a dream, desiring a "pure thing" in her, the thing only, and terribly fearing that she could suddenly disappear in the civilization of bars, cars, and highways, having, as it were, merged herself with all *other* things. Let us note, by the way, that modern civilization is not soulless, as it is usually thought to be by those stupid observers who scold it together with modernism in art and literature. It is ourselves who lack soul to animate this civilization. I think that the modernism of Nabokov's thinking in *Lolita* expresses itself in the nightmarish contradiction of the thinking of Humbert Humbert; for Humbert Humbert Lolita is a thing, something deprived of a living soul, but, at the same time, as a thing she cannot belong completely to his thinking which deprives her of a living soul. (The name Lolita means "excited by desire" in Sanskrit, and there is another word from the same root, Lolita, which means "erotic play.")

Philosophically, the plot of this novel is a sort of "anti-Pygmalion"; the animated creature is converted into a thing for possession, by. . . thinking. (From a purely Buddhistic point of view such an experiment is not only possible but also justifiable, but only as far as one does it with one's self, not with another person.) Lolita is a butterfly who at one moment is a soul, at another—a thing. The thinking here cannot find the interval between these two, and it cannot find a third entity lying apart from them, in a dimension different from that of thinking and of things opposed to the thinking. But to find the "third entity" one has to reject this damned habitual dualism of thinking and things, this dualism which was transformed into complete naturalism much earlier, in *Invitation to a Beheading* (according to Andrew Field the most philosophical of all Nabokov's novels)[4]—nearly as in a contemporary fantastic novel.

Well, the things remained material, but their matter was extenuated, worn out to such a degree that they became penetrable and permeable—so strongly was the matter changed in the "process of the world" (all this was excellently noted by Georgiy Adamovich, who stressed in his preface to the novel the obviously gnostic character of this idea). But what is particularly important is that our own intelligent being happens to be based on the very fragile balance between the states of the matter and the thinking (the latter has no state of its own). This balance depends not on the thinking but on the matter, or, let us say, on the degree of its thinness and fluidity. Therefore, the catastrophe of civilization is not expected to happen—we are used to revolutionary thinking, believing that we think in an evolutionary way. All that is very simple: Objects and even the place of the material world lose their definiteness with respect to thinking, the objects dynamize and change into one another. So a bit later, in the novel *Ada*, the pieces of

[4]Field, *Nabokov: His Life in Part*, p. 208.

Russia which is not Russia are grafted onto America which is also not altogether America. So even before *Ada,* in the wonderful short story "Solus Rex," the very idea of "the reconstruction of nature" (in this short story a mad planning engineer transforms the lowland into a plateau and commits suicide thereafter) appears not as a symptom of progress, but of the degeneration of life.

Well, the thinking remains the thinking. But what happens to "I," to one's destiny, to the truth and the knowledge thereof? This brings us back to the fantastic short story "Ultima Thule," where this sort of question is put to the omniscient A. I. Falter by Sineusov. The answer, if we may formulate it in an extremely concentrated way, is as follows:[5] (1) The truth, or, more exactly, our knowledge thereof, does not consist in the subjective thinking of an individual human being, but exists in its fullness only *objectively.* In respect to concrete thinking, this objective truth appears, as it were, dispersed, scattered, like the smallest fragments of a broken bottle. (2) To put all these fragments together, to reconstruct them into *one body of knowledge,* we need *Chance,* the probability of which is less than infinitesimal. That is, to do it we need the fulfillment of at least two main conditions: It is necessary to have *all* the fragments, and they must be put together in the only *proper* way. It seems that the state and quality of thinking of the given person play no more than a secondary or indirect role in this matter, like, let us say, skill in card games. Or to put it another way—not altogether skill and not altogether card games. That is why Sineusov divides all men into amateurs and professionals; with the former he associates himself and Falter. Chess player Luzhin and entomologist Nabokov are also "not altogether professionals," because for them their occupation is also "not altogether science" and "not altogether occupation" (not to say

---

[5] This motif was exactly repeated in the science-fiction novel *The Black Cloud,* by Sir Fred Hoyle (London, 1977, pp. 208–211), which was published fifteen years after "Ultima Thule" was published in Russian and fourteen years before it was translated into English. I would suppose that there is no borrowing here; rather, it is the congeniality of the famous British astronomer with which we are dealing.

"sport"), but rather *the game as such.* (3) As Chance, this knowledge is indefinable in the terms of the excluded third. By putting the question requiring of us "yes" or "no" we annihilate the answer, because Knowledge is the answer to a question which was never put. Therefore it is impossible to get the answer to a question like, let us say, "Is there life after death?"—because the answer is falsely included in the question itself. But one can put (or not put) various questions and get various answers thereto. However, even to put such a question is a matter of Chance. That is why it is totally senseless to put a question about *one's own* fate, for we do not know whose fate is in question, or what is one's own. (4) Falter's knowledge is not the knowledge of all things known simultaneously. Simply, whenever a *right* question is put (which is also a matter of Chance, let us remember), he can give the absolutely right answer, as if he had a gigantic dictionary of all the right answers at his disposition. That is, he does not know all of them by heart and in advance, but he can find out the answer immediately when it is needed. (5) A man's thinking cannot stand the objectivity of Knowledge, for (or unless) it works inside the framework of subjective human mentality. Or, more exactly, his mentality could not stand it. That is why a chance meeting with Truth is destructive psychically, mentally, physiologically, and biologically as well.

Thus, the human game is almost completely defeatable. Nabokov's hero perishes either from his own obsession (Luzhin is obsessed with chess; almost all other heroes are obsessed with women) when his thinking is hopelessly screwed into his only thing, or he dies when by mere chance his thinking meets with Truth, the Truth with which the subjectivity of his body and soul cannot cope. But where is Fate? In the unseen design of a carpet? In the untraced flight of a butterfly? Or would it not be the very moment where the thing and the thinking cease to be thought of as different? Nabokov does not answer. But let us return to what we have started with. In his novels and short stories Nabokov never looks Fate straight in the eye; as to the direct question—an answer would be impossible. It is only somewhere in the margin of the field of eyesight that one can notice something. I would call Nabokov's philosophical approach "the philosophy of lateral sight."

In order to have such sight one must constantly step aside. So stepping aside, estranging himself, he started seeing his Luzhin, but this habit developed fully in him much later (in *The Gift* it is still unnoticeable). Perhaps it was his departure from Russia that estranged him from Russia as a first step, and his deliberate transition from Russian to English that served as a second one? It is not easy to find another Russian writer in the twentieth century who was so completely alien to the feeling of tragedy as Nabokov was. The Tragic is a result of direct looking. But if you looked from a distance, then something could reveal itself, something the sense of which has not yet been discovered. Perhaps it is only from the rear that this something could be sought. And if you found it, by mere chance of course, it might happen that you found what you never sought. It might happen to be an answer which was never contained in the question.

In *King, Queen, Knave* the objectivity of description is unbelievable. The thoughts of the heroes, their lives as well as their dresses, socks, noses, and eyes are formed into *objects* so hard and so clearly measured in the author's knowledge that their own knowledge of themselves becomes altogether irrelevant. All seems to be so strongly predestined and preconceived here that the very problem of Destiny cannot be considered seriously. Let us think it over: The very concept of Destiny necessarily includes some lack of knowledge thereof, or, let us say, uncertainty is necessary here. I mean a sort of *objective* uncertainty in the sense of being observed from outside, not by an owner of Destiny himself. If a writer is an observer who knows *everything*, then Destiny itself vanishes and consequently real life vanishes too. This always happens when the thinking of a writer changes the thoughts of his heroes into *objects* of his knowledge. I only mean objects, not *things*, one must not confuse them with one another. We are not dealing with "reification" here. The world of thought and the world of things remain distinctly divided between themselves, but the former is automatically reduced to one point—solely to the point of the author's thinking.

But in the novel this is not a literary method, and not even a point of view, but rather a very elaborated metaphysical position. The heroes are described as various "I."

However, "I" of the various heroes cannot be converted into personalities if there is no destiny. They live without the sacred "Gnostic number" which *really* exists but which Nabokov deprived them of in his novel. No hints at a mystery would help if there were no mystery—Zinoviy Zinik said of this novel. The space of "I" is psychics and body; the space of a personality—the whole world. In the novel Martha wishes to enjoy Franz and hates Dreier, while Dreier enjoys life and loves Martha! Well, enjoyment and hate result in death. Enjoyment and love result in . . . death too. It is this field Franz happens to stumble into, just like the unhappy bohemian partner of Lolita did. Franz "by mere chance" evades his death, because—and it is the logics of "I"—his love disappears. Lacking personality, Franz simply could not support such a close combination of love and death in Martha. The capricious friend of Lolita, on the contrary, perishes by chance—he does not love her and never did. Lolita's friend always wishes to appropriate everything and to be all the time, as it were, out of the game. Well, speaking generally, nearly everything that happens to the majority of Nabokov's heroes is a matter of chance. And that is because of the fact that they possess their "I" only, which cannot substitute Destiny for them.

There is a long way between "I" and "personality" in the history of texts, in literature, and sometimes even in the life of an individual man, but very seldom during the course of one and the same novel. There cannot be a recipe for how to convert "I" into personality. Reflection and introspection—whether by the author or by his heroes—can exist as no more than an additional feature of such a conversion. In the history of philosophy the transition from "I" to personality was sometimes achieved by direct negation of "I" (as in early Buddhism) or by identification of "I" with one of the states of consciousness in the stream of conscious life (as in William James, Paul Carus, and, though in a completely different context, Edmund Husserl). In the new European literature the transition from "I" to personality was achieved during the two-hundred-year passage from Rousseau to the experiments with anti-novels of the sixties and the films of Antonioni and Bergman. And in such a short time (astronomically speaking) European literature repeated the essential stages of development of more than twenty-five hundred years of the history of philosophy, the history of philosophizing about personality, the essence of which can be summarized into two short sentences: Reflection still is not "I"; "I" is still not personality.

This movement toward personality was not unilinear, for personality did not always remain in the focus of the universal thought. On the contrary, it was very often the case that after being directed toward personality the literature returned to "I" again. Also, I do not think that this movement can be traced in the whole literature; it exists only when the very *problem* of personality exists, though there are many writers in whose work personality arises without any problem at all, that is, as something naturally given. This was the case with Joyce, Proust, and Faulkner, who have one thing in common in spite of all the differences in their artistic world-outlook; at the very moment when the writer took up his pen, or was about to do so, the personalities of his heroes already existed—without the existence of the heroes those authors simply could not have written at all. The personality already existed from the very origin in the embryo, in the ancestors, in the preconsciousness of the concrete lives of their heroes as a sort of initially given existence in the continuum of which the author included himself, and continued to think and write having been therein.

I allowed myself to indulge in this pseudohistorical excourse only to stress that to Nabokov personality was a problem, and a very hard one at that. He needed to overcome the personalism of Dostoyevsky, for to follow a Dostoyevskian personalistic approach was absolutely impossible.

But let us return to the novel. In the eternal triangle of King, Queen, and Knave, the Knave starts his existence as a mechanism wound by the author. The Knave desires the Queen. She is like a stimulus waiting for an unconditioned reaction. But at the same time, she desires the death of the King. The King, however (the author had supplied him with a lot of different desires, which he satisfied as they arose, and the Queen was only one of them, though, perhaps, the strongest one)—the King still plays, that is, strives to such an uncertainty which does not let life or the author have their way with him. Dreier, the King, possesses a much greater degree of freedom than the other two. That is why he is a King.

But two very important things are divulged here. The first is the fact that Dreier is still not altogether a personality. He is still a sort of "I" converted into an object, for, like the author himself, the King *plays* with objects. Even the Queen, whom he loves, is no more than an object to him. This is only stressed by his "affair" with a half-mad inventor from whom he awaits a wonderful Hoffmanian imitation of the living human body. But the dead object remains dead. Dreier's visit to the criminalistic museum provokes a very deep disgust of criminals as well as of their victims in him, because they are all exhibits—that is, they are objects existing in one and the same life together with the King. Actually, Dreier himself is not altogether a personality, only because the "I" of other people remains the object of his enjoyment and play. Humbert Humbert in *Lolita* is already a personality and not "I," because his only object, Lolita, runs out, slips out, and when Lolita becomes a soul —that is, a living personality—then Humbert Humbert is already done for. Done for, because he has already killed another personality. It is in the moment of death that each"I" becomes a personality again.

The second thing is revealed in *King, Queen, Knave* as yet another example of the law that does not know exceptions, at least in literature: If a hero is only "I," then he is always an obsessed, monomaniacal psychical automaton. He is a card, not a player. This started in the psychological novel of the last century (as in *Disciple*, by Paul Bourget, for instance) and was over very soon with *The Idiot* of Dostoyevsky, because Prince Myshkin is a perfect personality, not a psychical "I" of a human object. And since then, quite a different talk has begun, the talk of "pure personality"—a talk which lasted for decades and thousands of pages, a talk which irritated Nabokov himself enormously in such writers as Proust, Kafka, and particularly in Faulkner. Of course, anybody might have a psychosis, but "I" without soul is already a psychosis *par excellence*. In the novel we have Martha's mania, and Dreier himself as a bit of a maniac as well (he is "maniacal about play"). However, Dreier is able to awaken himself to reality: Each time somebody dies, he becomes a personality again. The death of the driver, the death in the museum—they *deobjectivize* him. The death of Martha is for Dreier the end of his play—and his own death as a king, a King-object. The Knave, Franz, disappears out of the play, like a card that falls under the table. Well, speaking generally, one cannot go on playing infinitely. For if there is such a thing as "I," then personality finally must appear sometimes.

The metaphysical difference between this novel and *Lolita* is enormous. Humbert Humbert is a personality, because from the very beginning (or more exactly, from the very end, for the novel begins with the end) he goes toward death. But there is another thing here. In these two novels we are confronted with two completely different apperceptions of literature (but by no means of *life* as described in literature). In *King, Queen, Knave* Nabokov desires very eagerly to work out and create a sort of "new classicism" (the same Zinik states that no classicism is possible without the previous modernism, but not the other way around) out of his own perception of contemporary modernism. But he perceived both Western and Russian modernism very badly. He perceived it irascibly, I would say. Perhaps it was due to the fact that the modernism was not his own. That is why the novel happens to be a splendid one, but by no means classical. The spirit of the twenties lives in the novel as if it were written in the forties. It may also be seen, by the way, in the stressedly manneristic and slightly archaic dialect of Saint Petersburg of the nineteen-tens, in which his novel was written. In *Lolita* we see a quite conscious motivation, as if there were an "order" (if not "social," then at least an individual one) to produce a total falling away from the classical principle, which was manifestly expressed in *The Gift* much earlier. It was in *Lolita* that he shouted out: "Well, take it, if *you* like it! I was able to do it, for I knew *how!*" And as a result he created a wonderful and well-nigh classical work. But of what sort? Russian? American? Nobody's?

Working "by order," Nabokov, it seems to me, set free spontaneous forces of his soul. The forces which, perhaps, would have had much more liberty in the no-man's-land of the "wild west" than within the Russian classical literature, between Pushkin and Dostoyevsky, which Nabokov had chosen in *The Gift* as a battlefield for his neoclassical exploit.

An Open Letter to the Director of Radio Liberty

BY VLADIMIR BUKOVSKY

Translated by Albert C. Schmidt

From *Kontinent* No. XI, 1977

The editors of the journal *Kontinent* herewith print a letter by Vladimir Bukovsky concerning the draft of guidelines

Vladimir Konstantinovich Bukovsky was born in 1942 in Belebey, Bashirla, U.S.S.R. His father was a Communist Party functionary in charge of writers. Bukovsky was first arrested in 1963 for possession—without permission—of Milovan Djilas's book The New Class (he had previously been rusticated from Moscow University). He was held for sixteen months and then arrested again in 1966 for demonstrating against the trial and sentencing of the writers Yuri Daniel and Andrei Sinyavsky (each was sentenced to seven years). On this occasion Bukovsky spent eight months in a psychiatric clinic. In 1967 Bukovsky organized a demonstration for the persecuted journalists Alexander Ginzburg and Yuri Galanskov (the latter, although a young man, subsequently died in prison) and was arrested a third time. This time he was sentenced to three years in a concentration camp. In 1970 he assembled a White Book entitled The Struggle Against the Misuse of Psychiatry for Political Purposes. In 1971 Bukovsky's book Opposition: A New Mental Illness in the Soviet Union was smuggled out to the West, where it was published. For this Bukovsky was arrested and held from March 1971 to January 1972, when he was sentenced to twelve years penal servitude. He was exchanged for the Chilean Communist leader, Corvalán, in December 1976. At present he is completing his studies in biology at Cambridge University, England.

for political programming of Radio Liberty and Radio Free Europe, distributed by the president of the Washington Council on radio broadcasting, Mr. S. Mikhelson. The editors hope that publication and discussion of the Bukovsky letter will be of aid to the work of the whole radio station as well as to that of the addressee personally.

Dear Mr. Francis Ronalds!

I have read the draft project for programming and political guidelines to be used by Liberty/Free Europe, as sent around by Mr. Mikhelson. I would like to voice my thoughts regarding the line of work of these radio stations as set forth in the draft, with emphasis on Radio Liberty—inasmuch as its broadcasts are of foremost importance for the U.S.S.R. at the present time. Over the past six years I have not had the opportunity to listen to Radio Liberty, to evaluate the quality of its broadcasts, or to grasp to what extent the line here laid down is already being followed in current broadcasting. Hence, I can only base myself on the text of the draft, as well as on my own conception of the needs of Soviet listeners and on that of my fellow prisoners.

Instinctively, perhaps, while reading and analyzing the text of the draft, I recalled my years of experience with Soviet bureaucratic papers, and this has affected my reaction. To a certain extent, this attitude has been prompted by the text itself and by the phrasing of the draft, the resemblance of which to normative documents and directives I have known is simply frightening.

From the text we learn that the draft must become OBLIGATORY guidelines for all personnel of the radio station, inasmuch as the management is charged with "constant supervision of the contents of broadcasts in accordance with the given guidelines." Amazing is the very attempt to make rules for everything, down to the tone of broadcasting: "to refrain from emotionality [!], cursing, anger, sharpness, militancy, arrogance, pomposity, pretentiousness or condescension [?]." And at the same time it is stated that the radio station transmits news and information, "submitting them to no censorship," taking upon itself in part the function of "local radio broadcasting and, as it were, replacing the free press, which is absent."

Maybe I am being too literal in translating the word Liberty as "liberty." But I was under the impression that the Western mass media regarded their collaborators not as shop clerks, but rather as people who devote their creative efforts to a cause in which they believe and which they desire to further. All the more so with regard to collaborators at the radio stations that broadcast to the Soviet Union and East Europe, most of whom are émigrés from the countries in question.

The Soviet reader (listener) is used to the fact that news as presented is not dispassionate or independent. Even the shortest information bulletin from Soviet sources is composed with a slant. For that reason he receives communications from Western radio with like suspicion. His ears buzz with noise about how Radio Liberty caters to American policy. And it would be naïve to suppose that implementation of this policy proposal would go unnoticed by listeners. What picture will the listener get of freedom of information as proclaimed in the West, of the independence of newspapers, radio, and the like? To him, you are a representative model of the Western press; in all your broadcasts he will only see American politics in action, and the absence of genuine freedom. Is that what Radio Liberty wants to convince its listeners of? Do the American media, operating on their own home ground, put the same restrictions on their employees as are now proposed for RL/RFE?

It is clear to me that such stringent regulation will cause the radio station to suffer the fate of *Amerika* magazine. That magazine aroused considerable interest, at one time, by virtue of its name alone; but it ceased to be attractive to anyone as soon as it became possible to familiarize oneself with its lack of content. Probably these proposals, if followed, can lead to success in negotiations concerning cessation of jamming (and I can understand why people are worried about this); but might it not happen that, when jamming stops, having been bought at such a price, the very same people who now listen despite the jamming ("KGB jazz") will turn off their radios and go back to trying to eke out information between the lines of the Soviet press?

In characterizing this paper, which so strongly reminds me of official documents of the dear old MVD, I should like to point out the following features:

1. Amazing inner contradictions. On the one hand, it is stated that "RL and RFE help the citizens of the U.S.S.R. and East Europe with dissemination and discussion of their own opinions, which, owing to censorship, they are unable to express via the media." On the other hand, right away a restriction is imposed on the utterances of the citizens: "Wherever appropriate information may include statements by citizens who, deprived of opportunity to express themselves through the mass media in their own country, are obliged to turn for help to foreign correspondents or to resort to uncensored publications—*samizdat*. BEFORE USING SAMIZDAT MATERIALS OR OTHER DOCUMENTS COMING FROM THE U.S.S.R. OR EAST EUROPE, THEY MUST BE CAREFULLY EXAMINED."

It would be interesting to know, by the way, how RL envisages such examination. The draft proposes: "If the facts appear dubious, it is necessary for them to be corroborated by two mutually independent sources." I find it hard to imagine how this can be done in practice. For example, if a communication has been brought out of a concentration camp at risk of liberty, through whom will RL check it? Will they call the camp commander?

In the draft paper it is proposed to give the listeners "examples of free discussion between different viewpoints and approaches on national and international problems"—but then, at the same time, to "avoid invidious comparison," and not to permit "criticism of the Soviet system from purely Western positions" (isn't that one of the possible viewpoints?). "Radio Liberty neither supports nor encourages any movements pursuing the goal of secession in any form and DOES NOT BROACH territorial questions." Thus, from the activity of RL is excluded not only a viewpoint, but an entire problem complex; a direct ban is imposed on a specific theme. The only thing proposed in this context is to "take a sympathetic stand regarding the right of all nationality groups to prosperity, to pride in their historical and cultural achievements, and to the use of their own language." As it turns out, the proposed policy does not even take into account the right of each Soviet republic to secede freely from the U.S.S.R., as set forth in Article 17 of the Soviet Constitution, and that policy automatically eliminates discussion, for instance, of the Ukrainian political prisoners who have made a broad appeal based on this constitu-

tional provision. All that RL promises the national groups
is to "support the right of every person freely to defend his
national origin as well as his religious and political convictions, and not to fear discrimination along these
lines." Absorbed as I am in the problem of individual civil
rights, I cannot forget—Soviet reality does not let me forget—the existence of problems of entire peoples which
cannot be summed up under the right to "take pride in
their achievements."

2. *Total lack of precision in terminology; vagueness of phraseology.* In compiling broadcasts on internal affairs in the
country beamed at, it is proposed first of all to "inform listeners about IMPORTANT EVENTS in their country's life
which are either unreported, distorted or insufficiently
explained by the official media." But who will decide on
the "importance" of an event and on the "sufficiency" of
official coverage? "Internal affairs must be commented on
in a CONSTRUCTIVE way." That ambiguous word has been so
frequently exploited by official Soviet sources (at home
and abroad) that it cannot be regarded as trustworthy.
"Avoid criticism for the sake of criticism"—a permanent
slogan of the Soviet press, which brands as criticism for
criticism's sake anything objectionable to chiefs on any
level. "Critical remarks with respect to policies or practical
action of the governments of the given countries must be
founded on DEEP knowledge of the factual side of the matter and must be presented in RESPONSIBLE fashion." Who
shall determine depth and degree of responsibility? At any
moment, any broadcast may be declared shallow and irresponsible if it diverges from the momentary demands of
the deep-thinking and well-informed American politicians.

3. *A degree of political helplessness which is astounding in a
policy document.* The authors of the draft do not realize or
try to find out who their Soviet listener is, whom they will
take as a guiding pattern, or what is the goal of this kind of
broadcasting. In the positive portion of the document we
read that the purpose of broadcasting is to draw the listeners "into the atmosphere of a less closed world, where their
problems and the problems common to many nations are
discussed freely, objectively and without ideological or
other preconceptions." And "RL and RFE make an effort to

adopt the viewpoint of the interests of their listeners." How can this be reconciled with the negative portion of the text, which imposes ELEVEN cowardly restrictions on broadcasting?

It is embarrassing for me, as a person who spent his whole life in unfree conditions, a person whose world was circumscribed by the four walls of a cell in Vladimir prison, to explain to free people in a free society that objectivity and impartiality are attained not by prohibitions and restrictions, but rather by breadth and diversity of information and viewpoints alike. The more different "unobjective" views a man hears, the easier it is for him to draw really objective conclusions. I think objectivity consists in a sum total of nonobjectivities; it is born in discussion. From this angle I should like to examine all of the proposed restrictions.*

The first restriction, having to do with the tone of broadcasts, has already been mentioned above. Which gives greater objectivity—a dispassionate and well-rehearsed announcer, who reads without vocal emphasis on sensitive points, or a varied, emotional and disputative chorus of excited people? (Naturally, individuality or excitement of tone should not be simply an acting trick.) The expression of a human viewpoint is impossible without emotional coloring.

The second restriction consists in "correcting the gaps and distortions in the official media, they do so by presenting the facts, avoiding polemical treatment of the kind the audiences are known to resent." But Soviet citizens need more than just information: They need editorializing, they need discussion, and not only between RL writers but also arguments with the official line. In essence, we in the U.S.S.R. are deprived not so much of information in the narrow sense of the word as of qualified elaboration on this information. The absence of a free press in the U.S.S.R. robs us, above all, of the opportunity to comprehend what is going on. For example, under Stalin everyone knew about the persecutions in progress (though not to fullest extent), yet they took this for an inevitable phenomenon

*The author omits the seventh restriction which deals with editorial opinions.—ED.

justified by the situation and by "great goals." Another example: Soviet emigrants with a certain amount of objective information about the West before they leave nonetheless often go there with the idea that "if it's bad here, then it's good over there"; they realize only vaguely that the West has its problems, and when they run up against those problems they get confused, they get depressed, and all because naked information without development in discussion does not form real conceptions. All of the information on Western difficulties and problems, so generously provided by the Soviet press, cannot break through the inner mechanism of consciousness that filters the facts.

If you analyze the political platforms of various groups arriving at the camps, you are struck not by any ignorance of events but by an abundance of antiquated conceptions and doctrines that have been refuted by life. The life these people see is one and the same life; the information they receive is homogenized; but their ideas and conclusions are often diametrically opposed and equally distant from reality. It is not a result of personal peculiarities or political preferences on the part of these people, but rather it is due to the lack of a chance to discuss their home-grown conclusions, to debate in the open, to hear counterarguments and to correct the results of their reflections. An expansion of polemics will allow people to avoid rediscovering the wheel.

The tragedy of people living in the U.S.S.R., in the information context, does not only consist in the fact that a monstrous propaganda and agitation machine rubber-stamps them into unthinking Communists. On the contrary, Soviet propaganda furnishes us with apodictic enemies of Communism. Even the stupidest individual will ultimately see the discrepancy between propaganda and reality, and the persistent monotony with which the former is inculcated will infect him with an itch to contradict. Yet a high degree of culture and intellect are necessary to keep that machine from turning out "Communists in reverse." The information tragedy is that Soviet propaganda turns out Fascists. Patent lies repeated day after day, mockery and violation of the truth, cause even those who have well-developed minds to look for countermeasures of violence as reprisal. Too few realize that every form of vio-

lence leads to Bolshevism in all its manifestations. Under
these circumstances, merely broadening information or
"filling up gaps" will not further the development of political thought, of political maturation, or promote perception
of democratic principles. I have met masses of people who
were overjoyed at the atrocities in Chile as though their
own personal success were involved—people who seriously believe it justified to torture the torturers.

The task of broadcasting to the U.S.S.R. as well as, no
doubt, the countries of Eastern Europe, consists not only in
broader dissemination of objective information: People
must be given other alternatives for escaping from the
present hopeless situation. This can be done only through
extensive discussion. In this regard, of great interest to Soviet listeners is the opinion of the "new" emigration—
those who only yesterday lived in the U.S.S.R. but who
have already gone through, or are going through, the stage
of rethinking their values.

Objection to the next limitation follows from the fore-
going. Almost exactly like the Soviet authorities, the authors of the policy draft believe that a problem can be removed by closing down discussion of it. The third
restriction consists in eliminating from the broadcasts "any
programming the content of which could be legitimately
construed as inflammatory," and "judgment must be exercised as to the potentially inflammatory nature of any program." Aside from the fact that here again there is no clue
as to criteria for defining the potentially inflammatory, it is
perfectly clear that such a point does not permit correction
of the above-described tendencies arising among Soviet
citizens under the impact of Soviet propaganda. I had
thought that American society had outlived the prejudices
of McCarthyism as a universal as well as local problem and
had dropped the term "inflammatory" as dangerous for
democracy. Then why is that which is an outlived phase
for Americans offered as the latest achievement of political
thought for Russia?

Almost the same objections may be raised to the fourth
restriction, recommending avoidance of "any comment or
broadcast of any material which could be reasonably construed as incitement to revolt or support for illegal and violent actions." Would this evaluation apply to news items or

stories about uprisings in camps, strikes and demonstrations in Poland, recollections of the Hungarian revolution?
It probably would: These are examples of mass action, some
of it violent (I am not talking now about causes). So should
this information and its discussion be excluded? That is the
logical conclusion to be drawn from the restriction in
question.

I should like to quote the fifth restriction almost in its
entirety: "Avoidance of tactical advice, by which is meant
recommendations for specific action in particular cases, except in unusual circumstances—and then only to calm
moods in tense situations. . . . Such advice is likely to be
resented and, if acted upon might cause harm to the people
involved." And yet RL, in the first sentence of the guidelines, calls itself an independent broadcasting service. In
contrast to the Voice of America, it assumes the function of
"local broadcasting." Unquestionably, the American government cannot give advice to people in other countries,
but a local radio is obliged to do just that. Why don't you in
America forbid your newspapers to give advice to their
readers? And in "extraordinary circumstances," when the
reader needs help, tell the newspapers to wage reassuring
propaganda only, not to analyze the causes of the extraordinary circumstances, and to use sedatives for the solution
of political problems. Of course, directives and ready reci-
pes are "likely to be resented," but a man must have possible escapes, alternatives, and possible solutions! Particularly since putting forth various opinions and conceptions
of that sort via RL/RFE should most certainly be done in
the first instance with the participation of representatives
of the peoples living inside the country as well as outside
its borders. Let me remark, by the way, that the term "advice" may be interpreted at will: Any discussion will provide some sort of advice, directly or indirectly; and this restriction could be used to shut off almost any discussion,
particularly the necessary discussion regarding the country's future paths of development.

The sixth restriction has to do with "rumors" and possibilities for using them. In the U.S.S.R. a rumor is considered to be anything not reported in the official press or not
confirmed by TASS and APN. To a Soviet citizen, I am ru-
mored to have been liberated in exchange for Corvalán. In

a closed society, any piece of information is a more or less credible rumor. Reports of this or that arrest by foreign correspondents in Moscow are always "rumors"; they were not present, someone told them about it. This brings us back to the previously mentioned topic of "two sources of information mutually independent of each other."

The eighth restriction, prescribing avoidance of anything that might be understood as "encouraging defections," and careful avoidance of any hint that someone might do well to follow the example of defectors, demonstrates that the authors of the draft paper interpret escape from the Soviet Union not in the spirit of Article 13 of the Declaration of Human Rights, but rather in the spirit of Article 64 of the R.S.F.S.R. Criminal Code, which equates flight from the U.S.S.R. and nonreturn with going over to the side of the enemy. An amazing and almost literal coincidence! Such a summons is in fact any broadcast concerning positive sides of life in the West, and particularly on the good life enjoyed by émigrés.

The ninth restriction is utterly superfluous. To avoid "any suggestion which might lead audiences to believe that, in the event of an international crisis or civil disorder, the West might intervene militarily." (!) Even if the Western governments were to make daily promises of armed assistance in "civil disorders," who would believe them? After Yalta, after Hungary, after Czechoslovakia, after Helsinki?

In the tenth restriction the authors of the draft are worried lest broadcasts might contain petty (?) gossip, vicious statements, or insulting remarks about the personal lives of state and party leaders. Milovan Djilas began his opposition activity by waxing indignant over the amoral habits of the government, and only later created his conception of the "new class." If Djilas were to appear with his statements today, he would obviously be unacceptable to RL/RFE, whose main concern is protecting the image of Communist leaders. One gets the impression that this worries these radio stations more than it worries the defendants themselves.

The eleventh restriction: "Do not respond or reply to attacks on RL and RFE without prior coordination of the form and content of such reply with the Director of the radio station in question." The answer to this is elementary. Every journalist (and every person) has a right to reply to attacks and to refute slander, as well as to select the form of his reply as he sees fit.

In my opinion the last point, the twelfth, calls for no comment. It says that in the event of extraordinary circumstances in the countries to which broadcasts are beamed, the directors of both radio stations should turn off the switches and urgently fly to Washington for instructions. During that time, light music may be played on the air, inasmuch as "none of the departments of RL or RFE have the right to broadcast any materials relating to such circumstances."

And then, after all of these restrictions, the authors calmly announce in the next section that "in this way the stations take upon themselves the function of a forum for local political, social, religious and philosophical thought."

In summing up what has been said, it remains to be pointed out that the American officials responsible for RL/RFE are in fact adopting the Soviet viewpoint on détente, interpreting free information as being interference in the internal affairs of a country. What is more, information is seriously regarded as a powerful medicine which may be dispensed in larger doses to nations accustomed to it, while other nations, situated to the east of the prewar borders of the Soviet Union, should be given only homeopathic doses, since they are not yet capable of taking "Western thought and cultural values."

I am amazed at the fear of life and naturalness oozing out of every line in this document. The people who wrote it do not believe in democracy, and they attempt to replace the natural process by substituting a set of vague instructions. In skillful hands the proposed guidelines will inevitably be transformed into a tool for strangling one of the last free channels of information directed toward the totalitarian countries. In practice it has been shown that skillful hands can always be found in time.

What would the American people, the American Congress, and the Senate say if the mass media of the U.S.A. were placed under this kind of control? THEN WHY IS RL/RFE BROADCASTING NOT POSSIBLE ALONG THE PRINCIPLES UNDERLY-

ING AMERICAN DEMOCRACY, PRINCIPLES WHICH I HOPE THE
AMERICAN PEOPLE INTEND TO GO ON DEFENDING IN THE   FU-
TURE?

All that remains is the hope that this policy draft will be
stopped in time and not go into effect. If this does not happen, I can only express to you, Mr. Ronalds, my profound
condolence at being the person who will be compelled to
implement it.

                              With sincere sympathy,
                              VLADIMIR BUKOVSKY

P.S. Please allow this letter to be considered an open letter,
in view of the importance to us all of the problems of free
broadcasting.

                              Zürich, December 1976

Farewell to the Voice of America

BY ALEXEI RETTI

Translated by David Chavchavadze

From *Kontinent* No. IX, 1976

My decision to leave the Voice of America was not an easy one; I won't hide the fact that it was a tortured decision. Fifteen years of my life were tied up with the Voice and with you. This is precisely the reason I consider it my duty to explain the causes which made me leave an interesting and useful job and the friends of many years.

Beginning in approximately 1965, I began more and more to be involved in work connected with Soviet internal affairs and with the affairs of Eastern Europe and the Communist Parties. My interest in these questions was no accident. I was involved with them long before I joined the Voice of America.

Having studied dialectical materialism rather seriously, I understood that the Soviet system is a direct consequence of Marxism and that it could not be different from what it is. But what holds up this faulty system? The answer to this question began to crystallize in my mind in the last decade, and in this I owe much to the Voice. The answer is complicated, and here I will touch on only one of its aspects,

ALEXEI RETTI (Alexei Georgiyevich Retivov) was born in 1926 in Prague. He studied at the Prague Russian Gymnasium and then at Munich University. In 1956 he graduated from the Political Science Department of Columbia University. He worked at the Voice of America from 1961 to 1976.

which directly relates to us an organ of information. The Soviet regime is upheld not just by the dictatorship; not only by the historical peculiarities of Russia; not only by the caste structure of Soviet society and by inertia and patience; but also by people's lack of knowledge of their own history, of historical facts, of everyday events, and by general and all-pervading ignorance.

Only through working at the Voice have I really understood how great were our possibilities, and how great could have been our influence in the fight against ignorance and disinformation.

It would be fair to ask me: Why bring up the Voice of America and the fight against Soviet ignorance? I think every one of us sometimes thinks about his own fate and the fact that, détente or no détente, many people understand that we are facing a terrible enemy which has never refuted and still does not refute Khrushchev's phrase: "We will bury you."

Perhaps quoting oneself is in bad taste, but I remember one episode that occurred in 1971. I was then asked to lead a seminar for new employees about the techniques and problems of news. Speaking of the importance of broadcasting news about dissidents, I permitted myself to make the remark that opposition in Russia is our only hope that the world will change; the alternative is nuclear disaster. Our chief at the time, who was present at this seminar, told me that he fully agreed with me, but that the State Department would not like the spirit in which I was trying to "educate" the new employees. I thank him even for this type of well-meaning remark.

Not only the fate of Russia, but that of the whole world, of America first of all, may depend on whether or not the Soviet regime is able to throttle its opposition. Our radio station, which millions listen to, has the strongest of weapons: the opportunity to spread the word about what is kept quiet in the Soviet Union. We not only can, but are obliged to do everything in our power not to let the Soviet regime throttle the opposition, if only because it is in our own interest.

If anyone thinks that these are merely loud words in regard to everyday work at the Voice, he is mistaken. By showing initiative, much can be done without leaving the framework of the Voice's general mission. Since my work mainly concerned Soviet affairs, I will confine myself to this field.

As in every editorial board, we have a general leadership for broadcasts to the U.S.S.R. This leadership is fully established, and within the framework of the Voice of America gives us great freedom of action. No canons are established —there are no censorship limitations, but the leadership wants certain rules to be observed in broadcasting material having to do with the U.S.S.R.

For instance, in speaking about Soviet affairs, we normally do not speak in the name of the Voice but cite other sources. In my time these rules did not change radically, but supervisors did change. I will bring up several examples of what, in various periods, was fitted into these rules. Perhaps some of these examples will now seem curious, but they were, nevertheless, typical.

In the first half of the 1960s, the main thrust was the amusement aspect of our broadcasts. We, so to speak, were putting jazz into production. We were very careful in regard to Soviet internal affairs and tried not to get into them deeply, as much as possible. The chief of the period even ordered us not to call the People's Republic of China "Communist China," exhibiting a gentlemanly concern not to hurt the feelings of the true Communists—the members of the CPSU, the Communist Party of the Soviet Union. That is what he said; I am not inventing anything. This regulation, incidentally, called forth a number of amusing problems: precisely *what* to call the People's Republic of China? Not "China," because someone might think we were talking about Nationalist China—but "People's Republic of China" was also impossible, since we did not then recognize Peking. So we called it either "Continental China" or something else, according to the depth of our fancies.

The trial of Sinyavsky and Daniel took place in this period, and this we did talk about on the air, though modestly. Before Sinyavsky and Daniel there was the case of Mikhailo Mikhailov for his book *Moscow, Summer 1964.* At that time such subjects were almost taboo, but still, the first part of my article about Mikhailov and his book, while somewhat cut, did go on the air. The second part was stopped, filed away by me for better times, and finally broadcast eight years later.

An extremely interesting, and for me productive, period at the Voice began after 1966. Then the voices of dissidents in the U.S.S.R. began to sound louder and louder, were caught up by foreign correspondents, and were broadcast by us. Everything was new and unknown; we had no experience in presenting the material; we were afraid of canards and provocations. If, as a journalist, I have the right to be proud of anything, it was that I participated in this work with all the strength and ability I could muster.

About the Czechoslovak events I can say that we presented them very broadly, and completely differently from the other—that is, non-Russian—services of the Voice. But even this "daring initiative" then somehow fitted into our regulations and did not call forth any objections from the talented chief of the time. It was not for nothing that he was later kicked out of the U.S.S.R.[1]

The tone and scope of broadcasts about Soviet internal affairs that started then continued without hindrance until the middle of 1973—that is, already in the conditions of the newly formed détente. But with the arrival of a new chief, things changed.

I remember him saying, at one of the first editorial meetings, that there was only a handful of dissidents in the U.S.S.R., that few people in the U.S.S.R. were interested in them, that they had no significance, and consequently, it would be better if we mentioned them more rarely. I will not begin an argument with this chief. I will only say that through lack of experience he always mixed up two concepts—diplomacy and information—and was completely convinced that we had not only an informational function but a diplomatic one as well, that international events could change from what we said or did not say. He practically placed on his own shoulders the responsibility for the fate of our foreign policy. And it was quite natural that broadcasts of a purely informational nature seemed diplomatically dangerous to him.

Here is an example: Once the writer Maximov, whose name this chief had never heard before (he explained that

[1] McKinney Russell was declared persona non grata.

the people with whom he socialized for years in the U.S.S.R. never mentioned Maximov's name) wrote, while still in the U.S.S.R., an open letter to Willi Brandt, accusing the West German government of a new Munich betrayal. The chief blocked the reporting of our Bonn correspondent on this story on the basis that we, the Voice of America, did not have the right to broadcast such a hostile attack on our ally.

Another example: At the height of the persecution of Solzhenitsyn and Sakharov in 1973, in the "American Press About the Soviet Union" department, I described in rather great detail the interview that Sakharov had given to a Lebanese correspondent and quoted sections of an article by Lydia Chukovskaya about Sakharov. The chief of the time found my material overly expanded and not deserving of so much attention, evidently not understanding that the Soviet regime was then trying to deprive the opposition of leadership in the person of Sakharov and Solzhenitsyn. And the fact that it did not do so was due only to the interference of the West, including the Voice. In a note attached to my article, this chief remarked that he fully agreed with Kissinger that for us foreign policy and not dissidence was important. Again a confusion of diplomacy and information. But the material was broadcast before the chief made his comments. And, as you know, words cannot be retrieved from the air.

And all this fitted into our regulations, and the chief successfully implemented his line of "diplomatic information."

Soon after the article, in which I included, citing *The New York Times*, excerpts from the first volume of *Gulag Archipelago*, I was gradually prevented from writing these articles and then completely removed from the position. At the time I did not even receive a real reprimand, but I hoped that I would be told, in a comradely manner, to hang on until a time when we could broadcast what was necessary again. But nobody said anything of the kind, although I had a direct relationship to the creation of these articles. Finally, a long time later, I asked the question myself, and here is the answer I received: "We waited for you to straighten up, and since you didn't want to or couldn't, we decided it would be better to remove you." This "straighten up" was something I never expected. It even reminded me a bit of my schooldays.

And, finally, an example out of the recent past, at the time of the last chief. We were broadcasting the award of the Nobel Peace Prize to Sakharov in a scope unprecedented for the Voice of America. Not counting the reporting of our correspondent, Yelena Bonner's press conference took up twenty minutes on the air. The Nobel speech was broadcast in full, directly from Oslo, and even interfered with the news broadcast. The decision of the new chief to give this event the coverage it deserved was, in my view, correct and corresponded to our mission as a medium of information.

This also occurred during the détente epoch and fitted into the framework of our regulations, even into the one about "noninterference in internal affairs."

About this famous "noninterference." Is it possible that after all this time there is someone who does not clearly understand that everything we broadcast, from A to Z, is pure interference in the internal affairs of the U.S.S.R.; that noninterference, from the point of view of the Soviet regime, is only what is written in *Pravda*? Would it not be simpler to use more appropriate terminology? Specifically: Instead of "We may not interfere," why not say, "We must not irritate the Soviet leaders," or else they might shake a finger at us or begin to jam us. If we are not jammed now, it is not because the Voice often did not speak in its own voice during the last few years, but because they have their own, more important, considerations. Jamming and the occupation of Czechoslovakia were connected only because the Soviet situation then changed, and not at all because of the specific content of our broadcasts.

But still, the Voice of America is an unpleasant phenomenon for the Soviet regime, and it is forced to fight us, if not with jamming, then by other means, above all by all sorts of myths. The myth of "interference" is a specially efficient one. For not believing this myth they even have a punishment ready for us in the form of the myth of jamming. From among the old myths which have passed their time but which used to work well, we can mention the myth that by broadcasting about dissidents we are hurting them. This "humane" myth existed in the middle of the 1960s, and my arguments with the management on this subject ceased only after this myth was exposed by the dissidents themselves. Now there exists a myth about the enormous diplomatic influence of the Voice of America, so great that we even influence the decisions of the Politburo. One can only be amazed at the fact that all these myths are created and have their followers.

We have often been accused of censorship, but those critics are wrong. The censorship that they imagine does not, or almost does not, exist. We truthfully broadcast everything that is important. But there is a self-censorship, fed by the myths. It is reflected in everyday work and expresses itself in emasculation, in the smoothing of sharp angles without the slightest necessity, in the reduction of the scope of some "risky" article or other, in order to, so to speak, acquire modest capital, but to retain innocence at all costs. When there was talk about "risky" subject, the same argument was almost always used: "Was this covered in the news broadcast? If so, we are not obliged to return to this subject."

The effectiveness of this self-censorship in broadcasts about Soviet internal affairs lies in the fact that it is done consciously and out of the best motives to anticipate every nuance of the highest policies of our government.

The influence of the chiefs on the level of the U.S.S.R. Division is very great. But they are replaced too quickly, and not all of them possess journalistic experience and enough knowledge about the Soviet Union, although most of them have some Soviet experience—but it is isolated, embassy experience. All this is reflected in our broadcasts. Instead of listening to the myths I have described, we should hold fast to a simple journalistic rule: to broadcast, without looking over our shoulders, everything about the Soviet Union that is important, checked-out, truthful, authoritative, and not very much available to our listeners. That is the way that I understood the mission of the Voice. It seems to me that our new chief understands it in the same way. I hope that he stays with us for a long time.

As concerns me, I think that fifteen years is enough time to work under the circumstances described by me, and given my views. One can just, in a human way, get tired. And I got tired, although I do not intend to capitulate.

The Voice of America is doing a tremendous job. Taking our possibilities into account, every day of our work is a remarkable miracle.

I wish productive work to all my colleagues and hope that nobody will be insulted by my frankness.

Washington, March 29, 1976

The Psychology of Contemporary Enthusiasm

BY NAUM KORZHAVIN

Translated by Edward Van Der Rhoer

From Kontinent No. VIII, 1976

Foreword

In 1970 I read in *samizdat* a letter, "To All People of Good Will—Fidel Castro, Sartre, Russell, and Many, Many Others . . ." written by a leftist Israeli journalist, Amos Kennan. The author protested against the behavior of his colleagues of the Left who suddenly turned against Israel. Amos Kennan rebukes his former comrades for inconsistency and injustice, he is offended by them because of this. But he is nevertheless a leftist, and the same motives which permitted his comrades to act in this way have not ceased to guide him as well—only in other cases.

In connection with this, his letter at that time became a

NAUM KORZHAVIN *was born in 1925 in Kiev, Ukraine, U.S.S.R. In 1959 he was graduated from the Literary Institute A. M. Gorky of the Writers' Union of the U.S.S.R. The lateness of his graduation date is attributable to the fact that his studies were interrupted by several years sojourn in Lubianka Prison and Siberian exile. Korzhavin is a poet, playwright, and critical essayist. His works appeared in most of the major literary publications of the Soviet Union. His play,* Once in the Twentieth, *was produced by the Moscow Dramatic Theater K. C. Stanislavsky and enjoyed a long run, but was denied publication in the U.S.S.R. It appeared in translation in both Poland and Hungary and was produced by the Contemporary Theater in Wroclaw (Breslau), Poland. Korzhavin was admitted to the Writers' Union in 1963 and expelled ten years later after he had voiced his desire to emigrate. He lives in Boston.*

very convenient excuse for my dialogue with the leftist Western intelligentsia, which I had been long impatient to begin. Thereupon I fulfilled this task, but only in part, since I did not resolve to transmit the work to the West. Now, after coming to the West, I have convinced myself that it has not lost its timeliness. With this feeling, I am sitting down to retype it. (I brought only a poor copy with me.)

To be sure, any retyping is also editing at the same time. But I have no desire to do too much updating of a work written at a particular time and in a particular place. The majority of the alterations, no matter how significant they may be, are purely of a stylistic character. The only part I considered it necessary to rework, i.e., to write from a present-day attitude, was the chapter about the "Chilean revolution" in view of Allende's tragic demise. It goes without saying that I did not change my earlier negative attitude concerning everything that he proposed to do (the rightness of this attitude, in my view, has only been confirmed), but I somewhat altered the tone in which I expressed this attitude.

This work is in no way devoted to an examination of the Near East crisis, it merely examines its moral aspects. It is simply that in relation to this crisis there has rather sharply appeared the general cultural and spiritual crisis of the West, and it is precisely this latter crisis to which my work is dedicated.

Unfortunately, only one of the phenomena of this crisis —the radical psychology—is subjected to scrutiny in it. But also related to this crisis is, of course, the general attitude of the Western citizen and the democratic governments which depend on him toward critical contemporary problems. Regretably, I touch on this attitude only in passing. But Solzhenitsyn and Sakharov, with whom I agree, have written very well about this on numerous occasions since then, since 1970.

It remains to be said that I unconditionally support Israel's right to exist and do not wish to conceal my personal interest in this (in order to have the possibility of *voluntarily* remaining Russian).

And I do not consider that Israel has exhibited or exhibits a lack of willingness to compromise, since the sole negotiations which the opposing side agrees to conduct with her are negotiations for a voluntary modification of the front line to its advantage in time of war without any agreement as to its cessation. From my point of view, one should not conduct such "negotiations."

In the years which have passed since 1970, the situation, of course, has changed (for the worse). The West has frequently agreed to the terrorists' demands and created among the latter a sense of impunity. Kreisky, the Austrian premier, in response to their demands, closed the transit point at Schoenau Castle, giving the Arabs confidence in their general impunity and, perhaps, unleashing the October war. The West submitted to oil blackmail. Matters are getting to the point where Israel will be betrayed by America. But there is nothing about all of this in the work written at that time. I think, however, that in it there have been noted tendencies which permitted all of this to happen, and, if people do not understand the situation in which they are living, will permit anything to happen.

Dear Mr. Amos Kennan!

Probably you are more accustomed to the salutation "Comrade." But, as is apparent from your letter, the people whom you are accustomed to address in this manner betrayed you and you are no longer a comrade to them. They are now concerned about establishing comradeship with those who wish to destroy you. It is not out of the question that this is also unpleasant for them, but the power of dialectics over those who permit it to replace their consciences is great. They believe that this injustice will turn out to be historically just. Such is their faith. . . .

Besides, in this letter you display considerably more self-reliance, maturity, and personal integrity than your former "comrades" can allow themselves, you appear to be and in reality are a "master," the master of your thoughts and your conscience. Perhaps the vital alternative facing humanity comes down to the question of what people will become in the process of the struggle for equality—all as one, masters or slaves. Slaves are undoubtedly comrades in terms of their fate, but it is hardly worthwhile because of this to strive for slavery.

One case of the manifestation of such comradeship can be recalled. When the now remote but then recurrent Paris negotiations on Vietnam began, the North Vietnam head-quarters sent a notice to all units in which the recommendation was made that nothing be communicated about these negotiations to ordinary "comrades" in order to maintain their "spirit" at the proper level. Are you impressed by this attitude toward each person's spirit as if it were state property, confiscated clay out of which the revolutionary creative intelligentsia can fashion anything that enters its head? Have you yourself not been at some time the object of such touching comradely concern? And have you not concerned yourself in the same way about somebody else? I can say about myself that I have been surrounded by such concern since early childhood. I was perpetually being formed into something for purposes which, incidentally, also frequently changed. And were replaced.

Unfortunately, this training does not merely relate to those of us living behind the "iron curtain." This is in general one of the main problems, misfortunes, crimes, and mysteries of the twentieth century. Surely the ones being trained are often far more intelligent, educated, and spiritual than the trainers. Nevertheless, they submit (sometimes considering it an honor to submit) to this training. Although later they often find themselves in the most ridiculous situation when, having already submitted to training (and having partly lost themselves because of it), these trainers abandon them in the middle of the road to the mercy of fate. . . . Like you, for example. . . .

The translator of your letter "to all people of good will—Fidel Castro, Sartre, Russell, and many, many others" for some reason rather ironically called this letter the "lamentation of an exile from the progressive Eden," notwithstanding the fact that by translating this letter and distributing it he risked a great deal. To be sure, a large part of this irony pertains to the "progressive Eden" itself, but of course some of it falls to your account. You endure this exile much too passionately. . . .

Our experience has been too vast and bitter to let us react without irony to the fact that a man of good will suddenly turns out to be the liar and dictator Fidel Castro. Or that Jean-Paul Sartre, who, as his behavior shows, has no will of his own—only a pathological striving toward ecstatic capitulation to someone else's will. And for some reason unfailingly to an evil will.

You must forgive me for the tone of speech an adult uses to a child. I do not at all wish to belittle you or your numerous like-minded colleagues in all countries. But in the context of social experience any of my fellow citizens is really more adult than his Western counterparts. Now more adult by almost sixty years. This is sometimes revealed externally. Many words which for you are still covered by a romantic veil have been at times nakedly exposed to us, and their nature was not in any way romantic. Many trains of thought in which your comrades today long (and, in a spiritual sense, somewhat cowardly) linger at the beginning have long ago been studied by us to the very end, against our will.

In the light of what we have understood, your indignation with your like-minded colleagues looks absurd. What really surprises you? What if they betrayed you? After all, we have been betrayed for about sixty years! By the same people who did it to you—the leftist intellectuals of the West. Sometimes calling themselves liberal, sometimes together with liberals, but they are betrayers. For about sixty years they have calmly and inspirationally sacrificed our destinies, health, lives (not to speak of freedom and dignity) for the sake of what seems to them (but not at all to us) historical progress, i.e., for the sake of their—but by no means our—love. Of course, we understand that you will not be able (even with the help of your governments) to aid us in any real way, even if you greatly wished to do so, and we do not have the slightest pretension to this. We are speaking of things which are purely emotional—one does not need to sacrifice us with such alacrity. Or to show too much solicitude for the "complicated position" of our executioners and oppressors, even if it seems to you that they are building on our bones some sort of marvelous world. After all, it is impermissible that the blood and suffering of some people should be regarded by others as nothing more than insignificant spots on the sun of their faith. Of course, no one says it so directly, but they behave in this manner—proceeding in their behavior from this attitude and attempting at any price to avoid the posing of the question, as if they did not notice it. This is a proven method, it is used by such people in an examination of all questions: the Near East, Indochina, or any other question. For that very reason the psychology of this method requires the most detailed examination. Even if this somewhat violates the genre of a "letter." So let us talk about the method.

The Tragicomedy of Faith, or, A Tale of Unrequited Free Love

This title should surprise no one, since what lies at the base of the method under consideration (and, in general, the psychology being discussed) is really love. Moreover, unrequited love is based on deception and self-deception. It is precisely with such love that this intelligentsia for many years has loved the Soviet system of repression. It loves this system for qualities which do not exist and never have existed. It loves without mutuality, for the representatives of the system simply make no reply to such ideological ardor, it only irritates them. True, they sometimes wink at this intelligentsia but always do so with an aim that is not good—to make use of it, to utilize its ardor for other aims. But love is blind. The intelligentsia interprets these winks entirely differently; it is able, generally speaking, to explain the actions of the Soviet leaders by motives which could not even come into their heads. This, however, is only the case if these actions cannot escape notice. Ordinarily it simply tries not to know the truth and sometimes succeeds in this for decades.

For many years it was greatly aided by an approach based on world-outlook—self-censorship. This approach is simple. Inasmuch as one felt that a press which was "bourgeois" (i.e., alien to this world-outlook or sometimes only to the party) could not by its nature tell the truth, one did not read it. Only veracious Soviet sources were utilized, thus helping to preserve, in the first place, loyalty and, secondly, peace of mind. But the method failed. Today there is hardly anyone who doubts which press is closer to the truth. The situation has been saved by dialectics, i.e., faith in the turns and twists of progress, when Good looks like Evil, and vice versa. This aids these intellectuals in their service to Evil, which for some reason simply does not turn into Good.

This intelligentsia still had the possibility of learning the truth from live witnesses, i.e., from people forced to live with it in the emigration. But since in its view society is divided not according to people but by classes, that was also impossible: Living impressions were not taken into account. What sense was there in interesting oneself in the impressions of representatives of the exploitative classes (or one's own impression of them, as of people), if it was known in advance that all ideas (and that also meant impressions) of these people were restricted by class? It is completely clear that they cannot reconcile themselves to their material and other losses from the revolution and are, in general, reactionaries. Their sufferings, even if regarded as real, do not merit sympathy.

At the same time, even among the most narrow-minded reactionaries, far from all people are motivated in their testimonies solely by their property and other personal losses. Not to speak of the fact that not all of these people were liars. When a man tells about the horrors which he or those near to him had to endure (and which by no means all of them survived), he seldom lies—he has no need to do so. With all the divergences in views (even now I do not agree with many of them), it was necessary to listen to them, if only as sources of information. But the Western intellectuals have not only failed to listen to them. They have not listened more to the most genuine "progressives," of whom there are more than a few in the emigration. They have preserved the aforementioned love. Yes, whatever one says, the Russian proverb that "love is evil" remains true. Especially if it depends upon the dialectical attitude toward the sufferings of strangers.

In these conditions, the higher intellectual and spiritual elite of Russia, also found abroad in large numbers—most frequently of all against its will—has been able to accomplish all the less. This was quite a special elite, possessing particularly rich spiritual and intellectual experience. It passed as a whole through revolutionary, often Marxist, sympathies and—under the influence of life—overcame them. As early as 1905, this elite was the first to begin to study carefully that crisis of culture which the twentieth century bore in itself (believing, in truth, that this was only a Russian phenomenon), and it defended its soul as a value of universal significance and indispensability for all. The tragedy of 1917 and the subsequent years further enriched its intellectual and spiritual experience and whetted a sensation of human and cultural values. It was exiled because the rulers of that time, leftist intellectuals—and what leftist intellectual is not aware of himself as a thinker?—did not feel sufficient competence, if not sufficient rightness on their side (this was replaced by the awareness of power), to win out over these "idealists" in an open dispute. It was another matter to beat them demagogically at a meeting—but the epoch of meetings had just ended. Thanks for only exiling and not shooting them.

But the left intelligentsia did not even think of utilizing this opportunity to find out the truth. Indeed, how could it listen to these people if they came to Christ, and this, from its point of view, was not only reactionary but even uncultured! This intelligentsia did not itself notice that its absolute rejection of God was also a faith, it only dimly felt that this faith (the foundation of its life and world-outlook) was shaky. It protected its wholeness from the influence of external impressions and alien, corroding opinions all the more harshly and fanatically. This is how one always protects weak faith. Once again it had at its disposal dialectics, with whose help it was possible to change the sense of any fact. As well as the constant possibility of declaring any opinions and arguments that are contrary to dialectics, any demonstration of real sense, as class-restricted and bourgeois—hence vilely egoistical.

Of course, it was a faith, although this faith does not inspire much respect. Really, Mr. Kennan, haven't you noticed that there isn't a single atheist in the world? As soon as a man turns away from God, he turns to idols, i.e., he begins to cast out of material at hand the usual calf, not necessarily of gold. In our time such calves are not merely objects (say, things—furniture, money), not only position and fashion, but finally what is worse—words.

These words quickly lose or repeatedly change their original meaning but remain all the same an object of worship for the person who once believed in them. Such a word could be "sex," it could be "emotionality," but it could also be NATION or SOCIALISM. It could be a whole system of such terms, positive and negative idols, delimiting the "only possible" meaning of a worthy life. This only possible meaning can be linked in our consciousness with an activity or simply with the name of some man (for example, Lenin, Stalin, or Hitler), and they can later make out of us anything that comes into their hot heads: We can always find a clever explanation for contradictions in their words and actions. Today's behavior of the French Communists or the Israeli party of Meyer Willner shows the extent to which this awful idolatry can lead. Genuine religion is good in providing liberation from it and its bewitching dialectics.

Precisely idolatry and the fear of violating the idols' will assisted the left intelligentsia in bypassing the extraordinarily rich philosophical and biographical literature of the Russian emigration. But, you know, it was possible to learn from it very much (and opportunely) about the red terror, about collectivization, about the self-destruction of the Bolshevik party, about decades of misinformation, and about much, much more. I could recommend to you Berdyaev's writings, S. Melgunov's *Red Terror in Russia*, A. Avtorkhanov's *Technology of Power*, the complete set of *Sovremenniye Zapiski* (Contemporary Notes), a magazine which came out in Paris between the two world wars, and many, many other books. This is in addition to the contemporary ones: those of Solzhenitsyn, N. Ya. Mandelstam, etc. I believe that any person who still thinks about socialism should carefully familiarize himself with its history in Russia, but this cannot be done without Russian books which have come out in the West. It is necessary if only to be honest with oneself. True, there are people whom no books and no facts will sway, but, judging from your letter, this cannot wholly apply to you. I think that, reading these memoirs and studies, you will feel the nature of the vivisection to which people of our country have been subjected for so many years. Possibly you will also consider how moral it was to close one's eyes to this and, in this regard, to feel enthusiasm.

Mr. Sartre's Enthusiasm, Grandeur, and the General Level of Culture

Yes, we are old victims of this enthusiasm. Nevertheless, it has now become somewhat easier for us. Half of the enthusiasts, disappointed in the U.S.S.R., have now deserted to

Now it is their, not our, sufferings which become nothing
in the face of great achievements. Of course, no one has
gotten any closer to the truth as a result: The Chinese Communists are an even more terrible anticultural force than
the Soviet party hacks. But still . . .

In truth, there are enthusiasts who, having deserted to
the Chinese, do not miss the chance to sacrifice us, too.
First of all in this line, as in many others which are equally
little-respected, stands J.-P. Sartre. The same one to whom
you address yourself as a man of some sort of will. He is
now widely known as a defender of freedom. Any sort.
Against anybody. In general, anything that comes into his
head to call freedom. True, in the process he leaves out
what is usually called freedom. But as we shall see, he does
not prize banal values in any way.

Anyway, this Sartre now publishes (or once published) a
magazine under the eloquent title *International Idiot* (*L'idiot
international*), whose aim apparently is the protection of idiots cramped by bourgeois society. (And it is true that under
socialism idiots, in contrast to normal people, are far better
off.) In one of the articles carried in this magazine it is
argued that the insane are people oppressed by a class
society and by doctors. (Evidently doctors are agents of this
society.) Nevertheless, I would not react to it. But the fact is
that the author of this article, so touchingly solicitous
about the sick, is more than indifferent to the fate of
healthy people (who for all that are more numerous and
are also being incarcerated in insane asylums in some
countries). Particularly instructive is his attitude toward
the Soviet opposition, i.e., toward those who at any moment can find themselves in such a situation. He re-
proaches it, even extremely severely. It turns out that it is
too much occupied with the acquisition of bourgeois freedoms (i.e., exactly the ones whose abuse allows Sartre to
publish his interesting magazine), at a time when the author of the article (and, apparently, its editor), for whom
some forefathers once obtained these freedoms, has long
been above such banal demands. Even the Soviet regime,
which they mildly castigate for conservatism, they nevertheless consider more progressive than us, since our opposition, in their opinion, is of a purely bourgeois character.
Ethically these judgments look the same as the judgments

of a feasting company that starving people think too much about bread. For the moment I intentionally do not focus attention on the intellectual unsoundness of this manipulation of terms which have lost any real significance. I wish to emphasize another side of this reasoning—its dishonesty and shamelessness.

Nevertheless, Sartre apparently has long since freed himself from such a bourgeois survival as shame. All his attention is now concentrated on how to remain as long as possible a ruler of men's minds. But for this it is constantly essential not to slip up and to keep in step with current opinions, each time attempting to seize them in the stage when they are still thought to be original. Here it is no longer a question of conscience. Probably it is not worthwhile to take Sartre seriously. But for all that one feels ill at ease when a man who enjoys complete freedom writes thus about people who are silenced, who, because they dare to think and express their views, are daily threatened, at a minimum, with Soviet camps of strict regime[1] if not psychiatric hospitals—dissenters are not confined in other places.

The consequences of such statements are far from harmless and are by no means of an academic character. They

[1]Incidentally, "strict regime" is not an empty term. Normal criminals are subjected to this regime in terms of extra punishment, dissenters from the very beginning, as established by law. Nevertheless, as we now live generally in an epoch of legality, "strict regime" has been formulated entirely legally in the "Corrective Labor Code of the U.S.S.R." so that anyone who desires could learn what that means. Those who are familiar with the works of Solzhenitsyn, Shalamov, and especially Marchenko, could observe that those procedures which existed without any code in Stalinist and post-Stalinist camps are now entirely legalized by this code, and some have been changed in the direction of greater cruelty. For example, the number of letters and food packages which a prisoner may receive is strictly limited. This is legalized torture, not only of the prisoner himself but of his relatives. The present leaders do not possess Stalin's cruelty, but in return they do not consider it necessary to be embarrassed, to hide their petty vindictiveness. Or perhaps they know that there is no one from whom to hide it—today's fighters for a better future in the West are not very interested in finding out what lies ahead of them. In any case, nothing is known to me about protests in the free world in connection with the adoption of this barbaric code.

divide the public opinion of countries where such an opinion exists and have significance in that they bring into dispute a question which was previously indisputable for everybody (except, of course, the Communists): Should one sympathize with the victims of dictatorship? Certainly as a result our position, the position of thinking people in totalitarian countries, thereupon worsened. In truth, no secret police in the whole history of mankind has enjoyed the support of such a number of refined thinkers as the Soviet secret police.

Nevertheless, these are thinkers of a special kind. Particularly that same Sartre. Really, it seems, the radical of radicals. In the June days of 1968 he practically broke into prison (an imperialist one, of course, not a proletarian one —there, I dare say, he would not break in under any circumstances). Suddenly he rebukes Nabokov and other Russian émigré writers for total "rootlessness" and for the fact that they "do not care about any community if only to revolt against it because they themselves do not belong to any community." He even adds: "Hence their writings are reduced to empty subjects."

No, I am not about to defend Nabokov or other émigré writers against Sartre. One cannot judge writers as a group at all, and Sartre is too imprecise a man that his esthetic judgments could have any significance (except purely for publicity). I am struck by something else. It develops that Sartre—aside from the fact that he is such a terrible radical —also wishes to be what is called in Russia a *"pochvennik."*[2] That's nice. As the saying goes, the rogue has a finger in every pie.

In our day it is difficult to surprise anybody with anything, but Sartre—a man who has never had or wanted to have any ground under his feet except the fluctuating waves of public agitation—reproaching someone for groundlessness nevertheless beats all records.

It is obvious that the spiritual and cultural level of France must have fallen to a low level if such a man can be regarded as a thinker in a country with such traditions. Is it

---

[2] *Pochvennichestvo* (grass-roots populism) is an attitude diametrically opposed to radicalism. Incidentally, I myself am close to it, but then, I am not a radical.

conceivable that the very culture of the country is now only history? Unfortunately, the intellectual content of the policy of "grandeur" introduced by de Gaulle and continued by his successors confirms the worst assumptions. The Sartre irresponsibility, in truth, makes itself felt in this policy. The policy consists of an open permanent betrayal of everyone who can be betrayed, in the name of grandeur (this is now how grandeur is conceived) and the interests (frequently imaginary) of France herself. Apparently this government, according to the ideas of the policy's creators, must emphasize the significance and role of present-day France in the contemporary world. And really all peoples already feel France's significance and, if things continue in the same way, will feel it even more acutely in the future. The significance of an ally who may at any moment abandon his sector of the front always makes itself felt acutely.

Certainly France has achieved more than a little. After all, the escalation of betrayals which has infected the free world today began precisely with her. It is as if she wittily decided to set fire to the house in which she lived in the hope of swiping the next-door neighbor's family jewels in the midst of the confusion. Or simply luring him away while he put out the fire. An infantile policy whose lack of foresight possibly exceeds its unconcealed baseness. When Sartre wanted to go to jail, de Gaulle quite sensibly prevented this, saying: "Leave the clown alone!" Undoubtedly Sartre is a clown, but did de Gaulle have the right to the feeling of superiority which can be detected in these words? If "grandeur" is a policy, then Sartre is a thinker and a philanthropist. The level of profundity and responsibility here is one and the same.

By a strange coincidence almost all Frenchmen whom I have had occasion to see were reasonable and cultured people whose level was superior by far to this policy and this opposition. Why is it, however, that this level is not reflected today in France's national life? What is the mystery?

All of this may comfort you in the sense that it is not only the leftists who are engaged in suicide. That is true, but it also happens to be true that everything is taking place in a situation created by the leftists, sometimes not without their influence, direct or indirect. Furthermore, this cannot change the fact that the leftists occupy themselves with suicide not from time to time, like all the others, but always, as I have already written in this work.

It is startling that nothing teaches them. Each time they hope again that now everything will work out, that they will not be the first to employ terror which in the end would turn against them. And each time—for love is evil— they carry out acts which force them to resort to terror as the only means allowing them "not to destroy the revolution." They are masters in convincing themselves that nothing bad can happen to them. They somehow forget that even if they succeeded in carrying out a revolution differently (and I do not believe it), then, as the song goes, the U.S.S.R. possesses "strong armor and swift tanks." The Soviet leaders will not tolerate any other socialism: It does not pay to forget Czechoslovakia. The majority of the comrades of these seditious socialists—even the ones who oppose this action—will nevertheless ultimately regard this as a private question and avoid spoiling their relations, because of it, with the country where there is no exploitation. Or even just adapt themselves to the "correct" point of view. As in the case of Israel.

"Comrades!" How glad I am that I no longer have such comrades and that there is absolutely no one to whom I can write letters like yours.

Useless Password

Your comrades lie. You are hurt by that. Not, however, because of revulsion toward falsehood but only due to the fact that methods which you also considered permissible, although solely in regard to things which were, so to speak, placed out of bounds (let us assume Class or Progress), now are applied to their full extent to you yourself. That is, you yourself have been placed out of bounds, converted from a subject into an object. Your situation is reminiscent of the situation of an Old Bolshevik (or, still worse, a Chekist) in a Stalin jail or on the defendants' bench at one of the big trials. One is wounded, slandered, and there is no one (and nothing) open to appeal: All laws, those of God and man, have long since been violated.

It is evident from your letter that abstractness of ideas and fiery spirit at progressive banquets are even now dearer to you than concrete truth. Very dear to you, too, is the lie which, by virtue of your being an accessory to it, assures you of such interesting comradeship. One does not have to go far in search of examples. They begin with the first phrase.

"I am for Cuba! I love Cuba!" you exclaim passionately.

If one has no idea of what it is all about, one might even be surprised. You love it—so love it, but why shout about it? People who love something are hardly rare. There are even those who like Antarctica. . . . But we are not surprised. For we know very well that neither love nor Cuba herself has any connection with your assertion. For this is not an assertion nor an exclamation but only an accustomed password through which you passionately wish to tell a sentry that you are on his side. Formerly, pronouncing this password, you found yourself accepted by your people in the progressive camp, and now you repeat it as an invocation and as proof that you have not become a traitor. But the invocation does not work. Whether the password now is different (for example: "Long live progressive Arab nationalism! Death to Israeli aggressors!") or the sentry simply had received orders not to respond to any password whatever in the event of your appearance, the fact of your fidelity does not impress anybody here and you are not allowed to pass. As a matter of fact, you yourself know that you will not be allowed to pass—the disciplined conscience of those to whom you appeal is well known to you—but you still cry out. With this cry you also wish to remind yourself that you are you. For you have no other picture of yourself for the time being. (I hope that it is only for the time being!) Cuba does not come into this at all. In general, in order to be accurate, you should have replaced the word "Cuba" with the word "Castro" in your exclamation: "I am for Castro! I love Castro!" For, properly speaking, you apparently do not care about Cuba. You are interested in revolution, not in Cuba.

Meanwhile, Cuba exists as such. This is not a password nor a symbol nor a synonym for the word "Castro." It is the name of a country in which flesh and blood people are living. True, now they have become the object of an ignorant experiment of the left intelligentsia directed by Castro.

Nevertheless, strictly speaking, you have also long since ceased to love him at all. Indeed, he suppressed people like you, your left intelligentsia of which he was a representative, long ago, changing, as is customary with your leaders, from an ignorant experimenter into a brutal dictator. But it is more pleasant for the left intelligentsia not to see this, as it did not see anything earlier.

It is true that the leftist German poet Hans Magnus Enzersberger visited Cuba at one time and departed in horror, a feeling which he did not conceal from some of my friends in Moscow. But that was evidently due to nervousness. By all appearances, he has already assumed a dialectical attitude toward what he saw there: The wind is blowing in the same direction. Generally speaking, it is easier to look at things dialectically at a distance than close up—you do not see with your own eyes.

At times, however, one nevertheless has to see something. For example, the *barbudo* Fidel threw the Cuban poet Ernesto Padilla into jail not so long ago. He only released Padilla after the latter publicly recanted and abased himself. On this occasion the leftist intellectuals were also unable to restrain themselves—even they do not believe in such spectacles today. So they got together and wrote their idol and spiritual brother a communication which was in part a friendly protest, in part a petition from loyal subjects: "Is it possible that things are so bad in Cuba it has become necessary there to forbid people to speak the truth?" The anticipated negative answer is implied by the very tone of this question. (Just as, by the way, it implies agreement with the idea that, if things are bad, one can and should forbid people to speak the truth.)

Apparently, however, Fidel Castro has somewhat more information about affairs in Cuba than his enthusiastic admirers, their obsequious sobs did not touch him in the least, and he at once, without entering into any discussion or straining his ingenuity, settled the problem, losing no time in calling his unbidden well-wishers hirelings of imperialism (he went so far as to place these words in Padilla's mouth). After this any need to explain the situation in Cuba vanished automatically. Right now his disheartened admirers are probably searching for the root of their error and some higher (to the extent that they do not discover an elementary) mystical-dialectical meaning of his philippic.

Nevertheless, as in any country where the party of the new type is in power, things in Cuba are, frankly speaking, bad. People are hungry and, judging by everything, will continue to be hungry, and there is not enough of the most essential things. Moreover, the Cubans receive a large part of their meager rations at the expense of the Soviet people, who are not delighted about this either.

Anyway, I even somewhat excuse Castro's unethical treatment of his admirers. What is this "Is it possible . . . ?" Things are bad. There is terror because things are bad. Always after a historically indispensable victory there is terror because the material (not to speak of other) things after this victory are invariably bad, but it is awkward to admit this: You see, everything that has been done was done solely for the greater development of productive forces.

Only terror can soften the effect of this horrifying reality: For, when a man convinces himself with his own eyes that he may lose his life at any moment, hunger and privation cease to appear to him the most awful things in the world.

Nevertheless, this will not convince you in any case. You are firmly convinced that all of this is only the cost of progress, Castro is just getting a bit of training in administration (on people) and everything will turn out splendidly. The more so as even now there have been such successes! An unskilled or even a nearly illiterate man can develop into a big person. Of course, accepting the authority of such a person will not afford much pleasure, but what do these trivial considerations matter in the face of such a rampage of democracy? One should be ashamed of such feelings! And so one is ashamed.

According to this code, for example, you ought to be ashamed that you oppose the destruction of Israel and do not believe lies about it. Although you do not yield to your former friends and although you know that they, not you, have betrayed the ideology, you are still ashamed and seek to justify yourself, you still, without even confessing it to yourself, feel your guilt before the insensate Moloch of progress. But, you see, this is really strange. They are the ones who—in defiance of all their own canons—define born nationalists as fighters for world revolution, racial war (against women, children, and defenseless people, against the population—so that there will be none left) as class war, and people who attack defenseless human beings, fearing those who are armed, as heroes and brave men. Moreover, as has already been said, such a reinterpretation (previously those friends of yours were on Israel's side) only occurred after a corresponding reorientation of Soviet foreign policy. The *fedayeen* likewise did not suspect they were so transformed that all their savage lusts became associated with the "bright dream of mankind." . . .

But your friends do not justify themselves, you do. Except as justification, what is the meaning of your password (or heart-rending cry): "I am for Cuba! I love Cuba!"?

The Saga of Che Guevara

Since, however, we have touched on fairy tales about Cuba, I suppose that we simply cannot avoid the related "Saga of Che Guevara." True, here we enter a dangerous zone, the area of precious myths. It is said that if I dare to treat this heroic "Saga" with my unromantic pen, all of the Earth's genuinely revolutionary people will instantly begin to hold me in contempt. And not only them, but all those who sympathize with them. And not just the sympathizers, but even those who are not sympathizers yet experience in relation to the sympathizers an inferiority complex (i.e., they regard their lack of sympathy as baseness of nature and incapacity for a real flight of spirit). Some of them will therefore even wish to kill me. Nevertheless, as the saying goes, if you're afraid of wolves, don't go into the forest. Don't renounce because of this the expression of thoughts and attitudes toward things. All the more so since I believe more than any socialist in the ultimate victory of socialism (without fail changing into national socialism) and therefore I do not greatly value my life. So I am going to give an account of this Saga anyway. In truth, it turned out to be too humorous for such a form, but what can you do! . . . There are things in the world which are serious only in their consequences, and in addition I am more interested as a writer in empirical coloration, while humor sometimes can arise apart from the author: due to an unforeseen conjunction of the play of colors and the whim of fate.

In any case, here is the Saga as it appears to me today.

To begin with, the prehistory. At first, as is known, there was a war in Cuba against Batista. During that period Che Guevara lived life to the full: He burned with ardor, feeling friendship and elation of spirit. (Such people generally fear death less than life.) But no matter how much rope is woven, there comes an end. The *barbudos* were victorious. Burned out, in all likelihood. Submitting to the logic of events. And they did not even notice that they had fought for freedom but dictatorship had triumphed. (Guevara also did more than a little, one must think, in imperceptibly bringing about this transition.) But victory had arrived. It appeared as if that was everything. Ah, no!

Suddenly there occurred unforeseen difficulties. Food was needed, manufactured goods were needed—to cover nakedness and write slogans—much that was so indispensable every day was needed, but it was not available. Certainly it would have been possible to say to people: "Go ahead, boys, feed yourselves, any way you can, and we'll arrange things later—however it works out for you." But then spontaneity would begin, and everyone would have a longing for bourgeois life. That would not be good. Later, if people started trying to be independent, what would there be to do for a left intellectual, a real revolutionary? Be bored? For what had blood been spilled? Was it not really for the creative joy of directing the life process?

Well, so one started to direct—to create reality. At first it was not bad—warehouses from the old regime still remained. But later it became quite bad. The tedious aspects of life so hateful to the leftist intellectual not only did not decline but even began rapidly to increase. Backwardness became a burden. If people do not wish to cope with objective difficulties, what do you want, do it for them. They crowd around, get excited. Give to this one, and give to that one, one to this, something else to that. . . . Everybody shouts. . . . Everybody demands. . . . Where are you to get it? On the whole, it is bad.

And annoying, of course. The most important thing of all, power, has been seized! . . . Nothing but trifles remain to be done. Oh, rubbish! Nonsense! . . . Such a mess!

Still, once it was like that, time-servers appeared. These are people who can do something, but they cannot forget

themselves. You will not catch such people bare-handed—
they demoralize everything, but you will get nothing on
them. They have accommodated themselves, the scum! Cry
if you like!

As a legendary hero, Che Guevara endured and endured,
thought and thought, and at last made his historic decision,
for which all the Earth's potential heroes still do not tire of
glorifying him. He gathered all his friends and comrades-
in-arms and said to them:

"O.K., boys! . . . There are still some things to finish up
—finish it without me. I'm off. To another country—to
start a revolution there, steer it onto our radiant path. If it
turns out to be inexpedient, our specialty is wasted."

As is known, the Bolsheviks are great admirers of expediency, and later, those who wished to rule outnumbering
those who wished to revolt, they released him.

"O.K.," they said, "go, dear comrade! We shall replace
you at your battle station! . . . " (One had in mind the minister's private office. Wicked tongues, however, maintained that everything began with this office, i.e., they un-
ceremoniously pushed out the dear fellow, but that does
not change the essence of the matter and cannot disturb
the tenor of the present narrative.)

In any case, strictly speaking, this is how the "Saga"
really begins. The new Don Quixote starts out in search of
the new Sancho Panza. He started out . . .

But it developed that now Sancho Panza was a different
man. Whether he had heard a lot about the Cuban experience, or rumors about Russian collectivization had reached
him in the form of a horror story, or he simply figured out
with his peasant brain that there was something suspicious
about the affair, the landing of Che Guevara on Bolivian
soil did not arouse on the part of the comrades the planned
conflagration of revolution.

In response to the fiery speeches of the young enthusiasts, the Sancho Panzas only remained silent, shook their
heads enigmatically, sometimes even expressed in the local
dialect their international—equally incomprehensible in
all languages—"I see, of course," but resiliently evaded
any participation in partisan warfare. Obviously they
thought: "It looks now as if there are a good many of them,
Don Quixotes. Their speech is incomprehensible and they

travel in gangs, like bandits—it's better for a peasant to stay as far away as possible from them." Nevertheless, I cannot say exactly what the Sancho Panzas thought, I do not know—I was not the one who sought to lead them into battle—but the fact remains: The ingenious plans to start a civil war, which, most important of all, had been approved by Castro, failed. And they failed so obviously that even such a high-principled man as Che Guevara could not help but see it. Sancho Panza this time did not long to become a follower of Don Quixote.

But a real revolutionary never loses presence of mind or faith in victory. Obstacles only increase his efforts but do not discourage him. Well, in those days Che Guevara wrote in his famous *Diary* the following sentence about his attitude toward the peasants, for whom, as is known, he was ready at any moment to sacrifice his life: "Judicious terror (in conjunction with something else, but this is not important in the present case: the tactics of revolutionary struggle as such do not interest us now) could give the movement real scope." That is what he wrote—"judicious terror." I do not vouch for the accuracy of all quotations, but I can vouch with my life for these words, the general sense, and the emotional coloration.

What leftist intellectual will not sigh when he hears this sad tale? He will say: What a tragic personality, how hard for this man due to the masses' backwardness and lack of spiritual resources. He will say that there is no telling what we have to do in order to herd them into paradise and deliver them from exploitation. . . . I also sigh. But about something else—I picture how it all looks in reality. . . .

A certain little peasant, let us say, lives in some remote Bolivian village. He is poor but still unconscious of class interests. (It should be said that not everyone has the opportunity to read pamphlets about these interests in secret during university lectures.) Well, he has a wife, of course, and five children, or not much fewer. He and his family live from hand to mouth in their Bolivian way, and on the whole it is bad. His wife is again carrying a child, the children are hungry, in the stall a cow is mooing (or some sort of buffalo), she wants something to eat. Don't ask her for milk. . . . Melancholy!

"Oh!" thinks the little peasant. "Here goes! There is

nothing to do! . . . I'll go and mow hay on the sly." (Or reeds, who knows what Bolivians feed cattle?) Especially as he is aware that the landowner has just gone away yesterday—either to amuse himself or to revolt as well (such things also happened), and the caretaker is on his second day drinking with friends. You never can tell!

No sooner said than done. He goes. He mows. He is satisfied that he has gotten away with it. "I'll make the children happy," he thinks, "my wife will be overjoyed, she has become quite thin, poor thing." He finishes. He is just about to go home, look, there come the fighters for his happiness out of the dark forest toward him. The evil of the evil: due to general ignorance and backwardness. And behind the back of each of them a submachine gun.

They see the little peasant and come up to him. "You're from this village?" they ask. "From this one," he replies. Why not reply? "You're the one we need." The peasant remains silent. He is probably surprised. "Why," he thinks, "do they need me?" But all of a sudden they launch into yells and begin to grab him by the throat: "What's with you, you bastard, you don't fight for freedom? You rely on others?" The peasant understood in no way what they wanted from him (he had never in his life relied on anybody), but he sees—the situation is bad. To make sure, he begins to whimper: "Oh, but we—but you—but the children are small, my wife is carrying a child. Besides, the field has not been harvested. . . . " And he mentions other trivial things which are inessential for a real revolutionary. But revolutionaries cannot be moved to pity so simply, they have been steeled by dialectics, all their lives they have been accustomed to get at the root of a problem, they distinguish the essential from the nonessential in an instant. The more so as they do not spare their lives for the cause—not to mention the fact that it is a foreign one which has, moreover, not yet been seized by revolutionary passion. "Stop that!" they answer. "There's your justification! Everybody has a wife, everybody has children. Anyway, if you want to know, that's all a survival. Now we have free love and a sexual revolution. Understand?" "How could I not understand?" the peasant temporizes. "I see, of course. But still, people need to eat and drink." "You will eat in a crystal palace! At a time of universal happiness!" says the greatest idealist. "Everything will be there. It's just that, having such disagreement as you do, will you build this palace? Oh . . . Louse . . . Only puts a brake on progress! Give us a straight answer—are you going with us or not?" "But what am I to do?" The peasant makes excuses: "I'll do it at once if you like, with the greatest pleasure. But there are the children, I have good friends . . ." "Ah, you're giving us that again! . . . Well, this is what you get for sabotage!" And with these words the greatest idealist takes the submachine gun off his back and, with a short burst, finishes the representative of the unenlightened working peasantry, who is somewhat surprised by this turn of events. Later the population of all the surrounding villages is solemnly informed through reliable people: "So-and-so was shot by us for his refusal to fulfill his revolutionary duty. Anyone who follows his example will meet the same fate." The old saying, of course, is also added: "He who is not with us is against us."

Now, of course, seized by fear, all the villages would fill up the partisan detachments, an insurgent army would soon come into being, and the civil war dear to the heart of Che Guevara would begin, then there would be victory, and then . . . Again a humdrum life and the next country to uplift the soul. As is known, there are still, for the time being, many countries on this planet. True, the peasant's children have become orphans, his wife is a widow, and for the most part the whole family has to beg for a living. But these are trifles to a man who lives solely for world development.

This is no doubt how judicious terror presented itself to Che Guevara. That was how it would happen. (The Vietnamese and many other peasants could tell a lot about this if they did not fear vengeance, and, of course, if the progressives had any interest in listening to them.) But that was not how it happened this time. Ignorance got in the way, and also gross materialism without any tinge of dialectics. It happened in the following manner. One of the Sancho Panzas, who for lack of time was little interested in the distant future, somewhere spelled out an official notice of an immediate cash reward to anyone who revealed the whereabouts of the great revolutionary. By chance this was known to him. Making out the sense of this notice, the peasant was very glad at the possibility to somewhat better his position at last by such an uncomplicated and, as it then³ appeared to him, legal means. He immediately set off for the city and there, as the saying goes, informed the necessary individual about what was necessary—in short, informed on his possible liberators.

To tell the truth, I even now do not know how to regard him. On the one hand, I cannot stand informers; on the other, without knowing it himself, this man has saved countless people from the above-described judicious terror. I can only say one thing straight out: Fool! He seized the bird in the hand too quickly and let two in the bush get away. He only needed to wait until Che Guevara had won, he could have gone far with such information! Particularly in the subsequent stages. (To be sure, if he lived that long.)

But, on the other hand, how would he know about stages? Or about birds? Ignorance!

Well, that is the whole "Saga." I do not vouch for the details, but the sense has been reproduced precisely.

The Fruits of Unrequited Love, or, About the Subsequent Stages

Thus we have touched on a subject which is sore for many revolutionaries—on the subsequent stages. Somehow the left intelligentsia does not like to focus attention on them. It is reluctant to recall that the thirties unexpectedly and inevitably come after the twenties, which are dear to its heart. . . . Of course, the left intelligentsia is enraptured about those years too (and how much more!), but . . . for all that, something is not as it should be. Nevertheless, an acceptance of reality (more accurately, a delight in it) comes harder to this intelligentsia in the subsequent stages than in the preceding ones. Somehow revolutionary romance is not the same. That is, it does not even resemble itself in the least, not to speak of the fact that it has gotten rid of its most fiery spokesman. . . .

No, of course this intelligentsia still does not doubt that

³Later some sort of revolution occurred in Bolivia. So that, who knows, perhaps it no longer seems so to him?

"everything is continuing," they understand, to be sure, that it simply comes down to the fact that "new conditions demand new forms," but . . . for all that it is no longer the same joy. Somehow it is unpleasant to observe that, while previously those who became inevitable victims of progress were more often an alien element—some noblemen, some bourgeoisie, as well as landed peasants and backward workers, i.e., more and more people of an unromantic character—now the left intelligentsia itself is beginning to suffer from mistakes, its inclinations and representatives. Somehow the mistakes are very persistent—I would say intentional. Of course, there are no protests. What kind of protests can there be—abstract humanism was a dead letter long ago, and all unnecessary victims have long since been written off in advance. It is impossible to oppose historical necessity because of such rubbish as the life and honor of your relatives and friends. There even begin, so to speak, soothing twinges of perverted conscience—quote, how does this come about?—while strangers are being sacrificed (then "mistakes" could not be avoided, you knew about that), you endured this—but when it applied to you and your friends—you reared up! (That is to say: When non-Party peasants were left without leg-wrappers and all "has-beens" were shot, there were not such complicated experiences.) This only proves that you still have not overcome your ancestral *petit bourgeois* origins. . . .

But no leftist intellectual can really bear this accusation (despite the fact that all "left" ideology was thought up by *petit bourgeois* intellectuals—and is no longer necessary to anyone). Something in no way romantic, shallow, shameful, egoistical, and vile seems to him to lie behind this accusation. He would betray his own mother if he could only prove that this was not so. One Moscow literary man spoke to me about the early thirties in Russia: "You see, it was necessary to convince people that to engage in trade was shameful, but to shoot people was not shameful!" Such people became convinced. (Now it has developed that these people are a global phenomenon.)

If, however, within the country this violence against oneself is not only supported and even in part explained by the state's total violence (even if approved—indeed, in other cases—by this intelligentsia itself), the same justifica-

tion does not exist for the leftist intellectuals abroad. But in
its entirety the intelligentsia does not stand up at all for
friends and colleagues but, on the contrary, agonizingly
proves to itself and others the realism (or necessity) of
senseless accusations raised against such people. Creativity
(but in reality one's own peace of mind based on a carefully
preserved "clear historical view") is dearer to them than
the lives and honor of its creators. True, creativity, too, is
no longer recognizable from its appearance today. But with
some internal work and with the aid of dialectics it is possible nevertheless to see (if only in draft or as a sketch) dear,
familiar traits. Strictly speaking, this is also called "engage-
ment," i.e., involvement, of which, as I heard, many are
even proud. It cannot in any way be confused with conviction, for genuine conviction does not require any involvement. Involvement is a renunciation of truth, justice, trust
in one's impressions and thoughts, for the sake of what has
once been decided and chosen. It sounds romantic, like a
certain dissolution into something high, but in fact it is a
cult of irresponsibility. This involvement also leads to
crimes against Spirit and Conscience. But it all begins with
an inspired little thing—you begin to regard some people
not as similar to yourself but as some sort of historical material. To be sure, in the name of a sacred cause, in
individual cases, on a narrow front. But if you entered into
a compact with the devil, the dimensions of your cooperation with him do not depend on you. Give him an inch and
he takes a mile. Any involvement is above all an involvement directed against oneself, against the best that is in us.
Terrible is the man whose conscience is controlled from
without. Do not set up an idol before yourself.

Very little remains of Western humanitarian culture in
this nonindividualistic approach to people and occurrences. Actually both the Communists and the "new Left"
are transmitters of an Eastern-feudal attitude into irreli-
gious Western consciousness. The renunciation of personality characteristic of the East and the strict regulation of
conduct are perceived as a certain wholeness and commun-
alism, as salvation from isolation and a new relationship to
life. Even depersonalized sex worship is an Eastern phenomenon. True, in the East such an attitude, acknowledged
as normal and natural, is nevertheless kept within limits,

while here it has broken through to freedom. The contemporary emancipated girl (if she is not just following fashion) conducts herself as if she has just run away from a harem, while the youth behaves like a man who has surreptitiously slipped into that harem and found it unguarded. These considerations are only outwardly irrelevant to the subject. We are talking now about the same thing—about human values which are all interrelated. And about words, whose sense cannot be replaced—otherwise people cease to understand not only one another but themselves.

The Relativity of Prosperity and Possibilities of Terror

Recently the Communists and other advanced people of the West found a new love—Chile. Now in power there, they thought, was "our" boy—the staunch socialist, art connoisseur, and collector of figurines, Comrade Allende. Moreover, he had come to power entirely legally—the Chileans themselves elected him. So everything would be marvelous—socialism had at last been betrothed to liberty and legality.

Now, when that epic is finished, it becomes evident that Allende himself believed this more than anybody else. I cannot understand and do not dwell on how his respect for democracy could be reconciled with his revolutionary socialism. His obstinacy, however, led to a situation in which it was already too late when he finally understood that universal happiness could not be established without infringement of democracy. He was overthrown and perished. But before his death he was on the point of violating certain democratic rights to some extent, since the situation compelled him to do so: Defending socialist achievements in other ways appeared impossible. Properly speaking—this has already been discussed—other revolutionary socialists also became dictators largely for the same reason: Life did not bend to their will, and they had to shoot. This was always regarded as an exception and an untypical deviation, but the whole trouble is that no one has ever seen what is supposedly typical.

But, as is known, in reality Allende did not have to violate the constitution. The opposition violated it first—and this still outrages many people. It did not wait for Allende's promised actions but "went over to the offensive" itself, something that is rather rare. So rare that, predicting how events would develop in Chile in the first draft of this work (in 1970), I did not foresee their—relatively fortunate—outcome.

I understand that few people will agree with such an assessment of this outcome, and many (in the West, of course) will even be filled with indignation. They will be partly right, for the word "fortunate" cannot be applied entirely either to events in Chile or to the modern world in general. Besides, there is another obviously negative aspect of this outcome—it permits wishful persons to continue to think or even to say that, had it not been for the "wicked forces of reaction," everything would have turned out all right. Meanwhile those "wicked forces" only took action when (and in consequence of the fact that) everything—already!—had turned out wretchedly. When the economy fell apart and international bands of romantics increasingly got the upper hand in the country, boldly experimenting with other people's property and lives and straining for power, Allende either did not want or was unable to restrain them. The country was threatened with a left (i.e., permanent and absolute, as distinguished from conservative) dictatorship. In 1970, even before Allende's final victory, I predicted that this was the way it would be in the country and that the threat of such a dictatorship existed. It did not involve any wisdom at all—forcible nationalization of industry inevitably has that result.

That is why I regard what happened as a fortunate outcome. However bad it may have been, it saved the people from both romantic dictatorship and permanent judicious terror. I had thought it was already too late for any salvation. It cost the Communists nothing to explain the existing chaos by Allende's "halfway measures." ("Halfway measures" is a favorite epithet of Communists *before* the seizure of power.) It was by no means out of the question that street mobs stupefied by delusions and disappointments would believe them and become their followers, howling with open mouths. They might have gotten rid of Allende with all his figurines (and, in any case, with all his democratic prejudices) as the last obstacle on their path to a new life and—whatever the case—to the bread, which was disappearing. Then they could have covertly established their "people's" power.

After that there would have been no one who could be held responsible. Neither for hunger nor satiety nor for integrity nor for halfway measures nor for chaos nor for expediency. All of that would instantly acquire minor significance: In any case, Communists would not jeopardize what is most valuable to them—power—because of such a trivial thing. It would be sure to be too dear to them. To some as an instrument for achievement of universal happiness (this is a very fascinating pursuit—achieving happiness for all of mankind), to others for itself, since by this time it (i.e., power) would have raised them up high. But both groups would have sooner shot half the people than go away. Especially since this measure is effective. I do not maintain that any problem can be *solved* by executions, but to eliminate it is entirely possible. As long as people who insist on the solution of these problems can be entirely eliminated. This is not one and the same thing, but unfortunately the difference will not interest everybody.

And it is not at all important that in the given case it was not the pro-Soviet but the pro-Chinese-Communist party which conducted the action. This might have been all the same to Allende, beginning, as he intended, to employ Communist methods. Terror is terror.

By the way, to imagine the epoch of terror as something sad and sorrowful is to oversimplify. In a time of terror there are always far more satisfied than dissatisfied people. For the value of life—due to the awareness that you may be deprived of it at any moment—only increases. As well as the gratitude for the good fortune that you are, after all, still alive. But since stability is essential to a person, he turns the fact of his existence on earth into a metaphysical value—into a graphic proof that "everything is exaggerated" and that "no one is imprisoned without reason." So the joyful faces which Western journalists saw in Russia in the thirties and in China in the seventies is not an invention. There were really many genuinely satisfied people there. Incidentally, aside from this fundamental joy—to feel euphorically the acuteness of being—the citizen of a terrorized society has many more insignificant ones, still completely unknown to residents of the free world (which causes many of them to feel deprived). For example, the joy of obtaining eggs for breakfast, meat for dinner, a button for one's pants. A world of small joys. . . .

The attempt to expand this world only supports and justifies terror as a means of limiting human baseness. Romantic contempt facilitates its use for creative natures. Contempt becomes stronger after victory because these romantic natures now see well that it is difficult to rule a state (earlier, when they concerned themselves only with criticism, it was easy) and just hate the ordinary man because he does not understand their high aspirations and still—at such a great time!—is overanxious about the feeding trough. And they really do not pity him—as if he were an insect.

Yet, by the way, the situation of the creative natures is not at all bad "in a difficult time" precisely with regard to the feeding trough. Something mysterious suddenly appears: "special rations," a "special provision." Lofty revolutionary confidence is audible in these words. As in Russia, for example, the leather coat—a rather comfortable garment in an epoch of general ruin—is perceived as some bastion of revolutionary awareness, faith, and a sense of life. Nevertheless, relative comfortableness was also tolerated as an exception for the sake of the general welfare, so that creative natures were not distracted by base concerns from their high service. Of course, in comparison with what there is in later stages, these transgressions and temptations look almost innocent, but the foundation of everything that came later was laid exactly here. And all of this together accounts for the absence of freedom.

Banal Word

Taking the risk of evoking the smiles of the radical world, I must say that I consider the word *freedom* banal. I demand only "freedom in general," only "abstract freedom," and not some sort of social or class freedom. To be sure, one can speak of inner freedom, but that has no relationship to the subject. Inner freedom also may not exist even in an overflowing sea of any other kind of freedom, but if this external, banal freedom does not exist, few people can preserve the inner one.

In our time there are many people (all Communists and Fascists) who strive at all costs to change the meaning of this great word or to eliminate it altogether. It is implied that philosophers still have not clarified its meaning and that in general it makes no sense, since it is in any case impossible to be free from the laws of biology or, let us say, the law of gravity. There are many such assertions but only a single task: to prove that a person is equally unfree in a Paris café or a Lubianka cell.

I could perhaps reply that, as a person who has been in the one place and the other, I am acutely aware of the difference between these positions. But this would signify that I take these assertions seriously. I, however, regard them simply as a convenient way of avoiding unpleasant subjects and unpleasant reflections. Possibly the question of freedom can be considered in a broader context than I have given to it, but only when it has been solved at least to some degree in a narrow, i.e., simple, crude, and unintellectual sense.

In short, speaking about freedom, I speak about what is most simple: about the very thing that interrogators in the course of grilling or criminals in camps had in mind when they spoke to their next victim: "I'll teach you, you son-of-a-bitch, to love freedom!" About the very thing which allows workers to strike without the risk of being felled by bullets, as in Novocherkassk, or allows you to write and publish a letter in which, at no cost to yourself, solely out of allegiance to elusive convictions, you castigate the head of government and the war minister of your country. I do not approve such use of freedom, but it is freedom all the same. Freedom is what permits your friend J.-P. Sartre to publish his strange magazine (if it has not already gone bankrupt, although that does not depend on freedom) which would have hardly once constituted the favorite reading of de Gaulle or Pompidou and would hardly be the favorite reading of Giscard d'Estaing today. Freedom is what makes it possible for your acquaintance Meyer Willner or, before that, your acquaintance Samuil Mikunis to make trips in safety to Moscow and return (although I re-

gard this as an abuse of freedom: Moscow is the capital of
an enemy state). Finally, freedom is what would permit me
—even if at my own expense—to publish this work of
mine in the Soviet press, without anticipating for myself
any unpleasant consequences, material or even physical.

In this connection, I recall one American intellectual, a
physicist or mathematician, who dashed about the lobby
during one of the Moscow scientific symposia and collected signatures protesting America's involvement in the
Vietnam war. But that is not important. What is important
is that, while doing so, he complained bitterly about the
lack of freedom of the press in America. He proved this on
the basis that one of his protests (evidently protests were
his hobby)[4] was published in *The New York Times* only as an
advertisement costing a large fee ($250, it seems). But I
thought then about the amount of money, to the last bit of
it, we would have been willing to pay in August 1968 in
order to publish our own protest against the occupation of
Czechoslovakia in *Pravda* or even *The Medical Worker*.
Those involved paid with years of exile for displaying one
slogan containing such a protest for a few minutes in Red
Square, and, by common acknowledgment, that was light
punishment. . . .

Apparently real freedom would appear to that intellectual to be a state of affairs in which any newspaper, even
one that in no way agreed with his views, was obligated to
publish his protests and articles in the form of an editorial.
But only Stalin enjoyed such freedom. And this is called
tyranny—i.e., the imposition of one person's will upon
others.

It is further said that freedom of the press without
money is a freedom in name only. I always want to reply to
this: "Have you tried *samizdat*—self-publishing?" *Samizdat*
is not the best solution, but lack of freedom of the press is
when you are put in jail because of *samizdat*, not when you
do not have money to publish books or newspapers. Not to
speak at all about the fact that one can try and collect
money. If people are very interested in your publications—

[4]Now that the terroristic dictatorship of the North has won, he can
be completely satisfied with his handiwork. (Today's comment of
the author.)

make a collection. To be sure, people do not always under-stand soon enough what is of interest to them, but that is after all a natural difficulty of existence and development of culture, and not a lack of freedom of the press.

In 1968 in Paris some writers created a committee for defense of freedom of the press. Louis Aragon and Elsa Triolet, in particular, joined this committee. I shall proba-bly never find out what freedom the committee was sup-posed to defend. I think that even the committee members themselves vaguely realized this. What kind of freedom is it that sufficed for Thomas Mann but does not suffice for Aragon? Don't they wish to obtain complete, including material, independence from the reader, from his buying or not buying our books? I agree that these are far from being always the right criteria, but there is no help for it. This is a natural risk which is inseparable from creativity. In the U.S.S.R., for example, writers are completely pro-tected in a material sense against the whim of readers: It is important to be published, not to be read. For that it is scarcely worth striving. It sometimes seems to me that the solution to the riddle of numerous motivations underlying the intellectuals' enthusiasm is to be found in this commit-tee, in the dissatisfaction which it expressed. Then it is not surprising that all this is directed against freedom.

Nevertheless, the impression is created that all those undermining freedom think that freedom will still live, no matter how much it is undermined. Evidently, having lived all their lives in conditions of freedom, these people cannot imagine that it could be otherwise. They forget that in humanity there are always people who cannot advance themselves in any other way (but they yearn to advance themselves) than through absolute and uncontrolled power, for they are only capable of wielding power. When society functions normally, they are suppressed (and do not even suspect, themselves, who they are), but when an occasion arises, they immediately take revenge. They are in all camps and on all levels, and it is necessary to guard against them as one generally should guard against people with criminal inclinations. True, today in the free world an opposite tendency can be observed. This world (in the per-son of its pseudo-elite) is more inclined to protect genuine criminals than to guard against such people—potential ones.

May progressive people forgive me, but I am full of deep
regard and solicitude for the traditional "bourgeoisie"—
there is no other—for freedom and for the usual principles
of legality on which it rests. Both the one and the other are
lofty and significant achievements of humanity, social and
spiritual. Both the one and the other have existed and exist
not always and everywhere, and both the one and the
other may at times exist nowhere.

I feel no respect whatever for those Western students
who, in a sudden paroxysm of love of liberty, assault the
police and shriek "Murder!" when the police resort to
countermeasures. In the same way the man who shot an
American president in the second half of the nineteenth
century aroused no respect whatever among Russian terrorists belonging to the *Narodnaya Volya*, People's Freedom. They justly considered that Americans at that time
could express their attitude toward things in completely
legal ways. This is very unusual for a Russian intellectual,
but I believe that in 1968 the American police had much
more respect for democracy than many American students.
And even their professors.

In general, it appears to me that the contraposition "freedom—authority" (the stronger the authority, the less freedom) does not in any way withstand criticism. It appears to
me that freedom is not conceivable at all without authority
and the state, that maximum freedom does not exist without a state but under the protection of the state, if that state
is free. It alone can suppress various impulses of private
persons against freedom and the dignity of other people. It
alone can watch over observance of the law, without which
freedom is not at all conceivable. Freedom generally exists
as long as there is respect for the law. Otherwise society
begins to maintain law and order by other means. It will
find these means (or it will fall apart), for the interests of
the majority of people, the interests of the average man
demand above all law and order. Politics is not an art, in it
those interests cannot be ignored. The average man will
give up any freedom for the freedom to sit in his own
house and to walk the streets in safety. And he will call
upon the help of anyone, including storm troopers. It is not
necessary to drive him to that point. . . . Ah, it is not necessary. . . . He will not be the one who is to blame for it.

PART FOUR

Clues from the Past

History as Investigation and Reminiscence

The Seven Deaths
of Maxim Gorky

BY GUSTAV HERLING–GRUDZINSKY

Translated by David Chavchavadze

From *Kontinent* No. VIII, 1976

"History reminds one more and more of a detective novel,"
I recently read in a French magazine. At the same time the
Moscow *Literaturnaya Gazeta* was writing: "In the Soviet
Union there is a shortage of detective and adventure novels. We could use our Jules Vernes, Alexander Dumas, Jack
Londons, and Conan Doyles. After all, nobody would say
that we don't have our detectives. In addition, the example
of detectives would have a positive influence on Soviet
youth and would help develop observation, courage, and
initiative in Soviet people."

The combination of these two observations gave rise to
this near-detective story of the seven deaths of Maxim
Gorky.

GUSTAV HERLING-GRUDZINSKY *was born in 1919 in Poland. His studies at
the University of Warsaw were interrupted by the war. He was the
founder of one of the first anti-Hitler underground organizations in Poland. In 1940, while on Soviet territory, he was arrested by Soviet security
forces. He has described the two years he then spent in Soviet jails in his
book* Another World, *which has been published in several European languages. He was with the Independent Second Polish corps under General
Anders as part of the British Eighth Army in the Italian campaign. He is
the author of several books and a member of the editorial staff of the Polish
magazine* Kultura, *which appears in Paris. Herling-Grudzinsky lives in
Naples.*

I.

Death Number One. Gorky died in 1936. His death was declared to be natural and was squeezed to the last drop for propaganda purposes during the funeral ceremonies. Honored foreign guests (and among them André Gide, who was even at that moment beginning his famous *Return from the U.S.S.R.* to the beat of the funeral march), standing next to members of the Politburo on Red Square, reviewed a parade of Red Army units; a farewell artillery salute swept over Moscow with a booming echo, etc., etc.

Pravda published the following communiqué: "The Central Committee of the All-Union Communist Party (Bolsheviks) and the Council of People's Commissars of the U.S.S.R. with great grief announce the death of a great Russian writer, a word-artist of genius, a whole-hearted friend of the workers, a fighter for the victory of Communism, Comrade Aleksei Maksimovich Gorky, which took place in Gory, near Moscow, on 18 June 1936."

The medical announcement about A. M. Gorky's death, published on June 19, stated that as early as June 1 Gorky had fallen sick with "influenza, which later became complicated by a catarrh of the upper breathing tubes and catarrhal pneumonia." The disease was a serious one "in connection with chronical harm to the heart, blood vessels, and especially the lungs because of a tubercular process going back some forty years." Death came "as a result of paralysis of the heart and breathing." The announcement was signed by People's Commissar of Health of the R.S.F.S.R. Kaminsky, chief of the Kremlin medical department Khodorov, Professors Pletnev, Lang, Konchalovsky, and Speransky, Dr. Levin, and also Professor Davidovsky, who had performed the autopsy.

Death Number Two. Two years later, in March 1938, the trial of Bukharin and his "rightist Trotskyite bloc" began in Moscow. In the course of the trial, the former head of the NKVD, Yagoda, came forth with the sensational admission that he himself had killed Gorky. He had used an unusual and very original method: He had ordered Gorky's secretary, Kryuchkov, to make every effort to see that the great writer caught cold. When this happened, Yagoda ordered two Kremlin doctors, Levin and Pletnev, to use incorrect healing methods. As a result of this medical socialist planning, Gorky had fallen ill with pneumonia and died.

Yagoda's secretary Bulanov gave the court a few curious explanations in this connection: Professor Pletnev, Dr. Levin, and Gorky's secretary Kryuchkov had taken direct part in the murder of A. M. Gorky. He, Bulanov, for instance, had witnessed the fact that Yagoda had often summoned Kryuchkov and demanded that he make Gorky catch cold or get sick in some way. Yagoda reminded him of the poor condition of Gorky's lungs, stressing the fact that any disease called forth by a cold would increase the chances of death. The rest was up to Pletnev and Levin, who received corresponding instructions on this question.

Death Number Three. In Voronezh in 1940 a collection of articles and reminiscences about Stalin was published. Stalin's personal secretary, Poskrebyshev, with Boris Dvinsky as coauthor, wrote an extraordinarily instructive essay for this anthology, entitled "Teacher and Friend of Humanity," in which he semiofficially denied the official version of Gorky's natural death. I say "semiofficially," but one must remember Poskrebyshev's position during Stalin's lifetime. Without a doubt he was a person of significantly more importance than the normal personal secretary of a head of state. It is not surprising that after Stalin's death the first triumvirate cremated the loyal spear-carrier together with the leader, or at least removed him into the valley of political shadows.[1]

Death Number Four. The fourth version of Gorky's death we received thanks to Herbert Morrison. In 1951 *Pravda*, wishing to demonstrate that full freedom of the press existed in the Soviet Union, asked Morrison to write an article for the paper. Morrison, the Minister of Foreign Affairs

[1] Patricia Blake wrote in the magazine *Encounter* (April 1963) that Poskrebyshev was living in Moscow and writing his memoirs.

in a British Labour government, wrote an article, sent it to *Pravda*, and it was printed. The author of the article, however, inexcusably violated good journalistic tradition: Having been invited to demonstrate to the world the complete freedom of press in the U.S.S.R., he took advantage of *Pravda*'s hospitality in order to expose the total lack of such freedom in the land of the Soviets. The editors of *Pravda* provided Morrison's article with indignant commentary, stating, in particular: "Freedom of the press in the U.S.S.R. is denied to incorrigible criminals, saboteurs, terrorists, and murderers sent in by foreign intelligence services, the criminals who shot at Lenin, and those who killed Volodarsky, Uritsky, and Kirov, and poisoned Gorky and Kuybyshev."

It should be emphasized here that in spite of the significant similarity between Death Number Two and Death Number Four, there is a serious discrepancy between them: In 1938 Gorky was killed, if one can say this without insulting the noble medical profession, by "medical" means; in 1951 he was simply poisoned. Insofar as the killers are concerned, there is not a large difference between the two versions: In the last analysis, the whole "Bukharin bloc," together with Yagoda, was, according to the now classical definition of Vishinsky, "a weapon in the hands of foreign intelligence services."

Death Number Five. The year in which Gorky's poisoning came to light as a result of Morrison's article was also the ceremonially observed fifteenth-anniversary year of the writer's death. Not one of the countless anniversary articles appearing in the Soviet and foreign Communist press mentioned the mysterious circumstances of Gorky's death. This should have signified a return to Death Number One and Death Number Three.

Death Number Six. In the extensive article on Gorky published in the second edition of the *Great Soviet Encyclopedia* (1952), there was a short mention of the writer's death: "On 18 June 1936 Gorky was no more. He was killed by enemies of the people from right-Trotskyite organizations, agents of imperialism against whom he fought so bravely. A little earlier, in 1934, these same people killed M. A. Peshkov,

Gorky's son." From the same article we learn that "during his illness" Gorky had been able to read the draft text of the new Stalin Constitution, published in *Pravda*.

Death Number Six basically repeats the versions contained in Death Number Two and Death Number Four, with the sole difference that it does not make clear whether the fatal blow was administered by a cold later complicated by pneumonia or with the aid of arsenic without any complications. The expression "illness" can be seen either as a subtle allusion to the "medical" Death Number Two, or as a linguistic lapse indicating the influence on the author of the competing versions contained in Deaths Number One, Number Three, and Number Five.

A compromise formula is given in *Russian Soviet Literature*, by L. I. Timofeyev, a literature textbook for the tenth grade, approved by the Ministry of Education of the R.S.F.S.R. (1952): "The dispatched murderers, who were able to infiltrate Gorky's entourage, gradually brought him to a fatal illness which put an end to his days on 18 June 1936."

II.

Possessing such skimpy official materials, one should, of course, avoid questions such as "Who killed Gorky?" or "Was Gorky killed?" A correct and carefully formulated question should sound like: "Why, in the course of seventeen years[2] after Gorky's death, were two mutually exclusive versions of his death alternatively six times brought to the attention of the reading public?" But this question is also a hard one to answer without the benefit of the working hypothesis gradually developed below.

At all the Moscow "witch trials" the central point, along with accusations having definite political goals, was the relationship of the accused to Stalin. It is true that Gorky

[2]The author is analyzing versions of Gorky's death circulated in Stalin's time and continuing to circulate today.

never found himself on the defendants' bench, but nobody prevents us from investigating *his* relationship with Stalin as well. Another circumstance also encourages us to do this, namely a photograph published in all Soviet newspapers on the fifteenth anniversary of the writer's death, which set the tone of the anniversary observance. According to the idea of the organizers, the photograph was supposed to prove the unbroken and close friendship between Gorky and Stalin over the course of many years.

Place: Red Square. Date: 1931. On the photograph: Stalin in a military cap and Gorky in a Central Asian skullcap, in a pose which was supposed to give the impression of sincerity but looked unconvincing. Gorky looks like a person who is upset, exhausted, and offended; his appearance is somewhat alarmed, more typical for a Russian *muzhik* seeing a devil's photographic machine face to face for the first time than for a person who was photographed, painted, and sculpted more often than any other Soviet writer. Stalin on the contrary; Stalin completely fits his name. It would seem that this still does not tell us anything: after all, Gorky was quite a bit older than Stalin and, as far as we know, unlike the great leader was not famous for his good health. But nevertheless, in looking at the 1931 photograph one cannot get rid of the feeling that one is seeing an animal tamer who has finally been able to tame a wild animal and drag it before a photographic lens. Suspicion is called forth by the persistence with which articles and anniversary reminiscences were adorned by this photograph. A similar photograph, showing Lenin and Stalin, was for a long time circulated in millions of copies to mask the traces of Lenin's death-bed addition to his will.

Now let us go back and rummage about in the revolutionary and postrevolutionary years of Gorky's life in the search for roots for the "unbroken" friendship between the writer and the dictator.

Even the *Great Soviet Encyclopedia* admitted in 1952 that in the first days after the October revolution Gorky committed "serious errors." He underestimated then the organizing power of the Party and the revolutionary proletariat, as well as the possibility of its alliance with the peasantry, being overly afraid of the elemental pressure of anarcho-individualistic small-property elements; on the other hand, he exaggerated the significance of the old intelligentsia and its progressivism at this stage of revolutionary struggle. Gorky stated these "mistaken views" of his in a number of articles published in 1917 and 1918 in the pages of the "semi-Menshevik" newspaper *Novaya Zhizn'* (New Life). His position was subjected to sharp criticism from Lenin and Stalin. Stalin "warned" Gorky (in the newspaper *Rabochiy Put'*) (Workers' Way) on October 20, 1917, that the "position taken by him might bring him into the camp of those rejected by the revolution."

It might be worthwhile here to help the author of the official biography and quote an example of Gorky's "mistaken views." Here is what he wrote on November 20, 1917: "Blind fanatics and adventurers without conscience are breaking their heads to rush to the so-called way of 'social revolution.' In actual fact this is the way to anarchy and the destruction of the proletariat and the revolution. . . . The working class cannot fail to understand that Lenin is only making a certain experiment on its skin and on its blood, trying to bring the revolutionary mood of the proletariat to the final extreme and to see what happens. . . . The workers must not allow adventurers and maniacs to load onto the head of the proletariat shameful, senseless, and bloody crimes for which not Lenin but the proletariat itself will pay."

In the summer of 1921, the *Great Soviet Encyclopedia* continues to inform us, Gorky had a tubercular relapse and, on Lenin's insistence, the author of the novel *Mother* went abroad for treatment. From the fall of 1921 until the spring of 1924 Gorky lived at German and Czech health resorts, and in April 1924 he selected as a permanent residence—Sorrento.

The political mistakes noted above, the *Encyclopedia* continues, did not fail to affect the artistic production of the writer: Gorky stopped writing. But, living abroad, he maintained lively contact with his native land. The voluminous correspondence of those years bears witness to the "intense attention" with which Gorky followed all the changes taking place in the motherland, Russia. He twice visited the U.S.S.R., in 1928 and 1929, wrote a series of sketches "about the Soviet Union," and in 1931 returned permanently to the motherland.[3]

And now the last touch of the brush, finishing the portrait in the *Encyclopedia*: "Gorky was a friend and comrade-in-arms of Stalin. The artistic creativity, the journalism, and the social activity of this very great Soviet writer were inspired by the ideas of Stalin. In 1932, on the occasion of the fortieth anniversary of Gorky's work as a writer, Stalin wrote him the following letter: 'Dear Aleksei Maksimovich! From my soul I greet you and firmly shake your hand. I wish you many years of life and work for the joy of all workers, for the dismay of the enemies of the working class.' During his illness Gorky read in *Pravda* the draft of the new Stalin Constitution and, deeply excited, exclaimed: 'In our country even the stones sing.' His untimely death prevented him from accomplishing his plan for a number of works on the contemporary life of Soviet Russia. In the last years of his life he was collecting materials for an artistic essay about J. V. Stalin. His death cut off this work as well. But in his journalistic articles Gorky drew a majestic picture of the leader of the first socialist state in the world."

After studying this official portrait, how is it possible to avoid the persistent thought that, apart from the illness, there was a deep connection between the first, direct reac-

---

[3]The date of Gorky's return to the Soviet Union cited by the *Great Soviet Encyclopedia* corresponds neither to the inscription on the memorial tablet at the villa Il Sorito ("Here, from 1924 to 1933, lived and worked the great writer of the U.S.S.R. Maxim Gorky") nor to Vsevolod Ivanov's account of his visit to Gorky in Sorrento on New Year's night 1933. It is possible that, after finally deciding to move permanently back to Russia, Gorky spent another partial or complete two years "living and working" in Sorrento. The Soviet encyclopedia does not want to talk about this, because it would be an indirect admission that the two previous trips of Gorky had a scouting purpose, with the warning: "The doors of the cage are not yet closed."

tion of Gorky to a revolution in bloody diapers and his sudden and unexpected departure abroad.

III.

It would of course be a mistake to exclude completely the motive of health in considering Gorky's decision to leave Russia. In the words of the *Great Soviet Encyclopedia* about Lenin's "persuading Gorky to receive treatment abroad" there is in all probability a large measure of truth. For instance, two of Lenin's letters to Gorky have survived, witnessing the attention with which for many years the leader of the revolution followed the health of its bard.

The first was written in Poronin on September 30, 1913: "What you write about your illness alarms me terribly. Are you doing the right thing living without treatment in Capri? The Germans have first-class sanatoria (for instance in St. Blasien, near Switzerland) where they treat and cure *in full* indispositions of the lungs, achieve complete healing of the tissues, fatten you up and then systematically accustom you to the cold, build up the resistance against colds, and discharge healthy people capable of work.

"And you, after Capri in winter, are you going to Russia? I am terribly afraid that this will harm your health and undermine your capacity to work. Do they have first-class doctors in that Italy of yours? Really, go to a first-class doctor in Switzerland or Germany and spend two months in serious treatment in a good sanatorium. Otherwise, wasting government property, that is being sick and undermining your work capacity, is an inadmissible thing in every way."

The second letter, of August 9, 1921 was written just before Gorky's departure from Russia: "I forwarded your letter to L. B. Kamenev. I am so tired that I can't do anything at all. And you are spitting up blood and you are not going! This is both unscrupulous and irrational. In Europe in a good sanatorium you will receive treatment and be able to produce three times as much. So-so! Here we have neither treatment nor work—just fuss. Pointless fuss. Go away and get cured. Don't be stubborn, I beg you."

In the second letter, however, the observant eye will no-

tice not only the undoubtedly sincere concern of Lenin
about Gorky's health, but a strange tone for Lenin: "Here
we have neither treatment nor work—just fuss. Pointless
fuss." Who is saying this, when, and to whom? The leader
of the revolution, four years after its victory, to its greatest
writer. Why was this unexpected explosion of fatigue and
grief necessary?

One can suppose that Lenin wanted to send Gorky
abroad not only because he was concerned about the writer's health but also because he wanted to protect him from
all kinds of possible shake-ups and disappointments of the
postrevolutionary period, apparently fearing that they
could undermine even more his already shaken belief in
the revolution. There are many examples of Lenin's understanding and genial attitude toward Gorky. Here, for example, is a quotation from Gorky's book *Lenin and the Russian
Peasantry* (Paris 1924): "I often happened to talk to Lenin
about the cruelty of revolutionary tactics and morals. 'What
do you want?' he would ask, surprised and irritated. 'Can
you be humane in such a bitter struggle?' I was always
bothering him with requests of all sorts and felt that my in-
tercessions for certain people called forth feelings of regret, even contempt, toward me. 'Is it not your feeling that
we are engaged in foolishness?' he would ask. However, I
continued to do what I considered essential: I was not dis-
couraged by the sidelong irritated glances of a man who
knew the numbers of the proletariat's foes. He would sadly
shake his head and say: 'You are compromising yourself in
the eyes of the comrades, in the eyes of the workers.' I directed his attention to the fact that the comrades, the workers, were in a state of irritation and excitability which led
to their regarding the freedom and lives of valuable people
very often with excessive lightness and 'simplicity,' and it
seemed to me that this unnecessary and sometimes absurd
cruelty was not only compromising the honest and difficult work of the revolution, but was causing practical dam-
age to the revolution, depriving it of many far from insignificant forces."

Finally, let us listen to Trotsky, who immediately after
Gorky's death wrote about him in his Paris monthly (*The
Bulletin of the Opposition of Leninist-Bolsheviks*, July–August
1936): "He met the revolution almost like a director of a

cultural museum. . . . Lenin, appreciating and liking
Gorky, was very much afraid that he would become the
victim of his connections (with the intelligentsia) and of
his weakness, and finally Lenin got his own way—he convinced Gorky to go abroad voluntarily. . . . He was a
fellow-traveler of the revolution, and like all fellow-
travelers he went through various phases: The sun of the
revolution would light up his face at one time and his back
at another."

Consequently it may be said that Lenin—a political
genius—considered Gorky as a writer valuable above all
for his literary works and not for his amateurish excursions
into the political sphere. Possibly Lenin was afraid that
Gorky's direct interference in politics would infect the
writer with an incurable disgust toward Communism. Perhaps he preferred to keep his falcon in fighting trim in the
West, rather than watch him break his wings against the
bars of a Moscow cage. Even the *Great Soviet Encyclopedia*
makes a very substantive distinction between Lenin's attitude, on the one hand, and Stalin's on the other, toward
Gorky's furious antirevolutionary statements in 1917–1918.
At the same time that Stalin was openly threatening that
Gorky's position "might bring him into the camp of those
rejected by the revolution," Lenin "pointed out Gorky's
mistakes to him and helped him find a way to overcome
them in actual revolutionary activity, exhorting him to
learn from the revolution, and advising him to observe the
gigantic work being carried out by the workers." The *Encyclopedia* sums up this problem by stating: "Afterwards
Gorky many times acknowledged the complete rightness
of Lenin and his comrades in arms, and acknowledged the
wise policies of the Party." In this way, very subtly, the
great Stalin of the revolutionary years was reduced—at
least in the Gorky matter—to the role of an anonymous
and modest comrade in arms of Lenin.

IV.

Thus, in the light of available materials, appears Gorky's
departure and Lenin's role in it. And how did Gorky himself regard this departure? Of course one could guess that

the reasons compelling the author of *Mother* to leave postrevolutionary Russia in such a strange hurry were not as simple as the official biographers, such as Ilya Gruzdev, would have the reader believe, insisting that Gorky was never "an émigré by his own will," or a man who "broke with the Soviet Union or lost contact with his own country." Until now, however, there have been no more solid confirmations of Gorky's thoughts and feelings in the first years of his "involuntary" exile. Luckily, the émigré magazine *Novy Zhurnal* (Nos. XXX and XXXI) published the previously unknown letters of Gorky, from 1922–1925, to the Russian poet and critic Vladislav Khodasevich, with whom Gorky edited the literary-scientific journal *Beseda*,[4] which was published in Berlin.

Khodasevich himself, who in the year of Gorky's departure abroad (1921) was still in Russia, states in his memoirs (*Necropolis: Memoirs*, Brussels, 1939) that Gorky decided to pull up stakes not only because of his health but also in connection with his difficult relations with the then chairman of the Petrograd Soviet, Zinoviev. "Things went so far," writes Khodasevich, "that Zinoviev ordered a search to be made of Gorky's apartment and threatened to arrest many people close to him. At that same time in Gorky's apartment meetings of Communists inimical to Zinoviev were organized, masked as modest receptions for comrades, which other people also attended." And here are a few quotations from the letters that the "involuntary émigré" wrote to Khodasevich.

Letter from Günthersthal, undated, received by the addressee on June 28, 1923:

"Pil'nyak and Nikitin were able, in London, to penetrate the P.E.N. Club, an international but apolitical society of writers, in which J. Galsworthy is the president and the

[4]*Beseda* was meant to become a general platform for Soviet and Russian writers and scientists located abroad. This program, which today is impossible to imagine, turned out to be impossible in practice even in the 1920s. Letters sent to Gorky from Russia by Soviet writers were held up and checked by Soviet censorship. Manuscripts sent to *Beseda* were also held up by the censor and some were never delivered. (From the preface of Roman Jakobson to "Letters of Gorky to Khodasevich," published in *Harvard Slavic Studies*.)

membership consists of a great variety of people: R. Rolland Merezhskovsky, S. Lagerlef and Hauptmann, etc. . . . Our energetic boys had spread some talk there, and I— also a member of this club—have already received a question from the management: Do I consider possible an apolitical organization of Russian literary figures living in Russia and dispersed abroad? I answered negatively, pointing out 'Lef' and his attitude toward the writers on the one hand and the regime on the other. I also pointed out that some of us accept the Soviet regime, while others are impatiently waiting for its demise, and living off this; but they do not agree and will not come together with a third group, which awaits the help of Curzon, Poincaré, plague, and leprosy. But, in addition to this, there exists the Soviet regime, which cannot allow an apolitical organization in Moscow, since it does not recognize the existence of people who are not infected by politics from the cradle.

"It would be very important to find out what specifically our boys Pil'nyak-ized in London. Won't you talk about this with Nikitin?"

Letter from Günthersthal, dated July 4, 1923:

"The letters from Russia are bad, very bad. There is some sort of a slush there, a fatigue, a dejection. You can't even feel a simple skin irritation in the letters."

Letter from Günthersthal, dated November 8, 1923:

"Among news that stuns the mind, I can report that in *Nakanune* they printed 'Gioconda, a Picture by Michelangelo,' and in Russia Nadezhda Krupskaya and somebody called M. Speransky have forbidden the following reading matter: Plato, Kant, Schopenhauer, Vl. Soloviev, Taine, Ruskin, Nietzsche, L. Tolstoy, Leskov, Yasinsky (!) and many other similar heretics. And it was stated: 'The Department of Religion must keep only antireligious books.' All this supposedly [Gorky added the word "supposedly" above the line] is no joke but was printed in a book called: *Instructions about the Elimination of Antiartistic and Counterrevolutionary Literature from Libraries Servicing Mass Readership.*

"I added 'supposedly' above the line because I still can't make myself believe in this spiritual vampirism and won't believe it until I see the *Instructions*.

"The first reaction I felt was such that I began to

write a declaration to Moscow about my giving up Russian citizenship.

"What else can I do in the event that[5] this bestiality turns out to be true?"

Letter from Sorrento, dated July 13, 1924:

"Here, you know, there is a season of celebrations— almost every day there are fireworks, processions, music, and 'popular rejoicing.' And, in our country? think I. And —forgive me—I am envious to the point of tears, to the point of frenzy, and it hurts, and it's nauseating, etc."

Letter from Sorrento, dated September 5, 1924:

"In truth:

> Worse times there were
> But none more base!

". . . I give you my word, at night I, alone with myself, feel so awful that if it were not so banal and ludicrous— I would shoot myself."

In order better to understand the extremely important excerpt from the next letter from Sorrento, dated May 15, 1925, which upsets the Soviet myth about Gorky's unwilling emigration, it must be remembered that under the common editorship of Gorky and Khodasevich only seven

---

[5]The words "in the event that" somewhat weaken Gorky's indignation; he uses them to leave himself the opportunity for an honorable retreat. Khodasevich made a remark about this letter: ". . . At first Gorky wrote me about the publication of the *Instructions* as a completed fact, and then added 'supposedly' and pretended that the matter had to be checked and that he couldn't make himself believe in the existence of the *Instructions*. However, he could not have had any doubts, because the *Instructions*, a white book of small format, had long before been in his hands. Even on 14 September, that is, two months before this letter, in Berlin, I visited the publishing house Epokha and met Baroness M. I. Budberg there. In my presence the manager of the publishing house, S. G. Sumsky, gave her these *Instructions* for delivery to Gorky. On the same day M. I. Budberg and I left for Günthersthal together. Immediately after our arrival, the *Instructions* were given to Gorky, and during my three-day stay in Günthersthal much was spoken about them, incidentally in the presence of F. A. Stepun. But Gorky forgot about these conversations and about the fact that I had seen the *Instructions* in his hands."

numbers of *Beseda* were published. Not one of them received the right of circulation in Soviet Russia in spite of countless efforts, protests, and supplications on the part of Gorky. Even his refusal to work with the Soviet press until the prohibition on *Beseda* was lifted did not help.

"On the question—a question of huge importance—whether or not *Beseda* should be allowed in Russia, a large and special conference of the specially wise was called together. Three voted to allow it in: Ionov, Kamenev, and Belitsky, and all the others: 'Don't allow it in—then Gorky will come home.' But he won't go back. He is stubborn too."

The correspondence and friendship between Gorky and Khodasevich broke off suddenly in July–August 1925 for such a trivial reason that today this reason can safely be considered a pretext on the part of the Sorrento coeditor of *Beseda*. In July, Gorky, in a letter, got angry at Khodasevich over his article, full of enthusiasm, about the technical strong points of the famous shipyard in Belfast in contrast to Soviet shipyards. But under the mask of unnatural indignation over a stupid triviality, something much more important and substantive was hidden. In this same letter of Gorky's we read: "P. P. Kryuchkov lived with me here for three weeks, a man not at all given to exaggeration and very businesslike. What he relates is very important and significant."

Who was Kryuchkov? In the years about which we are speaking here he was Gorky's trusted literary and financial agent and director of the Berlin affiliate of Mezhdunarodnaya Kniga [a Soviet chain of bookstores abroad—Trans.]; at the same time, in all probability, he was a GPU agent, attached to Gorky with the mission of watching the writer and guiding him to the true path. Khodasevich writes: "Gradually and patiently Kryuchkov, like a mole, dug himself a passage to the management of all of Gorky's literary and financial affairs, as a result of which a rivalry, fully evident at the time, arose between Kryuchkov and Maxim, Gorky's son, [Maxim Peshkov] who also handled his father's affairs."

In saying that Kryuchkov was "in all probability" a GPU agent in the 1920s, I am erring on the side of caution. He was *definitely* one after Gorky's return to the Soviet Union,

when he took the post of the writer's personal secretary.
This is the same Kryuchkov who at the 1938 Moscow trial
was accused of the murder by order of Yagoda, of Gorky
and Maxim Peshkov (see Death Number Two) and stood
up against a wall.

What did Kryuchkov communicate to Gorky during his
three-week stay in Sorrento that was so "important and
significant"? Undoubtedly we will never find this out;
however, the direct result of his visit is completely obvious. The businesslike guest, apparently, succeeded in
guiding his impractical host to the path of truth, because in
the same letter in which the Belfast mouse with such difficulty gave birth to an iceberg which cooled the relations
between Gorky and Khodasevich, we find news that the
author of *The Artamonovs* had begun conversations about
printing *Beseda* in Petersburg, with the editorship of the
magazine remaining abroad. The motivation of this decision was in ideal harmony with the arguments that the
"businesslike man" might have presented. The cost of
printing, Gorky tells Khodasevich, is much lower in Soviet
Russia than in Germany.

In this way the first round of the match between Gorky
and Moscow ended, at first glance, as a draw, a compromise. In actual fact Moscow won: The man who said about
himself, "I am stubborn too," did not go home, but sent his
Beseda on ahead as a scout.

V.

People are still alive in Sorrento who were friends with
Gorky and his family, or who at least remember well the
long-ago occupants of villa Il Sorito. They willingly share
their memories.

The numerous, very varied, and constantly changing
group of people making up Gorky's entourage acquired in
Sorrento in 1925–1933 the reputation of being a very social
and pleasure-loving society (*mondano e gaudente*). On those
who knew him Gorky made the impression of being a
"socialist-humanist" who hated the cruelty and excesses of
the revolution, and who reacted sharply against any form
of violence. This trait, incidentally, confirms the writer's

well-known admission in *Lenin and the Russian Peasantry*: "I feel an organic revulsion to politics and am a very doubtful Marxist, because I do not believe in the rightness of the masses, particularly of the peasant masses."

Gorky's son, Maxim Peshkov, showed a special weakness toward the bottle, parties, and a frivolous mode of life. Actually all the inhabitants of Il Sorito—both permanent and temporary—(with the possible single exception of the writer himself) devoted most of their time to amusements; they often built huge bonfires on the beaches in honor of guests, threw a lot of money around, and even allowed themselves the somewhat perverted pleasure of the *nouveaux riches*—showy philanthropy. Everyone called Gorky's daughter-in-law, Nadezhda, a beauty, *"la bella"* or *"la bellissima."* A few of the older people still remembered Kryuchkov. They spoke of him as being the only antipathetic, suspicious, two-faced, and gloomy visitor at Il Sorito. Maxim Peshkov is remembered as a "drunken reveler," *un gagliardo bevitore,* and a passionate automobilist who spent fantastic sums of money on new cars. Gorky had at his disposal such huge financial resources that his whole family and all the hangers-on could live at the level of the most unbridled bourgeois. Traditional Russian hospitality was obligatory at Il Sorito and the doors were never closed: The guests came in crowds, particularly in the evening, streams of alcohol were poured out, and when there were not enough glasses, ashtrays and vases were used. In Sorrento everyone was convinced that Gorky received from Russia every month a chèck for a million lira (in the nineteen-twenties!). This is probably an exaggeration, but a very characteristic one.

Where did this golden stream come from? Where were its sources? It seems incredible that Gorky's author's royalties could allow him to lead a life in exile the broadness of which astonished even Neapolitan aristocrats. Consequently, whence did it come? Apparently not only from Soviet publishers. This supposition should be joined to an interesting and rather mysterious circumstance: In spite of his contacts with Neapolitan Communists, Gorky was never seriously bothered by the Fascist police. We can therefore make a deduction: After his compromise with Moscow in 1925, the author of *Klim Samgin* was under the guardianship of the Soviet authorities. They gave him financial means for his life, and they arranged for semidiplomatic immunity for him with the Italian Fascist authorities. (Gorky's exclusive position is confirmed to some degree by an interview which he gave to the famous Fascist writer Sibilla Aleramo, published in *Corriere della Sera* on May 21, 1928: "He is grateful to our government, which allows him to live in ideal calm.")

Against this background, how does the image of the shaman of the Gorky tribe, the writer himself, look? He took money from the Soviet authorities for the upkeep of his pleasure-hungry and merry court. He was in constant contact with Soviet publishing houses and magazines in order not to lose his tie with the Russian reader. At the same time, however, in the hothouse atmosphere of the blessed life at Sorrento, he felt as if cut off from life and often was gloomy, sickly, and eaten up by the rust of nostalgia. He experienced his greatest pleasure sitting by a roaring fire in the fireplace and listening to Russian songs performed by his daughter-in-law. Once a delegation of Russian workers came to Sorrento: "A vacation as a premium for outstanding work." Gorky talked with them for a long time and then suddenly began to cry. When asked why he was crying, the writer replied that it was not easy to listen to stories, repeated by everyone, about the tortures suffered by his countrymen. After everything that he had seen himself and heard from others, could he have been an enthusiast of the Soviet regime? Maxim Peshkov once said to one of his Neapolitan friends: "We are not Communists." Actually, it doesn't matter whether Gorky was a Communist or not. After the decision taken in 1925 he could no longer retreat. There was only one conclusion he could make—to return to Soviet Russia: through financial considerations, since, thanks to skillful tactics, he was sitting deep in the Soviet pocket; through considerations of prestige and pride, not wanting to admit a mistake even to himself; through partially political considerations, since he sincerely hated the petrified anti-Soviet position of Russian émigrés; under the influence of natural human vanity, because he wanted to taste glory in the Soviet Union and the privileges and authority of the greatest contemporary Russian writer; and, last but not least, for purely sentimental reasons, for he missed his country.

The Sorrento stories allow us to suppose with a large degree of probability that Gorky's trips to the Soviet Union in 1928 and 1929 were something akin to a reconnaissance. The writer granted the above-mentioned interview with Sibilla Aleramo after the first trip to the U.S.S.R. It contains the following sentence: "He will soon go there again, but only for a few months; he believes that he can work only here." It is hard not to believe one of the most frequent visitors to Il Sorito, who states that after each return from the Soviet Union, Gorky's family sank into a state of numbness, worry, and disappointment, conversing mainly about the changes brought about by the first years of Stalin's rule. Especially frank was Maxim Peshkov, who always liked to talk (especially while drinking) and who openly complained about the unbearable police surveillance. He remembered with bitterness that during both trips he could not take a step without being under surveillance. But the die had been cast. Stalin was not interested in Gorky's health, and his benevolent restraint (the price of living abroad) was no longer sufficient. Stalin needed Gorky to be in the Soviet Union at that moment when the Secretary General was preparing his final blow at the opposition.

Thus began the final act in the drama. In the footsteps of *Beseda* its editor ("also stubborn") returned to the Soviet Union, both the magazine and the man to perish. But whereas everything went smoothly, almost automatically, with *Beseda*, Gorky's death came only after three difficult years.

VI.

Among the numerous interpretations of the Moscow trials, the most extreme and superficial one is predominant: that the trials were exclusively a disgusting spectacle of delirious fiction and lies fabricated during the investigation. The superficiality of this is attested to by the famous incident with Krestinsky during Bukharin's trial. As is known, during an open session of the court Krestinsky denied the statements he had made during the investigation, and confirmed them only on the following day—in a broken voice, after a night spent in the cellars of the Lubianka. If he had been a coward thinking only about saving his life, he would have declaimed without hesitation, like the Lord's Prayer, these statements, coordinated with Vishinsky, without waiting to be reminded of them with the aid of "forbidden means of interrogation." But Krestinsky was no coward. Nor was Bukharin a coward. The death of both men was red-lined in the calendar on the day of their arrest, but the line was underscored additionally after what they dared say during the trial. Why did they not deny the false accusations consistently, completely, and to the end, knowing well that nothing could save them, that the wall was waiting for them in any case? This question is usually answered in three ways: Either that they were unable to bear the torture; or that they agreed to loyally play their part in the spectacle, having received the investigator's promise not to touch their families; or, finally, that they remained, in spite of everything, loyal to the revolution and found themselves beaten down by the iron dialectic of their opponents. The "iron strength of the dialectic" does not have to be taken into account; it makes an impression in A. Koestler's book *Darkness at Noon*, but is scarcely useful in a serious analysis. Families? It is hardly possible to believe that Bukharin and Krestinsky did not know what happened to the families of their predecessors on the bench of the accused, who sang their lesson through without hesitation. Is it possible to think that Bukharin and Krestinsky imagined that they could ransom the potential hostages at half price—that they were bargaining in open court with Stalin on the size of the ransom? It is hard to regard such a possibility seriously.

There is, however, a way out of the labyrinth: The accusations at the Moscow trials had one foot on the ground, while the other was waving in the air to a melody played by Stalin on a harmonica: Vishinsky. Would it have been strange and unnatural for Krestinsky, an opponent of Stalin's political line, to have met abroad with representatives of Trotsky? But Stalin wanted more. Stalin wanted Krestinsky to be simultaneously a German spy, covering his traces in the frock coat of the Soviet ambassador in Berlin. This was too much for Krestinsky. He refused to swallow the nonsense, tried to spit it out with disgust, like castor oil, but they beat it into his throat by force. This procedure helped, because, as we know, the patient appeared on the following day in court completely cleansed. Or Bukharin. One can be almost completely certain that a person of his makeup, gifted with such a temperament, would have sharply criticized collectivization in a circle of close political friends. And one may believe that he was ready to admit this without torture, since, when there is no way to avoid death, it is better to die in the role of the ideologue of the opposition than as an oppositional zero. But Stalin again wanted something more: To round out the act of accusation, Bukharin had to have given orders to his supporters to put ground glass in the *kolkhoz* oil. In reading reports of the Moscow trials, one should separate the chaff of Stalin's sick, sadistic fantasies from the grains of truth. This also applies to those episodes which were only indirectly mentioned at the trials or came out in a secondary way. In particular this touches on the case of Gorky.

The portrait of Gorky sketched above is beginning to come to life. He was not, of course, a monolith. He was not distinguished by strength nor by incorruptibility of character. Those who knew him well saw that under the mask of false modesty was hidden a megalomania, and the mask hid, above all, the tendency to consider himself an unerring prophet and moral super-arbitrator in political questions. Let us compare the editions of Gorky's memoirs of Lenin. This is a detail, but what a characteristic one! In 1924, in the first edition, Gorky cites Lenin's opinion of Trotsky: "Show me another man who in the course of a year could create a model army and earn the respect of military specialists. We have such a man." In the 1931 edition the writer strikes out this paragraph. But at the same time he is never deserted by his natural and elemental quick temper, the spirit of an eternal rebel, his simple and instinctive human kindness, combined with certain idealistic features of the Russian *Narodniki*. He had a trait typical of people who have achieved everything by their own efforts: When he was flattered, he bowed in exultant and proud conformity; when he was criticized or not honored enough, he hardened himself in stubborn and unbending resistance.

If, consequently, Gorky finally sold himself to Stalin, he undoubtedly did it for completely different reasons than,

say, Alexei Tolstoy, who upon returning to the Soviet
Union placed Stalin on a granite pedestal next to Peter the
Great and ecstatically (as he himself told Bunin in Paris) received payment for this in the form of luxurious country
houses, cellars full of wine, and the most expensive automobiles. Gorky prepared to cooperate with Stalin as an
equal, as a titan of Soviet literature with the leader of the
Soviet state. It never entered his head to express submis-
siveness, to flatter, to sacrifice to Stalin his human, artistic,
and political dignity. Moreover, he counted on becoming a
real advisor to Stalin and that he would succeed in intro-
ducing a more tolerant and restrained tone in Stalin's policy of destruction, personal vengeance, and slavery. But
this is not what Stalin was waiting for. Stalin needed Alexei Tolstoys.

At the same time, if Maxim Peshkov had wanted to bathe
in champagne in the Soviet Union, to play cards, seduce
women, and in rare moments of sobriety indulge his passion for automobiles, nobody would have prevented this.
But it would have had to be paid for by a feeling of the impossibility to say what he was thinking out loud; it would
have had to be paid for by making peace with the fact that
all the affairs of his father's court were firmly in the hands
of Kryuchkov. About Nadezhda, it is enough to say that
she soon managed to convince herself to what extent
Kremlin flirtations were more dangerous than romances in
Sorrento and Naples.

Under these conditions there is no basis not to believe
the act of accusation in the 1938 trial, which stated that Yagoda decided, partly out of political and partly out of personal considerations (his being in love with Nadezhda was
known) to send Maxim Peshkov to the other world.
Kryuchkov agreed to carry out the murder plan willingly
—to get Maxim Peshkov drunk and leave him in the snow
all night. Let us assume that Gorky did not know the real
reason for his son's death, which happened only a year after the family's return to the Soviet Union. But he could
not help but feel at least that something unusual had happened, something that could be either a plot or a warning.
After all, in the first days the murder of Maxim Peshkov
was not attributed to "Trotsky's agents." On May 12, 1934,
right after Maxim's death, Stalin wrote Gorky a letter: "To-

gether with you we mourn and suffer the misfortune that
so suddenly and wildly has struck all of us. We believe that
your unbending Gorky spirit and great will power will be
victorious over this terrible experience." It could be that
Gorky, in reading this letter, understood that an elusive
and sinister shadow had crept into his relationship with
Stalin.

VII.

In accordance with the guilty verdict of the 1938 trial, two
years after Maxim Peshkov's death, Yagoda gave the irreplaceable Kryuchkov a new order: to prepare, with the
Kremlin doctors, the "medical" murder of Gorky. From
whom did Yagoda get this order? The bill of indictment
states that it was from the "Bukharin-Trotsky bloc," since
Gorky was too devoted to Stalin, praised Stalin too much,
was too enthusiastic about his policies. The stress of the bill
of indictment on this point calls forth special suspicion.
There probably is not a single statement made during the
1938 trial that does not underscore the very close symbiosis
existing between Gorky and Stalin. Here are a few excerpts
from the official stenographic transcript of the case of the
"anti-Soviet rightist Trotskyite bloc," published by the
People's Commissariat of Justice of the U.S.S.R.

> YAGODA: For a long period of time the rightist Trot-
> skyite center tried to influence Gorky and tear him
> away from close cooperation with Stalin. With this aim
> Kamenev, Tomsky, and others contacted Gorky. But no
> real results were achieved. Gorky remained faithful to
> Stalin and was a passionate supporter and defender of
> his political line. Since the rightist Trotskyite bloc seri-
> ously considered overthrowing Stalin, the Center
> could not fail but consider the extraordinary influence
> of Gorky in the Soviet Union itself and abroad. We
> could not allow this to happen. If Gorky had remained
> alive, he would have raised a voice of protest against
> us. We came to the conclusion that it was impossible to
> separate Gorky from Stalin. The united center was
> forced to make the decision to get rid of Gorky. . . .

RYKOV: I know that Trotsky, of course, realized that
Gorky considered him to be a scoundrel and adven-
turer. On the other hand, the heartfelt friendship between Gorky and Stalin was known everywhere, and
the fact that he was an unbending supporter of Stalin
created hate toward him in our organization. Bukharin
stated that in 1935 Tomsky said to him: The Trotskyite
group in the United Center of the bloc proposed the
organization of a hostile act toward A. M. Gorky, since
he was a supporter of Stalin's policies. Bessonov con-
fessed that in one of the meetings Trotsky announced:
Gorky is very closely tied to Stalin. He plays a colossal
role in capturing democratic opinion in the world for
the U.S.S.R., particularly in Western Europe. Gorky is
very popular as Stalin's closest friend and as an ex-
presser of the general line of the party. Our former
supporters among the intelligentsia have left us
mainly under the influence of Gorky. From this I conclude that Gorky must be removed. Give Pyatakov the
following instruction in the most categorical form:
Gorky must be physically destroyed at any price.

We see that the organizers of the 1938 trial climbed out
of their skin to emphasize the friendship of Gorky and
Stalin.

Let us return to Yagoda. From whom, in actual fact, did
he receive the order to kill Peshkov and Gorky? Among all
the accused at the last Moscow trial, Yagoda was the only
one in regard to whom the accusation of belonging to the
opposition camp sounded completely absurd and unbelievable. As the head of the Soviet police, he was a blind
executor of Stalin's orders, and nothing more. Why did
they put him on the defendants' bench, and even at a political trial, instead of getting rid of him, if the need came up,
by administrative means?

Because there had been a change in circumstances, not
only explaining the mechanism of the trial itself, but un-
covering the means used in the Soviet Union for secret political murders.

Immediately after the end of the Moscow trial, Trotsky
published in his *Bulletin of Bolshevik-Leninist Opposition*
(April 1938) an extremely interesting article, "The Role of

Genrikh Yagoda." He wrote: "According to Yagoda's own words (at the meeting of 5 March) he gave his subordinates in Leningrad an order not to interfere with the terrorist act then being prepared against Kirov. The orders, given by the head of the OGPU, were the equivalent of a command to organize the murder of Kirov." Why was such an order given? After listening to Trotsky, let us recall the facts. Kirov was killed on December 1, 1934, by a Leningrad student, unknown to anyone, called Nikolayev. The trial of the killer and his accomplices was held behind closed doors. All fourteen accused were sentenced to death and shot. But on January 23, 1935, however, a strange thing happened: A military tribunal sentenced twelve important officials of the Leningrad directorate of the GPU, headed by the chief of the directorate, Medvedev, to prison for periods of from two to ten years. In the text of the sentence published by the Soviet newspapers it was stated, in particular: "The accused knew about the terroristic act being prepared against Kirov, but showed criminal negligence in not taking necessary measures for his security." Could one possibly imagine that Medvedev and his colleagues, knowing about the preparations for Kirov's assassination, would not have reported it to their immediate superior Yagoda? There are only two possibilities: Either they did not report it, in which case, in a country in which nonreporting in questions of special governmental importance was punished by death by the firing squad, whereas the Leningrad GPU officers were given laughably small sentences; or they did report it, and then Yagoda, who also did not take the essential measures to protect Kirov's life, should have been tried in 1935 together with his Leningrad subordinates and not in March 1938. Consequently it seems probable in the extreme that Yagoda reported the terrorist act being prepared to his highest superior, or else organized the killing himself by order of Stalin. Somebody was desperately seeking an alibi in the Kirov affair and found it in the person of the twelve scapegoats from the Leningrad GPU.

Trotsky writes about this in his article: "The Circumstances of Kirov's assassination called forth whispers in the top echelons of the bureaucracy to the effect that in his fight against the opposition the Leader had begun to play

with the heads of his closest comrades in arms. There was
not a single straight-thinking person who doubted that the
chief of the Leningrad GPU, Medvedev, reported daily to
Yagoda about the progress of his most important operations, and that Yagoda, in turn, reported everything to Stalin and received instructions from him.

"The whispers could only be cut off by sacrificing the
twelve Leningrad executors of the Moscow plan."

Continuing the very accurate and logical arguments of
Trotsky, it is easy to come to the following conclusion: If in
1935 it seemed sufficient to Stalin and Yagoda to sacrifice
twelve scapegoats from the Leningrad GPU to obtain an alibi, it later became obvious that the blanket was too short to
cover the two partners for a long period of time. One of
them pulled it over to his side, exposing the other. What
Stalin did was completely obvious. In 1938 Yagoda appears
at the trial as the person responsible for the murder of
Kirov. The alibi now became the complete property of Stalin. Something similar took place in the case of Gorky: Yagoda was tried for what was done by the order of Stalin.

The question arises why the fact of Gorky's murder was
not publicized immediately after the writer's death in
1936, as was done with Kirov, if in any case the guilty parties could be found later. One can suppose that in 1936
Kirov's murder was still too fresh in memory in order also
to use Gorky's death as a proof of terrorist activity on the
part of the opposition. As a result there appeared the first
version of the writer's natural death. But only two years
later the moment was ripe for declaring to the world that
Gorky had become a victim of the opposition, and for finishing off Yagoda with a second accurate shot. However,
the repetitive tactic of using scapegoats, first employed in
the Kirov case (twelve officials of the Leningrad GPU) and
then in the cases of Kirov and Gorky (Yagoda) not only
could not dispel the doubts of the party leadership, but on
the contrary—by its repetitiveness it increasingly concentrated suspicion on the real criminal. That is why in 1940
the irreplaceable Poskrebyshev received the order to return to the natural-death version. And that is why to this
day Gorky's death is explained by two mutually exclusive
causes. Let us say that Stalin, in part, was caught in his own
trap. Because even the most careful conclusion must be for-

mulated in this way: If Gorky by chance did not actually die of catarrhal pneumonia, all the psychological and political circumstances of the last years of his life in the Soviet Union point to the fact that the *seventh* death of the writer was the deed of Stalin's hands.

Trotsky, in his articles about the Moscow trials, referred to the anonymous "letter from an old Bolshevik," written immediately after the trial of Zinoviev and Kamenev in August 1936 (i.e., a few months after Gorky's death). Trotsky calls this letter semiapocryphal. Today we know that its author was Boris Nikolayevsky, an old Menshevik, who emigrated in the 1920s, but who maintained close contacts with many Bolshevik leaders. The "letter from an old Bolshevik" was written after Nikolayevsky's conversations with N. Bukharin, who came to Paris not long before his arrest, and on the basis of Bukharin's words. The "letter from an old Bolshevik" mentions, in particular, that after returning to the Soviet Union Gorky wished to play the role of an arbitrator and achieve an agreement between Stalin and the opposition. For a while his efforts produced results, but more or less in 1935 Stalin selected the final path of liquidating his opponents, stopped visiting his "friend and comrade in arms," and did not answer his phone calls. Things went so far that there appeared in *Pravda* an article by David Zaslavsky with attacks on Gorky. The ferociously angered writer demanded a passport to go abroad, but the postrevolutionary episode with Lenin was not repeated.

In conclusion there is evidence which can be called posthumous. In 1954 the German Social Democrat Brigit Gerland, freed ahead of time in 1953 from a camp in Vorkuta and allowed to leave for the Federal Republic of Germany, wrote in the *Sotsialistichesky Vestnik* an article entitled "Who Poisoned Gorky?" I cite her text with significant abridgments:

. . . One of the most colorful and unforgettable personalities met by me during my time in Vorkuta was our hospital doctor, an old man of almost eighty years. For some time I worked with him as a medical orderly, and we became great friends, if one can speak of friendship between people so far apart in age and cul-

ture. This physician was Dimitriy Dimitryevich Pletnev. His name had caused quite a stir during one of
the famous trials of old Bolsheviks. [See Death Number Two, and also death Number One, in which Pletnev is mentioned as the physician who signed the official medical document on Gorky's death.] On one
occasion the professor told me the following story:
"We treated Gorky for heart disease, but his sufferings
were not so much physical as moral. He never stopped
tearing himself apart with attacks of conscience. He
could no longer breathe in the Soviet Union and passionately desired to return to Italy. He tried to run
away from himself, but he lacked strength for a serious
protest. Nevertheless the suspicious Kremlin despot
was afraid of an open statement against the regime on
the part of the famous writer. And, as always, in a
moment of necessity he thought up the most effective
method. This time it was a candy box. Yes, a light-pink
candy box, tied with a little silk ribbon. It lay on Gorky's night table; he loved to treat guests who visited
him. Soon after receiving the candy box he generously
treated two medical orderlies with chocolate candy
and ate a few himself. After an hour all three felt sharp
stomach pains, and an hour later death came. The au-
topsies were done immediately. Our worst fears came
true. All three had been poisoned. We, the doctors,
kept silent. Even then, when the Kremlin dictated a
completely false version of Gorky's death, we did not
protest. Rumors began to circulate around Moscow
that Gorky had been killed, that Soso had poisoned
him. This was very aggravating to Stalin. It was essential to distract society's attention, to direct suspicions
into other channels, to find other culprits. The simplest thing was to accuse the doctors of the crime.
What was the point of the doctors' doing it? A naïve
question. Of course, by order of the Fascists and their
agents. How did the affair end? How it ended, you
know."

Brigit Gerland finishes her story: "Pletnev's words engraved themselves on my memory forever." That is why
she repeated them with maximum accuracy, "not adding or

subtracting a single word. I would never have believed," writes Brigit Gerland, "in this cheap detective story with its pink candy boxes and poisoned chocolates if I had not on my own skin become acquainted with Stalinist methods of arrests, interrogations, and trials." She adds: "I never would have told anyone about this meeting in Vorkuta if Pletnev were still alive, but he died at the age of eighty-odd in Vorkuta and the NKVD cannot do anything more to him."

The NKVD could not do anything more to the dead Pletnev. But the KGB continues to try to do everything possible to prevent the solution to the mystery of Gorky's death and finally to expose the official "Gorky legend." Happily, today's "all-powerful" KGB is significantly weaker than yesterday's "all-powerful" NKVD. Today in the Soviet Union —under very difficult circumstances and not always successfully in everything—an unofficial "court of history" has begun to work. To include the Gorky case in the agenda of this "court of history" is an important task for the Russian intelligentsia, to which the regime has presented Gorky as a saint. Possibly, having uncovered the truth about Gorky, the intelligentsia will understand the truth of its own history.

Klim and Pannochka: A Tale

BY LEONID RZHEVSKY

Translated by Edward Van Der Rhoer

From Kontinent No. XII, 1977

1. Notice of Induction

Renouncing in advance that type of author's intrigue against the reader called a "suspenseful plot," I state frankly that Pannochka, the part-heroine of my tale (partly a documentary), is a horse.

Not I but others thought up this coquettish literary name; even if I had wished to do so, I would not have been able to change it, for to me it was picturesque and highly visible (like a movie still), it haughtily tossed its little head with pitch-black, silky forelocks falling over the eyes, and stepped out with legs (as slender as strings) in khaki stockings made from soldiers' puttees, and it seems to me that it, this name, must prance in the reader's imagination.

So Pannochka was a horse, English by blood, Polish in nationality, and now you can read further or not, as you wish; I entirely understand that people may not be interested in that sort of understated romance.

We liberated her (that is, Pannochka, not romance) with our Belorussian brothers from the yoke of Polish landown-

Leonid Denisovich Rzhevsky, born in 1905, was a candidate of philosophical sciences at Moscow Pedagogical Institute, named for V. I. Lenin. In the period 1953–1963 he lectured at Lund University (Sweden). He has lived in New York since 1964, and is a professor emeritus of Slavic Literature at New York University. He has published a number of books—both fiction and literary criticism—in the emigration.

ers and capitalists in the fall of 1939. The solemn inauguration of this victorious campaign occurred, as is known, in a
brilliantly simple manner: Some thousands of liberators,
who hitherto had no suspicion of the noble mission that
lay in store for them, were conducted past blue-eyed frontier lakes, I recall, to a clearing of wavy sand hemmed in by
a thin pine forest, and there assembled for a meeting. A
certain divisional or corps commissar of enviable size, with
a gesture that was estimable although imitative ("Hence
we shall threaten the Swede . . ."), pointed out to us the
west, the frontier posts that could not be seen from this
place, and said:

"Comrades! Polish laboring people, workers and peasants, have revolted against their oppressors. We must extend to them a helping hand. The Party and government
. . . and so forth . . . Hurrah!"

We cried out, "Hurrah!" and went across the sand.

We came— No, I cannot continue! Without speaking
about the stylistic weakness of this "went" and "came,"
which acute critics will instantly expose, I am obliged to
acquaint the reader from the outset with the preceding history of this story, and at the same time with some of the
dramatis personae—yes, perhaps above all with myself, in
the sense of how it happened that I, a civilian rather than a
military man, suddenly was cast in the distinguished role
of an armed liberator.

It happened rather simply: Unexpectedly, like hail out of
a clear sky, an induction notice from the military registra-
tion office flew into my peeling mailbox on the front door.
Unexpectedly—because no summons for military call-ups
had been sent up to that time—and, with perplexity and
constricted heart, I collected in my briefcase brushes, razor,
and a change of linen instead of précis and notes of lectures, and made my way to Lefortovo, headquarters of the
Moscow proletarian infantry division, and to the registra-
tion point.

This was a building formerly occupied by a military
school, to which I had been summoned—a dirty-yellow
Empire-style quadrangle with an enormous parade ground
in the middle.

It was just beginning to get dark. From the park across
the way came a smell of bitter autumn rainfall and slime
out of flower-filled ponds.

These odors stirred in me recollections of twenty years earlier, and the thought of why I had been called up stopped drumming in my brain and was replaced by something entirely different: Was the wooden summerhouse for trumpeters and the review of cadet parades standing as before in the place where I was going, on the very same parade ground? In the bare year of 1919, when the troika of our family—I, mother, and sister—were almost expiring of hunger, I put aside my high-school textbooks and went to work in this red military-school block, for the generous ration of a troop's horse groom, with assignment to the office. At that time there were courses for commanders there, and their chief, a Latvian commissar, had a young secretary whose name was Rozochka (little Rose)—the name was entirely descriptive of her. One early June evening, when I had the night telephone duty, I listened with her in that summerhouse to the nightingales. Yes, I beg you to believe me—at that time real nightingales still lived in the willows hanging over the park ponds; the nocturnal stillness, unshattered by any motors, carried their melodies far and wide and to my and Rose's ears. I had left a tongue-tied messenger to tend the phone in the hope that no one would call at night; but the commissar himself called. . . . A commander's heavy footsteps thudded across the courtyard to the summerhouse, and the duty officer of the training courses, pulling his sword out of the scabbard (my God, I thought for a moment that he was going to cut off my head), escorted me under arrest to the former cadet guardhouse, in which bedbugs had been breeding for two years with unheard-of freedom. . . .

These recollections of mine were submerged beneath a rumble that increased in intensity—I approached an entrance surrounded by a motley crowd. "Motley" because among the gray caps and backs of inductees there glowed kerchiefs of all colors as well as diminutive, delicate white ones, dampened, in all likelihood, with tears of parting. What is it? Mobilization? Maneuvers?—if everything turns out for the best?

But inside the courtyard, where one was told to wait—no, why speak of a summerhouse any more!—there was a roaring turmoil of thousands. A tobacco cloud over those sitting alone or in batches, the hoarse commands of local military ranks, a great crowd before the gaping jaws of storehouses; the yelling of quartermasters, who heaped up piles of overcoats, mess kits, gas masks, and shoes; it smelled of leather, pitch, mustiness, and rifle grease.

I received an unusual greeting: "Commander?" Some crazy supply clerk rushed up to me (why me?) and practically dragged me by my sleeve to the counter, where I was given a uniform that, by some miracle, fit the first time, even the boots and the cap. Any reservist who has been to an annual camp knows that such good fortune would make you feel it was your lucky day. I too felt that way and, screwing on my lieutenant's bars, mentally exchanged greetings with those who belonged to the regular army and hence had nothing to do with the economic mess I had hated since my youth.

But— "Don't count your chickens before they're hatched!" In the smoke-filled office, which I just reached by evening, a red-haired, stoop-shouldered major in a tunic with unbuttoned collar, his cheeks haggard from lack of sleep, grabbed me. "Lieutenant?" he asked hoarsely, leafing through my military booklet. "Postgraduate work is supposed to be *higher* education, or what?" His eyelids with yellow lashes sagged downward with fatigue, but with an effort he assumed on his face a firm expression of command.

"You are appointed commander of the headquarters platoon of our regiment. The platoon is to be formed by 0900 tomorrow morning. Do you have any idea of the mission? No? Well, apparently the state wasted its money on your military training. Here's the mobilization notice, with the roster and tables of organization. For guarding the headquarters, choose a combat-ready rifle squad. And a machine-gun squad—heavy machine guns. Yes, and also a housekeeping unit, so that there will be shoemakers, blacksmiths, and cooks of the best sort in the platoon. Obtain field kitchens of the latest model, double ones. Vehicles of higher quality . . . How many horses do you have there? Hmm . . . twelve? So that there'll be a full complement. That's all!"

"But how can I—"

"No 'hows'! Personal initiative, will, tenacity, a sense of duty. Carry it out!"

He wished, more than anything else in the world, I saw, to throw himself down to sleep, but he uttered all of this with his last strength, in a metallic patter, glancing past my face into the corner.

"But where . . . ?"

"No 'wheres'! I don't have an information bureau. Carry out the order!"

I doubt whether I can now convey the astonishment I felt then. In Afanasiev's collection of Russian fairy tales there is one in which an evil czar, seeking to destroy the hero, orders him: "Go thither, I know not where; bring that, I know not what"—it seems that this was what the fairy tale was called. Did the red-haired major also wish to bring about my ruin? In the fairy tale the hero is helped by a beautiful sorceress, and anyway he was himself a bright fellow; but who would practice sorcery for me? Double field kitchens, large-caliber machine-gunners, cooks, and a herd of horses!—the table of organization must have been established as long ago as the Crimean War. Double field kitchens struck me as crematoria on wheels, bluish clouds of smoke from burnt porridge hiding them from famished eyes. A dozen horse throats neighed in my ears and forty-eight hoofs tapped out a refrain on my eardrums.

"Carry out the order!"

Report sick? Submit a report on my unfitness for the housekeeping unit? I dwelled on this alternative, mentally selecting a suitable clerk and raging at the red-haired major. What a brutal tactic! Why on earth did he pick me as his victim?

When you recall this remote event (it's no joke: nearly forty years have passed since then!), there is a danger of overestimating all this by contemporary emigrant standards, in terms of tyranny over the individual, antihumanism, and the rest; but I am simply trying to remember how it was.

This was how it was: "Brutal tactic . . . victim . . ." My vain attempts to escape from this plight concentrated on such matters, and all of a sudden a green light lit up! I felt a well-fitting uniform on myself, two bars on the collar, and in my breast a cynical notion: In order not to become a victim oneself, it was necessary to find one's own victim and extend the red-haired major's tactic downward! . . .

Above the parade ground hung a thickening twilight that was half composed of the smoke of *makhorka* tobacco; half of the herd had obtained uniforms, rolled up over-coats, and wound footcloths the color of swansdown on raised feet; some people had already received weapons—had clicked bolts and set up rifle pyramids with oiled bayonets pointed upward.

I pictured the face of my victim distinctly: necessarily young, necessarily with a firm chin (perhaps separated by an energetic cleft) and expressive eyebrows.

Then, through the crush, swinging about the courtyard and banishing the darkness with my own flashlight when necessary, I discovered such a face.

"Name."

"Stroganov."

"A distinguished name. What have you done in your army service?"

"First sergeant—the last year, Comrade Lieutenant!"

"Then you are appointed a first sergeant. Headquarters platoon. It must be formed by morning. Familiarize yourself with the list—personnel and what needs to be obtained. Take the flashlight!"

And a little later:

"It's now nine-thirty. Report here at ten o'clock, at this same spot, with four squad leaders: two combat men, one of them a machine-gunner, then a housekeeping type, preferably a supply man, and an intelligent driver, one who knows horses. Choose the best of the best!"

"But how, Comrade Lieutenant—"

"No 'hows'! Personal initiative. Tenacity. A sense of duty. Carry out the order!"

"Yes, sir!"

I know that others will refuse to believe it, but in a half hour there were precisely five smart soldiers, partly with breaking voices, surrounding me in a circle, receiving their assignments. By midnight there were thirty-three first-class reservists—if not supermen—noted on my list. And on the outside parade ground, beyond the buildings, double field kitchens stood out side by side in flashes of lamplight, the harness smelling of leather and tar piled on wagons, while twelve horses with varied coats snorted and pawed the ground.

We even had time to get some sleep before dawn, but at daybreak there turned up, of course, the red-haired major, who had also managed a nap, and he identified himself as chief of staff; after receiving my report and inspecting everything, he blinked his eyes (as became clear later, he always blinked when he succumbed to unofficial emotion) and, after ceasing to blink, expressed gratitude to me in the name of the regimental command.

2. On the March

"Comrade Lieutenant, where are the revolting workers?"

At this point we are going along narrow, lancetlike Polish roads lined, it seemed, with ash. I and my thirty-three. I was destined to serve in the army both before and after this campaign, but I never again encountered such a glorious selection—what a fine fellow that first sergeant was! Excluding half a dozen older specialists, they were all young —Komsomol members—and he himself (after an initial halt) became a Komsomol organizer. On the command "Attention!" all thirty-three straightened up like one man. But about that—later.

Meanwhile we keep going. While on our way I am asked the awkward question about revolting workers. I evade the question half-jokingly: "What are they, these workers— partridges, running through the stubble?" But as we go deeper and bypass villages, I send to the commissar for answers.

Yes, in my platoon there was a battalion commissar, with two rectangular tabs. Either it was not enough for me, a non-Party man, to take care of regulars, or there was nowhere to place this commissar. His name was Kashirin, he came from the quartermasters, his body was slightly flattened in some places and somewhat encased in fat elsewhere. Responding to my messages to him, he at first snapped back ("Don't you see yourself what to answer?"), but I reminded him of his rank and his closeness to the commanders, and he lapsed into a dignified silence.

About him also later. But now, in order to be precise, still another case of someone assigned to my platoon, among those coincidences that have accompanied me all my life.

This "case" involved someone named Foma, who was known to all of the country's poets because he had managed the corresponding sector of its largest publishing house. At one time I had shared a school desk with him, then we parted for some twenty years, and now fate had brought us together again. He was, like me, a reserve lieutenant, but he suffered from a stomach ulcer, and, probably because of that infirmity, he was pushed into my more comfortable headquarters platoon. In all, therefore, our personnel amounted to thirty-six men.

Our platoon moved at the head of our regimental column, very possibly at the head of our whole line of advance as well. That is, there were battle outposts and patrols ahead of us, of course, but farther ahead, evidently, there was nothing—we felt this vanguard situation very acutely, and together with the creeping morning fog there moved with us along the sides of the road an almost morbid watchfulness.

It was intensified ceaselessly by various menacing words like "vigilance," "combat-readiness," and "snipers," the latter especially having significance: This was the name given to Polish farmers, who had established themselves on this Belorussian soil and supposedly threatened us at any moment with ambushes and surprise attacks. On the march and at halts, the *politruks* concentrated on this bugbear:

"Sni-pers . . ."

". . . ni-i-pers . . ."

". . . i-pers . . ."

And so, when shots suddenly rang out about five kilometers ahead, to judge by ear, the column came to a standstill without awaiting a command and stiffened. From behind came the snorting of the team harnessed to the wagon carrying the machine guns where Foma, racked with pain, was also riding, the fugitive tramp of boots on the tarred road, and muffled commands. "Battalion runners to the chief of staff!" resounded the cry behind my back, echoing along the column. I waited for the order to spread out, pondering what would then have to be done with the wagon. With a face that was growing gray, Kashirin kept stealing glances at me, as if asking what to do. I requested him to give the order to take the covers off the machine guns.

In the meantime the shots, which were at first like volleys and then sporadic, ceased altogether. A mounted scout rode on ahead. A little later the chief of staff himself, the red-haired major we already knew, came up beside me at the edge of the road, looking into the distance with binoculars.

Divided in two by the line of the road, the distance was empty and whitish. On the stubble to the left, flocks of crows formed black dots like currants; to the right there was a depression, a hillock, and beyond that, already at the horizon, the gray summit of some roof and the pointed tips of poplars.

"Lieutenant!" The major turned to me. "Take a runner and—look over that building behind the hill, well within gunshot from here, do you see it?"

"I see it, Comrade Major."

"Take a weapon, it's not a date you're going to!"

In regard to a weapon: Then and later, at the beginning of the great war, reserve officers were not supplied with weapons, except for a rifle. This old-fashioned rifle interfered with the handling of maps, making notes and sketches, and simply moving about, damn the old thing!

"Sergeant!"

There and then a Berdan rifle flew into my hand (it was somewhat lighter), and the runner stepped up beside me.

And we started out.

It was about two hundred paces to the hillock, and I remember them as the first test of courage in my life.

Because instead of courage I felt only fear that, climbing up to the crest, I would be fully exposed to the view of the presumed snipers' nest, in the sights of some partisan gun. I was under great strain, seeking not to give in to fear, not to stumble, under the gaze of thousands of eyes, on the damned mounds over which we were passing. Half a dozen soldiers among my relatives, famous for their combat efficiency and fearlessness, came to mind, but their descendant felt weak and vulnerable. . . .

"What do you think, Lieutenant—should we go straight over this rise or go around it?" asked the runner, coming up with me.

He was perhaps the least athletic of my thirty-three, that runner, coming nearly to my shoulder and not very young, but he posed the question as if we were out mushroom-hunting and thereby jarred me out of my sense of vulnerability—in another hundred steps I had already switched from "I" to "we." Indeed, it was possible to go around the rise, descending to nothing at the edge of a gentle slope—i.e., without becoming the target of a sniper's bullet—but that meant going by a circuitous route in sight of the column waiting behind us.

"Straight over!" I said. "Or are you frightened?"

"Well, I volunteered to go with you. If you're under arms, try to be brave. As the saying goes, it's a case of either a chest full of medals or hiding yourself in the bushes."

He half turned to me as he was speaking, and I immediately recognized those pale-blue lively eyes, darting here and there—on a recent night he had begged me to transfer him to combat status from the transportation unit, and because of those clever eyes I authorized the transfer.

"What's your name?"

"Klim. My father's name was also Klim. And Klimov is our family name. . . . Once it gets into your head, you don't have to rack your brain any more."

From the summit, once we had climbed up, the guerrilla farmstead seemed as if it was in the palm of your hand. The house was extended like a box along an orchard of what seemed to be apple trees, with Lombardy poplars on the sides. Six dim windows looked so much like a pillbox that we froze again, but we immediately aimed our Berdan rifles and descended. Our flank patrol should, of course, have combed through here, but . . . By and large, we went without thought toward those windows as, probably, one goes along at the beginning of an attack before one sees the enemy, and can you call that bravery? . . .

As we approached, we separated, Klim going behind the house to inspect the garden and outbuildings, I approaching from the front to the main door. With the Berdan rifle at the ready, I kicked the lower panel with my foot.

The house was empty, with all the signs of a hasty flight and the sweet, syrupy odor of apples piled in the pantry or in the cellar. The kitchen door stood ajar. Here I had hardly filled my pipe when Klim appeared.

"There's nobody, Comrade Lieutenant. Do you mind if I roll a cigarette?"

"Roll it, but we'll smoke on the way."

Holding onto a sack with a briquette, he rolled his own cigarette, which he folded in two and bent upwards—much in the shape of his small, partly folded penknife manipulated by his adroit fingers under the roving, lively creatures of his eyes. For some reason I spoke to him with the familiar "thou," although I called the others by the more formal "you," and he was by far older than they. I wanted to ask him which was his year, but somewhere a plane droned, and we both leaned across the threshold. Noisy as a threshing machine, a U-2[1] flew toward our rear, but we had scarcely followed it with our eyes when this was followed by a clatter—a gallop that sounded hollow on the country road but growing impetuously louder. It came to a standstill and froze close by, within arm's length: Someone, it was clear, had galloped into the courtyard and dismounted.

Pressing against the wall, we rounded the corner—nothing in sight. Still another corner, approaching the front of the building, ready for an encounter—nobody!

"What deviltry?"

"By no means, Comrade Lieutenant—I see. There it is, a horse, under the apple tree. Saddled . . . do you see?"

Indeed: a horse. It was in the farthest depths of the garden, and for that reason I had not noticed it immediately. It had a saddle on. When we came close, my gaze was struck first of all by this saddle, belonging to an officer, of yellow leather, with a second stirrup thrown across it on the other side.

The bay filly, clinging to the trunk of the apple tree, was panting, slightly trembling throughout her body and emitting short snorts through nostrils that were red below. An agate eye squinted wildly at Klim, who had seized the bridle.

He himself was trembling, Klim. I recall that I was struck by his face—rapturous, with eyes that had ceased to wander, strengthened and seemingly iluminated from within —when he viewed the steepness of the neck, the glossy sleek coat, slightly sweating under the cream-colored saddle cloth, which bore a monogram in one corner. "Com-

[1]The Uchebni-2, a light Russian training plane.

rade Lieutenant . . ." he said, plucking at the tar-black withers and almost gasping with excitement, "this is a marvel, isn't it? You know, she's really part—or even one-hundred-percent—thoroughbred. What pasterns, look at that!"

I partly shared his delight. Somewhere in Chekhov there is a description, of which I always remember one line: "Before me there stood a beauty, and I recognized that from the first glance as one recognizes lightning."

This prisoner of ours was a beauty. Not, incidentally, just because of her equine points, but also, I would say, due to a generalized expression of beauty, wherever it might be encountered—in modeling, in painting, in the play of chiaroscuro, in the secret emanation of harmony and femininity. Yes, femininity as well. The infantry in spirit may guffaw at me as much as they wish, but under the two pairs of eyes that observed her, this filly undoubtedly sensed her natural female essence: Still without ceasing to tremble, she shifted her finely molded legs several times; laying back one ear, she moved her small head in some expectant quarter-turn (in the same way one sometimes awaits an invitation to dance at a ball), and in her bulging black eye —I was prepared to swear—curiosity now filtered through the fear.

With his hand, Klim lovingly straightened the silky forelock that hung over this brilliant eye.

It is only now that I recollect, or partly conjecture, all of this in such detail, but at that time I found an explanation for our unexpected booty swiftly and in the style of an intelligence officer: Her master, a Polish officer, had been felled in the firefight that had just taken place, and she galloped away from the shots and, I suppose, from our U-2.

"So, Klim, we have a prize. Take the bridle and let's go."

With his hand on the pommel, he turned to me with a jerk, prepared, I realized, to give the prize a trial, but, guessing what I would reply, wilted, pulled up the stirrups as far as they would go, and, poking his finger underneath, loosened the saddle girth.

"I see, Klim, that you're a horseman!" I said to him when we started out.

"Oh, but I work on the ———— horse-breeding farm with draft horses. And still earlier I worked at the Tersky stud

farm in the Stavropol region, where they bred thoroughbred saddle horses, Arabians and an English strain. Siglavi,
too, closely resembling our own, and as for the gait—pour
tea in a saucer, it won't spill out. We have bred many kinds
—Budenovsky, Kustanaisky. The Budenovsky are more
coarse, though there are none hardier. The Akhalkatinsky
breed, from the Kapet-Dag mountains, are the most famous
of all. The English were envious, they obtained stallions
from us. But perhaps, Lieutenant, you're not interested in
hearing about horses?"

"As a boy I grew up in a cavalry regiment. My father's.
But certainly I am not such an expert in this area as you."

"I would have been certified as a practical veterinarian,
but I lacked a year, I didn't get through the seven-year
school . . . As I noticed, however, it came to you through
our prize as if by inspiration: One of your own! . . ."

The dialogue that I am now reproducing so smoothly
really took place entirely on the move, in hops and dance
steps; at times Klim lagged behind, at other times he
caught up with me and went along leaning sideways with
the reins over his head, looking at the movements of the
small hooves, which resembled little shells.

I let them go ahead—so that I could also look. The slender legs in yellow stockings, extending from the fetlocks
nearly to the knees, glided over the sparse grass more me-
lodiously than a bow over strings, spraying to each side
fine drops of dew. Before reaching the crest, Klim suddenly turned onto an intersecting path and started to trot,
checking her gait. The gait was also a wonder.

"Eh? Comrade Lieutenant!" he shouted to me, backing
up a step and beaming all over his face. "What a gait! Czar-
evna! Pannochka!"

"Pannochka? Let's leave it at that, just as you thought of
it. Anyway, she needs a name."

Pannochka! Just that. . . .

The column revealed itself to us from the summit, having already been dispersed to the sides of the road; obviously the order to halt had just been given, and the company quadrangles, with bayonets gleaming and rolls
shouldered on the run, fell apart like pods split lengthwise
by a finger. It was entertaining to look at.

The chief of staff stood with the regimental commissar at the edge of the ditch. I hesitated slightly about whom to report to, but it seemed that he had long since fixed his gaze on the little horse that Klim was leading, and went toward them without listening to my report. For some time he patted her croup and neck, running his fingers through the glistening mane and at the same time dilating his nostrils, which sprouted red hair. Then he turned to me:

"So tell me, where did you get the horse?"

"A military prize in the execution of a combat mission," said the commissar, approaching. He was a regular, young and very concerned about appearances. "Well done, Lieutenant! Congratulations!"

"A horse is not authorized for staff lieutenants."

"Why isn't it authorized? A military prize? Drop it, Major. Register it, Lieutenant, as an allowance."

"Yes, sir—it will be registered!"

I ordered Klim to bring Pannochka to the transportation unit, to the horses. "Later I'll be over myself!" I said to him.

But I did not come "over" until twenty-four hours later —the atmosphere on the march was so charged with nervousness and commotion. The top command itself, I think now, hardly could have feared anything, but, as I have said, calls for vigilance showered down upon the lower ranks. At this very moment, during the halt, the subject of "snipers" was being bruited in every way.

After sending off Klim, I began to look around for Kashirin and the top sergeant, but they were not there. With legs lowered into the ditch, Foma sat on a grassy slope. Judging from the notebook in his hand, with which he waved at me, his pains had temporarily left him.

"I saw, saw your cavalry, how about that!" he said. "Pretty! And even—

> Sweet ballerina in her tights,
> She tiptoed o'er the dew alone
> As I fixed her in my sights
> Down in the target zone.

I was left here as the senior officer," he continued more prosaically. "Kashirin and the top sergeant with the first section have gone on a truck somewhere up ahead. A mission. What sort of mission we'll learn later."

I was the only one who learned about it—the secrecy we had about everything was preposterous, but apparently Kashirin was ordered to tell me. The skirmish up ahead, it seemed, had taken place between our screen and some Polish outpost accidentally left behind by its own forces —a second lieutenant, corporal, and five soldiers. But in actuality there was no skirmish, our side only saw people wearing a strange uniform, opened fire, and killed all of them. "Well, we had orders, you understand," Kashirin said to me, "to insure, so to speak, the political coloration. Remove dead soldiers but leave officers on display. An educational suggestion, you understand."

We were already striding along again, and he had rejoined us with his group on the move, and we went past the "suggestions" (two light-green military jackets trimmed with silver), and I thought, not for the first time, what subtle masters and even fanatical devotees of this kind of suggestion ruled over us. I was reminded of *Iron Stream*, by Serafimovich—complete trash from the literary standpoint but declared a great epic, again for the sake of suggestion: The heroic leader forces an exhausted and starving human avalanche to make a detour of thirty versts in order to show them five persons hung by the Whites. . . .

"Klimov is missing, Comrade Lieutenant!" said the top sergeant, pointing at me his heavy jaw, reminiscent of Marshal Zhukov's portrait. "Or did you send him somewhere?"

"Yes, to the transportation unit, to look after our prize. Temporarily. . . ."

3. In the Hamlet M.

This is referred to in the textbooks as "exposing the method," but it doesn't matter, let it be! "Ugh, that's a load off my mind!" I say, having finished the first two chapters, that is, after providing the plot twist of my partly documentary tale in my part-heroine and the triangle partly in love with her: I myself, Klim, and the red-haired major.

I recorded our later cooperation at some time while it was still fresh in my memory. The notes remained in Moscow and were lost, but can be recovered rather easily because of the durability that the word on paper acquires for the writer, and further, perhaps, because of the very situation with which they were associated. Briefly interrupting the narrative's continuity, I shall now tell you about this situation.

That was already at the end of our campaign of liberation. A bluish September and October had been followed by a November with a tarpaulin-colored sky and roads flooded by ashy, bubbly waste water. It was also necessary to jump across streets on bricks haphazardly cast here and there. We were billeted in the miserable hamlet of M.

In my capacity as commander of the headquarters platoon, I was likewise guard and quartermaster and director of services for everything in the space occupied by the staff and its adjuncts. I requisitioned for myself a house with five windows and pink lintels and shutters that looked exactly as if it had been transported here from some remote spot in Moscow's Zamoskvoretsky district. In the cellar there was a wine vault whose key I had to guard like a Cerberus, suppressing any outside lusts. A middle-aged *petit bourgeois* (the landlord's son, as it later developed), fearsomely sprouting dark hair all over his face, opened the door for me. I'll postpone telling something amusing about the vault until later; I'll mention now something about the house.

Three of us lodged there (I, Foma, and Kashirin) in a large chamber, partitioning it off with cupboards and utensils.

On the following morning, when it was scarcely light, a delegation of local citizens called on me.

"To the *Pan* commandant . . ." said the head of the delegation, dressed in a formal three-piece suit and derby, pulling out from under his arm an office folder tied with tape, and bowing. He unwrapped it with trembling fingers, and from it there came something resembling a kite, with a paper tail that instantly hung down to the floor, covered with a great number of signature scrawls.

"*Podanie!*" said the chief delegate, bowing again. "A petition, if you please, sir . . ."

In the petition, which had been painstakingly written in Russian script with adroitly drawn d's and u's, there appeared a request to return Czar Nicholas to his former residence and his former occupation, whose usefulness (examples followed) was confirmed by seventy local residents, "providing signatures to this in their own hand and as loyal citizens."

Recalling now this episode, which is not contrived, I detect not without discomfiture an element of fear in my consternation of that time; it lasted only half a minute, for it became clear at once that *Czar Nicholas* was the surname and given name of our landlord, who had been "dispossessed" by the main wave of liberators that preceded us, but—fear nonetheless! Senseless, from nought, injected under all our skins by the insanity of our times; therefore it was by no means accidental that I immediately called on Kashirin, who was still sleeping, for assistance.

He was on the point of leaning out of the door in his underpants, but, hearing what it was about, he became gray in the face, got dressed, and hastily brought the petitioners to our commanders.

From that day on we started to call the landlord's unshaven son Czarevich. He was somewhat unsociable and somehow undeveloped, associating only with a woman who came in to cook and prepared for him one-dish soups or stews that lasted several days, and a hog he called "Petrusek" and was fattening for Christmas. Petrusek lived in the passage behind a latticed wall, enormous and gluttonous, and when he heard steps going by he began to roar like a bear and hammer with his hoofs on the tied-up door, inundating the passersby with the sour stench of his stall. I could not stand him.

Due to homesickness and idleness, we spent our nights playing cards. At first we played *chemin de fer*, and Czarevich, in whom, it seemed, the explosive force of gambling had been concealed, joined us with wistful shyness. In one of these nocturnal vigils he lost to me all his available cash—a stack of bills he fetched a little at a time from some earthenware banks. I was lucky and had a real duel with him.

"The wine cellar, please! Three thousand zlotys!" he said, gasping, and an awkward silence ensued, since the key to the wine vault was in my pocket, while certain principles of "liberation" had not yet been grasped by

Czarevich. Kashirin came to the rescue, inserting in some sort of gibberish the words "sequestered" and "for the time being."

"Then—Petrusek. A thousand zlotys!"

He also lost the hog. And when, toward morning, getting up from the table, I returned to him everything I had won, he was as overjoyed as a five-year-old who had gotten back a toy, and still sought to think of a way to even accounts.

He burst through the door when we had already laid ourselves down to sleep. "Gentlemen, I am going to slaughter Petrusek tomorrow. Perhaps you won't be here for the Christmas holidays, and I want to give you a treat."

The next day, at his request, I shot the hog with the Berdan rifle without any pangs of conscience, and for weeks afterward we received provisions in addition to our official rations.

Meanwhile we three continued to play cards, *preference*.

I realize that I am shamelessly slowing down the pace of my story, but there was no pace at all in the life we led then, and this is exactly what I have to tell about.

In the morning I usually occupied myself for about three hours with the platoon. Officially with the regulations, but more than that with all sorts of academic matters. I have already praised my subordinates above, but I also wish to say now that I never encountered elsewhere young people who were so eager for knowledge.

Later Klim, who had forced himself upon me as a runner, brought orders from the staff. After carrying out those orders that pertained to me, we went to see Pannochka. If it was not raining, Klim saddled her, and I went out beyond the outskirts—by way of the garden plots so as not to become an eyesore to the major (he would not let me get away, he wanted to have her for himself). Beyond the outskirts there was a good dirt road, which still had not been torn up by machines, and it led into a bare beech grove, where I rode around on paths or simply over the earth, across ruts and borders. This workout lasted an hour.

If, however, there was rain or snow, our activities were confined to gifts of sugar and consideration of Pannochka's prize points. "Comrade Lieutenant, I got a tape measure—140 to the withers! An Arabian, exactly! . . . Our veterinarian came the day before yesterday, he even has the bars of a senior officer, but he's a dense fellow. 'The withers,' he said, 'are right, but the diagonal length is short.' What, I said, short! Exactly 152, a real Siglavi! Even I was surprised by her size—but you can't fool me! Furthermore: 'She's mixed,' he said. 'Her tail is black.' Oh boy, I thought, strike me dead! This is a real Arabian breed, I told him, when she's a genuine bay or even rust-colored, the mane and tail are pitch-black."

She condescendingly listened to our enthusiastic talk, Pannochka, shifting her hooves, which Klim cleaned with polish, and twitching her ears. One day, with her head between the two of us, she even neighed slightly, feeling flattered and affectionate. "She usually greets me this way in the morning!" boasted Klim, and she shook her head at him entirely like some Carmen waving off suitors who complimented her, with her fan; then, perhaps scenting my jealousy, she touched my elbow with an extended velvety lip.

Foma had brought with him from home a little selection of verses for a future collection. On dull evenings, if he was not lying with a hot-water bottle on his stomach, he pored over sheets, wrote additions, and crossed out things, considerably wrinkling his forehead over the yellow circle of a sort of primitive oil lamp. I do not know whether the local dynamo was out of order, but we used kerosene lamps with flat wicks for illumination—which very well suited Kashirin, who repeatedly exclaimed in pathetic terms during political instruction: "But look at *our* country! Where is it we still don't have Ilyich electric bulbs? Eh? What do you say?" I can also mention in passing that he possessed another trump. It had its inception when, at some morning roll call, the top sergeant took me aside: "Comrade Lieutenant, you have lice on the bridge of your nose, allow me to remove them."

Czarevich was ordered to heat the bath and, fussing over me, nearly led me by the arm, equipping me with an extremely long towel embroidered with roosters. The bath, however, was heated without a chimney, as it turned out, and—a shameful admission—I proved to be totally unfit for the job: A caustic peat smell hung just above the floor; the water in the cask, warmed by red-hot cobblestones, was a dirty red, and it was impossible to scoop it out without standing up, that is, without exposing one's eyes to the smoke. I was unable to coordinate all of this, and on top of everything I was summoned to the staff unexpectedly in the very middle of this effort.

In the morning Kashirin said during political instruction: "Have you heard? Yesterday our lieutenant washed himself—he only had time to rinse his ————! A bathhouse without a chimney! That's bourgeois civilization for you. Eh?"

But I have digressed again. The essence of the matter is that the sight of Foma and his pages made me wish to write, myself. In my partitioned nook I had a folding bed and a wobbly table, but my writing was rapid. Sparingly and without generalizations, I made a record of our campaign and of some of the more striking episodes, for there was no place to hide the notebook. Kashirin! Either because of boredom, remaining alone without his card-playing partners, or because of vigilance, as he understood it, he looked at my and Foma's writing with apprehension, grumbled "Writing devils!" and was angry at us. He was suspicious and carping. In our rare conversations at supper on current events he interrupted Foma, who had inserted some verses in the discussion, himself overwhelmed us with quotations from editorials, and looked at me expectantly. "You're holding your tongue, Leonid?" he asked with an unkind squint, calling me by my given name for the first time.

I was frank with Foma. "Why are we in Poland? The fourth partition?" I inquired. "Military necessity, perhaps. Aren't these places, where we're sitting, *our* White Russia? . . . Incidentally, I wanted to ask: You haven't let anything seditious get into your notes? So that you don't tweak anyone's nose?"

"I understand. No, everything of mine is tame."

At that time I already knew that Kashirin was reading my notebook. Perhaps the very recording of facts on paper seemed to him a crime, like the divulging of military secrets. What was to be done? He was not a dyed-in-the-wool informer, Kashirin, but there was something of the scavenger in him—an instinct for opportunities to display his vigilance. Thinking a little, I ended my next entry thus:

"In days of doubt, in days of painful meditation about the fate of our Motherland, how good it is that we have Commissar Kashirin in our platoon! You will make no mistake ideologically, you will not be diverted from the correct path as long as he is here."

Plagiarism from Turgenev, I knew, would not be identified by Kashirin, and the spelling of Motherland with a capital letter and everything as a whole should work out well.

That was the way it turned out: a day later he looked at me with a tender gaze.

As I have already said, my notes were not preserved. Separate sketches, however, remained vividly in my memory, even the titles. These were: "Lida"—the first city that we entered at that time—"Night in Dunilovichi"—a tragic apotheosis of fear with which we were imbued by the command and the *politruks*—and, as the reader will see further on, the romantic "Podlipki."

Now, however, back to the beginning, that is, anew to our march headed west.

4. *Lida*

We are on the move. . . .

We have been on the move for about two hours without a halt. The lancetlike highway is empty up ahead. Roofs without any trace of smoke remained few and far between, off to the sides of the road. Nobody greeted us with offerings of bread and salt.

I am not much good at marching, and I had fallen slightly behind twice, to the vehicle with the machine guns: a couple of words with Foma, a hand on the heel of my shoe—and it was as if the next step became easier.

From behind:

"———irin, come to the chief of staff!"

"———sar ——— shirin, come to the chief of staff!"

The chief of staff was somewhere in the middle of the column, mounted on a tall gelding with fading spots; he rode on it like a makeweight on top of a loaf of bread.

"Commissar Kashirin—come to the chief of staff!"

Kashirin was mincing along in the rear with a perplexed face. He had two faces: a perplexed one, as at the moment, when he would have his mouth half open, and an official one, when a swelling came out over his cheekbones and a wrinkle on the bridge of his nose.

He returned with the wrinkle: There would be a halt, an inspection, and political-educational instruction—we're going into a large city! "We're the first ones, you understand? Straighten up, look happier, and—most important of all—no absenting yourself from your unit. Leave to be granted only in extraordinary cases. So that the men won't go rushing into stores. Here they have all kinds of food, goods—private trading, you understand. So as not to stain our honor. . . ."

And at the halt Kashirin spoke out:

"Discipline! Order! And don't stare at the different junk there. You can buy something only with special permission."

"How can we buy anything? They have another kind of money!"

"If you receive permission, then it will be this way: The zloty, their money, is the same as the ruble. Understood?"

"But which city is it? What's its name?"

"City?" After some hesitation—was it a military secret?—"The city of Lida."

Under a hail of questions, I intervened:

"An industrial city. In the former province of Grodno. There are ruins of the castle of Gediman, a Lithuanian prince, dating back half a millennium."

I told about this prince, who had once held our Kiev and Novgorod princes in fear and trembling. I suddenly began seriously to wish to see these ruins. Particularly when we were already in the city, and I was surrounded by red, up-turned tile, which, in my imagination of old, was always a tangible sign of another spirit, another land.

But tourism did not come about, instead something unexpected and totally different.

"Aha, Lieutenant!" The regimental commissar (I knew his name: Grishin) intercepted me just when we were being billeted. "You are being entrusted with the war against junk dealers. Well, look here." He ran his finger over the board with a map of the city. "This is the area with the town hall and the surrounding quarters—our places, and the devil might have guessed! All around here is the local department store and shops. Patrol directly from store to store. To stop junk dealing on the spot, chase anybody and everybody away!"

"But if they're senior commanders . . ."

"They'll turn out to be mostly junior. But introduce yourself to the senior ones, say 'the Commandant's office' and 'It is requested, Comrade Captain—or whatever he is—that you don't remain here.' That's all. Find an orderly and get moving!"

One of my worst memories is that "Get moving!" and those four hours of our stay in Lida—a squirrel cage, my battle with the many-headed Hydra running amuck due to the splendor of the counters and show windows. I particularly shall not forget the eyes of this Hydra—rapturous and greedy, replacing their rapture and greed with bewilderment and hostility when they were directed at me. My own orderly, Ryabov, a glib barber from the Moscow region, looked at me with reproach: How could you forbid others that which you so passionately desired yourself! How could you look on with indifference while other hands were snatching at the rare goods on the shelves! A unique chance! And you hide your covetous fists behind your back. . . .

My fight with the Hydra was a kaleidoscope, the devil's own carousel: faces, scowls, grins, entreaties, and a shout that was strangled somewhere in the larynx, submission and rebuff, sweetness and scorn. "It's all right, Lieutenant!" a tall major said through set teeth in response to my presentation. (He and someone else wearing bars were selecting silver cigarette cases in a jewelry shop.) "Everything's all right. You may be at ease."

I could not make up my mind to have any more to do with them.

"Lieutenant, my dear, or aren't you married?" A puny captain from one of our engineer units, I think, was speaking. He had spread out with five fingers something of cotton lace on a stand with ladies' fashions, and on the face he presented to me there appeared amiability and tenderness. "You're not married? Well, I have three females—my wife and two daughters. Six legs, three backs. Just so they don't go crazy with joy if they get this. I bought for each of them two pairs of stockings such as we don't see at home. The old fellow who is the salesman speaks Russian as well as the two of us. And what a wit! Can you press these stockings, I asked him? 'You can,' he said, 'but not above the knees.'"

In "leather goods" (*Wyroby skórzane*) there was suddenly Kashirin. I almost thought he was there on the same assignment I had—but no, the pockets of his overcoat were bulging, and in his hand there openly dangled a nicely wrapped box. Perhaps, however, he had an assignment, but it was of a different sort. . . . Pushing up to me, he spoke in my ear, keeping Ryabov off with his elbow:

"I sympathize with you! How about getting something for you?"

"Pipe tobacco," I said, "would be good."

"What else?"

"I also saw some chocolate, two bars for one zloty."

"It'll be taken care of!" he said, and headed for the door.

At the very end, returning when the bugler blew for muster, dead tired, we ran into Klim on the corner of the square, the hem of his overcoat tucked up to his belt, and in it there could be heard a clink.

"Who let you go, Klim?"

"The top sergeant. He stayed for the headquarters platoon."

"What's clinking in the hem?"

"Ah, nothing, Comrade Lieutenant. A new curry-comb for our Pannochka, some canned chicken, and this stuff. . . ." He held out the hem, and Ryabov and I saw a heap of tableware—forks, spoons, and knives.

"Where did you get all that? There's more than a dozen here."

"At home, when we get together, no fewer of us sit down to the table."

"Take it back."

"That's absolutely inconceivable, Comrade Lieutenant. First of all—why? everything was paid for exactly as the commissar instructed us: The zloty is equal to the ruble. Secondly—the owner had really left home, everything was bought up completely. There was a lot, but there was an excess of purchasers too, they fought like cats and dogs.

One fellow took five times as much as I did—he settled
with hundred-ruble bonds of the State loan. . . ."

"He was swindling, it seems."

"Is it really a sin to swindle them—the hucksters?"

Later, toward evening, once more walking kilometers, I
recalled to myself this "Is it a sin to swindle?"—some mu-
tation of Proudhon's popular nonsense in regard to property as theft. By what roots did it cling to the souls of Klim
and legions of others? Savagery? Envy? Rebellion? And
how contrary to their—the legions'—thirst for acquisition
and craving for things, which are organic and perhaps
even salutary: The material environment of man in its turn
creates and expresses him: Whoever expresses himself is
stronger. Isn't the label of "junk dealing" contrary to this?

A night halt in the enormous barn of some landowner
with unthreshed sheaves on drying racks. We are sitting
on sheaves that have been thrown down: Foma, the top sergeant, I, and Klim with a large kerosene lamp in his hands,
from which shadows resembling huge birds appeared under the roof. It was not possible to smoke, and that produced gloominess.

"In regard to junk dealing, many of our commanders
didn't miss an opportunity!" the top sergeant said grimly.

He said it and looked around: Behind us, likewise in the
light of a large kerosene lamp, Kashirin was conducting a
political discussion. I could not see but guessed that he was
waving a box of matches that he held in his hand—the
birds in the drying racks began to flutter their wings.

"Our Soviet matches!" he proclaimed. "What a trifling
amount we pay for them at home. But have you noticed
how much they get for matches here? How many times
dearer they are here? Eh? I ask you, can a poor individual
peasant avoid thinking twice before striking every match?
Eh? What do you say?"

"Lebedev-Kumach, the singer," continued the top sergeant after a pause, "came to Lida with the divisional orchestra. Anyway, I was told that he nearly filled a one-and-
a-half-ton truck with lengths of cloth—cheviot, drap,
serge, and castor . . ."

"Stop!" Foma suddenly became animated and, wrinkling

his forehead, moved his lips. "Just a minute! I'll have it for
you right away . . . Listen:

> Beat hard the drum. Call out the watch!
> Now sing a mournful dirge!
> Our poet Lebedev-Kumach
> Has become Lebedev-Serge!"

5. Night in Dunilovichi

I preserve here the genuine name of this hamlet, not quite
a village or a settlement—I did not have time to look
around, or to find out about it later, but it impressed itself
so much on my memory that to replace the name would be
like deceiving oneself.

We found our way there when night was falling, worn
out by the hurried march in overcoats soaked by a drizzle,
and more than that by nervousness driven into us by the
command. "What does a fighting man do, on duty at a sentry post, if he sees a figure approaching from the front?"
the *politruks* kept asking at halts. The equipment with
which we were burdened pulled us toward the ground; we
had to sit in slush; a thin rain slanted against us; bluish twilight crept up around the flanks. "The devil take it!" I
thought. "On both sides of us there are other units of ours,
patrols are combing the places between us and the forward
area. Why all this incitement of fear? Is the command conducting war games with us? Or simply yielding to the incredibly stupid pressure of our political nursemaids?"

"We are traveling a historic road!" Kashirin, walking
alongside, raised our morale. "Of Jeremiah Wishniewski, a
Polish baron, gonfalons have gone along here, and the cossacks of Bogdan Khmelnitsky from the Ukraine. The sev-
enteenth century! . . . And, of course, our own regiments
moved westward more than once."

"Correct, they did move," I thought, noting to myself
this lore acquired from Senkevich's novels. "But could a
Russian army have really moved at some time or other with
such caution, so disgustingly timidly?"

We stopped here toward evening, as has been said, and
bivouacked hastily in order to get settled before dark; the

staff in the town hall and the platoon next door, in a shed; the guard and machine guns along a wall, facing the traffic. Around us the gardens and—farther off—the hills darkened. The village night was total and impenetrable, as if everything surrounding us had been dipped in ink. Extinguishing the lamp, I observed through the gates of the shed, however, that the horizon was marked by a whitish streak above the hills; below it lights glowed—the companies were settling down for the night—and then went out.

Later the rain stopped, the black clouds dispersed, the sky grew silky, and in the light fissures a few stars twinkled. I wanted very much to suspend the moon above the space that had suddenly appeared, but it was nowhere to be seen. I even went out to look for it on the other side of the town hall. My machine-gunners, sheltered in waterproof tents, snored together, and it seemed as if the machine guns under the covers also snored in concert with them.

There was no moon on the other side either; a neighing faintly drifted over from the gardens—I had placed four wagons and the horses there. Klim was already running toward me from over there, completely shaken and almost crying: Pannochka, it turned out, had cast a shoe on her right front foot, and it was absolutely impossible to do anything before a long halt. "I led her on three marches over a dirt road, Comrade Lieutenant, I'm dead tired myself, possibly I'll ride farther."

Night. Distant neighing. Klim. Pannochka . . . If I were writing something that was less of a documentary, I would certainly play up the whole thing. And invent a dream.

But there was no dream, there was only some drowsy sequence when I returned to the shed: the square, mouse-colored frame of the gates, with a starry fissure above—and a gap into nowhere; again the gates before my eyes—and again the gap; gates—gap . . . And in the last gap—this was long after midnight, as I determined later—suddenly there came a shot, accompanied by an echo, spreading in a circle as if drawn by compasses, that cut through the surrounding darkness. After that, in a spurt, there was a whole cluster of shots, distant and near, hollow and sharp —as though in the night someone had shaken firecrackers out of a sack and they were exploding all around us at random. Next came a crash on the floor, the banging of doors thrown wide open, and a panicky "Stop firing!" and "Where are you, son-of-a-bitch . . . with the lamp!"— a pounding of feet on the road, and a tumbling of bodies into the deep ditches on both sides.

I recalled later that in the last war tracer bullets helped to determine where you were being attacked in the inky night; just now they whistled away blindly.

The covers were stripped off the machine guns. The platoon was in a defensive position facing west. Everything had been done according to logic and by the manual, and yet wholly absurdly: Ahead, along the road, I knew, were our medical unit and the band section. Ahead there was haze, and while you looked, live shadows grew dense and seemed to move. But your own people were also there!

Sometimes the shots ceased, sometimes they crackled again in volleys as if crossing over from one side to the other; it might appear that we were surrounded! Yet on our flanks there were also our own people.

"Zoom" . . . "zoom" . . . Two bullets sang by, and still another pinged into the machine-gun shield, ricocheting above my head. There were pings from our side, and it dawned on me: This is panic! We're shooting at one another!

"Maybe I should fire a round, Comrade Lieutenant?" A machine-gunner turns to me.

"At whom? Do you see the enemy?"

Again a bullet, and one of my flankers, unable to bear the tension, presses the trigger. A shot.

"Don't fire!" I yell, becoming furious.

"Who's ordering not to fire?" A voice shrilly asks from the road. "That's demoralization!"

"And who are you?" I ask.

"The *politruk* of the first company."

"Then go to your company, don't babble around here!"

"I'll report you tomorrow to the regimental commander."

"I'm going to report *you*."

The following day, after a hastily convened party meeting, this *politruk*, still young and awkward, came to me to apologize.

Right now, however, Grishin, the regimental commissar,

comes up from the rear. I am well disposed toward him—he possesses enviable integrity and an almost friendly tact.

"Well, what's the situation with you here?" he says, and, listening to my report, sits on a raincoat next to me.

I report to him about the bullets from the rear and in regard to the panic, but I see that he knows all of this already without hearing it from me.

"We'll establish liaison with the battalions," he says, becoming briefly silent, "but the fire is heaviest along the road; until we can see, don't send anyone."

"Oh-h-h . . ." a voice calls from the ditch, and a little later, hoarsely: "First aid!" Then another "Ah-h!" and the clatter of a falling rifle. From behind, beyond the gardens, where our stables are, an explosion resounds and shrill neighs come from several equine throats. Shouts are heard from there. We both prick up our ears. "Medic! Medic!" I make out. Isn't it Klim? . . .

"Something has happened in the transportation unit. Maybe I should send someone to see what's up? The rear areas are not so dangerous."

"Go ahead!"

I call Ryabov, the runner. "But you must only crawl!" I tell him, and he dives into the darkness.

The groans from the ditch subside, perhaps the man is bleeding heavily. But it is as if time has been frozen.

"An hour until dawn!" Grishin gets up. "Report if there is anything unusual!"

And he goes away. Ryabov still does not come back. While waiting for him, I fidget, at the same time trying to shake the water off my shoulders, and think that if Foma or even Kashirin were here, I would run down to the staff to warm myself and get a smoke. Unexpectedly it begins to grow light. On the hazy shroud before my eyes a network of naked branches becomes revealed; beneath it there are the trunks of elms at the roadside. A little later the road, with a descent and a slight bend, can be detected. Above this bend someone traces a roof, a gate with a wicket, and a little bridge over the ditch, with hardly distinguishable india ink. . . .

The shooting imperceptibly ends. All around there is the still unawakening gray coldness, without the predawn chirping of birds and crowing of roosters.

There are footsteps behind me—again it is Grishin with his runner and the pink eye of a cigarette in his hand.

"You may smoke!" he announces, and a joyous movement goes along the line. I fill my pipe too.

"I'll go with you to the medical unit, Lieutenant." He says this simply, but we discern a challenge in his voice: not to me—am I not afraid?—but to all of those around him who had just shaken off their panic.

"Take my place, Sergeant!"

We have only begun to walk when something bangs up ahead—the small wicket of the house on the curve—and a small figure runs across the bridge and goes down the road. An old man. A tuft of beard shows white over a fluttering dark robe.

A shot. The old man falls and, rolling over several times, stiffens at the side of the road.

"Don't shoot!" I yell as loud as I can. "Don't shoot, I tell you! . . ."

I reinforce this by leveling a semiautomatic, perhaps for the first time in my life, but the compulsion to add weight to my command is irresistible and in a strange way gives me courage. Probably not only me.

"Well, well, Lieutenant!" says Grishin. "Let's get going!"

We walk along the road past the body of the old man at the side, now resembling a pool of black oil, and—as we are going straight on—another unexpected and surprising incident happens to us.

Like a monkey, a soldier without a garrison cap, in a tattered overcoat, suddenly scrambles out of the ditch ahead and, not even straightening up, crawls over on all fours and throws himself at our feet.

"*Pan* Officer . . ." he mutters in a choked voice, mixing, as if in a bowl, Russian-Ukrainian and Polish words. "*Pan* Officer, I am no Communist, I'm an enemy of the Soviets, of Stalin, that cruel dog. Don't let me be shot, noble sir, I'm not—"

"Are you drunk?" I say.

"Silence, Lieutenant." Grishin cuts me off and, with distaste, pulls the hem of his overcoat out of the soldier's clutching fingers. "So you're an enemy?"

"Yes . . . yes . . ." The soldier nods and suddenly becomes paralyzed, turning his face up at us. Even now I cannot recall without a shudder that chalky face, with the black hole of his mouth, distorted by a surmise.

"Where is your rifle, former soldier of the Red Army?"

"In the ditch, *pan*—comrade . . ."

"Show us!"

The rifle really is at the bottom of the ditch, half-submerged in the brown water. "Get it!" Grishin says to his orderly, nodding at it. "And take this one to the staff. Guard him until I return."

We walk for a while in silence. Not far from the medical unit two corpsmen come toward us with a stretcher.

"On the double!" the commissar orders them. "You have to mobilize everybody there completely. And send a section to help them. Search all around there personally. I'm afraid that there are a lot of wounded!"

"Thirteen!" the first sergeant reported to me, with a list in his hand where he was recording the wounded, when, about forty minutes later, I returned to the medical unit. "We're taking them to the medical battalion!" A Ford one-and-a-half-ton truck with a bloodstained side thrown open stood nearby. I tried to avoid turning my gaze toward what was in the truck. "There are also dead. . . ." the first sergeant added in a low voice.

The Ford was already moving off when Klim came running up, out of breath and almost beside himself. "Ryabov!" he cried out already from a distance. "Ryabov has been wounded! There, in the gardens!"

I took with me medical corpsmen with a stretcher.

Ryabov lay on his back, stretched out full length at the wall—the garden vegetation next to him nearly hid him from view. I bent over: The wound was in the stomach, the bullet had torn up the cartridge pouch. I carefully touched the lacerated leather corner. A crimson stain was spreading below, bloodying my fingers.

He opened his eyes to look at me:

"I carried out your order, Comrade Lieutenant . . ." he said, almost soundlessly moving his lips. "Now, well . . . it's the end . . ."

"Not at all. It hit the cartridge pouch, so the wound isn't deep. They'll fix you up at the medical battalion!"

They carried him off, but Klim stood there rigidly, hands

dropped at his sides. then he abruptly walked up to me, his lower jaw quivering.

"Comrade Lieutenant, I was the one—I did it to him . . ."

"What kind of nonsense is that?"

"It's not nonsense. By no means. I was the one! . . . Precisely when the commissar pulled the pin of the grenade, I saw—"

"Stop! What commissar?"

"Ours, Kashirin. When it began, he came to us at once. He thought about getting farther away from the firing. He ran up—and immediately went beyond the shed: 'Going to take a leak!' he said. The boys said later that his hands were shaking, he couldn't take his own—excuse me—penis out of his pants. And when we were being hit, he threw a grenade, wherever he got it from. Then he chased all the horses. And I imagined: It's an attack! I noticed that someone was rushing at us, all bent over. So I picked him off. . . . It was him—Ryabov . . ."

"Stop that! A stray bullet came in, it wasn't yours at all."

"No, Comrade Lieutenant, it was mine!"

"Get it out of your head. And don't say a word to anyone. That's an order! There are no guilty ones in such a panic. Understood?"

"Understood, Comrade Lieutenant."

An hour later we went on our way.

Beyond the outskirts, on the road, a soldier's felt boots protruded from a waterproof sheet covering a body. They were persistently directed toward us with soles washed clean by dew, as in some battle scene by Vereshchagin, it seemed. They were like a question, those boots that belatedly remained to be taken off. "What about us?" they asked. "Why us? And there are no guilty ones?"

6. Podlipki

What thoughts, completely out of tune with place and time, overcame me when we were billeted on this estate! I believe that the great shamans of regimented societies, putting to death suspect grandfathers and grandmothers and

—in droves—their descendants, are partly right in their watchfulness: The spirit that developed of old suddenly takes hold and comes to life anew.

It came to life in me: This noble estate very much resembled the one on which I was born.

That one of mine was in no sense "hostile," it belonged to a member of the People's Will, it sheltered other subversives, even Ilyich's[2] brother Alexander Ulyanov was among them. But it was filled with such an all-pervading romance of antiquity and ease, avenues of linden trees and terraces with balustrades, faded ancestral images and creaking garrets, that class-consciousness remained somewhere in the background there.

Here there was also an avenue of lindens. Dense and dark like a tunnel: Bare branches were interlaced over the heads of Kashirin and myself when we went to billet the staff, but in my imagination they immediately became clothed, sprouted leaves, and exuded the scent of honeyed flowers. Only in my imagination—right now nothing existed here but silence and haziness, while a draft blew hard against our backs.

It blew us right up to the pedimented façade, to a portico of six pillars, almost in Bazhenov's semiclassical style around Moscow, from which, it seemed to me, just now there came something that sounded like "Did you hear?" and it smelled of strawberry jam poured into a shining copper pan.

"A nest of vipers!" said Kashirin. "The whole family ran off to the West. In the house, I've been told, there are only an old woman housekeeper and a young housemaid."

And it really was a nest, still preserving here and there the warmth of suddenly startled life—a small book with a bookmark on the smoking-table, a confusion in the cupboards, and, in a hall with a double row of windows, a cashmere shawl thrown down beside a bust of Chopin on a rosewood harpsichord.

"We'll have our Red Corner here," Kashirin declared, observing the waxed floor, mirrors in the corners, and scrolled backs of Louis ——teenth chairs along the walls. "Let's get rid of that doll of the Polish gentry. Who is it?"

[2]Lenin, referred to familiarly by his patronymic, or middle name. —ED.

"Chopin, the composer."

"All right, if it's Chopin."

It was a very spacious house with rooms in two rows as houses were built at one time: formal rooms and family ones. A double staircase led to the family rooms from the entrance hall.

"We three will be in the garret—O.K.? And check the attic to see if the reptiles have hidden arms anywhere."

He received a severe reprimand through party channels for his grenade, as I learned from Foma, and now, as Foma expressed it, Kashirin was trying in every way to put on a show for the command, in the area of everyday well-being and extra food beyond the official ration.

Jumping ahead, I'll say that those eight days of our life in Podlipki were like being in a rest home.

Klim, who was now my orderly, relieved me of the cares of purchasing and established good relations with Madame Yadza, the elderly housekeeper, with her supplies in cellars and storerooms, and brought her a cook from our platoon to work in the kitchen. Our table compared favorably with that of the Metropole Hotel.

The laurels, that is the command's approval, were presented for some reason to me—to Kashirin's secret annoyance. I do not know why, but he behaved toward me very inconsistently: At one moment he clapped me on the shoulder and even confided secrets to me ("You know, you've been recommended for a medal because you didn't lose your head there, in Dunilovichi, but the divisional commander sent someone else to his mother—he said she should award him a medal for panic!"), at another he looked askance at me as if I had concealed a gun in my bosom.

About guns, incidentally: He dragged me along after all to check the garret, but, not finding bombs or machine guns, he got caught up in piles of old clothes—a veritable Klondike of consumer items covering several generations.

I stood to one side, escaping the dust and smell of camphor balls, when he came over, holding in his hands two pairs of slightly shriveled ladies' shoes and with something green and sparkling over his shoulder.

"I found this, we'll share it. One pair is yours."

"No, I don't need it."

"Are you squeamish?"

"It's not that. . . . There's simply no one to whom I can give it."

"All right, I'll take it myself. And the classy curtains, you understand. The moths will eat them in any case. Eh? What do you think?"

"Certainly," I said.

But that's enough about Kashirin. The real hero of the subsequent story I am writing is Klim.

He did not fail to provide Pannochka with the good things of life, of course, and put her up in the carriage house, and in her feedbag there was always the best selected oats.

I reprimanded him for the carriage house—it was too close to the staff.

"The major came to our Pannochka. He stared, touched her . . . What does he want?"

"That's why he came, because it's next door."

The major did not leave me alone either—after supper he stopped me at the table and said with bristling mustache, although still good-natured:

"Well, what are you going to do with that filly? You are our guest, after all. I would take care of her properly. You'll give her to me, won't you? . . . If you are forced to ride somewhere, I'll send you my Shamil, although you're not authorized to have a horse."

"On no account!" I was accosted in the corridor by Grishin, who had overheard the conversation. "Don't give it up for anything! It's your prize! I'll support you. And that's what's meant by 'guest'? We'll go and send you to the Frunze Academy. And who will know at all what to expect in advance?"

In the coach house I had a portentous conversation with Klim.

Pannochka had just gobbled her oats, and on a nail nearby Klim hung the feedbag, embroidered on the edges with a red cross, that he had "appropriated" somewhere for her. Now she waited, breathing warmly on my hands with her suede nostrils, wanting me to give her sugar.

"I wished to ask you, Comrade Lieutenant," Klim began suddenly, glancing toward the gate. "We have just been given orders: Not one step away from our positions, no talking to local people, not to speak of going into their houses. Why is that?"

"We're on a military campaign, Klim. Not at home."

"But we're not fighting with local people. It is only seven kilometers in all back to Vilnius, across the border. Many of the commanders go there, but our top sergeant made a request yesterday and was turned down. The people around here, it is said, also travel freely all the time to Lithuania, without any hindrance. But now our patrols stop them, search for something, and sometimes turn them right back. People resent it very much. What are we apprehensive about? Are we breeding fear in ourselves? Recently in Dunilovichi—"

"Let's drop it, Klim. There's an order from above and it's not for us to judge."

"From the very highest level?"

"Exactly."

"Well, it's rightly said," he said slowly, as if speaking to himself, "'A regime of usurpers fears everything'!"

"Squad Leader Klimov!"

"At your service, Comrade Lieutenant!"

"Think over your proverbs before you speak."

"Yes, sir—I'll think them over!"

He stood at attention, responding, but in his eyes—I saw —the imps danced and laughed. "I wish to report something else to you," he said, stopping me at the threshold. "About my zeroing in . . ."

"What is that now? What zeroing in?"

"Well—as, for example, a setter points at a snipe or a woodcock, when it is discovered."

"What did you discover?"

"You've seen Madame Yadza's housemaid? The young-looking one?" he asked in a muffled voice, again looking around in a conspiratorial manner.

"I saw her. So?"

"Well, she's not a housemaid at all, but the daughter of the man who owns the estate. Pannochka!"

"Who told you?"

"She herself told me. That is, I heard it first from Madame Yadza. The old lady has always opened up her heart to me. And, you know, what a story! Just when they were about to flee from us, she had a heart attack—she has heart disease. Her mother is dead; the father—he is a colonel of theirs—ordered her to get in the carriage, but the doctor said she'll die before she gets to the border if you start out. So she was left in the care of the old woman."

"Well?"

"What's the 'well,' Comrade Lieutenant?"

"All of that's fascinating, but what business is it of ours?"

"It's also our business, Comrade Lieutenant. We have to help!"

He articulated the last words, drawing them out, with eyes that transfixed me, and instantly hurried on, fearing I would interrupt him:

"Well, you know, Comrade Lieutenant, we are the first ones here, a week only, and I'm afraid that the special types and others are coming. . . . Do you think they'll leave her alone? She will disappear, you know! And Kashirin already, Madame Yadza said, came, nosed around, and asked questions, writing down the answers— Who is the owner of the estate, what is his military unit, who else are members of the family, and you know the rest! . . ."

"I know, but I can't do anything."

"Just meet with her, with the young lady, her name is Marysya, talk to her yourself. There is one plan to help. You'll just go to Madame Yadza before retreat as always— to talk about tomorrow's menu or provisions. So at eight sharp . . . Comrade Lieutenant, really! . . ."

Now, recalling this episode, which would have made a good detective story or a tale of Bestuzhev-Marlinsky, I study it under a magnifying glass in the present light, but it is true that I have difficulty in saying how I viewed it some thirty years ago. It seems that I swore like a trooper at Klim and felt a landslide under my feet. . . . Go? . . . Not go? . . . Twice that day I saw Marysya, round-shouldered, in a quilted jacket, with something like a *povoinik*[3] head-dress. Stamping in her boots, she cleared the dishes from the table. There was no nobility, and even youth was missing from her sallow face with tightly pursed lips. Hadn't Klim imagined all of this? Wasn't he lying?

---

[3] A large scarf worn over the head and shoulders by older women. —TRANS.

When, at eight o'clock on the dot, I knocked at Madame Yadza's door (two tiny rooms in the garret across from the room that I shared with Foma and Kashirin), I already realized, by the very solemnity of the gazes directed at me by her and Klim, that the audience would take place. Madame Yadza instantly tapped lightly on the adjacent door, and then we expectantly looked for a long time at this narrow door, resembling a garret trapdoor—so long that I was again not myself and became annoyed with Klim; true, at just this time some party conference was going on in the Red Corner, in the hall, so that it was unlikely that Kashirin could have reported us, but this enforced conspiracy still irritated me.

Finally the door opened and Marysya came in.

More accurately, that which was Marysya in my imagination in the form of the headdress, gray cheeks, quilted jacket, and thumping boots remained apparently behind the garret door; the person who came in was utterly surprising and charming—"I understood that from the first glance as one understands lightning," to recollect Chekhov's lines. I will not undertake to describe her so as not to get mired down in clichés. I'll say only that under my dumbfounded and probably enraptured gaze a quick blush spread over her cheeks, from which the gray smear had been washed away, and flamed on the cheekbones so much that I wondered if she had a fever. Was this an aftereffect of her illness? . . . Something also ignited pity and a sudden capacity for any plot in me.

"*Pan nie mówi po polsku?*" (Can't you speak Polish, sir?) she asked. "*Może po francusku albo po niemiecku?*" (Can you speak French or German?)

I chose German.

"Madame Yadza told you about me . . ." she began, slightly stammering, clasping and unclasping her slender hands. "And I have heard—about you, that I can—can trust you, that perhaps you will advise what to do . . ."

She told me her story, which I had already heard from Klim, and how unhappy she was now, remaining alone, and how much the future frightened her, and asking what, for God's sake, could she do?

"I'm very afraid of your army, your soldiers . . . Maybe without reason, I see that they are not at all ogres, but . . . how should I behave? How can I be reunited with my own people? Can I appeal to one of your commanding officers? And—how? Reveal my identity or continue this masquerade?"

"You can't reveal your identity. I think that you also cannot remain here."

"Is it dangerous?"

"Today or tomorrow—no. Later, however, another command, other people will appear. They will take a closer interest in things. . . . In short, you must go away!"

"But—how, for God's sake? . . . The border nearby is closed for the Polish population. Directly west there are the Germans—you know that. Where am I to go? Jesus, Maria . . ."

Klim intervened during this interval of despair exactly as if he understood every word, once again with some sort of aspirated preceptorial emphasis in his voice. For the first time there was suddenly revealed to me the richness of nature of this horseman, potential horse thief, procurer, rescuer of drowning people, and schemer.

"I reported recently to our commissar Kashirin," he said, "that all the extra provisions we obtained from Madame Yadza have run out: There are neither fats, nor any sausage products, nor ham, nor cheeses, the mustard and all that are gone completely. What is there to give the command as a treat? The local landowners always went to Vilnius for cheeses and ham. They know a delicatessen there, have charge accounts and credit. So I assume, Comrade Lieutenant, that if you wrote out a pass from our staff for Madame Yadza on the morrow, she and Marysya could run over there. Just a pass so that our patrols would not stop them—and that's all. And Marysya would stay there."

The plan was simply brilliant and did not evoke any discussion. I remember that there was not time for it—the tramping of boots could be heard downstairs: The Party meeting had ended. I still remember those eyes that transfixed me to the floor, and the whisper in Polish: "May God bless you for your help!"

Everything thereafter was also simple. "Beautiful!" rejoiced Kashirin when I carelessly told him about the delicacies and the pass to Vilnius. "Right away—I'll organize everything and give it to them in a jiffy. Let them take off tomorrow. At daybreak."

Nevertheless, I breathed a sigh of relief when the next day, after noon, we received the order to move on.

Now we moved backward, to the southeast.

When I draw on a map our curving line of march, it looks like a lance: from Lida to the northwest nearly as far as Vilnius, from the Vilnius region toward Molodechno as far as the hamlet M., about which I have already written above.

When I recall the curve of our mental ebb and flow, however, I see Madame Yadza's tiny garret room, and in it, the transfigured Marysya, the second Polish maiden of my story. That image long accompanied me on the march from Podlipki; one day I also dreamt about this in a half-sleep when we were spending the night in some adjourned school with mice rustling behind the wallpaper. I dreamt about it as an extension of something unusually attractive and irreversible. It was as if I went out at night into the corridor, half-lit and creaking, with the door that led to Madame Yadza, and waited and waited . . . And as if the door opened and there appeared a figure muffled, head and all, in a dark cloak, like some medieval duenna; but that was not a duenna, the capuche was thrown back, and before me there were cheeks of alabaster pallor and great eyes blazing with anger. "What are you waiting for?" she asked, breathlessly. "I wished you happiness for your help, but you are a cruel enemy! You and your horde of wolves invading my land, plunging a knife into my country's back! I hate you!" . . . She was very beautiful in her anger! I wanted to object to this, but she immediately dissolved into the semidarkness like a cloud. Then I woke up and lay there a long time with this "very beautiful!" in my thoughts and—as frequently happened with me due to an overabundance of various literary quotations—I suddenly recollected something from Mickiewicz: *"Bo nad wszystkich ziem branki milsze Laszki kochanki, Wesolutkie jak mlode koteczki,"* which Pushkin translated as follows:

There is not in the world a czarina more beautiful
than a Polish maiden.
Gay as a kitten by the stove.
No, that was not gay.
And, probably, never will be.
But then, who will be? . . .

Later I thought (or perhaps not then at all, but now, as I
write): Am I not attributing too much significance to
events?

Somewhere in Pasternak it is said: "Life is symbolic because it is significant."

Were the things we experienced in this campaign significant? That about which I am telling?

It appears that it is significant, because, you see, behind
every human aspect, every act, and every incident there is
a certain unacknowledged fate. Aspect, act, incident—
mysteriously projected into all three phases of time. Into
the present? Certainly into the present as well, for how
could you understand it, the present, without this secret
and symbolic projection?

Let us jump now to the hamlet M., however, to round out
the story.

7. Again at M., and Denouement

"Lieutenant, my dear, don't refuse! Three of us engineers.
Don't tell me you're not going to try their Polish mead!
Judge for yourself! . . ."

"I can't, Captain. Only I have the key, but it is forbidden
to even stick it in the keyhole. Orders!"

"It's not of national importance, you can get around it.
Just a little jug. . . ."

This was the squab of a captain from the company of engineers, the one already known to us, who at one time had
bought stockings for his wife and daughters in Lida. As the
custodian of Czar Nicholas's wine cellar, I had to beat off
such attacks repeatedly. Our stay in M. was filled with minor oddities. The rare, more significant ones I recorded in
my notes. It is worth mentioning some of them now.

The oath of allegiance, for example. Under the effect, probably, of the treason committed by the soldier who had taken Commissar Grishin and me for Polish liberators, orders were issued to determine which of the reservists had not taken the military oath and to rectify this oversight. Amid the garden plots a lectern painted red had been set up and some slogan was stretched between two poles driven into the earth. In the face of this slogan and a solemn Kashirin, who conducted the ceremony, those taking the oath read the text. It was sunny, and the ground, frozen by a November frost, had slightly thawed; it smelled of outhouses, and rooks that for some reason had not yet left for a warmer clime croaked loudly. . . .

The second oddity was the trial of that same traitor: by all the rules, with the regiment drawn up in a rectangle open on one side, a prosecutor, and members of the tribunal. Sentence: "Death by shooting," after which the criminal, without a garrison cap and belt, delivered a last word that amounted to complete nonsense, and then he was placed in the cab of a truck and driven away.

"Will he really be shot?" I asked Grishin.

"Hardly, he'll be sent to a camp."

But let us come closer to the denouement of our narrative.

It began to take shape on one of the last days of this most abominable month in those parts, in the form of an orderly from the chief of staff.

"There is a summons for you, Comrade Lieutenant."

Only yesterday, to my annoyance, I met the major when I rode Pannochka beyond the outskirts, and I had the impression that he was lying in wait for me, because otherwise there would have been nothing for him to do there. He stood near the last house beside a stand for notices and pretended that he had not seen us, but for some time I felt his gaze boring into my back. Was the summons connected with yesterday's encounter?

I could only partly guess.

"It's an unofficial invitation, the conversation will be of a private nature," declared the major, seated behind a desk, without inviting me, however, to sit down. "I should not tell you, but I hope that this will go no further, and make it a condition as well! An order has been received by the staff

of the corps concerning the demobilization of reserve officers who are scientists and scholars. It directly concerns
you. What are you going to say?" He turned the red bristle
of his mustache toward me.

"Orders are orders!" I said somewhat irrelevantly.

"Exactly. For a week, I suppose, they'll be busy making
up lists before it gets down to us, but then—you'll be
headed home. Wel-l . . ." He fell silent for a moment.
"About your filly. You can't take her with you. When you
depart, you can leave her with the others in the transportation unit or give her to *sovkhozniks* to replace horses that
were drafted, and she'll carry sacks of cabbages. But with
me she'll be ridden and be well cared for. In my opinion,
there's nothing to think about very long: give her to me—
and that'll be the end of it."

There really was not much to think about, but I was still
greatly taken by surprise.

"Good," I said, "we'll do it in a day or two."

"No, not in a day or two, but without delay, today. We'll
get it in writing before your departure. Take into account
that you may perhaps leave in a hurry, three minutes to
assemble—you won't have time even to say goodbye to
anyone."

"All right, let's make it today."

For several seconds he sought for words but could not
find any. Then, beginning to blink:

"I'll send you my Shamil so that you won't be bored, after all, without rides. But back there in civilian life we'll
probably meet. Come by sometime."

We shook hands and I went back to my place.

But then . . . Oh!

He came running to me only a half hour later, Klim, with
chalky face and trembling lips. It was fortunate that I was
alone at home.

"Did you give away Pannochka?" he asked in a half
shout, and he made that "give away" sound like "sell out,"
"betray," or "ruin."

"Sit down, Klim, and listen, I'll explain it to you."

He sat down guardedly and expectantly, but as I told him
about my conversation with the major he somehow shrank
before my eyes; toward the end he even interrupted me,
abruptly jerked up his head:

"Lord! Think of the thirty or more kilometers I led her over the furrows and stubble when she threw a shoe . . ."

He turned his face aside and sobbed.

"If we were demobilized together, Klim," I said after a pause, "I would give Pannochka only to you."

"You would give her?" He grew animated. "I would pay. . . . Payment for life."

"I would give her without payment. So now you see: It's impossible."

"Well, what *is* possible now, Comrade Lieutenant?"

Again there was a pause. A deep breath. Then:

"The major sent over his gelding in exchange. He himself sits on it, the old hand, like a cock on a fence. What is to be done with that couch?"

"Leave it for now. I'll see later. . . ."

The parting came sooner than the major had predicted—about three days later. But exactly as he had predicted, in a big rush: A divisional truck came to pick us up. I only had time to bid farewell to the staff and Kashirin. Foma was demobilized together with me.

Inside the truck it was crowded and shook devilishly; I could not shake off my disappointment, however, that I had not said goodbye to the two main protagonists of this story of mine.

This disappointment also plagued me on the troop train, which was unexpectedly long and jammed; nevertheless, in our car, which was, as usual, of the cattle variety, Foma and I found ourselves on commanders' plank beds.

Foma was blissful because he was going home and his ulcer had not been bothering him, and he blissfully listened to the clicking of the wheels, illustrating the rhythm with poetry. He gave me a whole lecture about prosody, assuring me that in Russian verse the most important thing of all was not iamb-trochee but' paeon. "Tonic structure, you see, that's how it is tapped out—listen: Ta-ta-ta-tá . . . ta-ta-ta-tá—the fourth paeon, as in Blok: '*I strannoi blizost'yu zakovanny, Glyazhu za temnuyu vual', I vizhu bereg ocharovanny, I ocharovannuyu dal . . .*'" (And shackled by a singular proximity, I look through the dark veil, And see the shore of enchantment, And the enchanted distance . . .)

I was not listening very much; behind my own en-

chanted veil there was visible to me everything I had just
left and, turned away from me to one side, Klim's cheek,
down which tears were probably still rolling.

Klim was quite ill-at-ease the last three days after my betrayal, and, like a jealous lover, watched every step of the
major touching Pannochka. "He is lunging her!" He came
running to me one day, sticking out his tongue. "He has
gone completely mad! What is she—an unbroken filly?"

The next day, which was sunny and frosty, I returned
with him after my attempt to ride the major's gelding—
huge, with protruding thigh bones and a jolting, powerful
stride. ("If you ride him, you'll have to learn afterward
how to walk, yourself, Comrade Lieutenant.") And suddenly we saw:

Behind the headquarters, on a vacant lot, which had just
been cleared of weeds and rubbish and sprinkled here and
there with sand, the major circled on Pannochka at a trot.
Her whole bearing in this unhurried circling, which
seemed to be on a stage, was jewellike and sunny: the
rounded set of small ringing hoofs, the steep inclination of
the head under an unnecessary restricting martingale, and
the brilliant luster of her satin coat.

"Look, look, how he's easing up! You know, he's hurting
her, the disgusting fellow!" sighed Klim.

Our military train barely moved along, stuck for hours
on sidings and in cul-de-sacs. Around us there alternately
drifted by forest translucence and the whitish emptiness of
fields; sometimes they did not drift at all but remained
stock-still for a long time, depressing us through the monotony and the persistence with which our approach to
home was being delayed. On the first day, Foma and I still
counted the stations and kilometers, but on the second our
snail's pace subdued us—toward evening we turned over
on our sides on the plank beds, tossing and turning and
trying to sleep—there was no light in the freight car, you
are not going to read!

Therefore, when the train, running back and forth and
clanking its buffers for the last time, came to a stop and
some voice called out "Mozhaisk!" it was as if we had been
sent flying from our seats.

Mozhaisk!

That was almost home, three hours from Moscow if the train stopped at every station; or if the train did not stop and went at full speed, it would be nearly two hours!

"Mozhaisk!" One of our fellow travelers was already speaking up. "They'll put us on a siding, you'll see, we'll stand there until morning. Give us your canteens, Comrade Commanders, and we'll get some hot water."

"Thanks, we'll go ourselves."

Mozhaisk! That sounded to me not only like the Moscow region but welcomed me like a relative: At one time I lived here in a *dacha* about an hour and a half on foot from the station to the confluence of the Moscow River with some small stream—I don't remember the name. One went through a pine forest that smelled, not just in a literary sense but in reality, of "resin and wild strawberries," passing the dacha of the well-known artist K., beyond which one soon came to my little hut on a sandy shore.

Mozhaisk appeared on the suburban timetable. Right now the time was almost eight. One of the suburban trains to Moscow that I used to take left at exactly eight in the evening. An idea!

Nearly racing each other, falling over the switches, we ran to the station. "Hot water is over there, by the last door!" one of our fellow travelers yelled from the platform. Who cares about hot water! We want the suburban train. Incredible as it seemed, it was on the first track. The train sign read: "Mozhaisk-Moscow."

A few minutes—and, fully out of breath, with suitcases, we were on board.

An illuminated passenger car. Varnished, comfortable contour seats. Nets overhead for the suitcases. And almost nobody else—spacious! Only someone who has never been released from long military service (not to speak of imprisonment), only such a person would not know this rapture and sense of freedom. Foma was more sentimental than I, and, really and truly, his eyes now became moist.

All of a sudden:

"Comrade Commanders, please leave the car!"

A rifle, a flashlight in hand, a red armband above the elbow. Evidently a top sergeant, on duty, probably for the commandant's office. He saluted with his free arm, but his face and voice were determined.

"What rubbish is this? Why should we leave?"

"It is forbidden to anyone from a troop train. Orders!"

"Nonsense!"

"I'll be obliged to hold up the train. And then, Comrade Commanders, we'll have to go to the commandant's office."

"But that's absurd!"

"Orders!"

"Let's go!" said Foma, and we took our suitcases out of the racks. From the platform we went to the opposite side, where the troop train was standing. The duty officer sent a salute after us and, once the darkness had swallowed us up, went off along the platform. Stopping, we observed how his flashlight receded behind the wheels.

Then, without any spoken agreement, we returned to the passenger train and sat by the car on our suitcases. Only a few minutes were left until departure, but as a precaution we had to wait.

"An idiotic order!" said Foma. "And how ridiculous—if you told somebody about it, he wouldn't believe it: two lieutenants of the Soviet Army—one an assistant professor, the other a poet and publisher—hide like rabbits under a car because they are forbidden to ride on the train they want to take. Again that defensiveness, stupid vigilance, fear. The question arises: Why?"

I recalled Klim with the same train of thought.

"'A regime of usurpers fears everything,'" I quoted from folklore.

Only someone hidden behind the wheels could have heard us, but Foma still looked around, for that "regime of usurpers" went pretty far even for him.

"Babble!" he muttered. "Who and when did anyone receive power as a gift, on a platter? Cromwell? Napoleon? Francisco Franco? From whom was it usurped and for what?—that's the question! But wait—it looks as if we're starting. . . ."

Several pairs of eyes regarded our return to the car with such animation (somebody even clapped his hands) that the earlier good humor and rapture descended upon us. I filled my pipe and started to smoke. Foma unfastened the hooks of his overcoat and sat there relaxed, in rapt concentration as if rhyming a sonnet. Lowering his eyelids, he moved his lips—perhaps the most felicitous rhymes now came to him.

We did not speak: Subjects related to our experiences had been filed away in the "hold" basket; we were still ignorant of current events (the most important of them was the newly-begun liberation, this time the Finnish one), and all of them had been totally driven out by one thing alone— early arrival in Moscow!

Both of us, Foma and I, had been born and brought up in Moscow. And so some irresistible force compelled us to leave our seats almost half an hour before we reached the terminal. Nothing was visible in the window except the night and the orange lights at small local stations whirling by in the blackness. Together our years added up to nearly seventy, but, like schoolboys, we pressed our noses against the glass, guessing the places that went flying past and the stops. "We passed Odintsovo!" I said.

Someone flung open the door to the platform—the shrill, impatient rapping of the wheels assaulted our ears. I looked at Foma—wouldn't he begin again to compose lines about this rapping? But no, he was not up to it, he had been wholly captured by his impatience, his haste to get home. The sensation of nearing one's home town is similar to the sensation experienced by a parachutist hanging in the shrouds as he approaches the ground under his feet: Closer, closer, now—now . . . and all one's anticipation is stretched like a string!

"Kuntsevo! It's already Kuntsevo!" cried Foma. . . .

Was It the "Vlasov" Movement?

BY ROMAN DNEPROV

Translated by David Chavchavadze

From *Kontinent* No. XXIII, 1980

I will take it upon myself to say: Our people
would have been worth nothing, would have
been a people of hopeless lackeys, if during that
war it had missed the chance to shake a rifle,
even from afar, at the Stalinist government, if it
had failed at least to shake a fist and curse at the
"dear Father."

—Aleksandr Solzhenitsyn, *Gulag Archipelago*

During the last ten years, and especially after Solzhenitsyn's *Gulag Archipelago* saw the light of day, it has
somehow become customary to call the Liberation Movement during World War II the "Vlasov Movement."
Which, of course, is not only inaccurate in fact, but is also
somewhat of a historical oversimplification.

There are a number of reasons for the sudden appear-

ROMAN DNEPROV (*Ryurik Dudin*) *was born in 1924 in the Ukraine. He re-
ceived his secondary education in Kiev. During World War II he was a
participant in the LMPR, serving in Cossack units. He graduated from
Heidelberg University and received a master's degree in history at Yale
University in the U.S., where he teaches. He writes for a number of
Russian periodicals.*

ance of this name. On the Soviet side this is an obvious
(and rather successful) attempt to pin a contemptuous label
on a movement of many millions and tie it to the name of
one person executed for treason in Moscow on August 1,
1946. It is as if they are saying: There was one principal
traitor and turncoat, and there were a few thousands or
tens of thousands of weak or unprincipled people tempted
by him. Hence the terms "Vlasovism" and "Vlasovites."
These terms are also thoughtlessly repeated by those recent
Soviet citizens who, having made it to the so-called Free
World, do not take the trouble properly to acquaint themselves with the undoubted phenomenon in the history of
our country represented by the Liberation Movement of
the Peoples of Russia (LMPR) during World War II.

At the same time the "Vlasovites" themselves, that is, the
participants of the LMPR and especially of its armed formations of all types and kinds, for completely understandable reasons do not wish to shed this name: The martyr
death of the commander of the armed forces of the Committee for the Liberation of the Peoples of Russia (CLPR)
and of his closest comrades in arms has made the term
"Vlasovite" an honorable name for us. However, most former LMPR participants with whom the author has discussed this subject agree with the historical inaccuracy of
this nomenclature. In this article, limited in length, an attempt will be made to put some things in their proper
place by returning to events which took place more than
thirty-five years ago.

A number of historians of World War II hold the opinion
that Hitler lost his war against Stalin before the beginning
of military operations, at some point between November
10, 1940, and June 22, 1941, that is, between the day when
the possible plan of attack on the Soviet Union, which had
carried the code name "Fritz" until that time, was renamed
"Plan Barbarossa" and the war against the Soviet Union
became a matter of firm decision, and the start of military
operations. These historians (with whom the author
agrees) consider that the 1941–45 war between Germany
and the Soviet Union was lost politically, and that Hitler
forced the Soviet people to defend their oppressors: Stalin
and the Communist Party.

It would seem to be difficult to argue with this, but still most historians have a different opinion and continue to search for the solution of the question in the unexpected halts and bends in the salients of Guderian's Second Tank Army and the incorrectly chosen directions of the main German thrust.

Nobody denies the purely military mistakes of the corporal who came to believe in his historical mission. The completely unnecessary destruction of the German Sixth Army at Stalingrad is sufficient example. But it is impossible to find a document or documents giving the advancing German Army instructions on how to treat the population of the occupied Soviet areas. No such documents exist, and there never were any. There are only delirious or semidelirious conversations of Hitler at his coffee table which have come down to us in memoirs, like those of Albert Speer or the recently published, in third edition, *Hitlers Tischgespräche* (Hitler's Table Talk). These books relate how the leader of the Third Reich, between mouthfuls of cake, foretold the future of Russia, with German knightly castles in the fertile strip with a semiliterate local population, and similar Nazi delights. But we are learning about all this only today. Then, however, in the summer of 1941, let us face it: A large enough percentage of the Soviet population, still remembering the Germans of 1918, having experienced collectivization only ten years before and the Yezhov purge only four years before, awaited the Germans as liberators. This included those Jews who, unwilling to believe Soviet propaganda, refused to flee to the east to an unknown future and paid for this at Babi Yar.

But let us return to the Liberation Movement of the Peoples of Russia.

First of all, this name had a tortured origin. It was born after long arguments with various German organizations, such as, for instance, the East Ministry of Alfred Rosenberg or the Propaganda Ministry of Joseph Goebbels, after discussions with various nationality groups, and finally was accepted by all: the Liberation Movement of the Peoples of Russia and later the CLPR, the Committee for Liberation of the Peoples of Russia. The name was rejected and is still rejected only by the extreme separatists of the type of both Ukrainian OUN's, OUN(R) of Stefan Bandera and OUN(S) of Melnik, as well as by extreme Russian nationalists, to whom not only the term "peoples of Russia" but other similar terms seem some sort of treason to Eternal Russia.

The armed struggle of the LMPR during World War II can be rather accurately divided into three periods.

First Period. From June 22, 1941, to the publication of the so-called "Smolensk Manifesto" of General A. A. Vlasov in the spring of 1943. This period was the longest, most unorganized, and unfortunately remains the least studied.

Second Period. From the spring of 1943 to November 14, 1944, when the "Prague Manifesto" with its fourteen points was adopted in Prague and published. Various historians of the LMPR—mostly foreigners—in examining this period mostly concentrate their attention on the negotiations of A. A. Vlasov and his entourage with various German organizations and their heads. The battles and destruction of separate volunteer units, large and small, both on the Eastern and the Western Fronts, are usually overlooked by these historians.

Third Period. From November 14, 1944, until the capitulation of Germany in May 1945. The writer Irina Saburova in one of her pieces called this time "the tragic fairytale dance of the ROA."[1] It would be difficult to think of a better name for it. This period, partly because of its brevity and partly because by November 1944 the territory on which the LMPR operated was limited to Germany itself, has been the most studied. But in my opinion it is the least interesting period, if only because by that time both the outcome of the whole Second World War and the fate of the LMPR could already be predicted. Although nobody could predict the stupidity and mercilessness of the Western Allies in their attitude toward former Soviet citizens, whether they were participants in the LMPR or simply prisoners of war or "*Ostarbeiter.*"

To these three periods of the LMPR's struggle one should, of course, add an epilogue, the forced repatriation of the leaders of the LMPR and the rank-and-file participants. However, a lot has been written about this, and this subject, in spite of its tragic nature, or maybe precisely because of its tragic nature, does not come within the scope of this article.

[1] Russian Liberation Army.

* * *

It is absolutely impossible to determine when and in which German unit the first volunteer formation of former Soviet military personnel was formed. It is known that in August 1941 a Soviet regiment under the command of a Don Cossack, Major Kononov, went over to the German side and became the basis for a volunteer unit. However, there is reason to think that even before this there occurred instances of small Soviet units going over to the German side, expressing their desire to fight the Bolsheviks, and not being disarmed by the Germans. Such things depended on one or another commander of one or another German division, acting at his own risk. And the risk was not small: In those months the Germans marched eastward as if on a parade ground, took hundreds of thousands of prisoners, and were certain that the end of the war was at hand. The formation of volunteer units easily could have been regarded as lack of faith in the strength of the German Army, with all the resulting administrative consequences.

In the city of Freiburg, West Germany, the military archives of the Federal Republic of Germany are located and contain everything that did not perish during the retreat and did not fall into the hands of Soviet Army units. In Washington, in the American National Archives, there are microfilms of German documents captured by the Allies, including military documents—almost everything contained in the Freiberg military archives.

Only when you spend a few weeks working in one of these archives (and the author of this article has worked in both) does the enormous scope of the volunteer movement in the first two years of the Soviet-German war become clear. Literally in every German division on the Eastern Front there was a minimum of one and sometimes several volunteer battalions, scouting troops, reconnaissance battalions and platoons, and so forth. Those were the people who bore arms; unarmed helpers, the so-called *Hilfswilliger*, or "Hiwi" in the short version, are not even counted here. Some of these units—they were rarely larger than 300–500 men—actually had the name of "Volunteer Battalion No. So-and-So" or, in those cases when some German general, a division or corps commander, was more careful, the unit

was called "So-and-So's Combat Group," receiving the
name of some German first sergeant or even lieutenant.
Later, when the Soviet hunters of live skulls threw themselves at these documents searching for LMPR participants
who were still alive and had not been handed over, this
German caution (or conceit?) was useful. In the documents
(which have to be searched for in the section "Eins Caesar," according to the staff code of German military counterintelligence) there are few last names typical of the peoples of the Soviet Union. These people perished
anonymously. Try and find out who was in "Kampfgruppe
Leutnant Gamfe"!

The commanders of German divisions were in no hurry
to release these groups and small units of volunteers when,
after the publication of the Prague Manifesto in November
1944, the armed forces of the Committee of Liberation of
the Peoples of Russia began to be formed. Actually there
were not too many left by that time. Most of them fell
breaking out of encirclement, expending their last cartridge when there was no hope to break out. The volunteers knew what awaited them should they be taken prisoner. Sometimes in Soviet literature one comes across
cautious lines about these doomed people shooting it out to
the death. And when one reads in that same Solzhenitsyn
about the soldiers of some nameless volunteer unit advancing like a storm to break through, our much-maligned
brotherhood feels a certain warmth: They fought well, to
the end! Russians have always loved and respected military
valor, maybe even especially in civil wars. But this is
merely a sentimental digression. May the reader forgive
the author for it.

German statistics of the war and postwar period state
that various types of volunteer units of every kind in the
German Army, the so-called *Ostverbaende*, numbered at
their height from 900,000 to 1,500,000 men. These are just
the ones who bore arms; the "Hiwis" were not counted.
Considering customary German accuracy, such approxima-
tions—thirty percent in either direction—are indicative in
themselves. In the German Army until 1943 there was no
central point for collecting data about such units and formations. And when a volunteer office under the command
of the aged cavalry officer General Koestring was finally

formed, it still did not take over a number of volunteer units, mainly because of individual considerations on the part of one or another German general. They were jealous of their "own" volunteers as they might be about their own estate.

What types of volunteer formations were there? These were battalions of the RNNA (of which we shall speak later), Cossack companies and regiments, and a large variety of national units: Georgians, Armenians, North Caucasians, Central Asians, and even Idel-Ural legions—let somebody explain to me what that is—Kalmyk regiments, and various Ukrainian units, up to and including the SS "Galichina Division," created in 1944. Let those zealous accusers of "Fascist collaborators," who are now on this side, not hasten to attribute to this division "deeds" usually blamed on SS troops. This was a normal, although elite, volunteer unit of Ukrainian nationalists, clothed in the uniform of the SS. It should not be forgotten that the *supply* of most volunteer formations was in the hands of SS headquarters. It is also essential to distinguish between the front-line divisions ("Waffen-SS") of which there were more than twenty by the end of the war, and the units of the so-called "Algemeine SS," which were involved in concentration camps, executions, and so forth, and from the ranks of which came the "Sonder" and "Einsatzkommandos" of all types and duties.

In the early fall of 1941 in the region of Lokot, Bryansk Oblast', a unique phenomenon arose which still waits its objective historian. There, there was created by two civilian representatives of the Soviet intelligentsia, Voskoboinikov and Kaminsky, a sort of autonomous region with its own ten-thousand-man army (the RONA—Russian Liberation People's Army) and various administrative offices. There were no Germans there, with the exception of a few liaison officers from the Second Tank Army. There were also no partisans, who looked for places where it was easier to operate.

Out of this pair, Voskoboinikov was obviously the one with higher moral qualities, but in the winter of 1941–42 he perished. The partisans attacked his headquarters with grenades. A. N. Saburov, the famous Soviet Bryansk partisan, describes this event in dramatic tones in his two-volume memoirs, *Recaptured Spring*. Orders from the Party, preparations for the raid, and the traitor's death. All this, to be polite, is baloney. A few individual partisans were able to get past the sentry posts of the "Kaminskyites" (as they were later called) and throw a few grenades into the house where Voskoboinikov was spending the night. Voskoboinikov himself and, if I am not mistaken, a woman secretary of his staff were killed. Bronislav Kaminsky, who had before this been Voskoboinikov's deputy, took over command and immediately hanged a few partisans, captured in this or some other operation. (This has not been established.) That is all there was to Saburov's heroic raid.

Quite a bit has been written, and rather badly, about Kaminsky, who after the battles at the Kursk salient led his "army" and a train of fifty thousand civilian followers to the West and, having detached a small formation from among his units for the crushing of the 1944 Warsaw rebellion, was shot by the Germans in the fall of the same year. He was really, to put it mildly, a complicated and rather frightening man. But not everything was as black as it is described by writers. His main biographer, the American historian Alexander Dallin, the son of the famous Menshevik David Dallin (who, by the way, along with other well-known Menshevik leaders, "recognized" the Vlasov Movement), either by chance or deliberately overlooked a number of documents in the German archives which put Kaminsky in a somewhat different light. For instance, Kaminsky's letter to Hitler which, if the Germans had forwarded it to the addressee, would have brought death to Kaminsky much earlier than the fall of 1944.

The autonomous district of Lokot could exist almost a full two years because of the extremely benevolent attitude toward the principle of Russian resistance and toward Kaminsky himself on the part of the commander of the German Second Tank Army, Colonel General Rudolf Schmitt. Schmitt replaced Guderian at this post after the latter was relieved as a result of the German defeat at Moscow. But when Colonel General Schmitt proposed to Berlin that the whole Bryansk *oblast'*, including the city of Bryansk itself, be made into a self-ruling Russian area, he was immediately relieved from command and, so to speak, "squeezed" into retirement. The war was already over when Schmitt was searched by East German police officials on the train from West Berlin to West Germany. In his suitcase there was found a general's uniform, which the old Prussian soldier had not wanted to leave behind. Schmitt was immediately detained, and after that his trail is lost: The Soviet authorities, naturally, were in no hurry to free the general who had agitated for Russian self-rule. Perhaps one of the new arrivals happened to meet this friend of national Russia on one of the islands of the "Gulag Archipelago"?

1942 can probably be considered as the year in which the formation of volunteer units reached its zenith.

In Osintorf, Belorussia, the battalions of the RNNA (Russian People's National Army) were formed with the aid of three émigré officers who arrived from Germany: General Ivanov, Colonel Kromiadi (also known as Colonel Sanin), and Colonel Sakharov. However, soon two former Soviet officers, who later became important functionaries in the LMPR, appeared in Osintorf: Zhilenkov and Boyarsky. Between them and the émigré officers there was immediate friction, due to some unfortunate misunderstandings. The Germans, for their part, having seen that the Osintorf operation was headed in the wrong direction from their point of view, quickly shut it down and the RNNA fell apart into separate battalions, which began to operate against the local partisans.

Later, in 1943, these battalions were transferred to the Western Front, to the Atlantic Wall. A number of critics of the LMPR and Vlasov personally blame the latter for addressing a personal letter to the volunteers of these battalions during this transfer, supposedly approving this transfer, which in fact transformed the anti-Communist volunteers into German mercenaries who didn't care where and against whom they fought. These historians and nonhistorians, who never examined the position in which Vlasov found himself at that time, should be advised to read with greater care this letter, written in Aesopean language to a significant degree. It began with the words: "*By order of the German command.*" Anybody who knows how to read will understand this.

In the summer of 1942 the victorious German march to the east on the southern flank of the Eastern Front began. The Soviet defeats at that time were different in principle

from the terrible defeats of the summer of 1941. If then the
Germans, in the encirclements they organized, captured a
million prisoners at a time or nearly that many—which
merely testifies to the fact that Soviet soldiers did not want
to fight, since you cannot make an army of a million men
surrender—in the summer of 1942 a terrible *military* rout
took place. This rout resulted from Stalin's "geniuslike"
spring counterattack near Kharkov, in the course of which
several Soviet armies were destroyed. Having finished
with them, the German divisions tore on toward Stalingrad
and the North Caucasus. Military specialists to this day
puzzle over this strategic plan devised by Hitler, who had
assumed supreme command after the defeat at Moscow.
But the analysis of the strategic mistakes of Hitler and Stalin is not part of this report: In this, as in many other aspects, they deserved each other.

In the late autumn of 1941 the Germans on the southern
flank reached Rostov-on-Don and fortified themselves
there. At the beginning of their 1942 advance, the Germans
went through Cossack lands, first through the territories of
the Great Don Army, and then through the Kuban and partially the Terek Cossack areas. Perhaps more than any others, the Cossacks had scores to settle against the Soviet regime. Entering Cossack villages, the lead German units
often came across Cossack troops all prepared and armed
with weapons thrown away by the Soviet Army, sometimes even heavy weapons. If a German general commanding one of those divisions had a sympathetic attitude toward the national Russian cause, these troops were
immediately given the opportunity to join German units
and along with them to chase the Soviet armies eastward. If
not, they remained in the rear, and sometimes, more rarely,
were disarmed and sent back to their villages. Neither the
Cossacks nor the Germans at that time had any idea that
the Soviet regime would return.

It is finally time to call by their proper name the lies in
the works of the Soviet writer Anatoly Kalinin. The commander of the German Army Group "South," Field
Marshal von Kleist, had a positive attitude toward the idea
of a mass creation of Russian volunteer formations. In addition, Hitler himself, with his delirious racial ideas, considered that the Cossacks were not Russians but some special

nation. It is essential to admit that here he was seconded by a number of Cossack separatist leaders. In any case, the Cossacks at that time were not considered to be "*Untermenschen*," and the winter of 1941–42 had taught the Germans a solid lesson. The formation of a limited—and I emphasize—a *very limited* number of Cossack units was permitted. There are some people still alive who remember those times. The formation of Cossack units took place, more or less, in the following way: In the company of several Germans, Cossack officers, sometimes from the "old" emigration, and sometimes from among Soviet citizens, were sent to a number of villages with the aim of forming a Cossack cavalry squadron. Usually in the first and often in the second village the permitted number of volunteers was enlisted in the course of a few hours, and many who wanted to go had to be rejected. Grinding their teeth in rage, the recruiters cursed German stupidity, but there was nothing they could do. A similar situation occurred in prisoner-of-war camps, where volunteers were also recruited, and the recruiters paid no attention to ethnic origins. Thus many Leningraders evacuated to the North Caucasus found their way into Cossack units, and among them there were even, in a few individual cases, some Jews. The author knows of no instances when such volunteers were delivered up to the Germans.

How many Cossack troops, squadrons, and regiments were formed in this way? Only God alone knows. The German Sixth Army with its files and staffs, as is known, perished ingloriously and unnecessarily at Stalingrad. It is only known that in its ranks there were quite a few Cossack companies and battalions. At this time in the United States there is an officer from these volunteer units who reached Stalingrad with the Sixth Army, and was badly wounded in the first street fighting and thus evacuated in time. He considers that in the ranks of the Sixth Army there were perhaps several tens of thousands of Cossacks— who, naturally, fought to the last bullet. This officer came to the U.S. in the guise of a Pole and maintains this guise until the present time. He doesn't like to talk about his military experiences, except sometimes in the fall, in the days of the Protection of the Virgin, the Cossack holiday, with a very large glass to drink and in carefully screened com-

pany. The forced repatriations of 1945 and the "chase" after volunteers that followed for many years by anybody
who had the energy for it have not been forgotten even after thirty years....

When, after their Stalingrad debacle, the Germans rolled
back to the west, the civilian population followed them
through the snow and slush of the winter of 1942–43. The
Germans did not force anyone to go with them—these are
all fables—but they did not chase them away either, knowing what would happen to people who had taken up arms
against Stalin and to their families. Many thousands perished on the road, many fell in battle. Not many made their
way to Central Europe. Out of these later, in Northern Italy, a so-called Cossack camp and the Second "Domanov"
Cossack division were formed. It is precisely about the repatriation of these units by the British that so much is
being written now so touchingly. Thirty years later.

The most combatworthy Cossack units, which had been
strongly roughed up in battles in Mlav, in East Prussia, in
the fall of 1943 were consolidated into the First Cossack
Division, which by the end of 1944 had been enlarged into
the XV Cossack Cavalry Corps, numbering by the end of
the war about fifty thousand effectives. A German cavalry
officer, Helmut von Panwitz, who had received an Oak-
Leaf Cluster to his Knight's Cross while commanding a
mere squadron, took over the command first of the Cossack
division and then the corps. This was the only volunteer
unit which, all alone, came face to face with large Soviet
units. And beat them. In December 1944 several Soviet divisions fought their way into Yugoslavia, where the Cossack corps was then located. In Slovenia, in the large village of Pitomach, the regiments of the Second Brigade of
the corps annihilated the Soviet 233rd Infantry Division,
taking more than a thousand prisoners. The Soviet soldiers
hardly fired at the Cossacks, even at that time, when the
outcome of the war was already clear to everyone. Many of
the Soviet prisoners entered the Cossack units and shared
their fate. The XV Cossack Cavalry Corps was repatriated
almost to the last man. Not much has been written about it,
simply because almost nobody remained from its ranks. At
most only a few hundred men who were in hospitals at the
time were, by some miracle, saved. And they prefer to

maintain silence even now, after the passage of more than thirty years.

As far as von Panwitz himself was concerned, he, being a great friend of the Cossacks and National Russia, was the first to send a telegram to Vlasov after the publication of the Prague Manifesto, putting himself and his corps under the command of the commander-in-chief of the armed forces of the Committee for Liberation of the Peoples of Russia, for which he was almost shot by his own superiors but got away with only a few days house arrest. In November 1944 the Germans were afraid to irritate the Cossacks, who adored their German commander. This whole incident can be confirmed by the former chief of General Vlasov's personal office, Colonel K. Kromiadi (Sanin) who is still in good health in spite of his advanced age.

In the spring of 1945 the Cossacks of the XV Corps elected von Panwitz as their field chief (*ataman*). And he did not betray their trust. He led out the regiments of the XV Corps, damaged in constant fighting, to the British positions in Austria, whence, after first disarming them and calming them with all sorts of promises, the British turned them over to the Soviets. And with them the then Lieutenant General von Panwitz.

In the fall of 1946 Stalin indirectly recognized von Panwitz's status as Cossack field chief (*ataman*) by hanging him, the only German, together with the Cossack generals Krasnov, Shkuro, and others, a few weeks after the execution (perhaps it would be more accurate to say murder?) of General Vlasov and his comrades in arms. General von Panwitz's birthday coincided with the Cossack holiday of the Protection of the Holy Mother of God. In the corps this was always marked with great ceremony. And even now, the survivors of his men, some alone and some in small groups, lift a glass on this day for the soul of this strange man, a German who considered himself a Cossack and proved it by his death.

On July 12, 1942, approximately at the time when Stalin was signing his famous order about the creation of punishment battalions, Lieutenant-General A. A. Vlasov was captured—I emphasize that he was captured and did not surrender—in the Volkhov area. He had been sent by Stalin in the spring to bring order to the northern part of the front,

and in particular to take over command of the Second
Shock Army. However, this command consisted of carrying out orders from above, for the most part inane and illiterate in a military sense; as a result the Second Shock Army
was smashed and its surviving personnel ran off in all
directions, which was very customary in those times.

Soon after his capture, Vlasov was taken to a special
camp for Soviet prisoners under the German high command near Vinnitsa. There he had the opportunity to exchange thoughts with a number of Soviet senior officers
and generals. These conversations, which for the first time
in his life Vlasov could carry on *freely*, without fearing the
consequences, changed his view of the world.

Yes, personally, Vlasov had not been harmed by the Soviet regime. But is that so important? One should not forget that if before 1935–36 in the Soviet Union people in
Vlasov's position could still chat with each other to some
extent, after that such conversation became completely impossible. For the first time in all those years Vlasov could,
being a prisoner of the Germans, come out with everything
that had accumulated in his mind during the years of Soviet power in Russia. He could talk and listen to the others.

In the Vinnitsa camp, which was, incidentally, organized by Count Klaus Schenk von Stauffenberg, the same
man who on July 20, 1944, placed his briefcase with a bomb
in it at Hitler's feet, Vlasov formed an especially close relationship with Colonel Vladimir Boyarsky, the commander
of the 41st Guards Division, who had been taken prisoner
wounded. Boyarsky stated quite frankly that he hated the
Soviet regime and was ready to cooperate with the Germans, but only on the basis of full equality, and only if the
Germans were planning liberation and not conquest.

In private conversations Boyarsky sometimes related an
incident during the battle of Moscow when he and his
unit, led by tanks, had to cross a main highway which was
flooded with civilian refugees leaving Moscow and moving east. There was no possibility of halting this flood of
people. Boyarsky queried his superiors by radio and in reply received unprintable curses and a sneering question:
What's the matter, don't you have any tanks? Send the
tanks on through them!

In the last days of the existence of the Russian Liberation

Army—or more accurately, to correct myself, the armed forces of the Committee for the Liberation of the Peoples of Russia—when units of the First Division were leaving Prague, which they had saved, this same Boyarsky fell into the hands of Czech partisans together with General Trukhin. They say that when the teen-age partisans tore off his shoulder boards, Boyarsky "blew his stack." He was immediately hanged on the nearest tree branch. It is impossible to establish now whether this story is true or not, but it was like Boyarsky, and his name is missing from the list of those hanged in Moscow on August 1, 1946.

In the spring of 1943 in one of the buildings of the high command of the German Army in Berlin, Viktoriastrasse 10, there was a department which, according to plan, should have become the headquarters of the already recognized Liberation Movement of the Peoples of Russia. One of the colorful figures of that time was Major Melenty Aleksandrovich Zykov, according to rumor a Jew, and also according to rumor one of the co-workers of Nikolai Bukharin when he ran, in semidisgrace, the newspaper *Izvestia*. Zykov was undoubtedly one of the ideologists of the LMPR. Always inseparable from him was his adjutant, Valentin Nozhin, who never parted from the seditious little volume of Antoine de Saint Exupéry. Later, if I am not mistaken, in the fall of the same year, 1943, officials of the German state security service summoned Zykov for a business meeting to an apartment, and after that he disappeared. There is no doubt that they killed him, perhaps because he was a Jew, perhaps because he was a Bukharinite, and perhaps because he was a Russian patriot. Who knows? At the same time Valentin Nozhin was killed. And having killed them, they began to spread rumors that Zykov, it seems, had been an agent of Soviet intelligence from the very beginning.

Here, going forward a bit, it would seem to be appropriate to say a few words about the attitude of the "Vlasovites" toward Jews. First of all it should be known that in the first months of the war the Germans shot Jews and "commissars" on the spot, unless they managed to hide their nationality. Later they stopped killing commissars but continued killing Jews. The famous "Commissar Order" was not rescinded but was no longer applied. When the time

came for the publication in November 1944 of the so-called
Prague Manifesto ("halfhearted" as some people who have
not thought it through or do not have enough knowledge
call it) the Germans strove for a long time and without success to include an anti-Jewish point in it. Vlasov absolutely
refused, declaring many times that the attitude of the
LMPR toward the Jews was no different from its attitude
toward any other nationality of Russia—or, if you like, the
Soviet Union. This stubbornness on the part of a former
Soviet general, who never put on a German uniform or
German shoulder straps, cost a few fatal months, if I may
be forgiven my possibly excessive pathos. Actually, in the
ranks of LMPR units there was a certain number of officers
and soldiers who were Jewish, but whom nobody betrayed.
Let that serve as a certain food for thought for those who
have insisted for a long time that the Soviet regime has
been able to turn the Russian people into a people of betrayers without exception. Some of these Jews who wore
the uniform of the Russian Liberation Army are still alive. I
will not name names: To tell or not tell about one's past is
everyone's personal business.

Throughout 1943 and 1944, the Germans, suffering defeat after defeat both in the east and the west, bargained
with Vlasov, who stubbornly insisted that any agreement
between the Germans and the leaders of the LMPR must
not be an agreement with collaborators who, as Vladimir
Ilyich Lenin expressed himself in his time, were willing to
spit on Russia. Books have already been written and more
could be written about these negotiations, into which the
head of the SS himself, Himmler, entered, apparently understanding better than his boss that the party was over,
and therefore grabbing at every straw.

At present certain famous and less famous critics reproach Andrei Andreyevich Vlasov and his entourage for
allegedly not showing necessary toughness, for not banging their fists on the table and shouting "No!" to the Germans and not forcing them either to come to a real agreement or to go to hell.

I recommend that these critics read the numerous books,
written both in an academic way and as memoirs, about
how Polish representatives held discussions with—no, not
with Stalin, but with the Western Allies—about the crea-

tion of new Polish divisions, and how these actions were conditioned upon whether the Polish units in Italy would take the Monte Cassino monastery, defended by German paratroopers nicknamed "green devils" for their combat bravery. About that battle a wonderful song has been written, beginning with the words: "The red poppies on Monte Cassino instead of dew drank Polish blood," under the sounds of which it is so pleasant for old soldiers to drink, regardless of where and how they fought! And these were not people without rights, like the volunteers of nameless Russian units declared to be outside the law, but representatives of the legally recognized government of a country the violation of whose territory officially started World War II. And remember how Eden and Churchill and Roosevelt literally drove these representatives to come to an agreement with Stalin, who naturally had his own special plans for Poland.

Vlasov, of course, could have banged his fist on the table, which he actually did many times. And he could have told the Germans to go to hell. And so? He would have soundlessly been shot somewhere in the cellars of a big house on Prinz-Albrechtstrasse in Berlin, where the headquarters of the Reich security service was located. Vlasov was not particularly afraid of death, even such a death. But he knew something that his critics now forget. In German units at that time already about a million volunteers were serving, whom in those days the German command would stick into any gap where enemy fire was particularly thick. These people had to be given something, some sort of unifying idea; they had to be given at least the chance to tell their children, growing up in the Motherland whose government had betrayed them, that no, simple collaborators their fathers were not. That they died not for Hitler but for Russia, that they fought not for the "Thousand-Year Reich" but against Stalin and the Communists, against—and I have come to like this definition—the "stinking roots of socialism" on Russian soil. And Vlasov and his entourage gave them the Prague Manifesto, literally torn from the Germans with blood.

If anybody develops the opinion that I am indulging in apologetics here, this does not in any way enter into the purposes of my very schematic article. Of course, some things could probably have been done differently. But the history of the LMPR should be examined only in the context of its time. And it should not be forgotten that its participants, and particularly its leaders, were threatened from all sides with only one fate—a bullet. And it is not by chance, in expressing the mood of that time, that one of the best poets of Russia, Ivan Yelagin, wrote, already after the war was over:

> Because I did not reach for a weapon
> With my rested hand,
> Because I did not take the soldier's road
> To the barbed wire of Plattling,
> Because I did not fall under the three-flamed
> Banner of martyrs—
> For this the ruins of all cities
> Are piled into my eyes,
> For this all those mowed down by war
> Are thrown into my eyes,
> And instead of my perishing honorably,
> The shadows of those gallows
> That towered over Moscow
> Drank my blood drop by drop.

After the publication of the Prague Manifesto, the first divisions of the armed forces of the Committee for Liberation of the Peoples of Russia began to be formed. One must be fair to the Germans: They sabotaged the formation of the CLPR troops as much as they could. Tens of thousands of volunteer declarations, coming from prisoner-of-war camps and "East-Laborers" camps, and from literally everywhere, remained without an answer. There was nothing to arm these people with, and no place to form their units. Instead of this the Germans continued to try to form various separatist formations which did not recognize Vlasov, the appointed commander of the CLPR armed forces.

However, I consider it necessary to make a reservation here. When I write "German," I naturally have in mind the Hitler government and its followers. Hundreds of thousands of officers of the German Army—mostly, but not only, front-line officers—supported the ideas of the LMPR as well as they could, and helped Vlasov in every way. Many of them paid for their faith in a future free Russia with their lives. Their names will someday be remembered with gratitude.

At last a division and a half, the First Division, and partially the Second, were formed not far from the Swabian village of Muensingen. But the German Eastern Front—this was already after the beginning of Zhukov's 1945 spring offensive against Berlin—was cracking at all seams, as was the Western Front as well. The First Division was sent to the front and put under the command of Field Marshal "the butcher" Schoerner. Instead of this, the commander of the First Division, Bunyachenko, decided to save from ruins the city where the Prague Manifesto had been signed and support its citizens, who had risen in revolt against the Germans. Vlasov, as far as it is known, had no part in making this decision, which many LMPR officers to this day consider to have been a mistake. Then came the capitulation, the repatriation of the generals—Malyshkin and Zhilenkov came to the Americans in their deep rear, and still were turned over—and the repatriation of the officers and soldiers. History, naturally, continues to be falsified, and not just from the Soviet side. Thus in most American schoolbooks on the history of Eastern Europe it appears in black and white that Prague was liberated by Soviet troops. About the "Vlasovites," of course, there is not a word.

This article is directed at, basically, the reader of the so-called "Third Wave" of emigration, in its mass either hostile to the LMPR or knowing nothing about this movement. And also at those in the Motherland who may happen to receive the issue of *Kontinent* containing this article. For this reason I would like to take up the remaining space in the article by listing those books published in the West through which, given the desire to do so, readers could acquaint themselves with the history of the LMPR more closely. Naturally there is no point in speaking of the article once published in *Novy Mir* under the name of "At One O'Clock, Your Excellency," as a historical source.

In the first place, about ten or perhaps more years ago, at Columbia University in the United States, a broad detailed bibliography of historical materials on the LMPR—not, however, complete for the present day—was published under the editorship of M. Shatov.

In the Russian language at various times and by various publishing houses, the following books were published: *The Third Force*, by A. Kazantsev; *Against Stalin and Hitler*, by W. Strick-Strickfeld (which also came out in German and English); *Vlasov*, by S. Steenberg (also in German and English); *The First Division of the ROA*, by V. Artemyev; *Andrei Andreyevich Vlasov*, and *The Birth of the ROA*, by Colonel V. Posdnyakov; and *The Spiritual Image of General Vlasov*, by Father Aleksandr Kiselev.

In English there exist: *Soviet Opposition to Stalin*, by D. Fisher (one of the first); and A. Dallin's *German Rule in Russia*, which is about the German occupation during the war but contains a lot of material on the LMPR. The very first book about Vlasov and the LMPR written in the West was published in German: *Whom the Gods Want to Punish*, by Juergen Thorwald. This book was something of an ancestor to the extensive literature about the LMPR in World War II, and it was written with the aid of Karla Steenberg, the daughter of a German front-line officer and friend of Russia. She, who later married Sven Steenberg, a Baltic German who fought the whole war on the Eastern front, inspired him to write the book *Vlasov*, which in the opinion of the author of this article throws the best and most objective light on the events of that time.

All the books listed above—and the list is far from being a full one—examine the LMPR of World War II, generally speaking, from a very positive viewpoint.

If anyone is interested in negative views of the LMPR, he should be directed in the first place to Reitlinger's book, *A House Built on Sand*, which came out in English. However, this book cannot be considered as a historical source because of its obvious prejudice.

At the end of the 1940s, after the war was over, the foreign delegation of the RSDRP, as the Menshevik émigrés called themselves, split up because of its attitude toward the "Vlasov Movement." The three "whales," R. Abramovich, D. Dallin, and B. Nikolayevsky, together with other Mensheviks of lesser status, "recognized," so to speak, this movement. But the group of Aronson, Dvinov, and Sapir took an openly hostile and accusatory position toward the

"Vlasovites." A number of their articles criticizing the Vlasov Movement can be found in the issues of *Novy Zhurnal* in those years.

And now the last. Aleksandr Isayevich Solzhenitsyn, whose attitude toward the "Vlasovites" notably changed from the first volume of the *Gulag Archipelago*, through the "Vestnik RSKhD," to the third volume of the same *Gulag Archipelago*, writes in that third volume:

"It is now time for us to look into the *Vlasovites* again. In the first part of this book the reader had not yet been prepared to accept the whole truth (and I don't even possess the whole truth. Special studies will be written. For me this is a secondary subject)."

Now here I am forced to doubt the words of Solzhenitsyn, whom I respect so much. Will special studies be written? By whom and when?

There is no point talking about the Soviet regime. There indeed "special studies" are being prepared and sometimes even published, such "special studies" that I have to wonder whether I slept through those years.

As far as the West is concerned, the hope here is also weak. The "Vlasovites," or the LMPR of the Second World War, is a slippery subject. If only because of those bloody forced repatriations about which Julius Epstein, Nicholas Bethel, and very recently, in the book *Secret Treachery*, Nicholas Tolstoy have written. And also, a completely understandable hatred toward Hitler and those who, often through simple ignorance, are connected with him, blind even historians whom God Himself has commanded at least to *try* to be objective.

At Columbia University for more than ten years there existed the so-called Project Mensheviks. Young historians, and others not so young, spent years sorting out what, in his time, Lenin said to Martov, and vice versa, and who controlled VIKZHEL or who controlled VIKZHEDOR. But for a thorough study (superficial ones were undertaken at the end of the 1940s and the beginning of the 1950s) of a phenomenon which had never happened before in Russian history, when a million and a half citizens of the former Russian Empire put on the uniform of a most cruel enemy just to hit the "beloved regime" on the head—for this no money was found in Columbia University or in other

Western universities. And attempts to create an interest, to
start a project for such a study, were undertaken many
times, until the people who made the attempts got tired
and gave up on them.

I imagine that all this takes place completely consciously. There are thousands of captured German documents having to do with the history of the LMPR, which I
have already mentioned at the beginning of this article.
But these are dry military papers, written by far from
friendly people, having reason either from fear of superiors or from the eternal German disdain of Russians to dis-
tort or hide reality. About a dozen books have been
written, either by foreigners or compositions of a memoir
type. Several hundred articles have been written, usually
in foreign newspapers. That is the material that future historians will have to work with. But the witnesses, the live
witnesses of those events, will be dead by that time, not
having left their eyewitness accounts: Soldiers, as is
known, don't know how to write as a rule and don't like to
write. And they are dying, these witnesses. In the last two
years—and I will list only a very few—Vlasov's personal
adjutant, Captain Rostislav Antonov, has gone to a better
world; Colonel Vladimir Pozdnyakov died, having left behind, it is true, the two books listed above, but not having
had time to write his memoirs; Colonel Igor Sakharov perished in Australia, a man who went through the various
stages of the LMPR "from the opening to the closing bell."
And so many are dead from among those ordinary soldiers
and officers, whose testimony would have been of extraordinary value! The hour is not far off when we shall hear of
the death of the "last lieutenant" of the White Movement.
Soon after that the last "Vlasovite" will close his eyes. And
the Soviet regime, as well as some people in the West, is
eager for that moment to come. That's when we'll write the
history of the LMPR! By anybody's order!

In my opinion the history of the LMPR must consist of a
minimum of three thick volumes, one for each of the periods listed by me at the beginning of the article. In order to
write it, a group of qualified historians must be assembled,
both Russian—and there are such in the emigration—and
foreign, both witnesses of the events of the period and persons who were not connected with it. But participants in

the LMPR must be present in this group, if only to have the opportunity to explain how things were. This group must contain persons who could take a tape recorder and record the testimony of witnesses who are willing to give such testimony. A great difficulty will be the fact that people still feel forced repatriation in their bones. Western historians already have work experience with such testimonies: In almost every university there now exists a department of "oral history," working with tapes. One need not go far: Let us remember the notorious memoirs of Nikita Khrushchev.

To achieve all this, funds are needed, and substantial ones. Such sums are not to be found in the emigration. Private patrons have somehow dried up. There remain either Western governments or Western private foundations. There is scant hope here, in my opinion. And who is interested in all this, in the general bloody mess of the loss of twenty millions of our people during World War II? Maybe just the "Vlasovites," who wait in vain to hear the truth about themselves, and perhaps their children, grown up without their fathers. In a word, sit down and write your memoirs, my comrades-in-arms!

War

A Chapter from an
Unpublished Manuscript

BY ISMAIL AKHMEDOV

Written in English by the Author

From *Kontinent* No. XX, 1979

There probably was a deliberate element of drama imposed
on that mid-November suspension of the War College. It
was early afternoon and we were at map class. Without
knocking, an orderly entered and whispered to our in-
structor. Class was halted immediately and we were ordered to report to the conference hall on the double. At the
doors, armed sentries checked our names off lists before
allowing us to enter. After other classes had been checked
in, the chief of the academy entered and went to the platform, flanked by his commissar and chief of staff. Quickly
and sharply our chief told us that by a top-secret order of
the Chief of the General Staff of the Red Army, we were to
report immediately to headquarters of the Leningrad Military District, "to perform special tasks of our Party and

*ISMAIL AKHMEDOV was born in 1904 in Orsk in the region of Orenburg. He
was graduated from the Military Academy for Electrotechnics in Leningrad and the General Staff Academy in Moscow. With the rank of Lieutenant Colonel and diplomaed engineer, he worked in the Scientific Research Institute Intelligence of the People's Commissariat for Defense of
the U.S.S.R. and thereafter on the General Staff of the Soviet Army. During a duty trip in 1942 he broke with the Stalin regime. Since 1953
Akhmedov has lived and worked in the United States.*

government." He then gave us four hours to order our affairs and board a special train for Leningrad.

The next morning we arrived in the former capital and were billeted in an officers' hotel run by the provost marshal of the city. We were not confined to quarters, but there were no passes for longer than six hours or for overnight.

For ten days we waited there. We used the passes to renew acquaintance with the city, stroll along the Neva, and visit old friends.

Among our group, as a fellow student, was a dashing, almost swashbuckling colonel who had been in the operations section of the Leningrad Military District before attending the War College. He was a professional, had been decorated with the Order of the Red Banner for gallantry in the civil war, and was a graduate of the Frunze Military Academy. Although a Communist, he was very outspoken and could get away with that because of his ability. He used to regale us with scandals about distinguished Soviet generals. Among those was an account that Marshal Semeon Budenny had killed his wife, a beautiful ballet dancer, after accusing her of being a German spy.

On the afternoon of November 26, 1939, that colonel returned to the billets after a visit with old friends at the military district. Quite excited, he came up to me and several other students in the lobby and said: "Well, comrades, acting on orders from Moscow, our own artillery shelled our own troops on the Karelian Isthmus. Tomorrow the war is starting and this evening we will all leave to join the troops. A 'protest' has already been delivered to the Finns accusing them of the shelling. Isn't it funny?"

His information about our departure was very correct, indeed. That night, we all received orders to report to our respective units and moved out immediately. Later, I saw secret reports that it was also true the Soviets and not the Finns had done the shelling. The incident happened near the highway to Viipuri[1] in the Soviet village of Mainila, separated by the little Sestra River from the Finnish settlement of Tamisspeni. In a quick flurry that stopped as suddenly as it had started, seven Soviet artillery rounds were

[1]Now shown on maps as Vyborg, then in Finland but now in the Soviet Union.—ED.

fired. Four Red Army soldiers were killed, nine were wounded.

In the early hours of the next morning, I reported to headquarters of the 7th Army, north of Lake Ladoga and some two hundred miles north of Leningrad. Promoted to the temporary rank of major, I was to be the 7th Army signal officer.

Only after I had seen maps at headquarters did I realize how extensive, how massive the Red Army preparations had been. Sending us from the War College was just a trifling last-minute addition. Hundreds of thousands of men, thousands of tanks and artillery pieces, great dumps of matériel had been in position all along the Finnish frontier for weeks before our arrival.

The 7th Army was just a part of the entire plan and not a major one at that. To its north were three other armies, the 8th, 9th, and 10th, and to the far north, opposite the Finnish Barents Sea port of Petsamo, was a special army corps. Despite that array, it was to the south, south of Lake Ladoga and up the Karelian Isthmus toward Viipuri, that the main effort was to be made. Concentrated there—and later reinforced—were twelve rifle divisions, a tank corps, and two separate tank brigades and special ski battalions, supported by the air force and the heavy artillery of the fortress island of Kronstadt, as well as by fire from the Red Navy. The reason for that concentration of forces in the south was that their task was to break through the redoubtable steel-and-concrete fortifications of the Mannerheim Line, a little more than a score of miles north of Leningrad. Those southern troops formed the Leningrad Military District and were under the personal command of Stalin.

On November 29, two days after I had arrived at 7th Army, we heard Molotov declare on the radio that relations had been broken with Finland as a result of the Mainila incident. The next day the war started and the Red Army attacked all along the Finnish frontier, meeting able and determined resistance.

I saw practically none of the fighting in the 7th Army sector because I was transferred almost immediately after hostilities started. That army was under command of General Stern (later purged), who had been made a Hero of the Soviet Union for his conduct of the campaign against the

Japanese on the Manchurian border a year earlier. His chief of staff was the officer responsible for my transfer. He had been one of my instructors at the War College and had several times praised me for my work there. From the moment he laid eyes on me at 7th Army, he said I should be doing staff work, not signals.

The next day, I was sent north to 9th Army headquarters at Kem, on the White Sea coast, to be the assistant G-1 officer. The 9th comprised two corps, the northern one consisting of the 44th and 163rd Divisions, the southern one of the 54th Division and a Siberian Ski Brigade, and both were supported by artillery and tank units. The commanding general of that army was Vasily Chuikov,[2] then a three-star general. His commissar, whose party connections made him the real chief of the army, was Lev Mekhlis, once an editor of Pravda and a former chief of the Political Department of the Red Army. Mekhlis was a four-star officer.

The mission of the 9th Army was to advance across the border in the general direction of the town of Suomussalmi and across the waist of Finland to the port of Oulu (Uleaborg) on the Gulf of Bothnia and occupy that city, destroying Finnish forces and defenses en route. The border was 175 miles east of Oulu. Between the two points lay difficult terrain, heavily forested, with few roads and spotted with scores of Finland's thousands of lakes. The original Battle Order of the 9th, signed by Stalin, specified that Oulu be taken on the "18th day" of the offensive. Even Chuikov laughed at the optimism of that order.

My first three days at Kem were spent on map work, an attempt to coordinate the positions of the various units. It was particularly difficult because the maps of Finland supplied us by military intelligence were extremely poor, an indication of sloppy work, indeed, by those responsible for that area.

[2]Vasily Chuikov, born 1900, went on to command the 62nd Army at Stalingrad. Not long after the war he became Commander of the Soviet Forces in East Germany. Later, as a Marshal, he became Supreme Commander of the Soviet Army and Deputy Minister of Defense. His book, The End of the Third Reich, has been translated into all major languages.

At midnight of the third day, I was awakened and summoned to the chief of staff's. There I was ordered to proceed immediately to the most advanced battalion of the 44th Division, then just east of the town of Suomussalmi some twenty miles into Finland, observe its situation and operations, and report back. More than 18,000 men strong, the 44th Ukrainian Rifles was made up not only of Ukrainians but also of Kazakhs, Azerbaijanians, even troops from Turkistan. It was regarded as a crack outfit, although, having been trained in the steppes, it was not familiar with operations in forested areas or accustomed to the severe cold of the north. Its mission was to push beyond Suomussalmi on the shore of Kianta Jarvi (lake), already thickly encrusted with ice, so as to relieve the inadequately equipped and poorly trained 163rd Division which was on the right flank and in bad trouble.

After I had been given my orders, I was introduced to a Major Nikolayev, a political-school graduate. Nikolayev, who had had practically no military training, was to accompany me as my commissar. For the trip, we were given a staff car and soldier driver. For arms, we carried light machine guns, machine pistols, and grenades.

Our starting point, Kem, was some 140 miles east of the frontier, although later the army headquarters was advanced to Ukhta, less than a third of that distance from Finland. Ironically, we soon found that the maps of that part of the Soviet Union were just as poor as those we had for Finland. As a result, over the snow-covered route, we had to rely upon our own ingenuity and what advice we could get from advancing units of the 9th that we passed. The longest stretch was west to Ukhta, from where we paralleled the frontier in a southerly direction until we reached the headquarters of the 44th at the small town of Raate, right on the frontier.

When we left Kem that night, some of our fellow officers had shaken hands with us as if they never expected to see us again. The weather we faced was no more cheerful. It was mid-December, the temperature about 20 degrees below zero Fahrenheit; snow loomed four to eight feet high on either side of the icy ruts we bounded and skidded over, and a cutting wind blew from the north. There was only one advantage to that cold. It had formed such heavy ice on lakes and marshes, so common to that territory, that tanks and artillery could travel without trouble. That was the reason the offensive had started when it did.

North of Raate we overtook elements of the 44th moving toward headquarters and the front. Some were resting, others were on the march. I checked the schedule of each unit we passed, and whenever possible I talked to individual officers and men. Some of those we passed were pretty young girls, part of the medical and signal units. None of those hundreds seemed in the least bit enthusiastic about the campaign as party papers we read at headquarters had reported. Their faces were sullen, their bodies tired, their spirits low. Men, machines, artillery, tanks, horses, all moving on to their final destination, Suomussalmi, which also proved to be, for most of them, their destruction.

At one stop among those troops, a soldier, a simple Ukrainian peasant from the Poltava area, asked me a question. "Comrade Commander," he said, "tell me, why do we fight this war? Did not Comrade Voroshilov declare at the Party Congress that we don't want an inch of other people's land and we will not surrender an inch of ours? Now we are going to fight. For what? I do not understand." Nikolayev, giving me no chance to reply, butted in to tell the soldier about the Finnish danger to Leningrad.

At another halt, my attention was drawn to a middle-aged soldier, a horse driver who was having trouble with one of his pack animals. The horse was very obstinate and did not want to go on one step further. Yet the driver did not beat or curse the stubborn beast as a *muzhik* would have done. Instead, the man looked as if he were ashamed of not understanding the horse and was trying his best to convince him to go on. The soldier was clean-shaven and his face was that of a man from a different world. Puzzled, I asked his name and background. He explained that before being drafted he had been a professor of physics at Leningrad University, that by some bureaucratic error he had been made a horse driver. He smiled and said he had no objection, but I made a note to do something about his case. When I did, however, it was far too late for him.

Near Raate, our car broke down and the driver said it would take at least two days to repair it. We walked a few miles to the nearest service unit and commandeered the car of that outfit's commissar. He protested loudly, but it did him no good. We had army orders.

Just before nightfall, we arrived at the Raate headquarters. There we passed the night in the only quarters available, a small house filled with about a hundred officers trying to keep warm. Only a few lucky ones could sit. The others had to rest standing. Everybody was drunk. Vodka —250 grams daily for officers and men alike—was a chief item in our rations. And those who liked to drink could get more from those who did not.

By evening, the stench of the smoke of cheap cigarettes, as well as that of too many bodies in too small a place, sickened me. I went out to get some air, not caring if I lost my standing place.

I had only barely cleared my lungs when I heard someone approaching in the dark slip, curse, and fall. Upon impact, there came the cracks of two sharp explosions, a scream, then silence. I went forward with my flashlight. There on the ground dead, his guts torn out, was a lieutenant. The fall had tripped his grenades somehow. He was only a boy.

Sicker than when I had left the house, I wandered around until a sentry stopped me. Ahead of us, a few yards away, were the houses of the Finnish town. They were dark, abandoned—but first the Finns had stripped them of everything. All the people were gone, all the livestock. The streets and roads leading out of the town were mined. It was a hostile land; dead, too. Nearer by was the building of the Finnish border post, likewise abandoned. By the light of the stars, I could make out several figures on the ground at the door of the building. They were Russian soldiers and they were dead, very dead. The sentry told me that these men had tried to loot the border post of a radio, a record player, and a bicycle, left behind by the Finns. All three of those prizes had been booby-trapped. The soldiers' bodies had been left there as a warning to others.

At dawn the following morning, the three of us left Raate on our quest for the isolated advanced—or vanguard, as we called it—battalion of the 44th. From the moment of crossing the frontier we went slowly and very cautiously. Our slow speed was due to the fact that we were not traveling a real road, only a dirt path beneath packed snow and ice. Our caution came from the knowledge that until we reached the battalion, some twenty miles to the west, we were alone in enemy territory. Often we halted and prodded at suspicious-looking humps in the road, wary of mines. At other times, through the darkness of the forests to either side of us we saw, out of the corners of our eyes rather than full on, flitting figures all in white. We had no ski troops in the area. Those were Finns, but they evidently thought our single vehicle was not worth their trouble.

Every once in a while we came across the single body or groups of bodies of Soviet soldiers killed in the advance of the battalion. There had been no chance to recover and bury the dead. There never was any chance to bury our men in that short but terrible war.

The eyes of some of the dead were wide open. All were in exactly the same positions as they had been at the moment of death. The cold had frozen them to stony hardness, and they looked like figures in some museum of horror. One corpse stood stark upright in deep snow beside the road, both arms stretched upward toward something. Another was half crouched, his bayoneted rifle still in firing position. Most, however, were lying face down, the bodies covered with frozen blood.

Everywhere, except for the sound of our motor and the noise of the tires crunching in the snow, the silence was absolute. Occasionally that deathly stillness would be broken suddenly by explosions, some like rifle shots, others sounding like high-velocity artillery shells. At first we flinched, until we learned that the lesser sounds were ice cracking on some unseen lake or stream nearby and the bigger ones were frozen sap bursting in some unfortunate tree.

Everything was terribly unreal. I thought of the haunted forests of the fairy tales of boyhood. I was very nervous, but tried not to appear so. I looked at the faces of Nikolayev and the driver. They were ashen. I guess mine must have been the same color.

That first ordeal of fear ended a little after noon when we caught up with the vanguard battalion. The entire outfit was dug in behind snow pits on either side of the road. The earth was too frozen for real defense positions to be made. Nor could the men be deployed off the edges of the road as they should have been. The snow was too deep. They had no skis or snowshoes.

At the battalion command post—also right on the road—the commander told me that his outfit had undergone heavy harassment from Finnish ski troops the day before. That accounted for some of the bodies we had seen on the road up. In a combination of three raids, from both flanks, the rear and forward, the enemy had tried to slice the battalion into pieces like a salami. The battalion had been kept together, but at the cost of heavy losses.

The commander said he had orders to attack the following morning. But where, where, he asked, were the Finns? Where was the front? Where were the Finnish fortifications? The Finns were everywhere and nowhere. From ambush, up in the trees, they attacked with machine guns, then disappeared into the forests on skis and in uniforms of the same whiteness as the snow. They were gone before counterfire could be brought into position. Here was a very harassed commander. His orders were to get through to Suomussalmi, dig in there, and await the rest of the division. Where was the division, he asked, and who was securing the road behind him? I felt very sorry for him. The Finns had sucked him in and he was getting none of the support promised from the rear.

Evening came and then darkness. Outposts were doubled and orders were given that there would be no fires. Two nights before, the battalion had been badly punished when the men had lit fires to warm themselves and heat food. From treetops the Finns had machine-gunned every fire, easily picking out the dark silhouettes of the men against the snow.

The men had learned their lesson about fires, but they were miserable with the cold as I walked among them. Some were terrified, too, so afraid that they did not leave the positions where they were dug in to relieve themselves. Whole units stank with the smell of offal and the sharp odor of men long in the same uniforms and too long unwashed. It was a sorry sample of the glorious Red Army, I mused. Good soldiers reduced to such a lamentable condition because higher echelons, currying political favor, had sent them into battle without proper equipment, without adequate maps, with no knowledge of the terrain, with no information about the enemy's tactics and defenses. It was criminal. And it was certainly no occupation, as ordered from on high, no destruction of the Finns and their defenses. Except for that one piece of road, the Finns had control of everything else, were free to move practically everywhere. Unlike our men, they knew where they were, what they were doing. My conclusion was that it would take the 9th Army not eighteen days but at least eighty to reach Oulu.

The next morning, the battalion was put into attack position at dawn. Then the commander held a briefing. Present were company commanders, artillery officers, commanders of supporting units. Also there were all the political officers, the battalion commissar, the party organizers, even the editor of the battalion newspaper, *Bulletin Board*.

Under the critical eyes of those political troops, the commander started to give the battle order. As I watched, I felt very sorry for the battalion officer. If the attack were a success, the politicos would get the credit for it, would get medals for bravery in action. Those types carried weapons but actually were very poor soldiers and only by mistake got into dangerous areas. If the attack were a failure, the commander would get the blame, with the politicos describing that he had done wrong in great detail. This system was later changed, but at that time troop commanders had no freedom of action. The purges were still going on. Political zealots had the real control.

"Comrades, commanders, and political instructors," said the battalion commander. "The enemy is entrenched in front of us. The battalion must advance to Suomussalmi and dig in there in preparation for the arrival of the main forces of our glorious division which will be concentrated in this area. Company A must attack from the right, Company B from the left. Battalion artillery, after preliminary shelling of surrounding trees, will support the companies..."

The shelling started. Not only were some trees hit, from which the Finns had earlier fired a few machine-gun rounds, but all the trees in sight. It was a senseless and terrible harvesting of timber, but the commander knew—as did every other officer of that division—that his troops, accustomed to the open plains, were afraid of the forest. The soldiers thought that every tree in sight was a deadly trap, that every treetop was a machine-gun nest. *Boom, boom, boom* went the guns on and on, but not a single Finn fell from the trees.

Only after that artillery display did the infantry start to move forward down the road. That, too, was a great noise. Forward, to both flanks, to the rear, went the staccato of machine-gun fire, the single shots of many rifles, the bangs of grenades, and the *whumps* of mortars, all directed at imaginary but completely nonexistent Finns in imaginary foxholes or in treetops.

Not a Finn was hit, not a Finn was seen, not a Finn was taken prisoner. Prisoners were badly wanted for information. But in the whole campaign, even after sending out the Siberian ski troops to get some, the 9th Army never took a single Finn. Only one man was caught in Finnish uniform. A great prize, he was taken all the way back to army headquarters, stuffed with food, and almost drowned in vodka. Then, when it came time to really interrogate him, we found out that he was not a Finn, but a very recent Swedish volunteer, and knew absolutely nothing at all.

That noisome attack continued throughout the morning. Really, it was not an attack at all, but a slow move westward with much waste of ammunition. From time to time, from the flanks and from the rear, a few machine-gun shots, a few rounds from light mortars coming from treetops, hit the column. Seconds later, the Finns up there would drop out of the trees and disappear into the forest as if by magic. At noon, a halt was called to that "attack." The troops again began the sorry process of digging in along the roadside. They had moved up a few more miles toward Suomussalmi.

That evening, Nikolayev, myself, and the driver started on the road back to Raate. The battalion had both signal line and radio contact with division headquarters, but that was not adequate to send my report to Army. First, my findings had been lengthy, secondly, they had to be sent in cipher. Division had teleprinter connection with the 9th. We were nervous, of course, on that trip back, but we had no trouble at all, never saw a Finn. It was as uneventful as a visit to the corner store.

We found Raate humming with activity. The main ele-

ments of the 44th were pulling in, plus supporting tanks
and a great amount of artillery and service units. All were
preparing to move forward down that same little road to
the west. The easy trip back to division headquarters had
made me very uneasy because of its very simplicity. That
and the relatively light harassment taken by the vanguard
battalion gave me a feeling in my bones that the Finns
were just waiting for the main forces of the division.

The morning after I had filed my report to Army, I got
orders from the chief of staff to stay with the 44th. We were
told that further information was wanted on the advance
of the main elements. That meant another trip up that road.

Before leaving division headquarters, I saw special orders just issued to regimental commanders. The division
emphasized that better efforts must be made to secure the
flanks and rears and that service units should get special
protection. Those orders were correct, but I did not see
how they could be carried out. They were in accord with
standard field regulations that reconnaissance troops and
other patrols should be deployed forward and on the
flanks and that rear guards should bring up the tail of each
column. That was what it said in the manuals, but it was a
procedure impossible to follow. There was only the one
road west, not a single flanking path within miles. Also,
with no skis or other equipment to negotiate the snow, reconnaissance or deploying in depth was impossible, with
the snow shoulder high in the forests. The Siberians
should have been used for that task, but they had all been
assigned to the southern corps.

Again the three of us traveled the road to Suomussalmi
without incident. By midafternoon we reached the command post of the most advanced, or vanguard, regiment.
Within moments of our arrival, pandemonium broke loose.
Eerie silence was suddenly replaced by the chatter of machine guns from treetops, the crunch of mortar and even
more distant artillery shells into our position. At first the
confusion was terrible. Some of our men shouted, some
threw themselves flat, some were hit, some had been killed
instantly. Near me, a big Ukrainian fell, crying like a baby
from the pain of his wound. He had been hit in the stomach. There was blood, cursing, and agony.

Then our troops recovered from the surprise and started

to return the fire. Everyone fired at everything. But it was not effective, just a lot of noise and waste of ammunition. Nobody knew what to fire at. It was a textbook situation. The Finns were in control of the area.

A message came from the rear. The Finns had cut the column in half and were chopping up the rear echelon. It was a sausage-cutting operation. Moments later we lost communications with the rear. The signal line had been cut and the radio units knocked out.

Darkness was falling and the Finnish firing becoming heavier. Our casualties were mounting so rapidly the medics could care for only the most seriously wounded. The dead, of course, were left where they fell. (After the war, a special corps was sent into those forests to collect and bury sixty thousand Red Army dead, well decomposed by then because the spring thaws had set in.) The situation was clearly becoming critical.

Fortunately, that twilight onslaught proved to be the final major attack of the day. With the coming of darkness, the firing slacked off, except for sporadic shots. The survivors around me were badly shaken, and many doubted they would see the dawn of another day.

At ten P.M. I was handed a radio message from Army. We were ordered to return to the 9th, then at Ukhta, immediately. Nikolayev protested, said he wanted to stay with the regiment and distinguish himself. A T-34 tank and two platoons of infantry in two trucks were assigned to us for the trip to Raate.

When it came time to go, Nikolayev could not be found. He must have been very frightened, to disobey that order. Certainly I was nervous too, but not to that extent.

I left the regiment a quarter of an hour after getting my orders. The tank was in the lead of our little convoy, with the two trucks of soldiers following. I rode in the turret of the tank, at the machine gun.

As we left, a thin sliver of a moon was just rising in the east. By that and the light of the stars, we could see about a hundred yards ahead of us. Our parting glimpse of the regiment was a grim one. Strewn all about, making our passage difficult, were the dead men and burnt-out vehicles of the rear echelon, which had been chopped up late that afternoon.

We had made it safely about half of the some twenty miles back to Raate, when the tank driver called that he thought he saw mines in the road ahead. Sure enough, scattered across our path, I made out a half dozen or so little humps. As I fired into them ahead with the machine gun, they exploded one by one. With the first of my shots, several men in white, Finns, jumped from the side of the road and ran into the forest. I tried, but I could not bring any of them down.

Then we went on. The tank rolled over the mined strip safely. The first truck following was not so lucky. Its wheel spread narrower than our tracks, it hit a mine I had missed. With a crashing roar and cries of pain, pieces of the truck and bodies of soldiers flew into the air. I got out of the tank and did the little I could to help—order the survivors and casualties crowded into the second truck before starting on again.

Several miles farther on, we met another regiment, halted for the night in its march up the road. I left the truckload of troops, wounded and dead with them and continued to Raate in the tank without further trouble. From there on, a staff car took me to Ukhta, where I reported to Army in full on the troubles and deficiencies of the 44th.

Some two weeks later, in early January of 1940, the chief of staff ordered me to accompany him to the headquarters of our northern corps, the one to which the 44th and 163rd divisions were assigned. Our destination was the corps command on the eastern shore of Kianta Jarvi, a few miles north of Suomussalmi. The mission was to get the corps and the 163rd to beef up their operations in support of the 44th.

We never got to the command post and the mission was never accomplished. As we approached the area where the CP was supposed to have been, we found everything in great disorder. The CP had been abandoned. The corps was in full retreat up the lake, to the north and east. So was the 163rd, but for that division it was more of a rout than a withdrawal. I, a lowly junior officer, was amazed that the chief of staff of army had been unaware that such a mess was imminent.

The senior officer and I joined the retreat.

We finally located corps headquarters on the move and joined them on the retreat up the lake that followed the luckless attempt of the 163rd to take Suomussalmi. Never had I dreamed of such disorderly retreat—horses, artillery, men, running in every direction, trying to get back across the frontier. To make matters worse, Finnish planes attacked the fleeing units. Big holes were blasted in the lake ice over which we were moving. Scores of men and much matériel vanished into the cold waters opened up by the bombs.

On the anguished trek back, I personally met Mekhlis for the first time. He had been with the corps headquarters, perhaps in search of battle honors just like the lesser commissars. What else he could have been doing there was beyond me. He was the real boss of the army. He alone had the connections to get it the equipment, the supplies, the troops it needed. He should have been back at Ukhta. There, and only there, he could have done something about the great danger facing the army.

During the retreat, Mekhlis asked me about the 44th. Since our days, if not hours, might be numbered, I told him quite bluntly. I told him how fine were the soldiers in that division, but how inadequately trained they were for fighting in such terrain. I told him of the dearth of proper maps and intelligence about the enemy. I told him of the lack of ski troops in the right places at the right times.

Mekhlis did not regard it as an impertinent outburst, but heard me out. And I regarded him highly, as a man. A fine type of Jewish intellectual, he was broad and high of forehead and his eyes were large, deep-set, and extremely intelligent. His manner was urbane, his voice usually low and modulated.

Most of the routed corps and division made it back across the border without further serious trouble, although all corps artillery, about half of the troops of the 163rd, and almost all of its equipment had been lost. Four days after that rout on the lake and two days after return to Ukhta, we received word that the 44th had been annihilated, or, as the official report put it, "more than seven hundred men overcame all difficulties" and made it back to Raate.

Mekhlis named a commission to investigate the disaster.

He had to. It was his army and he had already lost almost all of one of his two corps.

I, no doubt because I had talked so frankly on the lake, was made head of the commission. There were two other members, the routed army corps chief of counterintelligence, which was the role of the KGB with the troops, and a commissar under Mekhlis. As a War College student, I was supposed to have the technical knowledge for the inquiry, while the presence of the other two men was to give weight to the commission.

We went to the staff of the northern corps. We went to the staff of the 163rd and finally to the remnants of the 44th at Raate. Among those survivors were the division commander, General Vinogradov, and his commissar, Gusev.

After interviewing scores of men from the three units, we composed our report. We listed as principal reasons for the disaster: (1) faulty coordination with the 163rd on the right flank; (2) poor organization by army staff; (3) the lack of sufficient machine guns and other automatic weapons; (4) the lack of ski-troop support. Other causes we gave were scanty intelligence about the terrain and enemy techniques, poor maps, inadequate training, in fact almost everything we had learned, down to the smallest detail.

Mekhlis turned our report over to a military tribunal, with orders for severe consideration of Vinogradov and Gusev, who should never have returned. The trial was held almost on receipt of our report. The two men were found guilty of treason and ordered executed.

The day after that, as chief of the investigation commission, I had to go to Raate to be present at the executions. The general and the commissar were put before a counterintelligence (KGB) firing squad and shot. Also present at the execution—in fact, it was staged in front of them—were the 700 remnants of the 44th.

Among those survivors was none other than my former commissar, Nikolayev. He had become a physical and mental wreck. He cried steadily, babbled incoherently, shot blindly at anybody, was soon sent to an asylum. Nikolayev was one of the many commissars, too many commissars in proportion, who had made it back to Raate. Our report had mentioned how those types had torn their insignias from their uniforms, fearing capture, and then had run like beasts madly through the forests. Our report had also mentioned how the line soldiers had stayed and fought almost to the last man, fighting from behind the stacked bodies of their fallen comrades.

That report proved to be almost too much for my career, almost, even, for my life. Mekhlis had instructed me to make the report in an original and one copy, with both the original and copy to be delivered to him only.

A week after I had completed it and Vinogradov and Gusev were well under ground, orders came for me to report to Mekhlis's office posthaste. I found him in a terrible rage, stuttering and hardly able to control himself.

"You idiot," he screamed at me. "I'm going to have you hauled before a tribunal. I'm going to have you shot. Illegally, and probably intentionally, you let the NKVD (KGB) have a copy of that inquiry. It's probably in Moscow, in Beria's hands by now."

Ai, ai! Me, a simple Tartar, a mere temporary major caught up in a mess like that! I was literally shaking all over. I could hardly speak, but I did manage to mumble a denial. I had not done what I had been accused of, but neither was I too simple a Tartar not to understand the weapon against Mekhlis that report could be in high KGB hands, especially with purges continuing.

Also in the office during that awful session were the two corps commanders and Chuikov. The army general had looked on quietly while Mekhlis yelled and I mumbled in reply.

As I stood there waiting for the ax to fall, Chuikóv interceded. He turned to Mekhlis and said, "I believe Akhmedov is telling the truth. After all, the NKVD took part in the inquiry. It would have been no trouble to them to make not just one copy, but as many as they pleased."

Maybe Mekhlis recalled that he should have been at Ukhta and not with the corps at the time of the rout. Maybe he was the decent man I had thought him to be. I do not know the reason, but as Chuikov spoke, he cooled down. In the end, he said he understood what had happened, apologized for yelling at me, and excused me.

Some days later, in a letter from Tamara, clippings from Moscow newspapers were enclosed. They said that I—

among many others—had been cited for gallantry in combat on the Finnish front. Only Mekhlis could have been responsible for that.

After that very near thing, I spent almost a month quietly keeping my maps in order and carrying out my other duties at G-1. Work was not too strenuous, with everything static on the northern sector after the 44th had been wiped out, the 163rd mauled, and the corps had lost its artillery. Nor were things too busy with the southern corps and its 54th Division and ski troops. In that sector they were not advancing, but at least they were not retreating.

The lull for me ended early in March. Mekhlis again called me to his office. This time he did not bawl me out, but was smiling. Maybe he liked me. He had decided to visit the 54th Division—probably on another try for a medal—and I was to accompany him.

On March 8, we went in Mekhlis's special plane to the command post of the 54th. Aboard were also about fifty high-ranking officers from army headquarters. I was the junior rank among them.

Except for Mekhlis's whim, plus the fact he did not like my chief, the head of G-1, there was really no purpose in my going on that trip. With the 54th, I just wandered around, doing nothing of real importance.

On the night of March 12—exactly at midnight it was—I was in the headquarters teleprinter room, rather idly watching incoming and outgoing traffic. At the zero hour, the bell for an urgent message sounded. On the machine I read that the truce had been arranged and would become effective at noon the next day, March 13. The message was preceded and followed by the warning that the information was secret and was for distribution for staff officers only. The last sentence of the text was startling. It read: Until the truce hour, "spare not a single bullet."

My first reaction, since I had been involved in Mekhlis's affairs whether I liked it or not, and since I had been taken to the 54th by him, was to wonder what he was doing there at a time like that. I would not have thought that a man of his authority could not have had an inkling of truce arrangements being under way. Also, it was strange for him to be away from his headquarters at such a time.

I got the answer to the last question very soon. The next morning he and his plane had returned to Ukhta. And the next few days, before I made my way back to the 9th by staff car, I found Mekhlis gone from there too, and already in Moscow.

Early on the last day of the war, I went to a regimental command post to see it out. The commander was a fellow Tartar, a Colonel Ibragimov. He, not being a staff officer of army, had not the slightest idea that the truce was only hours away.

That poor man's outfit was involved in a very sharp fire fight all over its sector when I arrived. It was the Finns rather than the Russians who were not sparing bullets.

Shortly before noon, the Finns charged and our forward lines collapsed. At five minutes to noon, they had driven to within a handful of yards of our CP.

At that very moment, the CP came under direct fire. The colonel fell, shot through the head. I held him in my arms, and before he died I told him how narrowly he had missed the end of the war.

At noon exactly, messengers ran everywhere calling the cease-fire, and announcements came repeatedly over the radio. Finns, Russians alike threw down their arms. All embraced.

The war was over. Only later did we learn what had been lost: 60,000 killed, 200,000 wounded, 10,000 of those with feet or legs amputated because of frostbite; the respect of much of the civilized world for fighting so small a neighbor and so poorly at that. Gained was the town of Viipuri, some fortifications, a few thousand square miles of forests, lakes, and marshes; the downgrading of the commissars and the reestablishment of real rather than simulated grades and ranks in the Russian armed forces. The last was all that counted, and it was gained at terrible cost.

That disastrous war over, I was returned to Moscow to resume my studies at the War College, but not for very long. That period, the spring of 1940, was when Stalin had his eyes on other small border states, hopeful of grabbing some territory while Germany and the West were involved in World War II. His first of several of those efforts was a nibble at Rumania, a demand that she cede him her border provinces of Northern Bukovina and Bessarabia. Historically, he had some claim to Bessarabia, which Russia annexed early in the nineteenth century in war with the Ottoman Empire, but he had no clear right at all to Northern Bukovina.

In mid-June, when pressure on Bucharest was reaching its height, the War College was once more closed down. Again students and instructors were put aboard a special train. Our destination that time was Kamenets Podolskiy, in the extreme southwestern corner of the Ukraine near the Rumanian border.

I do not mean to be critical of Rumania, but as happened in so many affairs involving that nation, my brief role in that operation was comic opera as compared to my work on the Finnish front.

On June 26, 1940, I was summoned to the high command at Kamenets Podolskiy. There I was handed top-secret orders to deliver in person to the commander of the 12th Army, for attack in event Rumania rejected a Soviet ultimatum. A small observation plane and pilot were put at my disposal.

Our destination was Kolomyya—Polish before that nation's collapse—a small city on the river Prut, just north of Bukovina. It was good weather when we left, but by the time we approached Kolomyya, in the foothills of the Carpathian mountains, we were plagued by very thick and low-lying cloud cover.

Around and around we flew for several hours looking for an opening. We found none at all, and the clouds, instead of thinning as we had hoped, became ever thicker. The pilot seemed unconcerned, but I had seen some pretty impressive peaks on the map and just prayed we were nowhere near them.

Finally, when the time came that we had just enough gas to get back to Kamenets Podolskiy, the pilot jokingly suggested I use my parachute and jump. I had thought of that, not with any pleasure at all, but as a dutiful officer. However, my map-reading had showed me that in those clouds we might have been over Bukovina or the eastern tip of Czechoslovakia, which the Soviet Union grabbed at the end of the war. I was not going to run the risk of being taken prisoner or interned, especially with those orders on me.

In the end, I returned a bit shamefacedly to Kamenets Podolskiy. There I was given a staff car for the trip. Then, shortly after midnight, on June 27, while winding through tortuous roads paralleling the Bukovina frontier, I was advised by radio that my mission was over. The Rumanians, I was told, had agreed to Soviet demands.

For several days after the capitulation, I was with our troops as Bukovina was "liberated." Our radio broadcasts were making much of that occupation. They spoke about the "great joy of the liberated people," of the "great joy" with which they welcomed the Red Army. What I saw were sullen and frightened people and Soviet troops wide-eyed at the wealth of consumer goods in stores.

With Bukovina and Bessarabia duly "liberated," we were all sent back to Moscow and classes at the War College started again. I was glad to get back. I was far behind with my reading—although I well knew the value of the field work that had caused the interruptions—and the course was ending in August.

To be graduated, we had to acquit ourselves of two prime tasks, a thesis and an oral presentation on military subjects. Many of my fellow students took the easy way out with their final papers. They selected "The Achievements of Stalin in the Civil War" and were, of course, commended. I preferred "The Battle of the Marne" of World War I. That was work, not sycophancy, but I was commended, too.

I must admit, however, that my oral presentation played the Party line and was also very well timed. It was made before the chief of staff of the Red Army and many other high-ranking officers. The commissar of the college had just made a poor speech on electrification because it happened to be the very anniversary of a boring book by Lenin entitled *Electrification Plus Cooperation Is Equal to Socialism*. The speech was poor because its subject matter was limited to such mundane matters as supplying power to factories and cooperatives, forgetting the advances made since Lenin's death.

I was called to the rostrum to discuss the speech and was told: "Comrade Akhmedov, you have specialized on electrical subjects, let us hear your views." So I spoke for five minutes. I supported the views of the new breed of officers who envisaged sophisticated applications of electricity and power. I spoke about research with magnetrons (from which radar eventually was developed), about remote control of tanks, about military applications of television, about the role the atom might play some day, and about possible push-button wars of the future, running the gamut of new developments that might force modification of military doctrine. In closing, I said "...and all that, plus cooperation, will make socialism. Long live our Lenin." The generals called "Bravo," they clapped, they cheered.

Primarily on the basis of those remarks, but also with consideration of my decoration and my other work during the course, I graduated high in my class in August 1940 and was promoted to engineer major.

I Was Stalin's Secretary

BY BORIS BAZHANOV

Translated by Edward Van Der Rhoer

From *Kontinent* No. IX, X, 1976, 1977

Stalin's Coup d'État

Except for the Central Committee, I still worked in the Supreme Council of Physical Culture and in the People's Commissariat for Finance. It was more a case of recreation than work, in the Supreme Council. I took part in the presidium's sessions and directed two departments: the Section of Track and Field in summer and the Section of Skiing and Ice-Skating in winter. Work in the presidium proceeded lightly and smoothly. Council Chairman Semashko (he was also People's Commissar for Health) was an intelligent and educated man with whom one could easily cooperate. Moreover, he understood very well that the Central Committee's line had to be observed, and I was the one who determined this line. Krylenko, the former bloody Attorney General of the Republic, now People's Commissar for Justice, also came to the presidium's ses-

BORIS GEORGIEVICH BAZHANOV *was born with the century in Kazan, Russia, the son of a doctor. He was shot in the chin while gawking at the revolution in his home town. He joined the Communist Party of the Soviet Union at the age of nineteen. Two years later he became the corresponding secretary of the Politburo and hence secretary to the Secretary General of the Party, who was Stalin. He engineered his escape on New Year's Eve 1929 over the Soviet-Iranian border. His book* I was Stalin's Secretary, *from which this article has been excerpted, has been published in several European languages. He lives in Paris.*

sions. He was an ardent chess player; therefore we placed him in charge of the Chess Section. He appeared in connection with its affairs, too. While other matters were being discussed and he had nothing to do, I took a sheet of paper and wrote on it "1. e2-e4" [Pawn to King's 4—Ed.] and handed it across to him. There began at once between us a chess game without a board. After seven or eight moves, however, he could no longer play without a board, so he took out his tiny leather pocket-size chess set from his briefcase and became absorbed in the game. Semashko cast reproachful looks at us, but it was almost impossible to tear Krylenko away from a chess game once it had begun. When it turned out that he would lose, he became very sad.

The Section of Winter Sport provided the occasion for my first trip abroad. Soviet skates and skis were miserable even when they were brand new. As a result, it was decided that we buy them in Norway. The Council requested me to go for a very short time to Norway to inspect material on the spot and acquire whatever was obtainable. In December 1924 I undertook this short trip, which made a strong impression on me. I went abroad for the first time and saw normal human life that differed fundamentally from our Soviet one. Besides, the three Scandinavian countries—Finland, Sweden, and Norway—through which I traveled breathed an air which was unknown in the Soviet paradise. They were countries of astounding honesty and integrity. At first I was unable to accustom myself to this. In Norway I wanted to see the vicinity of the capital. The Holmenkollen, whose expanse is used for winter sports and walks, rises above Oslo. I climbed it with a colleague from the legation who accompanied me as a guide. It was rather warm, only two degrees below zero, we began to perspire as we climbed since we were dressed too much for winter. The legation colleague took off his knitted jacket, placed it on a stone along the way, wrote something on a slip of paper, laid it on top of the jacket, and weighted both down with another stone. Interested, I asked: "What are you doing?"

"It's very hot," my companion answered. "I'm leaving the jacket behind, I'll pick it up again on the way home."

"Well," I said, "your jacket is weeping, say good-bye to it."

"No, not at all, I've written that 'it isn't lost, please leave it there.'"

I looked at him as if he had made a bad joke. The path was heavily traveled, a lot of people were going up and down. Two hours later we came back and the jacket was still lying there. My companion explained to me that nothing was ever lost here. If something had been stolen in the city, the investigation always revealed that a foreign sailor was the thief. In Finland there were no locks or bolts on the doors in the country, theft is unknown there.

In Sweden I talked at the legation with our Counselor Asmus and his wife Koroleva. They had just arrived with their seven-year-old son from Russia. A workers' demonstration was just taking place next to the legation. Well-dressed people in neat suits, wearing hats, walked politely, gravely, and calmly back and forth. The child observed this procession for some time and then asked his mother, "Mama, where are all these bourgeois going?"

On the return trip we crossed the Soviet border at Beloostrov; it was thirty kilometers to Leningrad. The conductor warned us: "Citizens, you're already in the Soviet Union—keep an eye on your baggage." I looked at the scenery through the window. I had on one glove, the other lay on the seat. After a while I turned around and discovered that someone had already stolen it.

I had returned to the usual Soviet everyday life. In the People's Commissariat for Finance, the purchase of new light bulbs represented a consistently large expenditure. Since the population was suffering from a great shortage of these lamps, the employees of the People's Commissariat unscrewed the bulbs from the sockets and took them home. People's Commissar Sokolnikov hit on an ingenious solution to the problem, arranging with the supplying firm to engrave on every light bulb: "Stolen from the People's Commissariat for Finance." The thefts ceased abruptly; anyone who took a lamp home confirmed the theft, so to speak, with his own hand.

I returned from the Scandinavian countries with the strange impression that I had put my head out the window and breathed fresh air.

In contrast to the Supreme Council of Physical Culture, my work in the People's Commissariat for Finance was serious and attracted me more and more in the course of time.

Up to the revolution there had been a Learned Council, a group of the best financial experts, composed mostly of professors, at the Finance Ministry. Sokolnikov established in his commissariat a similar body, the financial management office, which was supposed to assume the functions of the Learned Council. It was divided into the Institute for Economic Research and the Market Institute. Sokolnikov obtained the best specialists, mainly old advisers of the prewar ministry. There were no Marxists or even Communists among them. Sokolnikov employed them on good terms, and their views were highly esteemed; since their advice was even followed, the difficult and complicated monetary reform could be carried out, the hard gold ruble created, and finances put in order. The activity of this office was looked after by a collegium member, Professor Mechislav Henrikhovich Bronsky. When I asked Sokolnikov whether Bronsky was really a professor, he replied with a smile: "Anyone can call himself a professor so long as the contrary has not been proved." Bronsky's real surname was Warschauer (Varshavsky); this Polish Jew, a highly educated and well-read old emigrant (he had been with Lenin), occupied himself with journalism. There was very little of Bolshevik spirit to be noted about him. Nor did he possess any administrative talents. Moreover, he did not supervise the financial management office in any way. His principal—indeed the only—activity that interested him was the publication of *Socialist Economy*, a thick monthly. In Bronsky's opinion, he was without doubt Soviet Russia's best economic journalist. And this was probably the way it was. In addition, Bronsky edited the *Finance Journal*, which appeared weekly. The finance institute was left to itself and had not suffered any disadvantage from it until then. Sokolnikov proposed to me that I take over the direction of this institute. Apart from everything else, he had in mind my Politburo experience in economic questions and calculated that I would bring the office's work more into line with current practice of financial management; in reality, the office of professors, being remote from all organs charged with practical solutions, was devoted more to abstract and theoretical work than the practical side.

I really entered into this work as an anti-Communist already, although people still regarded me as a trustworthy adherent of the regime and therefore considered me a friend. Most amusing of all was the fact that the professors cherished the illusion that one could cooperate with the regime and perform useful work for the country. I was far better informed in this regard than they.

In any case, the office and the professors saw in the appointment of a very young Communist as head a grave threat to their free, independent existence. The Director of the Institute for Economic Research, Professor Shmelyov, approached Sokolnikov on behalf of the whole collegium. He said that the professors were getting ready to leave the People's Commissariat, as they saw no possibility of working under the conditions which the new head, as a Communist, would impose, particularly because, in view of his age, he would constitute no authority for them. Sokolnikov smiled and said: "Please, let's continue this discussion in a month's time. You are greatly in error about the new head."

Everything changed in the course of the first two weeks. The old and experienced professors from the prerevolutionary ministry—Hensel, Sokolov, Shmelyov—discovered to their astonishment at the institute's sessions that I not only had an excellent grasp of all problems of financial management but provided them further with the great advantage that I knew concretely on the basis of my activity in the Politburo what fitted in with government policy and where and how one had to initiate the practical work. At sessions of the Market Institute I also gave the necessary suggestions in order to orient its work in the required direction. But also in specific branches in which the professors considered themselves unsurpassable authorities I dealt with them on the same level, proposing at the very first session to include in the number of market indices covering market development an index of the utilization of cargo and freight transport routes, which at once proved to be one of the most valuable for market forecasts of trade in foodstuffs. Moreover, I was able very quickly to establish good personal relations with them. The Party cell and the little Communists no longer attempted to harass them in order to demonstrate Party vigilance toward these "suspi-

cious specialists." I put the Party cell in its place—due to
my work in the Politburo I represented an authority for it
—and induced it to leave the professors in peace.

At the end of two weeks Shmelyov came to Sokolnikov
and declared that the professors wished to retract their
statements about the new head, since cooperation with
him had developed splendidly. It should also continue in
exemplary fashion in the future. My relations with
Bronsky were also excellent, since he was a likable man.
Apart from that, he occupied a part of that large apartment
where Veniamin Sverdlov and his wife lived, and I also
had accommodations with them.

Perhaps the most congenial of my new subordinates was
the Director of the Market Institute, Professor Nikolai
Dmitrievich Kondratyev, a great scholar and a man of deep
understanding. The Market Institute was his creation, and
in market research, which was still new for Russia, he rendered through his observations and his survey of economic
development the greatest services to the leading economic
bodies, above all to the People's Commissariat for Finance.
To be sure, his work was based on the same naïve illusion
that knowledgeable people and specialists were not only
useful but necessary. Like other experts of the Commissariat for Finance, Kondratyev believed in the usefulness of
his work and did not understand the wolfish character
of Communism. He also worked in the agricultural section
of the State Planning Commission.

He was soon to have occasion to realize what sort of
power he was dealing with. In the Planning Commission,
which was struggling to develop a sensible agricultural
policy, his advice proceeded from the assumption that the
country needed an increase in farm production. Hence,
nothing was more essential than to allow the hard-
working and efficient farmers to work undisturbed, instead of plaguing them endlessly with agitation about rural
parasites, which was the essence of Bolshevik "class warfare" in the villages.

In the State Planning Commission, however, there
watched and ruled the Party cell, which immediately
attacked the experts. There was no Bazhanov on hand to
shut them up. So the Communists raised a wild uproar:
Kondratyev recommends giving up Bolshevik struggle in

the village, the "Kondratyevs" place their hopes on the *kulaks*—the "Kondratyevshchina" amounts to counterrevolution in the villages! There was noise, *Pravda* printed articles, a campaign against the "Kondratyevshchina" was set in motion. A couple of little Communist rogues tried with all their might to make careers on the basis of their vigilance: they had discovered and unmasked a secret class enemy. Finish him off! Naturally poor Kondratyev had no possibility of answering the whole witch-hunt with even a line; *Pravda* did not recognize his right to present a rebuttal. He was very depressed. Even the Party cell of the People's Commissariat for Finance was getting ready to seize him by the collar. After all, the signal had been given by *Pravda*! But I did not permit them to arrange the same spectacle, but explained to the Party cell that the subject of discussion was agriculture, and specifically the agriculture of the State Planning Commission, which was likewise the source of the whole fuss. On the other hand, in the People's Commissariat, where we were, Kondratyev worked in a totally different area, the market, which had nothing to do with his political view about the village; his work with us was very useful and he should be left in peace. As long as I was in the Commissariat, no one actually dared to touch Kondratyev. Nevertheless, the witch-hunt against him was already under way on an all-Russian level. Right at the beginning of collectivization the critical moment arrived, since the destruction of agriculture led to a shortage of food and to famine. According to traditional Communist practice it was necessary in such a case to find hidden enemies and to throw the guilt on them.

In 1930 the GPU "discovered" a "working peasant party" of its own invention. Professors Kondratyev, Chayanov, and Yurovsky were named as the leaders of this party by the Chekists. The latter was a Jewish economist, an expert on exchange and monetary questions, who had never had any connection with peasants or the village. The GPU blew up the whole affair enormously. This peasant party supposedly had more than a hundred thousand, if not two hundred thousand, members. In preparation was a big trial which would explain to all of Russia why there was no food—it was due to Kondratyev's sabotage! And the poor professor would of course have to confess all his crimes at the trial. But at the last moment Stalin decided that it all seemed hardly convincing, he rejected the trial and ordered the GPU to try the leaders and members of the fictional peasant party in "closed proceedings"—that is, they were sent after the verdict of some Chekist troika to a Soviet extermination camp. In this way the great scholar and wonderful person Kondratyev perished, not least of all as a victim of a professor's illusions that one could cooperate with the Soviet regime and with Communists and take part in discussions based on the assumption that one could thereby be useful to the country. The Bolsheviks used such people as long as it was advantageous for them, only to destroy them ruthlessly when somebody had to be saddled with the guilt for a senseless and destructive Marxist practice.

In 1925, the power struggle between Stalin and Zinoviev took place. The triumvirate of Stalin, Kamenev, and Zinoviev, a temporary alliance founded for the struggle against Trotsky, fell apart once and for all in March. In April Zinoviev and Kamenev energetically attacked Stalin's "Construction of Socialism in One Country" at meetings of the Politburo. The triumvirate thereafter did not gather again. Stalin alone approved the proposed agenda of the Politburo, which functioned over a period of several months as a collective body, apparently under the leadership of Zinoviev and Kamenev. This illusion was created by the fact that Stalin, as always (due to a lack of the appropriate knowledge), took little part in the discussion of various qustions. Kamenev still ran the country's entire economy, while economic questions always took up a great deal of the Politburo's work. The triumvirate sought to give the appearance of participating correctly in current work; as a result there reigned a shaky peace in the Politburo.

Since Stalin was not completely convinced that the majority of Central Committee members supported him, he sought to avoid having the final stage of the struggle take place at a Central Committee plenum and to postpone the final decision until the next Congress, but continued his underground work and brought nothing to a head; on the contrary, he even delayed setting the date of the Congress under many pretexts. During the summer political calm still reigned, but in the fall Trotsky published the pam-

phlet *Toward Socialism or Toward Capitalism?* and thereby renewed political struggle against the majority of the Central
Committee, which for its part slowly began to split up.
Concerned about his position as a political leader, Zinoviev
replied with the pamphlet *Leninism* in which he set forth
his philosophy of equality. Nevertheless, right at the beginning of October the question of the date of the Congress and of the main speaker to deliver the Central Committee's political-accounting report was decided in the
Politburo. The Congress was to take place in the middle of
December, and on Molotov's motion the Politburo majority
voted to have Stalin deliver the political-accounting report. Thus Zinoviev and Kamenev had lost the majority in
the Politburo. They instantly presented a resolution with
the demand to open the discussion. At the Central Committee plenum, which was held directly thereafter, it became clear that Stalin's preparation had borne fruit. The
plenum confirmed that Stalin was to make the political-
accounting report at the Congress, while rejecting the
opening of discussion, which Zinoviev regarded as his
chief weapon. Moreover, the plenum gave the impression
of attaching the greatest importance to "Party work with
the village poor" and, in order to open preparations opportunely for the campaign against the Zinoviev-Kamenev
group, also condemned the *"kulak"* right deviation and
"anti-srednyak" right deviation. On the basis of these resolutions, the Party apparatus began energetically to combat
the "new opposition." As always before each Congress, the
Central Committee had to proclaim theses for the Congress
and inaugurate a discussion in connection with their approval. Molotov and Stalin (who feared political discussions) skillfully bypassed this discussion and substituted
for it a simple "reworking" of the resolutions of the October plenum, according to which the elections for the Congress were supposed to take place. The pre-Congress
plenum of the Central Committee only approved the
theses for the Congress on December 15, with the Congress
itself opening on the 18th. Of course, there were polemics
in December in the organizations and at Party conferences.
The election of delegates to the Congress, which had taken
place at the beginning of December in the *raion* and *oblast'*
conferences, also anticipated the composition of the Con-

gress as well as Zinoviev's defeat. Since he did not have the possibility of supervising the whole local Party apparatus, with which only Stalin and Molotov in the Central Committee could occupy themselves, Zinoviev and Kamenev counted on the support of the three authoritative and leading organizations, namely the two big-city ones (Moscow and Leningrad) and the Ukrainian, which was the most important of the regional organizations. Kaganovich, who had been sent to Kiev by the General Secretary of the Central Committee, did everything necessary to insure the loss of the Ukrainian organization for Zinoviev. On the other hand, Zinoviev continued to maintain his control of the Leningrad organization. Stalin, however, had succeeded in unseating the secretary of the Leningrad organization, Saluzky, who prematurely and excessively sharply came out against Stalin and Molotov and their majorities in accusing them of "Thermidor degeneration." But Yevdokimov, secretary of the Northwest Central Committee Bureau, took over from Saluzky as Zinoviev's right-hand man and kept the Leningrad organization in line.

Nonetheless, a completely unexpected catastrophe for Zinoviev and Kamenev was the desertion of the most important organization—Moscow—to Stalin's side. This unheard-of development resulted from a betrayal on the part of Uglanov, opportunely contrived by Stalin and Molotov.

I have already told how the Politburo became dissatisfied with Moscow Committee First Secretary Selensky when the Right Opposition went into action at the end of 1923. In the summer of 1924 the triumvirate—still working hand and glove at that time—sent him off to Tashkent as First Secretary of the Central Asian Bureau. All three Party leaders agreed that he was too weak for Moscow. Still, who should be appointed in his place, in the most important Party organization? As usual, Kamenev had little interest in such organizational problems and left the decision up to Zinoviev. Stalin would have liked to see Kaganovich at the head of the Moscow organization, but Zinoviev, then still number one and consequently taking the lead, wanted someone who was devoted to him. Therefore he proposed Uglanov. The discussion of the matter took place with the triumvirate, at whose meetings I was always present as the fourth man.

In 1922 Uglanov had worked in Leningrad for Zinoviev and was faithful to him; when the question of the First Secretary of the Nizhni Novgorod Oblast' Committee came up, Zinoviev insisted on sending Uglanov. It was the first period of the triumvirate; Stalin very rarely spoke out and was obliged to accept this appointment. Nevertheless, soon afterward Molotov began to work on the secretary. When on one occasion in the summer of 1924 I went to see Stalin and failed to find him in his private office, it occurred to me that I would find him in the connecting room, a conference space between the offices of Stalin and Molotov. So I opened the door, entered, and saw Stalin, Molotov—and Uglanov. When the latter caught sight of me, he became deathly pale and looked so dismayed that Stalin had to reassure him: "This is Comrade Bazhanov, the Politburo secretary. Have no fear, we have no secrets from him, he knows about everything." Uglanov calmed down only with difficulty.

I understood immediately what it was all about. The day before, Zinoviev had proposed at the meeting of the triumvirate to appoint Uglanov as chief of the Moscow organization. Stalin asked if Uglanov was strong enough to lead this most important of all Party committees. Zinoviev insisted on his proposal. Stalin acted as if he opposed the idea and reluctantly voted in favor. In reality, however, Molotov had already turned around the secretary, and now a secret pact against Zinoviev was being concluded by Stalin and Uglanov.

In this way, Uglanov played a double game for a year and a half, assuring Zinoviev and Kamenev of his loyalty and—in the second half of 1925—his hostility to Stalin. In reality, he was cultivating and gathering the appropriate cadres, and at the Moscow preliminary conference of the Party congress on December 5, 1925 he suddenly went over to Stalin's side with the whole Moscow Party leadership and its supporters. That was the decisive blow—Zinoviev's defeat was sealed in advance.

It is well known how events further developed at the Fourteenth Party Congress, which took place at the end of December. Stalin delivered a skimpy and boring accounting report. The Leningrad delegation demanded an accompanying report by Zinoviev, and this was conceded, with-

out, however, changing anything. The whole Congress
voted obediently for Stalin, only the Leningrad delegation
for Zinoviev. Kamenev's report on "Current Questions of
Economic Construction" was dropped from the agenda of
the Congress. Zinoviev aside, Kamenev, Sokolnikov,
Yevdokimov and Lashevich spoke for the opposition.
Yevdokimov was shot in 1936, Lashevich committed suicide in 1928.

Many of those in the Leningrad delegation, however,
hastened to switch sides and to climb onto the victor's
bandwagon. For example: Shvernik, Secretary of the Leningrad Committee; Moskvin, Assistant Secretary of the
Northwest Central Committee Bureau; and Komarov,
Chairman of the Leningrad Oblast' Executive Committee.

At the Congress a new Central Committee, whose majority was already Stalinist, was elected. Stalin had become
the head of the Party. But the real Stalin times still remained in the future. Everything cannot be turned inside
out at once. Trotsky, Zinoviev, and Kamenev had still been
reelected members of the Central Committee. Naturally all
sorts of "organizational results" emerged from the new circumstances. Thus, Kamenev was removed as boss of the
economy at the first Central Committee plenum after the
Congress in January of 1926, also losing his post as Chairman of the Labor and Defense Council as well as that of
Deputy Chairman of the U.S.S.R. Council of People's Commissars. He was also reduced from full to candidate membership in the Politburo. Rykov was named as Chairman of
the Labor and Defense Council. The Politburo was enlarged: Candidate members Molotov and Kalinin became
full members, Voroshilov was immediately made a full
member. Zinoviev and Trotsky remained Politburo members. Other new candidate members, apart from Kamenev,
were Rudzutak, Uglanov (the reward for his betrayal), and
Petrovsky, the nominal founder of Soviet power in the
Ukraine. Stalin was elected General Secretary, Molotov
Second, Uglanov Third, and Stanislas Kossior Fourth Secretary. Stalin sent Kirov, who had been secretary of the
Azerbaijan Central Committee up to then, to Leningrad.

The following year, 1926, was filled with the gradual
smashing of the "new opposition." It became clear to the
whole world that a change of leadership was taking place

in Communist Russia and in world Communism. Nevertheless, hardly anyone saw and comprehended that a genuine coup d'état had occurred and that new circles and layers had assumed the leadership of Russia as well as of Communism. That requires an explanation.

In prerevolutionary Russia the Jews, whose rights were restricted, were overwhelmingly inclined toward opposition, while the Jewish youth in large measure provided the cadres of revolutionary parties and organizations. It was therefore hardly surprising that Jews had always played an important role in the leadership of these parties. The Bolshevik party was no exception to this rule, and about one-half of the Central Committee's members were Jews.

After the revolution this changed fairly rapidly, insofar as all the main organizations of power became united in the hands of this Jewish group in the Central Committee. That presumably reflected the centuries-old habit of the Jewish diaspora to stick firmly together and support one another, while the non-Jewish Central Committee members had no such habits. In any case, all the key positions and central posts of power were occupied by Jews. One could cite first of all Trotsky, head of the Red Army and number-two political leader, next to Lenin; then Sverdlov, who was formally at the top of the Soviet regime and remained Lenin's right hand and main assistant until his death; Zinoviev as leader of the Comintern and virtually all-powerful ruler of Petrograd, the second-greatest metropolis; Kamenev, Lenin's first deputy in the Council of People's Commissars, manager of the Soviet economy, and, in addition, master of the Moscow Party organization. In this manner, the Jews had far more influence in the Central Committee and in the regime than non-Jews.

This phase lasted from 1917 until the end of 1925. At the Fourteenth Congress, in December of that year, Stalin not only removed the Jewish Party leaders from the centers of power but also took an important step toward the complete elimination of the Jewish part of the Party leadership from all of the higher councils. Only Trotsky, Zinoviev, and Kamenev still remained in the Central Committee. At the succeeding Congress in 1927, however, they were already expelled from the Party so that Jews elected to the Central Committee constituted very exceptional cases. The Jewish part of the Party summit never again attained leading positions. Moreover, Kaganovich and Mekhlis declared quite publicly that they did not regard themselves as Jews. In the thirties Stalin allowed some of the most loyal and obedient Jews, like Yagoda, to rise to the point of becoming candidate members of the Central Committee, but he immediately had these newcomers shot. In the last decades no other Jew was taken into the Central Committee; after Mekhlis's death (1953) and Kaganovich's removal (1957) the last ones disappeared.

In concrete terms, Stalin brought about a revolution by once and for all ousting the previously dominant group from its command posts. But he went about this very carefully; it did not appear that the blow was aimed first of all at the Jews. That would have looked like a Russian nationalistic reaction, even if power had been transferred as a result to a Georgian; secondly, it was constantly strongly emphasized that the struggle was aimed at the opposition and the affair was being conducted by close ideological allies, and that therefore Zinoviev, Kamenev, and their like-minded colleagues had been removed exclusively because they held a different view about the possibility of construction of socialism in one country than the Central Committee majority.

This illusion was not only carefully cultivated but to some extent confirmed in the subsequent period by two characteristic elements. On the one hand, Stalin did not continue this purge from top to bottom after the removal of Jews from the Central Committee but brought it to a halt, so that in the following years Jews still occupied some of the more important posts as Deputy People's Commissars or members of the Central Control Commission. On the other hand, in the mass executions of leading party cadres which began in the mid-thirties, Jews and non-Jews alike were killed in adequate numbers.

Taking into account all these details, one can assume, some people have said, that Stalin got rid of all his rivals in an ordinary power struggle, and thus the circumstance that they were Jews was nothing more than a coincidence.

I cannot agree with this point of view for two reasons:

First of all, because Stalin was an anti-Semite. As long as he needed to conceal this, he concealed it carefully, aside

from some uncontrolled outbursts like the one involving
Faivilovich about which I have already written. In the
years 1931–1932 Stalin also had weighty political reasons
for concealing this. In Germany the self-professed anti-
Semite Hitler came to power, and since Stalin foresaw the
possibility of a conflict with him, he had no desire to
arouse the hostility of the Jewish world. This game proved
to be useful both before and after the war. After 1948, however, there was no longer any reason to continue this mim-
icry. Stalin laid down an almost open anti-Semitic Party
line. In 1952 and 1953 he even considered a plan for total
extermination of the Jews in Russia; only his death frus-
trated its execution and saved the Jews. His anti-Semitism
has been confirmed, moreover, by Svetlana as well. One
only needs to recall how he sent the Jew who courted her
to a camp and became completely cold toward her when
she married another Jew. The story of the "doctors' plot"
also became well known.

Secondly, I was able to observe preparations for the coup
d'état at the Fourteenth Party Congress very closely, as I
was in a special position, and therefore saw that Stalin's
underhanded work followed a very particular, specific
line.

It must be added that the Party makeup had changed a
great deal since 1917 and was constantly changing further.
If Jews had formed a relatively large group in the Party in
1917, that reflected the Jewish social level itself, which
consisted of tradesmen, craftsmen, and intellectuals, while
there were very few workers and no peasants at all. The
longer these changes went on, the more the Jewish Party
group became submerged by the mass of Party members.
At the same time, it held onto its leading positions and created the impression of being a small privileged class. For
this reason, in the Party there was growing dissatisfaction
which Stalin cunningly exploited. When the Jewish group
split into two camps, around Trotsky and Zinoviev, which
were fighting each other, Stalin could take excellent advantage of this without being noticed. He placed in important parts of the Party apparatus people who were dissatisfied, "embittered" because of the group of Jewish leaders,
this circumstance being camouflaged by the choice of
known anti-Trotskyites (including almost as many anti-

Semites). I observed very attentively the persons whom
Stalin and Molotov appointed in those years as secretaries
of *oblast'* and *raion* committees. They were clearly future
members of the Central Committee, if not perhaps of tomorrow's Politburo. They all yearned to overthrow the
Jewish leaders at the top and take their places. The necessary phraseology was found very quickly. The line put out
for the Party apparatus by the Stalin center ran: Genuine
Party members are those who come from worker or peasant
stock, the Party must become more "proletarian." Social origin was to play an ever greater role in regard to entrance
into the Party and advancement in it. The Party statutes
demanded that. Obviously the Jewish leaders, who came
from families of intellectuals, tradesmen, and craftsmen,
began to be looked upon as appendages. The training and
preparation for their elimination had an early start in the
persecution of the "Trotskyist" clan. Nevertheless, by the
end of 1925 there were already cadres in place to strike at
the second group of the Jewish leadership, based on
Zinoviev and Kamenev.

All the distinguished workers of the Party apparatus
whom Stalin helped with this blow gladly accepted the
posts that became available.

The upheaval was successful, but the camouflage lasted
until 1947 or 1948. It was only then that the cards were
turned up, at first carefully with the campaign against the
"Zionists," then against the "cosmopolites," and finally
with the addition of nationality to the passport: The designation "Jewish" finally brought the Jews into the special
position of internal enemies.

It is characteristic that Stalin's anti-Semitic line was not
recognized by the Jewish world diaspora before the war.
The incautious anti-Semite Hitler raised a tremendous uproar, the cautious anti-Semite Stalin concealed everything.
Jewish public opinion simply did not believe that the Soviet regime could be anti-Semitic until the "conspiracy of
the blueshirts," and even then this "conspiracy" was attributed to Stalin himself. It required a number of additional
years to comprehend the essence of the policy of Stalin's
heirs, who saw no need to alter his line.

Radek invented a considerable part of Soviet and anti-
Soviet jokes. I had the privilege of hearing some of them

from him personally—at first hand, so to speak. Radek's jokes concerned daily political occurrences. Here are two typical examples of Radek's jokes on the subject of Jewish participation in the leadership:

Two Jews in Moscow are reading a newspaper. One says to the other: "Abraham Ossipovich, a certain Bruchkov has been appointed People's Commissar for Finance. What's his right name?"

Abraham Ossipovich answers: "Well, that's his right name—Bruchkov."

"How come? His real name is Bruchkov? Is he a Russian, then?"

"Well, yes—a Russian."

"Oh, listen to that! These Russians are an astonishing people—they push in everywhere."

After Stalin ousted his enemies Trotsky and Zinoviev from the Politburo, I encountered Radek, who asked: "Comrade Bazhanov, what is the difference between Stalin and Moses? Don't you know?—A great difference. Moses led the Jews out of Egypt, Stalin led them out of the Politburo."

It appears paradoxical that a new form of anti-Semitism, the Marxist type, has been added to the old forms (the religious and racial ones). One can predict that it will have a great future.

The GPU as Foundation of Power

The GPU . . . How much meaning there is in this name for a Russian heart. . . .

In the same year I joined the Communist Party (1919), the Bolsheviks held power in my native city. On Easter Sunday that day's edition of the daily Communist newspaper appeared with a banner headline: CHRIST HAS RISEN! Editor of the newspaper was the Communist Zonin, a local Jew, young and good-hearted, whose real name was Kruemermann. This example of religious tolerance, even affection, greatly pleased me. I attributed it to the Communist Party nucleus. When Chekists came to the city some months later and began to carry out executions, I was horrified; the notion came to me of a division of Communists between good-hearted "idealists" who wished to build a better society and murderers and sadists who personified evil, hate, and cruelty. I did not immediately comprehend that this division was naïve and false—in short, that it was not a matter of people but of the system.

During my later stay in the Ukraine, I learned about the Chekists' bloody reign of terror. I arrived in Moscow with feelings that were not particularly friendly toward this institution. Nevertheless, practically I had no occasion to become better acquainted with it until my work in the Orgburo and the Politburo began. There I met mainly members of the Central Control Commission, Latsis and Peters, who at that time were also members of the GPU collegium. The same Latsis and Peters had on their consciences the horrible mass executions in the Ukraine and at other Civil War sites. The number of their victims amounted to hundreds of thousands. I had expected an encounter with somber fanatics and unfeeling hangmen. To my great astonishment, the two Latvians turned out to be very ordinary trash, flattering and fawning scoundrels, eagerly intent on anticipating every wish of the Party leadership. I had feared that I would be unable to stand the fanaticism of these death-dealers. But there was no fanaticism. The pair were civil servants, engaged in the processing of executions, who, greatly concerned with their personal careers and private welfare, attentively responded to every cue of Stalin's secretariat. My hostility toward this institution turned into disgust at its leadership.

The matter was less simple in the case of the GPU chairman, Felix Edmundovich Dzerzhinski. The old Polish revolutionary, who had headed the GPU from its foundation, remained only nominally in charge until his death, for he became Chairman of the Supreme Economic Council after Lenin's death, in place of Rykov, who had been appointed Chairman of the Council of People's Commissars, and in a practical sense, therefore, he took little part in its work. At the first Politburo meeting where I saw Dzerzhinski in person, he irritated me by his manner of speech. He had the appearance of a Don Quixote and spoke like a convinced ideologist. I was perplexed by his sport jacket with patched elbows. It was completely clear that this man did not use his position in order to obtain any personal benefit. I was no less astonished at first by his fiery speeches; one had the impression that he took everything very much to heart and had an empathy for all problems of Party as well as State life. This fire was in stark contradiction to the cold cynicism of many Politburo members. Later, however, I somewhat modified my opinion of Dzerzhinski.

At that time a freedom reigned inside the Party that no longer existed in the country; every Party member had the possibility of defending or relinquishing his viewpoint. The consideration of all problems was equally frank in the Politburo. Here we are not speaking of opponents like Trotsky and Piatakov, who were not afraid to argue for their standpoint against the majority. Even within the majority the consideration of questions of principle or current matters took place in the form of debates. There were countless occasions on which Sokolnikov, who was conducting the currency reform, would take a position opposed to various Politburo resolutions on the economy, saying: "You're wrecking the whole currency reform! If you adopt this decision, release me from the duties of People's Commissar for Finance." And in questions of foreign policy and foreign trade, People's Commissar Krassin very directly accused the Politburo and its members of lacking any comprehension of the subject and bluntly took them to task.

It soon came to my notice, however, that Dzerzhinski always went along with the ruling group, and when he spoke with fiery enthusiasm in favor of something, it was only a matter that the majority had already approved. Thus all of his fire was received by the Politburo members as feigned and unbecoming. They looked aside or at their papers, there was a painful silence. Once the chairman, Kamenev, said dryly: "Felix, you're not at a public meeting, this is a session of the Politburo." And, wonder of wonders! Instead of justifying his fire ("I take the affairs of the Party and the Revolution so much to heart!"), Dzerzhinski shifted from one second to the next from feverishly excited pathos into a very simple, prosaic, and calm tone. At one meeting of the triumvirate, when Dzerzhinski happened to be mentioned, Zinoviev said: "He has, of course, a frog in his throat, but he misuses it too much in order to create his effects." It should be added that after Stalin's coup

d'état Dzerzhinski began to defend Stalin's position with
the same fervor he had used a short time before to defend
Zinoviev and Kamenev when they were still in power.

My impression finally condensed to the point of concluding that Dzerzhinski never deviated an iota from the
prevailing line of the majority, and that consequently he
never had any opinion of his own. That was very advantageous. And if he defended the orthodox line, almost choking in his fervor and enthusiasm, wasn't Zinoviev right
that he took advantage of the external effects of the frog in
his throat?

This made a rather unpleasant impression on me. It was
the year 1923, I was still a Communist, and a man who
headed the GPU had an aura of rectitude and inner purity
for me. On no account could anyone reproach him for ex-
ploiting his position for the pleasures of life; in this sense
he was completely O.K. Probably the Politburo kept him in
charge of the GPU partly for that reason, thus ensuring
that his subordinates did not become too extravagant.
There was already enough temptation in an organization
that decided about the life and death of the whole non-
Party population. I simply do not believe that Dzerzhinski
really did justice to this role; he was rather far removed
from his agency's practices: the Politburo contented itself
in this respect with appearance rather than reality.

Dzerzhinski's first deputy was another Pole, Menzhinski, a man who suffered from a rare disease of the spinal
marrow and spent his life lying on a sofa; as an esthete, he
concerned himself very little with direction of the GPU. As
a result, the second deputy, Yagoda, ran the GPU, for all
practical purposes.

Incidentally, I was able to infer very quickly the Party
leaders' order of precedence at meetings of the triumvirate.
Since the GPU held the whole population in its hands
through its practice of terror, it succeeded in acquiring
very great power. The triumvirate consciously kept
Dzerzhinski and Menzhinski as nominal bosses of the GPU
and transferred active management to Yagoda, a poorly regarded individual who had no weight in the Party and also
clearly recognized his complete dependence on the Party
apparatus. It was essential that the GPU always and in
everything remained subordinate to the Party and devel-

oped no power position of its own—something that would have run counter to the intent of the Party leaders.

This intent could be recognized without any special difficulty. The leaders, who were purely concerned with their relationship to the Party and with the struggle for power, behaved with complete indifference toward the non-Party population and left it entirely at the mercy of the GPU, which acted as a curtain dropped between the people and the rulers, effectively preventing any political activity on the part of the people and eliminating the slightest threat to the political power exercised by the Party. The Party leadership could sleep peacefully, and it had little interest in the fact that the people fell more and more into the iron cage of the gigantic apparatus of the political police, which was permitted unlimited possibilities by the Communist dictatorial structure.

I saw and heard Yagoda for the first time at a meeting of the Central Control Commission, where I functioned as secretary, while Yagoda found himself among the functionaries invited to the meeting. All the commission members had not yet arrived and those already present conversed with one another. Yagoda spoke with Bubnov, who at that time was still the Central Committee chief of propaganda and agitation. Yagoda boasted about the expansion of the GPU's information network, which was being spread ever more tightly over the whole country. Bubnov expressed the view that the basis of this network was the Party members, who would quite normally serve the GPU as informants: as to the non-Party population, the GPU had to select those elements which were closest to the Soviet regime and would be loyal to it. "Not at all," replied Yagoda, "we can turn anyone into a *seksot* [secret collaborator], particularly those who have a hostile attitude toward the Soviet regime."

"How is that?" Bubnov asked curiously. "Very simply," answered Yagoda. "Who wants to die of starvation? When the GPU works over a person in order to make him an informant, we already have him in our hands no matter how much he struggles against it. We'll take away his job, he won't find another one without the secret approval of our organs. And, above all, if a man has a family—a wife and children—he'll have to give in quickly."

Yagoda. made a repulsive impression on me. The old Chekist Xenophontov, a former member of the GPU collegium and now an administrator of the Central Committee, who carried out all the dark assignments of Kanner, Latsis, and Peters, as well as the shameless secretary of the GPU collegium, Grisha Belensky, completed the picture of this institution as a band of sinister scoundrels, all apparently subordinate to Dzerzhinski.

About this time an acquaintance of mine, the assistant stationmaster at Podolsk, a thoroughly honorable man, came to see me in Moscow. Married to my aunt, he had known me from the time I was in high school and therefore addressed me by the familiar "thou" without regard for my high posts and rank, while I continued to use the more respectful form. He was in great trouble and asked me for advice and help. The local GPU railroad authorities demanded that he become one of their secret collaborators and spy on his colleagues at work. He was probably taken for easy prey as a family head, and besides, he was a very gentle person. Nevertheless, he rejected the idea of becoming a secret collaborator of the GPU. The local Chekist placed his cards on the table: "We'll take away your job. Say good-bye to the railroad, nobody will hire you, your family's bellies will swell up from hunger . . . You'll consent, you have to."

What could he do? Luckily he had me, a high-ranking *apparatchik*, to protect him. I obtained some stationery bearing the Central Committee seal and informed them curtly and plainly that my acquaintance was to be kindly left alone. The stationery did its work, no one bothered him again. This episode afforded a graphic illustration of Yagoda's system for extending his information net over the whole country.

Some time later I had a direct collision with Yagoda at the meetings of the Supreme Council of Physical Culture. Since I was the Central Committee's representative, I could put through a line that ran counter to the GPU's views. Yagoda was defeated and humiliated. Besides, I had a certain opinion of the GPU collegium and therefore did not hide my scarcely friendly attitude toward this bunch. That sounded an alarm in the GPU collegium. The GPU found it extremely unpleasant to have an enemy among Stalin's aides. The Chekists rightly felt that I could become very dangerous as the secretary at meetings of the triumvirate and the Politburo, and also because I was in constant touch with the secretaries of the Central Committee and members of the Politburo. And so they reflected over what to do. Finally the Chekists came to the conclusion that it would be most advantageous to make the mutual antagonism open and official, thus casting suspicion on any blow I might be able to deliver. Moreover, they made up their minds to play on Stalin's pathological suspiciousness. Yagoda therefore wrote Stalin a letter on behalf of the GPU. In this letter it was stated that the GPU collegium considered it as its duty to make Stalin and the Politburo aware of its general belief that Secretary of the Politburo Bazhanov was a secret counterrevolutionary. It was true that it could not yet supply any proofs and had to place more reliance on the Chekist intuition and experience. Nevertheless, it was obligated to bring this conviction to the attention of the Central Committee. The letter had been signed by Yagoda.

Stalin held out the letter to me and said, "Read this." I did. I was twenty-three years old. Stalin, who regarded himself as a great judge of men, looked searchingly at me. If the letter contained a particle of truth, the young man would become confused and begin to defend himself. I only smiled, however, and gave him back the letter without saying anything.

"What do you think about it?" asked Stalin.

"Comrade Stalin," I replied slightly reproachfully, "you know Yagoda, that's just trash."

"Nevertheless," said Stalin, "why does he write that?"

"For two reasons, in my opinion. On the one hand, he wants to arouse suspicion against me; on the other hand, I had a run-in with him at meetings of the Supreme Council of Physical Culture, where I succeeded in imposing the line of the Central Committee against certain harmful positions. But he not only wants to get revenge against me for that, but also because he feels that I don't have the slightest respect for him, not to speak of sympathy. As a precaution, he wishes to compromise anything that I might tell you or the members of the Politburo about him."

Stalin found this explanation quite illuminating. More-

over, knowing Stalin, I did not doubt for one second that
he was pleased by this turn of events. The Politburo's secretary and the GPU collegium in open hostility to one another! In that case, he could not doubt that the GPU would
watch every step of the secretary and, if the slightest cause
arose, report this to him immediately; and the Politburo's
secretary, for his part, would miss no opportunity to report
to him in case the secretary learned anything suspicious
about the GPU's operations.

My further relations with the GPU took shape on this basis: From time to time Yagoda informed Comrade Stalin of
his conviction that I was a secret counterrevolutionary and
Stalin indifferently handed me these notes.

I must add that I was very satisfied when I read Yagoda's
first report. The core of the matter lay in the fact that this
open hostility guaranteed me security in one respect. The
GPU possessed enormous possibilities for arranging some
unfortunate accident. An automobile crash, a murder camouflaged as a robbery, and other similar things. After the
declaration of our openly hostile relations, the GPU was
deprived of these possibilities, for now Yagoda would have
had to pay with his head if I encountered an unfortunate
accident.

Shortly before this letter there had been such an incident. Foreign-language courses were provided in the Central Committee for its personnel. I belonged to the groups
for English and French. In the English group I formed a
friendship with a beautiful Latvian girl named Wanda
Swerde, who worked in the Central Committee apparatus.
At that time I was completely free; we fell in love with one
another, but took everything else as a pleasant adventure;
Wanda was married to a high-ranking Chekist. They lived
in the Lubianka, the GPU building, where there were
apartments for the top Chekists. Wanda usually came to my
house, but on one occasion she invited me to her place. I
found it interesting to see how the Cheka cream lived
there. I arrived at her home in the evening after work.
Wanda explained to me that her husband was on a business
trip, and she proposed that I spend the night with her. That
struck me as suspicious . . . the "unexpected" return of her
husband, who surprised me in bed with his wife, he could
draw his pistol—and everything would take its course as in

an ordinary drama of jealousy. The husband would pretend that he had no idea who I was . . . Using the pretext
that I still had to attend to several urgent matters, I declined the offer. Anyway, I did not blame Wanda, I blamed
the GPU, which wanted to exploit an available opportunity.

Now, however, after Yagoda's letter, such possibilities as
an unfortunate accident or a murder due to jealousy no
longer existed.

All the subsequent years of my activity passed in this
open hostility, which was more or less known to everybody. Stalin had also become accustomed to it, so that cases
like the one with Anna Georgievna Chutareva did not affect him at all.

In the technical college I had a friend, a non-Party student named Pashka Simakov. He was not interested in or
concerned with politics in any way. After his father's
death, his mother married a very rich man, Ivan Andreyevich Chutarev, owner of a large factory for fine linens in
Sharapovaya Okhota, near Moscow. During the civil war,
in order to save himself from the Bolsheviks, Chutarev had
fled to the south and from there had made his way abroad.
Now, in 1924, he lived in Baden bei Wien. His wife had
remained behind with four small children; as the wife of a
"capitalist," she lived in extremely poor and difficult
circumstances.

Pashka Simakov informed me that his mother wished to
talk to me, so I drove out to see her. There I heard the following story. With incredible foolishness, Anna Georgievna had obtained a medical certificate from a doctor she
knew to the effect that the springs of the health resort of
Baden bei Wien would be very beneficial for her health.
Then she went to the administrative section of the Municipal Soviet and requested the issuance of passports for foreign travel to herself and her children for the purpose of a
stay at a health resort. The official of the Municipal Soviet
read her request. "You want a passport for the trip with all
your children?"

"Yes."

"Are you crazy, citizeness, or are you just pretending not
to be normal?"

"Why? I want to take the waters."

"Good, come back in a month."

The GPU issued passports, so her petition went there for review. The connection was immediately clear to the GPU. The bourgeois woman was brazenly asking for permission to flee abroad to her husband, a White Guard émigré and capitalist. When she came back a month later to the Municipal Soviet, she was called into the adjoining room, where three Chekists began a promising interrogation. From her answers it was instantly clear that she knew all about her husband, even the fact that he lived in Baden bei Wien. The Chekists asked: "You want to make fun of us, don't you?" Then the poor woman had an idea that saved her: "You know, I don't belong to the Party and understand nothing about politics; what if a prominent Party member vouched for me?"

"Who is the prominent Party member?" asked the Chekists ironically.

"Comrade Stalin's secretary."

"What? Just what are you trying to pull? Are you in your right mind, citizeness?"

"Yes, I assure you that he can vouch for me."

The Chekists looked at one another.

"Good, bring the guarantee, then we'll talk some more."

Anna Georgievna told me all this. I was fascinated. I had never encountered naïveté of such proportions. "In other words," I said, "you're asking me to go bail for you and to guarantee that you will return to the U.S.S.R. in a month's time?"

"Yes."

"But you're joining your husband in order to stay there and not to return again to the U.S.S.R.?"

"Yes."

Charming. "You understand," said Anna Georgievna, "that I'll die here together with my children. The only salvation for me is to join my husband."

"Good," I said. "Give me the paper, I'll sign it."

"I'll pray for you all my life," replied Anna Georgievna.

Everything else went smoothly. My guarantee was immediately reported to Yagoda. I pictured how maliciously he must have rubbed his hands. He at once issued passports for travel to Austria to Anna Georgievna and all her children. When the Soviet Consulate in Vienna reminded

her after a month that her visa was expiring and that she
had to return home, she answered that she was renouncing
her Soviet citizenship and remaining abroad as an
emigrant.

Yagoda had only waited for this, and immediately sent a
detailed report to Stalin about the way in which Bazhanov
had facilitated a capitalist woman's flight abroad. "What
kind of story is this?" Stalin asked me, handing over
Yagoda's report. "Oh, yes, Comrade Stalin, I merely
wanted to convince myself how dumb Yagoda really is. If it
was a bourgeois woman who wanted to flee abroad and
Yagoda knew that, why did he issue a foreign passport to
her and let her leave? If, on the other hand, there was
nothing bad about her departure, why does he accuse me?
Yagoda agreed to everything just to make trouble for me
but without realizing the dumb position in which he
placed himself." There the matter rested. Stalin paid no
further attention to the whole episode.

I understood very quickly the power which the GPU exerted over the non-Party population. It was equally clear to
me why no personal freedom could exist under the Communist regime. Everything had been nationalized; everything and everyone depended on the government in order
to live and be nourished. The least liberalism or the smallest desire for freedom—and the threat immediately hung
over an individual that he would no longer be allowed to
work or consequently to live. All around there was the gigantic information net of *seksoty* (secret collaborators):
Everything was known about everybody, everything was
in the GPU's hands. While this authority continually increased its power and constructed the *gulag* system, it was
intent on telling the Party leadership as little as possible
about what it was doing. The camps, an enormous system
of extermination, were developed, and the Party was informed about how cleverly free labor resources had been
mobilized for fulfillment of the Five-Year Plan. As to
"reeducation," it was a matter of "work improvement
camps" throughout the country. And what really happened there? Well, nothing unusual. I had the impression
that the Party leadership was satisfied with the GPU's
splendid functioning as a partition between it and the people, feeling no need to find out what the GPU was really

doing. Everybody considered it reassuring to read the official chatter in *Pravda* about the steel sword of the revolution (i.e., the GPU), which constantly remained on guard to defend the revolution's achievements.

I often attempted to discuss with members of the Politburo the completely uncontrolled power of the GPU over the population. Such conversations did not interest anybody. I soon became convinced that the introduction of this subject was fortunately attributed to my strained relations with that institution and hence was not used against me; otherwise I might have been accused on the spot of "intellectual softness" or a "lack of genuine Bolshevist vigilance in regard to the enemy" or some such "deviation." Due to long and continual training, the brains of Communist Party members tended in a very particular direction. A Bolshevik was not someone who had read and accepted Marx, but a person who had been trained to engage in constant detection and pursuit of all sorts of enemies. Meanwhile, the GPU's work grew and developed all the more as something normal for the whole Party. The essence of Communism, after all, was to grab someone by the throat without interruption; how could one reproach the GPU for anything when it was coping so splendidly with this task? I comprehended at last that it was not because the Chekists were vermin but because the system (man is a wolf to other men) demanded and allowed these functions to be carried out by vermin.

Yagoda was a criminal and a scoundrel. His real role in the creation of the All-Russian *gulag* is so unequivocal and well known that evidently nothing can be said in his favor. Only one episode in his entire life pleased me very much.

In March 1938 the comedy of a Stalinist "court" with Yagoda as the star reached the stage. Someone who was supposedly a human being, the not unknown Vishinsky, functioned as prosecutor before the "court."

VISHINSKY: "Tell us, Traitor Yagoda, during your disgusting, treasonable activity, haven't you once felt the least compassion, the least repentance? Even now, when you finally have to account for all your cowardly crimes before a proletarian court, don't you feel the slightest regret for the deeds that you committed?"

YAGODA: "Yes, I regret, I regret very much—"

VISHINSKY: "Listen, Comrade Judge. The traitor regrets. What do you regret, spy and criminal Yagoda?

YAGODA: "I regret very much that I didn't shoot you all while I still had the power to do so."

Perhaps one should add that only someone other than Yagoda, who had organized a long series of such trials, would have suffered from the least illusion about the outcome of such a "trial."

My personal position was paradoxical. The GPU hated me, the maniacally mistrustful Stalin paid absolutely no attention to the GPU's reports, all the secrets of the regime were in my hands. I, however, earnestly studied the question of what I could do to overthrow this regime. In doing so, I did not have any illusions. The masses of the people, no matter how far this slave-holding system went, could not overthrow the regime, the time of barricades and lances was long since past, the regime not only possessed tanks but also a police of hitherto unparalleled strength; moreover, the rulers would draw the line at nothing in order to retain their power. They were not Louis XVI, who did not wish to spill the blood of his subjects, they spilled as much as they liked.

The revolution could only come from the top—that is, from the Central Committee. But this was absolutely impossible, since for this purpose one would have had to keep secret from the people who were going to liquidate Communism that they were anti-Communists and wished to become the majority in the Central Committee. I saw the whole roster of personnel of the Bolshevik leadership before me, but not the people who might have been inclined to do away with it.

Did Stalin Kill Lenin?

An Interview with
Boris Souvarine

Translated by Edward Van Der Rhoer

From *Kontinent* No. XXII, 1980

Few people remain alive who knew Stalin in those distant
years when he was only "General Secretary," having not
yet become the "Genius Secretary." Among those few
there is Boris Souvarine, French revolutionary, publicist,
historian, and author of the first biography of Stalin, published in 1935, which continues to be the best. Republished
in France in 1977, the biography has been called "one of
the most important books of the twentieth century."

Boris Souvarine gives interviews very unwillingly, not
because they are somewhat fatiguing at his age but because

BORIS SOUVARINE *was born in Kiev in 1895 and grew up in exile in France.
During World War I he joined the French Socialist Party; he belonged to
the party's left wing. In 1917–18 he was the Paris correspondent of
Maxim Gorky's newspaper* New Life *which was published in Petrograd.
In 1920 he became one of the cofounders of the French Communist Party;
thereafter he was a member of the Party Secretariat and the Executive
Committee of the Comintern. In 1925 he was expelled from the Party because of "undisciplined conduct." Shortly afterward he became correspondent of the Institute for Social History in Amsterdam. Souvarine contrib-
uted to the* Encyclopaedia Britannica *and the* English Encyclopedia
for Social History. *He was founder and editor of the magazine* La Critique Sociale *(later renamed* Le Contrat Social*). The first edition of his
famous biography,* Stalin, *appeared in 1935. When a revised, expanded
version appeared in France in 1977 it was considered "one of the most important books of the twentieth century."*

he prefers to set forth his ideas on paper. It seems to him
that he can only express what he thinks on paper: clearly,
precisely, and fully. Boris Souvarine makes an exception
for *Kontinent*, agreeing to answer some questions about
Stalin on the eve of the centennial of the latter's birth.

*Boris Konstantinovich, the first, obligatory question: Where and
when did you meet Stalin?*

In 1921 I arrived in Moscow as a member of a French
Communist Party delegation. In accordance with a proposal by Lenin, I was given a post in the Comintern Secretariat and co-opted as a member of the Executive Committee and the Small Bureau. My acquaintance with Lenin
through the printed word had already taken place in 1916,
when I wrote an article criticizing "our friends who are in
Switzerland." Lenin answered me. Thus he knew about
me, and I, of course, knew the leader of the revolution. In
Moscow we became personally acquainted.

Lenin, Trotsky, Zinoviev, Bukharin, and Radek belonged
to the Executive Committee of the Comintern. I would
meet them occasionally. Stalin did not participate in the
Comintern's work.

In September 1923 I went to Kislovodsk on vacation. In
the train I severely pinched my finger. On my arrival I was
given a cot in a dormitory, but I was always an individualist. I went to the railroad station, the only lively spot in the
city. I bought a newspaper and read about the great earthquake in Japan. A train came in and Bukharin got out of a
railroad car, followed by Zinoviev. Bukharin, a jovial, emotional man, embraced me, calling me by the diminutive
"Suvarinenok." Zinoviev greeted me and asked what was
new. I replied: An earthquake in Japan. A big one?—Zinoviev asked, growing interested. Hearing that it was a big
one, he said with relief: "War has been postponed for several years." All the Soviet leaders then lived in fear, anticipating from one minute to the next an attack—by England,
Japan, it made no difference. They were convinced that the
imperialists would attack.

Hearing that I had been put up in a dormitory, Bukharin
suggested that I stay with him in a villa, where there were
numerous rooms and where Clara Zetkin and her son,
Safarov, and Lashevich were already living. Zinoviev lived

nearby. Trotsky occupied a separate villa on a mountain—he lived alone, like an eagle. Stalin lived at Yessentuki. Every day he came by trolley to talk and joke. One day I was present during a general discussion when local Communists told about "bandits." This was the name given to anti-Communist partisan mountaineers who attacked post offices and village soviets. Listening to the story, Stalin made a gesture as if he were firing a machine gun, and asked: "Why isn't it possible to shoot a few of them?" In the words and the expression on his face, cruelty and malice could be felt. I recall that someone once remarked that all the leaders were here and that Kamenev remained alone in Moscow—he was the boss of Russia, he was also Soviet power. If he was killed, there would be no regime.

We returned at the beginning of October. At every station there was a demand for a speaker—and someone made a speech.

We returned in order to assume power in Germany. In October 1923 a revolution in Germany appeared inevitable. In the Politburo, Trotsky proposed to set a date for the uprising, but other Politburo members objected. Trotsky published an article in *Pravda*: "Should a Date Be Set for the Uprising?" He maintained that the date of the revolution could not be set, but that it was possible to set a date for the uprising. He proposed a date—November 7. He wanted to repeat once again what had succeeded six years earlier. The leaders of the Communist Party of Germany, Brandler and Thalheimer, turned up in Moscow and asked for a "leader" —they had no confidence in themselves. Whom do you want as a leader?—they were asked. They replied—Trotsky. This answer enraged Zinoviev. What, the German Communists did not care to accept him, the Comintern chairman, as a leader?

Stalin undertook to resolve the conflict in the Politburo. He assumed the role of peacemaker, calmed and persuaded. No, he said, we will give them neither Trotsky nor Zinoviev, both are too important, too essential here at home.

It was decided that Pyatakov, considered a rightist, and Radek, considered a leftist, should be sent to Germany. That was a common Bolshevik practice—to choose a delegation in such a way that political or personal adversaries were included. In addition, all the Cheka bosses who knew the German language were sent to Germany: Unshlikht, Trilisser, and others.

In the days of preparation for a revolution in Germany, Stalin came for the first time to a meeting of the Comintern Presidium, being accompanied by Dzerzhinski. This was the beginning of Stalin's activity in the international revolutionary movement. He did not conceal his contempt for the Comintern, considered its personnel mercenaries, and called the Comintern "this clip joint." Stalin was not alone in his attitude toward the Comintern and its officials. Although more than a half a century has passed, I still remember the Russian word used by one of the leaders of the "Workers' Opposition," A. Medvedev, speaking about the Cominternist "menials" (*chelyad'*) because they always supported the "general line" against the factional elements. It cannot be said that his attitude was incorrect: The Comintern Executive Committee trusted the leadership of the All-Union Communist Party of Bolsheviks—VKP(b)—and always voted in favor of decisions adopted by the Politburo.

What did you know about Stalin in 1923? What did you think of him?

I didn't think anything of him. My close friend Amédée Dunois once came from France to a conference of the VKP(b). In the meeting hall he began to ask me: "Who is Stalin? Is he considered an important figure?" Glancing around, I discovered Stalin among the VKP delegates and pointed at him:— There he is, with the mustache . . . .

Stalin began to attract attention. I knew Russian affairs better than the others, for I already knew a little Russian and had friends who knew French—Shlyapnikov, Kollontai, and Safarov. In Stalin I recognized the General Secretary. Nevertheless, I understood the role of secretary, even a general one, as the role of a man who gave instructions to typists or who saw to it that lights were extinguished in offices.

What happened? How did Joseph Stalin's irresistible rise occur?

The secretaries of the Central Committee who preceded Stalin were Russian intellectuals—Krestinsky, Preobrazhensky, and Serebryakov (although he came from the working class). They never stopped discussing and talking, they neither replied to letters nor checked up on the fulfillment of decisions. Taking charge of the Secretariat, Stalin established order there. But, still more important, Stalin understood the role and significance of the Uchraspred, which later came to be called Orgraspred. He understood that a Communist's fate depended on this section of the Central Committee, whether he would remain at work in Moscow or be sent to Astrakhan or else to Turukhansk. When one voted for the "platform," one did not vote for "permanent revolution" or "socialism in one country," but for an apartment and a job in Moscow or Leningrad. I recall an anecdote which people then liked to tell. Filling out a questionnaire, a Communist wrote in the column for dependents: "Wife, three children, mother-in-law, 300 thousand English miners."

Stalin's opponents considered ideology and ideological arguments important. Trotsky cites in his memoirs an excerpt from the diary of his wife, Natalya Sedova: "Lev Davidovich returned from a meeting of the Politburo in a sweat." But why was he sweating? Did he quote Marx?

Stalin played his own game—he tried to be a good secretary of the Central Committee, supporting those who supported him. Trotsky did not hide his contempt for everybody. Stalin understood that, except for a handful of idealists, there existed a majority which thought above all about living well.

When, in your opinion, did Stalin understand that he would become master of the party and country?

When he defeated Trotsky. After that everything became possible.

The last question I would like to put to you—this is a question about Lenin, about his share of responsibility for Stalin's acquisition of supreme power. Should Stalin be regarded as Lenin's "illegitimate" or "legitimate" son?

First of all, I wish to begin with the fact that I arrived in Moscow at a time when everything was changing. Things and people changed. When I arrived, the NEP was in full swing. Many stores opened up. As if by magic, goods appeared from various cracks. The Sukharevka swarmed with people and was full of provisions. Private publishing houses appeared. I was shown a "Book of a Marquise" published in Petrograd. I met anarchists whom no one bothered (Sandomirsky, Aleinikov, Andrei Andreyev, my distant relative). The dissolution of the Cheka was announced (we Frenchmen could not foresee that the GPU would not be better)...

Lenin changed, and there was every reason to hope that this was not the end of the changes, that he would take into account the experience of past years. After all, he had said: "Facts are stubborn things." He had also changed his views earlier. In April 1917, like Plekhanov and Martov, he thought that the Russian Revolution would be a bourgeois democratic one .... Lenin changed his views only in September when he became convinced of the Provisional Government's impotence and the impatience of the people, who were discontented because of the war. He virtually adopted Trotsky's point of view on permanent revolution. Joffe wrote about this in his letter written at the time of his death.

Lenin changed once more after Kronstadt. At the end of his life he asked himself about further changes. My friend Dr. Goldenberg, who visited Lenin together with Semashko at Gorky, related on his return to Moscow: "Ilyich sees everything very clearly, he knows that nothing works, but he doesn't know what to do."

Trotsky also changed. Instead of using his intellect, as he had done until 1917, he attempted to adapt himself to Lenin's pseudo-Marxism, a Marxism which was primitive, anemic, skeletonized, and sterilizing living thought. He realized that the revolution had been made by the Party, that the regime only maintained itself through the Party, that the Party was Lenin's creation. In this connection, considering all the circumstances, he sought a "class" explanation. This would also be his undoing. Moreover, his activity in the post of People's Commissar for Military and Naval Affairs and his military successes poisoned his relations with people—he was convinced that all difficulties, any resistance could be solved with one word: Shoot! His doctrinairism turned into dogmatism and prevented him from understanding what happened after Lenin's death. He thought that everything could be explained by the influence of the *kulaks*, then the bureaucracy, when in reality Stalin had recruited a real gang lacking any principles whatever and determined to retain power at any price in human victims. With all its privileges and advantages.

Trotsky did not realize this, which was tantamount to suicide.

Stalin also changed as the scope of his functions broadened and his power simultaneously increased. Lenin valued Stalin's ability to bring about order in the Secretariat. Above all, however, Lenin and Trotsky, theoreticians of a terrorist dictatorship, willingly turned over to Stalin, who represented the Politburo in the Cheka collegium, the role of executor of bloody deeds, knowing that his hand would not tremble. Stalin remained indifferent to theory; he acquired just enough terminology to know the language spoken in the Politburo and the Central Committee; he was armed with the whole power of the Party, i.e., state apparatus including the Orgburo, Uchraspred, Rabkrin, and the GPU; and he had the opportunity to interpret arbitrarily "Marxism-Leninism," which had been converted into an official and dogmatic religion. Stalin gradually scaled the heights, where he began to grow dizzy with "success" and ended in paranoia.

Consequently, it is necessary, bearing in mind the facts which merit attention, to consider always *when* they occurred. Without forgetting that Stalin from childhood bore in himself seeds of vulgarity, malice, and cruelty which luxuriously blossomed out in the service of limitless ambition after he received the undeserved inheritance of Lenin's cause. His superiority to his rivals lay in his capability of disregarding words, and the ability to take advantage of human weaknesses, not stopping at anything. Thus he brought about his rise and consolidated his tyranny in the sphere of the omnipotent oligarchy created by Lenin.

Trotsky suspected that Stalin hastened Lenin's end by giving him poison. Possibly this suspicion is justified. In that case, however, Stalin only carried out Lenin's own wish. I can testify to the following fact: In 1923, just before the next-to-last crisis in Lenin's illness, I encountered Bukharin, who was attending a meeting of the Comintern Executive Committee. He had just returned from Gorky. Naturally I asked him how Lenin felt. Bukharin could not restrain his tears. "Ilyich," he said, "asks to be killed. He never stops repeating, 'Kill me, kill me.'" Embarrassed and searching for words that would be comprehensible to me (with my book knowledge of Russian) but not excessively crude, he gave me to understand that Lenin was soiling himself. Therefore Lenin pleaded, "Kill me, kill me." Unusually excited, Bukharin explained to me: "He's ashamed . . . he's ashamed." For that reason, I believe that, if Stalin did away with Lenin, he did so at the persistent request of his mentor.

Indisputably Trotsky shares with Lenin the responsibility for Stalin's election to the post of General Secretary, which made it possible for him to achieve total power.

It is also indisputable that without Lenin there could not have been Stalin. I do not agree, however, with those who place them on the same level or those who call Lenin a second Stalin. The difference between them lies in the fact that Lenin was a utopian who would undertake the most awful things for the realization of his idea. Stalin was a cynic who believed only in Stalin, who was prepared for everything and did everything—solely for himself, for the preservation and expansion of his power, for the satisfaction of his monstrous ambition.